Ethnic Canada
Identities and inequalities

D1262222

Leo Driedger
University of Manitoba

Copp Clark Pitman Ltd.
A Longman Company

ISBN 0-7730-4619-4

Editing: Pamela Erlichman
Cover design: Kathy Cloutier
Technical illustration: Catherine Aikens
Printing and binding: Webcom Ltd.

Canadian Cataloguing in Publication Data

Main entry under title:

Ethnic Canada

Bibliography: p.
Includes index.
ISBN 0-7730-4619-4

1. Ethnicity. 2. Multiculturalism – Canada.
3. Minorities – Canada. I. Driedger, Leo, 1928–

FC104.E74 1987   305.8′00971   C86-095065-4
F1035.A1E8 1987

Copp Clark Pitman Ltd.
495 Wellington Street West
Toronto, Ontario
M5V 1E9

Associated companies:
  Longman Group Ltd., London
  Longman Inc., New York
  Longman Cheshire Pty., Melbourne
  Longman Paul Pty., Auckland

Printed and bound in Canada.

Contents

Preface

Some may think that the time for ethnic readers is past, and that now we should write an integrated text on Canadian ethnic relations. Indeed, we should. Some of us are working on it. In the meantime, Patrick Burke and Copp Clark Pitman have given us this opportunity to review all the ethnic literature published and available. *Ethnic Canada: Identities and inequalities* is the result. This is a selection of twenty-one of the best writings we could find, introduced with a summary article. Note that most of the authors are very well-known scholars whose names you will readily recognize.

There were many challenges. First, the field of ethnic relations is still much in need of integration, so we were challenged again to design a whole which included some of the most important areas including perspectives on ethnic change, demography, identity, stratification, and inequalities. Second, it was a challenge to find a balance of equally solid contributions in each of the five areas to make a well-rounded set of readings. Third, we found that there are still many gaps especially in the theoretical, identity, and inequality areas where creative thought and mature vision are greatly needed. Fourth, much basic empirical research is still needed, using especially larger regional or national adult samples. Fifth, although with a few exceptions, census data are still the major form of longitudinal data, these data are much in need of indepth supplementation of better conceptualized works.

We hope that the reader will find this collection helpful. We wish to thank contributors to this volume, who gladly revised and updated previously published works of theirs which we were able to include. We also thank the several authors who wrote papers especially for this volume, which are first published here. Many thanks to Patrick Burke, the former Executive Editor of the College Division of Copp Clark Pitman who took a personal interest in this project. Thank you Pamela Erlichman for editing the diverse contributions. I wish to thank Darlene Driedger who often helped with the typing of the manuscript.

Leo Driedger
University of Manitoba
1987

Introduction

Canadian Pluralism: Identities and Inequalities

LEO DRIEDGER

Canada is indeed a pluralist nation comprised of a multitude of historical influences, regional patterns, and ethnic collectivities—a mosaic of histories, regions, cultures, languages, ideologies, and communities. At least five major ethnic forces have shaped Canada over the centuries— the aboriginals, the French, the British, the Americans, and more recently the multiethnic minorities. To what extent do the various ethnic collectivities continue to perpetuate and expand their identities, and to what extent are there inequalities that have become a part of the national and regional structure? This volume examines these complexities and explores trends of the future.

Finding a Theoretical Focus

A variety of approaches to ethnic persistence and change are reviewed. An examination of the literature about early sociologists such as Marx, Durkheim, and Weber shows that they were less preoccupied with ethnicity than we are today. Their approaches to any sociological questions (including ethnicity) varied considerably. Marx's concerns with macropower conflicts, especially in the economic and political fields, certainly can be applied to ethnic dominance in nation-building and the consequences for lesser minorities and their role and status in society. To some extent Joane Nagel's (1984) contribution explores such macroeconomic and political trends and the place of ethnicity in national and international arenas. She suggests that ethnicity is much more a part of modern mobilization toward revolution and ethnic nationalism than we had previously foreseen. Various economic, ecological, organizational, and labour market models, as well as political reaction and construction models, provide important macro perspectives in understanding change.

On the other hand, while Marx focused on macro national and international processes of change, Durkheim was more concerned with a focus on social cohesion and the organizational features of solidarity. Again, he wrote very little about ethnicity, but his frame of reference concerned with maintenance of social structures can be easily adapted and applied to ethnic enclaves and communities such as Indian reserves, Chinatowns, rural ethnic agricultural bloc settlements, Hutterite colonies, and the like. Few, if any, contributions in this volume focus explicitly on such structural and functional analysis, but social solidarity is often implicit in discussions of ethnic identity.

The focus here is clearly on a number of concerns best presented by Max Weber (1978). Thus, we present first a brief discussion by Weber on ethnic groups. First of all, Weber deals with some of the major categories and definitions, including the concepts of biological differentiations of race, variations of group consciousness of kind, smaller *gemeinshaft* groupings of *Volk* or tribe, and *gesellshaft* nations of *nationalgefühl* or nationalism and political power. In this short focus on ethnicity Weber is concerned with theoretical ambiguities of belief in ethnicity and he thinks that there is a disutility in the notion of *ethnic group*. He clearly brings out some of the conceptual complexities of definition.

Secondly, Weber suggests that the *Verkehrsgemeinschaft* (social circles which humans form) are symbolically linked often to some of the most superficial features of custom, language, and culture so that it is in many ways a "belief in common ethnicity" as much as actual important distinctions upon which differentiations are based. These subtle images of consciousness of kind, degrees of *Verstehen* (mutual understanding), memory of origin, and *heimatsgefühl* (feeling at home) in the minds of humans are often hard to differentiate empirically.

Third, in much of his work, Weber presented the historical and social context in which social phenomena emerged, and illustrated differential patterns in comparative forms. One of the ways in which we can illustrate distinctions, is to represent ethnic diversity in its multidimensional patterns. It will be a challenge to show such demographic patterns in a variety of ecological regions with their varied linguistic, cultural, ideological, and historical forms.

Fourth, Weber also emphasized multiple rather than unitary factors in seeking to probe the origins of social phenomena. While he did not use this method in research on ethnicity, he used it extensively in probing the origins of capitalism and its links with religion. Weber delved considerably into the importance of symbolism and the role of ideology, which is certainly important in ethnic studies. * Grd

Raymond Breton (1984) focuses on the symbolic dimensions of linguistic and cultural realities in line with Weber's construction of a symbolic order. Linguistic and cultural symbolism took many forms for the Indians in the northwest, the French along the St. Lawrence, and the British in the northeastern American colonies. When the British conquered the French in Canada their goal was to construct a British-type of Canadian society. Since then this symbolism has been modified to include multiculturalism in a bilingual frame; there have been recent attempts at restructuring the symbolic order. Such restructuring involves considerable resistence and potential for conflict increases as a result.

Jean Burnet (1979) reviews the extent to which Canada has indeed become multicultural within a bilingual framework. The policy of multiculturalism is not yet accepted by all, and many think it is a myth. Who came first and what claims can be made in light of early arrival? Claims of size are made by the aboriginal peoples, the charter groups (French and English), and other minorities as to how important and influential their proportion of the population is. The degree of ethnic solidarity and the salience of identity is a third myth; the degree and quality of British dominance is another. Thus, Burnet attempts to explore the extent to which multiculturalism is a reality in Canada.

Providing a Broad Empirical Context

To provide the larger demographic and ecological context for a perspective of the many peoples to be examined, we turn to demographers such as Warren Kalbach (1987) to lay the groundwork for ethnic comparison. It is important to examine empirical facts, especially longitudinal data presented over a hundred years in the Canadian census. Here we find: that government policy encourages immigration; that because of this we continue to have a sizeable foreign population; that this population changes so that no one ethnic group is a majority; and that the numbers of visible peoples from Asia, Africa, and Latin America are increasing. The ecological distribution of these populations varies considerably so that the British dominate Newfoundland, the French Quebec, the aboriginals the Northwest Territories, while Europeans create a mosaic on the Prairies. Larger Canadian cities are becoming more multicultural; non-Caucasians moving to the cities add visible racial, religious, and cultural heterogeneity. Such longitudinal data clearly show a move to a more multicultural pattern.

Darroch and Marston (1984) focus on the surprising persistence of ethnic residential concentration and segregation in urban areas and link these spatial patterns with demographic parameters and ethnic social organizational patterns of urban life. They propose a model showing the relationship between ethnic residential concentration and other variables such as urban size, critical ethnic mass, institutional completeness, and emergent ethnic communities. They see ethnicity as a social process that becomes increasingly heterogeneous in modern metropolitan areas as the demography and ecology becomes more complex. Signs are that ethnicity is an integral feature of urban proliferation just as political, economic, and religious pluralism also increase with modernization.

Black-white segregation patterns in the United States reflect that residential segregation is especially correlated with racial differentiation, a trend which Balakrishnan and Kralt (1987) also expected in Canada. However, this does not seem to be the case. Comparing the three largest metropolitan areas of Toronto, Montreal, and Vancouver, they find that although some ethnic groups usually are segregated, this varies city by city for others. The Jews are consistently the most segregated in all three cities, while the blacks, surprisingly in contrast to U.S. findings, are usually among the least segregated. On the other hand, the British are more segregated in Montreal (being a minority) than they are in the other two cities. The Portuguese (also Caucasians) are much more segregated than blacks, even though both groups have arrived recently. This diversity shows many factors operating; the symbolism (Weber's and Breton's concerns) varies by group, by race, by nationality, in patterns which are not always uniformly predictable.

Although researchers are fortunate to have longitudinal census data that span a hundred years (as used by Kalbach, Balakrishnan and Kralt), they usually lament the limited number of questions they can explore and the lack of indicators to probe indepth questions. Special national surveys are necessary to find salience of identity, or degree of religiosity, or dimensions of prejudice and the like. Fortunately, Reginald Bibby (1987) has made three such national surveys in 1975, 1980, and 1985, so that we have additional comparative data on ethnicity which greatly supplement demographic and ecological census data. Bibby reports that support for the official bilingual and multicultural policy is increasing in all regions, but there are important regional, educational, and age differentiations. Canadians are also increasingly optimistic about French-English relations and are becoming more at ease with Negroid and Mongoloid Canadians. These new data greatly enrich our knowledge of the quality of ethnic relations by reflecting positive changes over time. We report Bibby's results here because it is important background for our discussion of the extent of ethnic identity and solidarity in Part III and prejudice and discrimination in Part V.

Probing the Dimensions of Identification

In the social sciences there are several competing theoretical frameworks which are also used in the study of ethnic identity. Arnold Dashefsky (1975) reviews the literature and proponents of four perspectives— sociocultural, interactionist, group dynamicist, and psychoanalytic— and provides a means of separating confused ways of approaching ethnic identity. According to Dashefsky, the sociocultural and interactionist orientations are macro and micro approaches taken by sociologists, while the group dynamicist and psychoanalytic approaches are the macro and micro orientation of psychologists. Dashefsky suggests that these approaches will help the scholar to integrate individual theory within the larger body of theory and to develop a social psychology of ethnicity. The other contributions in this section focus on three of the four approaches presented by Dashefsky. Price, an anthropologist, presents the sociocultural approach to Indian culture. Psychologist Berry examines a micro interactionist-behavioural discussion of identity attitudes. Sociologist Rioux presents a macro sociohistorical view of the development of ideologies in Quebec.

John Price (1975) shows that "Micmacs, Mohawks, Inuit and Nootka are at least as different from each other as Canadians with Greek, French, English and Swedish heritages are different from each other." The descendents of more than fifty Indian cultures living in Canada have a complex prehistory which began at least 29,000 years ago. Five cultural areas are examined: language use, food preparation, constructions and crafts, rituals, and entertainment. Economic, political, religious, and family institutions have developed in stages—band, tribe, chiefdom, state—all of which survive today.

These cultural, institutional, and individual identities continue to change as Indians move to urban areas.

Like Max Weber, who examined historical context in order to reconstruct trends, Marcel Rioux (1973) traces the development of ideologies in Quebec. The clergy's resistence to Durham's attempts at assimilating Lower Canada (largely francophone) with Upper Canada (largely anglophone) gave rise to the ideology of conservation—it sought to preserve the French culture in a rural society dominated and directed by the Roman Catholic church. For one hundred years until the Second World War, "the clergy and other professionals were at leisure to disseminate their ideology since they controlled for all practical purposes, most of the information media, houses of learning, books, and textbooks." After the war, the ideology of contestation and recoupment by union leaders, intellectuals, journalists, artists, students, and some of the members of the professions resulted in enormous changes as Quebec became more urban, more industrial, and in need of dealing with modern problems. The ideology of contestation was soon followed by an ideology of development and participation with elements of both conservatism and contestation—characteristics of modern Quebec. Ideologies are an important part of the dynamics of ethnic identity and solidarity. The ingredients of these solidarities are complex and difficult to predict or shape. Rioux's paper was written in the seventies. Much has happened in the last fifteen years and it is difficult to predict the role ideology still holds in modern Quebec.

We have examined two of Canada's earliest peoples, the Indians and the French, focusing broadly on culture and ideology. Both are important dimensions of ethnic identity and social solidarity related to Dashefsky's macro types. Psychologist John Berry (1987) probes the micro dimensions of ethnic identity by asking two basic questions: "Is there value in maintaining ethnic cultural identity?" and "Should relationships with other groups also be maintained?" Depending on the combinations of answers, Berry comes up with separation, integration, assimilation, and marginalization types of ingroup and outgroup relationships which he tests with native people, French Canadians, and immigrants from Korea, Portugal, and Hungary. Berry finds that there are usually positive correlations between separation and integration perspectives, as well as between assimilation and marginalization perspectives. On the other hand, there are usually negative correlations between integration and assimilation perspectives, as well as separation and assimilation emphases. These correlations do, however, vary considerably by ethnic group. Studies such as this show that a simplistic pluralist-assimilationist unidimensional view of the phenomena of individual identity and group solidarity must give way to more options in the middle range.

Sorting the Strata of Ethnicity and Class

There are at least three views on the interrelationship of class and ethnicity: 1) ethnicity is a by-product of the class structure and reducible to class (Cox 1948, Bonacich 1972, Hechter 1975); 2) ethnicity may or may not be reducible to class, but it is a drawback to social mobility (Thomas and Znaniecki 1964, Wirth 1964, Wiley 1965, Porter 1965); and 3) ethnicity and class are separate phenomena that should be examined independently (Tepperman 1975, Darroch 1979, van den Berghe 1981, Isajiw and Driedger 1987). Proponents of the first theory hold that race and ethnicity are means of exploiting minorities by the capitalist class, although there are several variants of this approach. Proponents of the second, like Wiley (1965) and Porter (1965), are concerned that some ethnic and racial groups cannot compete in the market if they remain distinctive, therefore endorse assimilation wherever possible.

Pierre van den Berghe examines the third view. Some sociologists have been highly critical of the "mobility trap" hypothesis which assumes that ethnic identity is a hindrance to upward mobility. Tepperman (1975: 156) concludes that the hypothesis is in many ways "patently false" and Darroch (1979: 22) views it as "an exaggeration of any data available to date." Gordon Darroch (1979: 1-25) did an extensive review of the literature on the relationship between ethnicity and social class and found three major themes: 1) limited evidence of entrance of noncharter groups into positions of power; 2) an ethnic mosaic (maintenance of identities) impedes the processes of social mobility, which he suggests is exaggerated; and 3) evidence that continued ethnic stratification (lack of assimilation), can harden so that ethnic groups remain in their original low entrance class, which he seriously questions based on the data he found. In this volume van den Berghe (1981) maintains that ethnicity and class are separate bases of sociality, though at times they overlap. Each should be treated as an independent factor with its own influences. Evidence found by Isajiw and Driedger (1987) using Toronto data supports this view. The relationship between class and ethnicity varies enormously by ethnic group and numerous other variables. Van den Berghe makes the case that genes and social phenomena surrounding kinship are strong forces that often operate independently of social class, and these forces must be taken into account.

In measuring socioeconomic status, objective criteria show that some ethnic groups, like the Jews, rank very high on education, income, and higher occupations, while others, like native Indians rank low. Peter Pineo's (1977) national Canadian sample reports the prestige attributed to various ethnic groups and ranks the results. He found that although north Europeans ranked high and non-Caucasians low, perceptions varied considerably by ethnic group. Anglophones ranked the British much higher than did Francophones, while Francophones ranked themselves and the English equally on top. Comparisons between the prestige rankings by Canadians and Americans also varied with Americans ranking the British much lower. Another study by Burshtyn and Smith (1978) shows that such ranking studies vary considerably between native students in the Northwest Territories and southern Canadians; Northerners rate greater prestige to mechanical operators and less to professionals, for example. Studies such as this clearly show that prestige images vary considerably by ethnicity, region, ideology, and the like, making the study of ethnic stratification both complex and interesting.

In a short volume as this it is not possible to explore the many features of ethnic stratification; we can only focus on a couple of interesting cases. Since studies show that the British usually rank high in both prestige and socioeconomic status (Blishen 1967), the questions arise— how and where did the British emerge as the establishment? Frederick Armstrong (1981) traces the formation of the British Ontario establishment beginning 200 years ago. This study shows that Canadians of British ancestry have always dominated southern Ontario where they formed the industrial heartland of Canada. The role of the Empire Loyalists, various forms of Family Compact, British political connections, holding of important offices, control of land and economic influence, and educational and religious connections led to a British Ontario establishment which is now the most powerful Canadian establishment, increasingly centred in Toronto. The origins of this economic and political power can be traced to times when the British consolidated their establishment, extending its influence nationally, far beyond the southern Ontario region. Although Canadians of British origin are not a majority group (40 percent, 1981) in size, they represent the largest ethnic group in Canada, and they are also economically and politically the most powerful.

What happens on the other hand, to ethnic minorities that are much less powerful, but also wish to have some control over limited ethnic community solidarity? We have chosen a prairie Mennonite community to illustrate the potential for ethnic and religious conflict when industrial bureaucracies seek to wield power in minority ethnic enclaves. Using Laumann's et al. (1977) bargaining and oppositional community network models, Driedger (1986) demonstrates how a small rural ethnic minority kept Eldorado Nuclear's hexafluoride refinery out, by defining the issue as consummatory, and leaders consolidating internal community and external networks in opposition. The study shows that on occasion religious and ethnic solidarity can successfully keep large industrial bureaucracies from invading, but only if both traditional and liberated networks are used effectively by charismatic leaders. Urban bureaucracies will usually have their way, unless ethnic salience can be rallied around consummatory issues about which a religious or ethnic group cares deeply. While this may represent a model for successful ethnic defence, it is clear that many communities will not always have the resources, nor the will and commitment to organize themselves sufficiently to persevere. However, this small Mennonite minority on the rural prairies, far away from the centre of Eastern industrial power, did manage a "David over Goliath" triumph.

Establishing Standards of Rights and Equalities

The Western world has been influenced by numerous ideologies regarding human rights and freedoms, the Judeo-Christian ideology being one of the important ones. Many of these beliefs concerning the worth and equality of humans found their way into the American constitution so that the freedom of speech, assembly, and the pursuit of life, liberty, and happiness is a legal right upheld by the law (Driedger and Mezoff 1980). Canada has been slower in legalizing such rights. The British North America Act "made no express mention of the words 'human rights' or 'civil liberties' so that such human rights were not legally entrenched in Canada" (Crowley and Whitridge 1978) until very recently. The Canadian Bill of Rights became law in 1960:

> which declares and recognizes that the following human rights and freedoms exist: freedom of religion, speech, assembly, association and the press; the right to life, liberty, security of the person and enjoyment of property, and the right not to be deprived thereof except by due process of law. The above rights and freedoms exist without discrimination by reason of race, national origin, color, religion or sex (Crowley and Whitridge 1978).

Very recently the patriation of the constitution of Canada has taken place along with passing the Charter of Rights and Freedoms which has become law. Evelyn Kallen (1987) addresses the details of this new Canadian charter and its implications.

Kallen (1987) argues that:

> if the Charter of Rights and Freedoms is to pave the way for a national transformation predicted on the multicultural principle of unity in diversity, it must be amended so as to recognize and protect not only the individual human rights of all citizens, but also, and equally important, the collective cultural rights of all Canada's ethnic groups.

She reviews the distinction between voluntary and involuntary minorities and the complexities of serving these variations. She suggests a typology of collective ethnic rights claims that involve cultural, national, and aboriginal group rights. The first claim is the collective right to express and enjoy a distinctive ethnic language, religion, and culture in a community of ethnic fellows. The second is the right to seek politico-economic and cultural sovereignty within the geocultural boundaries of an ancestral territory, for example, the French claim in Quebec. The third is the collective right to occupy and use ancestral lands or claim compensation in exchange for "extinguishing" aboriginal rights as certainly involves our native people. Kallen outlines what has already been accomplished in Canada, and she challenges Canadians to a greater vision inherent in the concept of multiculturalism. Much still remains to be done.

Prejudice and discrimination are negative attitudes exhibited by a majority group to deny some minorities the freedoms and rights of all. John Hagan (1977) reviewed the literature in North America, and in his search classified his findings into four types of discrimination (differential treatment, prejudicial treatment, disadvantaging treatment, and denial of desire). Other researchers (Driedger and Mezoff 1981) used Hagan's typology and suggested that the first two types were attitudinal (prejudice) and the last two behavioural (discrimination). Hagan realized that finding prejudice and discrimination empirically is not easy and suggested a social construction of discrimination somewhat akin to Berger and Luckmann's (1967) social construction of social reality. Not only is it difficult to find discrimination, it is also difficult to define. A Ukrainian Canadian may choose not to marry someone who is Jewish (differential treatment) not because of prejudice, but because he wants his children to grow up Greek Orthodox. The other types of discrimination are equally difficult to operationalize especially when empirical studies are attempted. For example, hard evidence in the Keegstra case was difficult to document even though there appeared to be prejudice against Jews. Although lawyers found much alleged and circumstantial evidence, it was very difficult to document empirically.

While prejudice and discrimination certainly have to do with images and symbols mentioned by Weber (1978) and Breton (1984), ethnic stereotypes involve even more symbolic interaction. Walter Lippmann (1922) was the first to use the term "stereotype" and assumed that his readers were familiar with the concept as used in the printing press. In this context, a stereotype is a plate made by molding a matrix of a printing surface and from this, casting a metal typeface which is used to print many standard unchanging pages of the same kind. As in the world of print, once negative or positive stereotypes of ethnic groups have been formed they are often difficult to change. Taylor and Lalonde (1987) suggest that stereotypes can serve important functions, such as defining categories but such definitions may over-simplify complex material, may not give enough credit to others, and may not be redefined to change an image when new evidence comes in. In reviewing Canadian studies, Taylor and Lalonde find that the stereotypes French Canadians have of English Canadians is often at variance with what the British think of themselves and vice versa. Stereotyping is a complex symbolic process which is difficult to study, but nevertheless some progress is being made in research.

While the contributions by Hagan and Taylor deal with the complexity of finding and defining subtle prejudice, discrimination, and stereotyping, Thomas Berger (1981) reports the extent to which Canadians were willing to blatantly and unjustly banish the Japanese from the west coast during the Second World War. There was nothing subtle about this national atrocity and Canadians today have not yet officially acknowledged any wrong-doing. Berger describes the racial bias shown towards Asians on the west coast: Asian immigrants were banned; economic opportunities were restricted; the vote was denied them; anti-Oriental feelings led to hatred, riots, and destruction of property; and finally, the Japanese were shipped inland, destroying their ethnic communities with loss of property as well as freedoms and rights.

Actions such as banishing the Japanese, slavery of the blacks, the Nazi holocaust and South African apartheid could be attributed to the unenlightened views of the past, were it not for the fact that half of Canada's land area still belongs to Canadian aboriginals and it has not yet been justly dealt with by treaty.

The high standards of the Charter of Rights and Freedoms and the policy of multiculturalism is problematic for Canadians. Our ideals have not yet been achieved and in many ways progress is slow. Kogila Moodley (1984) reviews the "Report of the Special Committee on Visible Minorities in Canada" which illustrates that many Canadians are concerned, and study and work is in progress. Many issues such as the politics of combatting racism, entrenching racial stigmatization leave us in the dilemma of whether the mainstream or the victim needs to be changed. The committee advocated the extension of existing affirmative action programs but it is difficult to implement. It is hard to ignore racial and ethnic cleavages especially if we take our Charter of Rights and Freedoms and our policy of multiculturalism seriously. However, to restore a better balance by instituting quotas and affirmative action to provide more opportunities for those who are underprivileged or who have been unjustly treated is also difficult. Increasingly Canadians are faced with painful problems as they create a just, multicultural society within a bilingual framework.

In the pages that follow we present a selection of contributions by well-known ethnic scholars. It is only a sampling, because in a short volume it is not possible to deal with everything that deserves attention. Each is a fine contribution to some of the major themes in ethnicity.

part I

Perspectives on ethnic persistence and change

Ethnic Groups[†]

MAX WEBER

"Race" Membership[1]

A problematic source of social action is "race identity," common inherited and inheritable traits that actually derive from common descent. Of course, race creates a "group" only when it is subjectively perceived as a common trait: this happens only when a neighborhood or the mere proximity of racially different persons is the basis of joint (mostly political) action, or conversely, when some common experiences of members of the same race are linked to some antagonism against members of an *obviously* different group. The resulting social action is usually merely negative: those who are obviously different are avoided and despised or, conversely, viewed with superstitious awe. Persons who are externally different are simply despised irrespective of what they accomplish or what they are, or they are venerated superstitiously if they are too powerful in the long run. In this case antipathy is the primary and normal reaction. However, this antipathy is shared not just by persons with anthropological similarities, and its extent is by no means determined by the degree of anthropological relatedness; furthermore, this antipathy is linked not only to inherited traits but just as much to other visible differences.

If the degree of objective racial difference can be determined, among other things, purely physiologically by establishing whether hybrids reproduce themselves at approximately normal rates, the subjective aspects, the reciprocal racial attraction and repulsion, might be measured by finding out whether sexual relations are preferred or rare between two groups, and whether they are carried on permanently or temporarily and irregularly. In all groups with a developed "ethnic" consciousness the existence or absence of intermarriage *(connubium)*

†Guenther Roth and Claus Wittich, eds., *Economy and Society*, vol. 1 (Berkeley: University of California Press, 1978), pp. 385–98.

would then be a normal consequence of racial attraction or segregation. Serious research on the sexual attraction and repulsion between different ethnic groups is only incipient, but there is not the slightest doubt that racial factors, that means, common descent, influence the incidence of sexual relations and of marriage, sometimes decisively. However, the existence of several million mulattoes in the United States speaks clearly against the assumption of a "natural" racial antipathy, even among quite different races. Apart from the laws against biracial marriages in the Southern states, sexual relations between the two races are now abhorred by both sides, but this development began only with the Emancipation and resulted from the Negroes' demand for equal civil rights. Hence this abhorrence on the part of the Whites is socially determined by the previously sketched tendency toward the monopolization of social power and honor, a tendency which in this case happens to be linked to race.

The *connubium* itself, that means, the fact that the offspring from a permanent sexual relationship can share in the activities and advantages of the father's political, economic or status group, depends on many circumstances. Under undiminished patriarchal powers, which we treat elsewhere, the father was free to grant equal rights to his children from slaves. Moreover, the glorification of abduction by the hero made racial mixing a normal event within the ruling strata. However, patriarchal discretion was progressively curtailed with the monopolistic closure, by now familiar to us, of political, status or other groups and with the monopolization of marriage opportunities; these tendencies restricted the *connubium* to the offspring from a permanent sexual union within the given political, religious, economic and status group. This also produced a high incidence of inbreeding. The "endogamy" of a group is probably everywhere a secondary product of such tendencies, if we define it not merely as the fact that a permanent sexual union occurs primarily on the basis of joint membership in some association, but as a process of social action in which only endogamous children are accepted as full members. (The term "sib endogamy" should not be used; there is no such thing unless we want to refer to the levirate marriage and arrangements in which daughters have the right to succession, but these have secondary, religious and political origins.) "Pure" anthropological types are often a secondary consequence of such closure; examples are sects (as in India) as well as pariah peoples, that means, groups that are socially despised yet wanted as neighbors because they have monopolized indispensable skills.

Reasons other than actual racial kinship influence the degree to which blood relationship is taken into account. In the United States the smallest admixture of Negro blood disqualifies a person unconditionally, whereas very considerable admixtures of Indian blood do not. Doubtlessly, it is important that Negroes appear esthetically even more alien than Indians, but it remains very significant that Negroes were slaves and hence disqualified in the status hierarchy. The conventional *connubium* is far less impeded by anthropological differences than by status differences, that means, differences due to socialization and upbringing (*Bildung* in the widest sense of the word). Mere anthropological differences account for little, except in cases of extreme esthetic antipathy.

The Belief in Common Ethnicity: Its Multiple Social Origins and Theoretical Ambiguities

The question of whether conspicuous "racial" differences are based on biological heredity or on tradition is usually of no importance as far as their effect on mutual attraction or repulsion is concerned. This is true of the development of endogamous conjugal groups, and even more so of attraction and repulsion in other kinds of social intercourse, i.e., whether all sorts of friendly, companionable, or economic relationships between such groups are established easily and on the footing of mutual trust and respect, or whether such relationships are established with difficulty and with precautions that betray mistrust.

The more or less easy emergence of social circles in the broadest sense of the word (*soziale Verkehrsgemeinschaft*) may be linked to the most superficial features of historically accidental habits just as much as to inherited racial characteristics. That the different custom is not understood in its subjective meaning since the cultural key to it is lacking, is almost as decisive as the peculiarity of the custom as such. But, as we shall soon see, not all repulsion is attributable to the absence of a "consensual group." Differences in the styles of beard and hairdo, clothes, food and eating habits, division of labor between the sexes, and all kinds of other visible differences can, in a given case, give rise to repulsion and contempt, but the actual extent of these differences is irrelevant for the emotional impact, as is illustrated by primitive travel descriptions, the Histories of Herodotus or the older prescientific ethnography. Seen from their positive aspect, however, these differences may give rise to consciousness of kind, which may become as easily the bearer of group relationships as groups ranging from the household and neighborhood to political and religious communities are usually the bearers of shared customs. All differences of customs can sustain a specific sense of honor or dignity in their practitioners. The original motives or reasons for the inception of different habits of life are forgotten and the contrasts are then perpetuated as conventions. In this manner, any group can create customs, and it can also effect, in certain circumstances very decisively, the selection of anthropological types. This it can do by providing favorable chances of survival and reproduction for certain hereditary qualities and traits. This holds both for internal assimilation and for external differentiation.

Any cultural trait, no matter how superficial, can serve as a starting point for the familiar tendency to monopolistic closure. However, the universal force of imitation has the general effect of only gradually changing the traditional customs and usages, just as anthropological types are changed only gradually by racial mixing. But if there are sharp boundaries between areas of observable styles of life, they are due to conscious monopolistic closure, which started from small differences that were then cultivated and intensified; or they are due to the peaceful or warlike migrations of groups that previously lived far from each other and had accommodated themselves to their heterogeneous conditions of existence. Similarly, striking different racial types, bred in isolation, may live in sharply segregated proximity to one another either because of monopolistic closure or because of migration. We can conclude then that similarity and contrast of physical type and custom, regardless of whether they are biologically inherited or culturally transmitted, are subject to the same conditions of group life, in origin as well as in effectiveness, and identical in their potential for group formation. The difference lies partly in the differential instability of type and custom, partly in the fixed (though often unknown) limit to engendering new hereditary qualities. Compared to this, the scope for assimilation of new customs is incomparably greater, although there are considerable variations in the transmissibility of traditions.

Almost any kind of similarity or contrast of physical type and of habits can induce the belief that affinity or disaffinity exists between groups that attract or repel each other. Not every belief in tribal affinity, however, is founded on the resemblance of customs or of physical type. But in spite of great variations in this area, such a belief can exist and can develop group-forming powers when it is buttressed by a memory of an actual migration, be it colonization or individual migration. The persistent effect of the old ways and of childhood reminiscences continues as a source of native-country sentiment *(Heimatsgefühl)* among emigrants even when they have become so thoroughly adjusted to the new country that return to their homeland would be intolerable (this being the case of most German-Americans, for example).

In colonies, the attachment to the colonists' homeland survives despite considerable mixing with the inhabitants of the colonial land and despite profound changes in tradition and hereditary type as well. In case of political colonization, the decisive factor is the need for political support. In general, the continuation of relationships created by marriage is important, and so are the market relationships, provided that the "customs" remained unchanged. These market relationships between the homeland and the colony may be very close, as long as the consumer standards remain similar, and especially when colonies are in an almost absolutely alien environment and within an alien political territory.

The belief in group affinity, regardless of whether it has any objective foundation, can have important consequences especially for the formation of a political community. We shall call "ethnic groups" those human groups that entertain a subjective belief in their common descent because of similarities of physical type or of customs or both, or because of memories of colonization and migration; this belief must be important for the propagation of group formation; conversely, it does not matter whether or not an objective blood relationship exists. Ethnic membership *(Gemeinsamkeit)* differs from the kinship group precisely by being a presumed identity, not a group with concrete social action, like the latter. In our sense, ethnic membership does not constitute a group; it only facilitates group formation of any kind, particularly in the political sphere. On the other hand, it is primarily the political community, no matter how artificially organized, that inspires the belief in common ethnicity. This belief tends to persist even after the disintegration of the political community, unless drastic differences in the custom, physical type, or, above all, language exist among its members.

This artificial origin of the belief in common ethnicity follows the pattern of rational association turning into personal relationships. If rationally regulated action is not widespread, almost any association, even the most rational one, creates an overarching communal consciousness; this takes the form of a brotherhood on the basis of the belief in common ethnicity. As late as the Greek city state, even the most arbitrary division of the *polis* became for the member an association with at least a common cult and often a common fictitious ancestor. The twelve tribes of Israel were subdivisions of a political community, and they alternated in performing certain functions on a monthly basis. The same holds for the Greek tribes *(phylai)* and their subdivisions; the latter, too, were regarded as units of common ethnic descent. It is true that the original division may have been induced by political or actual ethnic differences, but the effect was the same when such a division was made quite rationally and schematically, after the break-up of old groups and relinquishment of local cohesion, as it was done by Cleisthenes. It does not follow, therefore, that the Greek *polis* was actually or originally a tribal or lineage state, but that ethnic fictions were a sign of the rather low degree of rationalization of Greek political life. Conversely, it is a symptom of the greater rationalization of Rome that its old schematic subdivisions *(curiae)* took on religious importance, with a pretense to ethnic origin, to only a small degree.

The belief in common ethnicity often delimits "social circles," which in turn are not always identical with endogamous connubial groups, for greatly varying numbers of persons may be encompassed by both. Their similarity rests on the belief in a specific "honor" of their members, not shared by the outsiders, that is, the sense of "ethnic honor" (a phenomenon closely related to status honor). These few remarks must suffice at this point. A specialized sociological study of ethnicity would have to make a finer distinction between these concepts than we have done for our limited purposes.

Groups, in turn, can engender sentiments of likeness which will persist even after their demise and will have an "ethnic" connotation. The political community in particular can produce such an effect. But most directly, such an effect is created by the *language group*, which is the bearer of specific "cultural possession of the masses" *(Massenkulturgut)* and makes mutual understanding *(Verstehen)* possible or easier.

Wherever the memory of the origin of a community by peaceful secession or emigration ("colony," *ver sacrum*, and the like) from a mother community remains for some reason alive, there undoubtedly exists a very specific and often extremely powerful sense of ethnic identity, which is determined by several factors: shared political memories or, even more importantly in early times, persistent ties with the old cult or the strengthening of kinship and other groups, both in the old and the new community, or other persistent relationships. Where these ties are lacking, or once they cease to exist, the sense of ethnic group membership is absent, regardless of how close the kinship may be.

Apart from the community of language, which may or may not coincide with objective, or subjectively believed, consanguinity, and apart from common religious belief, which is also independent of consanguinity, the ethnic differences that remain are, on the one hand, esthetically conspicuous differences of the physical appearance (as mentioned before) and, on the other hand and of equal weight, the perceptible differences in the *conduct of everyday life*. Of special importance are precisely those items which may otherwise seem to be of small social relevance, since when ethnic differentiation is concerned it is always the conspicuous differences that come into play.

Common language and the ritual regulation of life, as determined by shared religious beliefs, everywhere are conducive to feelings of ethnic affinity, especially since the intelligibility of the behavior of others is the most fundamental presupposition of group formation. But since we shall not consider these two elements in the present context, we ask: what is it that remains? It must be admitted that palpable differences in dialect and differences of religion in themselves do not exclude sentiments of common ethnicity. Next to pronounced differences in the economic way of life, the belief in ethnic affinity has at all times been affected by outward differences in clothes, in the style of housing, food and eating habits, the division of labor between the sexes and between the free and the unfree. That is to say, these things concern one's conception of what is correct and proper and, above all, of what affects the individual's sense of honor and dignity. All those things are objects of specific differences between status groups. The conviction of the excellence of one's own customs and the inferiority of alien ones, a conviction which sustains the sense of ethnic honor, is actually quite analogous to the sense of honor of distinctive status groups.

The sense of ethnic honor is a specific honor of the masses (*Massenehre*), for it is accessible to anybody who belongs to the subjectively believed community of descent. The "poor white trash," i.e., the propertyless and, in the absence of job opportunities, very often destitute white inhabitants of the southern states of the United States of America in the period of slavery, were the actual bearers of racial antipathy, which was quite foreign to the planters. This was so because the social honor of the "poor whites" was dependent upon the social *déclassement* of the Negroes.

And behind all ethnic diversities there is somehow naturally the notion of the "chosen people," which is merely a counterpart of status differentiation translated into the plane of horizontal co-existence. The idea of a chosen people derives its popularity from the fact that it can be claimed to an equal degree by any and every member of the mutually despising groups, in contrast to status differentiation which always rests on subordination. Consequently, ethnic repulsion may take hold of all conceivable differences among the notions of propriety and transform them into "ethnic conventions."

Besides the previously mentioned elements, which were still more or less closely related to the economic order, conventionalization (a term expounded elsewhere) may take hold of such things as a hairdo or style of beard and the like. The differences thereof have an "ethnically" repulsive effect, because they are thought of as symbols of ethnic membership. Of course, the repulsion is not always based merely on the "symbolic" character of the distinguishing traits. The fact that the Scythian women oiled their hair with butter, which then gave off a rancid odor, while Greek women used perfumed oil to achieve the same purpose, thwarted—according to an ancient report—all attempts at social intercourse between the aristocratic ladies of these two groups. The smell of butter certainly had a more compelling effect than even the most prominent racial differences, or—as far as I could see—the "Negro odor," of which so many fables are told. In general, racial qualities are effective only as limiting factors with regard to the belief in common ethnicity, such as in case of an excessively heterogeneous and esthetically unaccepted physical type; they are not positively group-forming.

Pronounced differences of custom, which play a role equal to that of inherited physical type in the creation of feelings of common ethnicity and notions of kinship, are usually caused, in addition to linguistic and religious differences, by the diverse economic and political conditions of various social groups. If we ignore cases of clear-cut linguistic boundaries and sharply demarcated political or religious communities as a basis of differences of custom—and these in fact are lacking in wide areas of the African and South American continents—then there are only gradual transitions of custom and no immutable ethnic frontiers, except those due to gross geographical differences. The sharp demarcations of areas wherein ethnically relevant customs predominate, which were not conditioned either by political or economic or religious factors, usually came into existence by way of migration or expansion, when groups of people that had previously lived in complete or partial isolation from each other and became accommodated to heterogeneous conditions of existence came to live side by side. As a result, the obvious contrast usually evokes, on both sides, the idea of blood disaffinity (*Blutsfremdheit*), regardless of the objective state of affairs.

It is understandably difficult to determine in general—and even in a concrete individual case—what influence specific ethnic factors (i.e., the belief in a blood relationship, or its opposite, which rests on similarities, or differences, of a person's physical appearance and style of life) have on the formation of a group.

There is no difference between the ethnically relevant customs and customs in general, as far as their effect is concerned. The belief in common descent, in combination with a similarity of customs, is likely to promote the spread of the activities of one part of an ethnic group among the rest, since the awareness of ethnic identity furthers imitation. This is especially true of the propaganda of religious groups.

It is not feasible to go beyond these vague generalizations. The content of joint activities that are possible on an ethnic basis remains indefinite. There is a corresponding ambiguity of concepts denoting ethnically determined action, that means, determined by the belief in blood relationship. Such concepts are *Völkerschaft*, *Stamm* (tribe), *Volk* (people), each of which is ordinarily used in the sense of an ethnic subdivision of the following one (although the first two may be used in reversed order). Using such terms, one usually implies either the existence of a contemporary political community, no matter how loosely organized, or memories of an extinct political community, such as they are preserved in epic tales and legends; or the existence of a linguistic or dialect group; or, finally, of a religious group. In the past, cults in particular were the typical concomitant of a tribal or *Volk* consciousness. But in the absence of the political community, contemporary or past, the external delimitation of the group was usually indistinct. The cult communities of Germanic tribes, as late as the Burgundian period (6th century, A.D.), were probably rudiments of political communities and therefore pretty well defined. By contrast, the Delphian oracle, the undoubted cultic symbol of Hellenism, also revealed information to the barbarians and accepted their veneration, and it was an organized cult only among some Greek segments, excluding the most powerful cities. The cult as an exponent of ethnic identity is thus generally either a remnant of a largely political community which once existed but was destroyed by disunion and colonization, or it is—as in the case of the Delphian Apollo—a product of a *Kulturgemeinschaft* brought about by other than purely ethnic conditions, but which in turn, gives rise to the belief in blood relationship. All history shows how easily political action can give rise to the belief in blood relationship, unless gross differences of anthropological type impede it.

Tribe and Political Community: The Disutility of the Notion of "Ethnic Group"

The tribe is clearly delimited when it is a subdivision of a polity, which, in fact, often establishes it. In this case, the artificial origin is revealed by the round numbers in which tribes usually appear, for example, the previously mentioned division of the people of Israel into twelve tribes, the three Doric *phylai* and the various *phylai* of the other Hellenes. When a political community was newly established or reorganized, the population was newly divided. Hence the tribe is here a political artifact, even though it soon adopts the whole symbolism of blood-relationship and particularly a tribal cult. Even today it is not rare that political artifacts develop a sense of affinity akin to that of blood relationship. Very schematic constructs such as those states of the United States that were made into squares according to their latitude have a strong sense of identity; it is also not rare that families travel from New York to Richmond to make an expected child a "Virginian."

Such artificiality does not preclude the possibility that the Hellenic *phylai*, for example, were at one time independent and that the *polis* used them schematically when they were merged into a political association. However, tribes that existed before the *polis* were either identical with the corresponding political groups which were subsequently associated into a *polis*, and in this case they were called *ethnos*, not *phyle*; or, as it probably happened many times, the politically unorganized tribe, as a presumed "blood community," lived from the memory that it once engaged in joint political action, typically a single conquest or defense, and then such political memories constituted the tribe. Thus, the fact that tribal consciousness was primarily formed by common political experiences and not by common descent appears to have been a frequent source of the belief in common ethnicity.

Of course, this was not the only source: common customs may have diverse origins. Ultimately, they derive largely from adaptation to natural conditions and the imitation of neighbors. In practice, however, tribal consciousness usually has a political meaning: in case of military danger or opportunity, it easily provides the basis for joint political action on the part of tribal members or *Volksgenossen* who consider one another as blood relatives. The eruption of a drive to political action is thus one of the major potentialities inherent in the rather ambiguous notions of tribe and people. Such intermittent political action may easily develop into the moral duty of all members of tribe or people *(Volk)* to support one another in case of a military attack, even if there is no corresponding political association; violators of this solidarity may suffer the fate of the (Germanic, pro-Roman) sibs of Segestes and Inguiomer—expulsion from the tribal territory—even if the tribe has no organized government. If the tribe has reached this stage, it has indeed become a continuous political community, no matter how inactive in peacetime, and hence unstable, it may be. However, even under favorable conditions the transition from the habitual to the customary and therefore obligatory is very fluid. All in all, the notion of "ethnically" determined social action subsumes phenomena that a rigorous sociological analysis—as we do not attempt it here—would have to distinguish carefully: the actual subjective effect of those customs conditioned by heredity and those determined by tradition; the differential impact of the varying content of custom; the influence of common language, religion and political action, past and present, upon the formation of customs; the extent to which such factors create attraction and repulsion, and especially the belief in affinity or disaffinity of blood; the consequences of this belief for social action in general, and specifically for action on the basis of shared custom or blood relationship, for diverse sexual relations, etc.—all of this would have to be studied in detail. It is certain that in this process the collective term "ethnic" would be abandoned, for it is unsuitable for a really rigorous analysis. However, we do not pursue sociology for its own sake and therefore limit ourselves to showing briefly the diverse factors that are hidden behind this seemingly uniform phenomenon.

The concept of the "ethnic" group, which dissolves if we define our terms exactly, corresponds in this regard to one of the most vexing, since emotionally charged concepts: the *nation*, as soon as we attempt a sociological definition.

Nationality and Cultural Prestige

The concept of "nationality" shares with that of the "people" *(Volk)*—in the "ethnic" sense—the vague connotation that whatever is felt to be distinctively common must derive from common descent. In reality, of course, persons who consider themselves members of the same nationality are often much less related by common descent than are persons belonging to different and hostile nationalities. Differences of nationality may exist even among groups closely related by common descent, merely because they have different religious persuasions, as in the case of Serbs and Croats. The concrete reasons for the belief in joint nationality and for the resulting social action vary greatly.

Today, in the age of language conflicts, a shared common language is pre-eminently considered the normal basis of nationality. Whatever the "nation" means beyond a mere "language group" can be found in the specific objective of its social action, and this can only be the *autonomous polity*. Indeed, "nation state" has become conceptually identical with "state" based on common language. In reality, however, such modern nation states exist next to many others that comprise several language groups, even though these others usually have one official language. A common language is also insufficient in sustaining a sense of national identity *(Nationalgefühl)*—a concept which we will leave undefined for the present. Aside from the examples of the Serbs and Croats, this is demonstrated by the Irish, the Swiss and the German-speaking

Alsatians; these groups do not consider themselves as members, at least not as full members, of the "nation" associated with their language. Conversely, language differences do not necessarily preclude a sense of joint nationality: the German-speaking Alsatians considered themselves—and most of them still do—as part of the French "nation," even though not in the same sense as French-speaking nationals. Hence there are qualitative degrees of the belief in common nationality.

Many German-speaking Alsatians feel a sense of community with the French because they share certain customs and some of their "sensual culture" *(Sinnenkultur)*—as Wittich in particular has pointed out—and also because of common political experiences. This can be understood by any visitor who walks through the museum in Colmar, which is rich in relics such as tricolors, *pompier* and military helmets, edicts by Louis Philippe and especially memorabilia from the French Revolution; these may appear trivial to the outsider, but they have sentimental value for the Alsatians.[2] This sense of community came into being by virtue of common political and, indirectly, social experiences which are highly valued by the masses as symbols of the destruction of feudalism, and the story of these events takes the place of the heroic legends of primitive peoples. *La grande nation* was the liberator from feudal servitude, she was the bearer of civilization *(Kultur)*, her language was *the* civilized language; German appeared as a dialect suitable for everyday communication. Hence the attachment to those who speak the language of civilization is an obvious parallel to the sense of community based on common language, but the two phenomena are not identical; rather, we deal here with an attitude that derives from a partial sharing of the same culture and from shared political experiences.

Until a short time ago most Poles in Upper Silesia had no strongly developed sense of Polish nationality that was antagonistic to the Prussian state, which is based essentially on the German language. The Poles were loyal if passive "Prussians," but they were not "Germans" interested in the existence of the *Reich*; the majority did not feel a conscious or a strong need to segregate themselves from German-speaking fellow-citizens. Hence, in this case there was no sense of nationality based on common language, and there was no *Kulturgemeinschaft* in view of the lack of cultural development.

Among the Baltic Germans we find neither much of a sense of nationality amounting to a high valuation of the language bonds with the Germans, nor a desire for political union with the *Reich*; in fact, most of them would abhor such a unification. However, they segregate themselves rigorously from the Slavic environment, and especially from the Russians, primarily because of status considerations and partly because both sides have different customs and cultural values which are mutually unintelligible and disdained. This segregation exists in spite of, and partly because of, the fact that the Baltic Germans are intensely loyal vassals of the Tsar and have been as interested as any "national" Russian (*Nationalrusse*) in the predominance of the Imperial Russian system, which they provide with officials and which in turn maintains their descendants. Hence, here too we do not find any sense of nationality in the modern meaning of the term (oriented toward a common language and culture). The case is similar to that of the purely proletarian Poles: loyalty toward the state is combined with a sense of group identity that is limited to a common language group within this larger community and strongly modified by status factors. Of course, the Baltic Germans are no longer a cohesive status group, even though the differences are not as extreme as within the white population of the American South.

Finally, there are cases for which the term nationality does not seem to be quite fitting; witness the sense of identity shared by the Swiss and the Belgians or the inhabitants of Luxemburg and Liechtenstein. We hesitate to call them "nations," not because of their relative smallness—the Dutch appear to us as a nation—but because these neutralized states have forsaken power. The Swiss are not a nation if we take as criteria common language or common literature and art. Yet they have a strong sense of community despite some recent disintegrative tendencies. This sense of identity is not only sustained by loyalty toward the body politic but also by what are perceived to be common customs (irrespective of actual differences). These customs are largely shaped by the differences in social structure between Switzerland and Germany, but also all other big and hence militaristic powers. Because of the impact of bigness on the internal power structure, it appears to the Swiss that their customs can be preserved only by a separate political existence.

The loyalty of the French Canadians toward the English polity is today determined above all by the deep antipathy against the economic and social structure, and the way of life, of the neighboring United States; hence membership in the Dominion of Canada appears as a guarantee of their own traditions.

This classification could easily be enlarged, as every rigorous sociological investigation would have to do. It turns out that feelings of identity subsumed under the term "national" are not uniform but may derive from diverse sources: differences in the economic and social structure and in the internal power structure, with its impact on the customs, may play a role, but within the German *Reich* customs are very diverse; shared political memories, religion, language and, finally, racial features may be sources of the sense of nationality. Racial factors often have a peculiar impact. From the viewpoint of the Whites in the United States, Negroes and Whites are not united by a common sense of nationality, but the Negroes have a sense of American nationality at least by claiming a right to it. On the other hand, the pride of the Swiss in their own distinctiveness, and their willingness to defend it vigorously, is neither qualitatively different nor less widespread than the same attitudes in any "great" and powerful "nation." Time and again we find that the concept "nation" directs us to political power. Hence, the concept seems to refer—if it refers at all to a uniform phenomenon—to a specific kind of pathos which is linked to the idea of a powerful political community of people who share a common language, or religion, or common customs, or political memories; such a state may already exist or it may be desired. The more power is emphasized, the closer appears to be the link between nation and state. This pathetic pride in the power of one's own community, or this longing for it, may be much more widespread in relatively small language groups such as the Hungarians, Czechs or Greeks than in a similar but much larger community such as the Germans 150 years ago, when they were essentially a language group without pretensions to national power.

Notes

1. On race and civilization, see also Weber's polemical speech against A. Ploetz at the first meeting of the German Sociological Association, Frankfurt, 1910, in *Gesammelte Aufsätze zur Soziologie und Socialpolitik* (Tubingen, Germany: Paul Siebeck Publisher, 1924): 456–62. Two years later, at the second meeting of the Association in Berlin, Weber took the floor again after a presentation by Franz Oppenheimer. Among other things, Weber said:

   With race theories you can prove and disprove anything you want. It is a scientific crime to attempt the circumvention, by the uncritical use of completely unclarified racial hypotheses, of the sociological study of Antiquity, which of course is much more difficult, but by no means without hope of success; after all, we can no longer find out to what extent the qualities of the Hellenes and Romans rested on inherited dispositions. The problem of such relationships has not yet been solved by the most careful and toilsome investigations of living subjects, even if undertaken in the laboratory and with the means of exact experimentation (p. 489).

2. See Werner Wittich, *Deutsche und französische Kultur im Elsass* (Strassburg: Schlesier und Schweikhardt, 1900), 38ff; for a French translation, see "Le génie national des races française et allemande en Alsace," *Revue internationale de Sociologie* 10 (1902): 777–824 and 857–907, esp. 814ff. Cf. also Weber, in J.C.B. Mohr, *Gesammelte Aufsätze zur Religionssoziologie*, 3 vols. (Tubingen, Germany: Paul Siebeck Publisher, 1920–21) 1, 25, n.I; *GAzSS*, 484. "Outsiders," in contrast to the pre-1914 custodian who showed Weber his greatest treasures, cherish the Colmar museum for one of the most powerful works of art of the late Middle Ages, Grünewald's "Isenheim Altar."

The Ethnic Revolution: Emergence of Ethnic Nationalism[†]

JOANE NAGEL

Item: On May 30, 1967, Lieutenant-Colonel Emeku Ojukwu proclaimed the independent Republic of Biafra and launched a civil war with the Nigerian federal government. The war ended two-and-one-half years later with over one million dead.

Item: In the autumn of 1968, in Minneapolis, Minnesota, Russell Means, Dennis Banks, and a small group of American Indians formed the American Indian Movement (AIM). Its purpose, to protest and improve the conditions of American Indians in United States cities and on reservations.

Item: On August 26, 1977, the Quebec National Assembly, under the leadership of Premier Rene Levesque of the Parti Quebecois, passed Bill 101. The bill's passage revoked the Canadian policy of bilingualism, making French the official language of Quebec.

Item: Beginning on September 16, 1982, Lebanese Christian Phalangist militiamen embarked on a two-day massacre of several hundred Palestinian refugees in the Lebanese camps of Sabra and Shatila. Questions about the complicity or indifference of nearby occupying Israeli troops led to the resignation of Israeli Defense Minister, Ariel Sharon.

Secession, organization, devolution, and genocide represent the many faces of ethnicity in the modern world. It is difficult to overstate the role of ethnic conflict and ethnic mobilization as a force in world affairs. The substance and rhythm of national and international politics are shaped by the various ethnic configurations confined within or spanning the

[†]"The Ethnic Revolution: The Emergence of Ethnic Nationalism in Modern States," *Sociology and Social Research* 68 (1984): 417–34. My thanks to Susan Olzak for her comments on an earlier draft of this paper. The research was sponsored, in part, by a grant from the National Science Foundation.

boundaries of the world's states. Once identified, the pervasive presence of ethnicity may be seen underlying such political issues as East-West relations, North-South inequalities, human rights abuses, and short- and long-term political stability.

There are several important questions raised by the widespread, apparently escalating role of ethnicity in the modern world. First, to what extent are we witnessing a new historical phenomenon? The majority of the world's states are themselves new—most are less than 40-years-old, and much ethnic conflict and mobilization occurs within their borders. India, Pakistan, Iraq, Iran, Zaire, Angola, Ghana, Ethiopia, and Guyana only begin the list of new states confronting ethnic challenges to nationalism. They are not alone. The old states of Europe and the Americas also face ethnic challenges. Great Britain, Spain, Belgium, Canada, the United States, the Netherlands, Switzerland, and Finland can all testify to the power of ethnicity as a political force. Even relatively homogeneous states as Sweden and Germany face the political consequences of imported ethnicity in the form of immigrant labor.

2. A second important question concerning the dynamics of ethnicity in the modern world stems from the variability of primordial differences as precipitants of ethnic mobilization. That is, it is clear that religious, cultural, or linguistic differences among a population do not result in ethnic mobilization at all times, in all places. The question to be asked, then, is to what extent can we specify the conditions under which ethnic movements will occur?

3. A third question centers on the political and economic implications of high levels of ethnic mobilization for the stability and structure of governments in the world's states. What are the likely outcomes of the tendencies toward Balkanization within a large number of states? Will we see the continued proliferation of sovereign states? Or will there emerge suprastate confederations of subnational ethnic units?

The widespread presence of subnationally organized populations in a great variety of states—new and old, East and West, industrial and developing—has been both puzzling and provocative to social scientists.[1] During the past two decades, sociologists, anthropologists, and political scientists have been engaged in an attempt to piece together the components of the ethnic nationalism mosaic in hopes of constructing a body of explanation that links diverse ethnic phenomena in diverse locales and answers some of the questions concerning the causes and consequences of ethnic nationalism. The mosaic is not complete, but the outline of a general model of ethnic mobilization can be discerned and some of the details of an explanation of the timing and shape of modern ethic nationalism can be sketched. The remainder of this paper outlines several major current models of ethnic phenomena, categorizes them, and specifies their points of similarity and divergence. The paper concludes with a discussion of unresolved issues surrounding ethnic nationalism and lists the questions remaining that will determine future conceptual and empirical research agendas.

Current Explanations of Ethnic Nationalism

Current models of ethnic nationalism can be sorted into two categories: 1) explanations that emphasize economic structures and processes (e.g., resource competition, patterns of industrialization, the shape of labor force participation), and 2) explanations that emphasize political structures and processes (e.g., the form of political organization, the structure of political access, patterns of political participation). Although these current models of ethnic nationalism represent diverse, often divergent points of view, they are distinguishable from traditional conceptions of ethnicity and ethnic processes in that they challenge the assimilationist/primordial assumptions of earlier models. Rather than presuming that ethnic divisions are atavistic leftovers from pre-modern forms of social organization, expected to disappear momentarily, the new vision of ethnicity emphasizes the *emergent* qualities of ethnic identity and organization, arguing that ethnic boundaries among a population are likely to be strengthened rather than diminished by economic and political processes underway in modern states. Before moving to a detailed discussion of the current economic and political explanations of ethnic nationalism, it will be useful to elaborate briefly on these points of divergence from earlier theory.

Challenged Models: Assimilationist and Primordial Explanations

One reason for the recent increased attention paid to ethnic phenomena by social science researchers has been the failure of earlier assimilationist, primordial models of ethnicity to predict modern ethnic mobilization (see, for instance, Lipset 1960, Deutsch 1961, Geertz 1963, Azkin 1964). In fact, these models foretold of a *decline* in cultural, linguistic, or religious divisions among populations in the face of industrial development and the expansion and consolidation of central state power. What occurred in virtually every country in the world was precisely the opposite: an intensification of religious, cultural, linguistic differences and a glorification of "the tribe" (Isaacs 1975a, 1975b). There are two major reasons why this negative evidence has been particularly damaging to the assimilationist/primordial model. First is the *timing* of the ethnic intensifications, and second is the *newness* of many ethnic groups.

Timing

The post-World War II period was expected by assimilationist theorists to be especially destructive of primordial bases of identification because of the proliferation of the number of sovereign states and the expected spread of industrialization and its accompanying urbanization. The construction of nationally-oriented citizens out of locally-oriented tribals was the anticipated result of the elimination of traditional regional political and economic organization in favor of modern national, political and economic organizations. The fact that the greatest levels of ethnic political mobilization in world history occurred precisely during this period of intense state building and urbanization in the new states and large-scale industrialization in the old states, discredited the assimilationist model.

Newness

The primordial model of ethnicity has shown itself to be somewhat more tenacious as an intuitive way of understanding ethnic phenomena, but has been no more consistent with empirical evidence than the assimilationist model. The view of ethnic organization and identity as rooted in earlier epochs, reaching forward to shape the attitudes and behavior of current group members does not mesh well with a multitude of examples of the *production* of ethnicity. The black renaissance in the United States (Singer 1962, Patterson 1977), the emergence of pan-Indian cultural and organizational forms in Canada and the United States (Hertzberg 1971, Ponting and Gibbons 1980), the construction of Sinhalese identity in Sri Lanka (Horowitz 1977: 160, Kearney 1967: 40–51), and the unification of Scheduled Caste (Untouchable) groups in India (Fiske 1972, Rudolph and Rudolph 1967) are all examples of the creation of ethnic culture and organization. They illustrate the ways in which newly forming ethnic groups construct history and culture partly by borrowing from historical or anthropological records (where they exist) of putative or actual ancestral groups and practices (Hodgkin 1956: 177, Horowitz 1977: 13–14, Young 1965: 266) and partly by creating new cultural forms (Spindler and Spindler 1978: 80, 83, Stanley and Thomas 1978: 117, Hobsbawm and Ranger 1983).[2]

Dynamic and Emergent Ethnicity

As it became clear 1) that ethnic boundaries would not disappear in the face of economic and political development, that indeed they would intensify, and 2) that much ethnic mobilization was not based on archaic forms of social organization and identification, but was in fact newly organized cultural and social organization, then the search among social scientists was underway for new ways of understanding modern ethnicity. The remainder of this paper presents the fruits of those efforts. As with all ventures into creative explanation, the results do not fall easily into a coherent, consistent, complete theory of ethnic group formation and action. The following discussion therefore will explicate the various understandings of ethnicity in current theory and provide some overarching structure of explanation to tie the arguments together. The review begins with economic explanations of ethnic processes followed by a discussion of political explanations.

Economic Models of Ethnic Processes

Two threads of theoretical and empirical research combine into a single strand of economic explanation of ethnic mobilization and intergroup relations. The first, which I shall label the "ecological model," mainly developed by anthropologists and extended by sociologists, explores the relationship between ethnic boundaries and economic production niches. The second thread, which I shall label the "economic organization model," arises mainly from the work of sociologists and examines the role played by the organization of the economy and the division of labor in subnational mobilization.

The Ecological Model

Cultural materialism stresses the importance of technology and environment in determining the form and substance of culture. According to this argument, environmental constraints on economic production and technological limits in overcoming the environment lead to particular cultural adaptations. For instance, Harris (1974) outlines various cultural and religious practices (e.g., the sacredness of cows in Hindu societies) as solutions to, rather than causes of, the problems of scarcity and competition in a number of societies. While this explanation has its critics, the role of environment and technology in producing one particular sort of cultural unit, the ethnic group, has produced a rich body of theory and research. This ecological model of ethnicity is best articulated in the work of Barth (1969) and his associates. Challenging the primacy of culture and asserting it to be essentially a reflection of economic organization rather than a major force in determining the shape of production, Barth links the emergence and maintenance of ethnic differences (which he calls "boundaries") to competition for resources in various ecological niches. An example may be found among the Pathans (Pushtu) of Afghanistan. Barth (1969: 127) argues that Pushtu identity can only be maintained where economic surpluses are very large since cultural prescriptions require hospitality and patronage. Thus, when economic conditions do not produce adequate surpluses, rather than lose face by violating cultural norms, Pushtu change ethnic identity (becoming members of other groups, such as Baluchi or Punjabi).

The importance of competition as a determinant of ethnic solidarity and inter-ethnic relations is central to the ecological model and represents its major contribution to understanding ethnic phenomena.

The Mutability of Ethnic Boundaries in Inter-ethnic Relations

Just as the ecological model links ethnic boundaries to economic production niches, it identifies resource competition as the underlying dynamic in inter-ethnic relations. Assimilation, pluralism, domination, conflict, and cooperation all characterize inter-ethnic relations. Which form relations take depends on several factors: population size, group organizational ability, technological strength, and political influence. Whether inter-ethnic relations are placid or combative, however, according to the ecological perspective, directly depends on the existence of inter-ethnic resource competition.

Resources can be economic or political. Economic resource competition has dominated the work of anthropologists employing the ecological model (Barth 1969, Harris 1964, Despres 1975). Sociologists borrowing and extending this view (Hannan 1979, Lauwagie 1979, Nielsen 1980, Olzak 1982) have focused on both economic *and* political resource competition. And, whereas most anthropological research has focused on ethnic relations in non-industrial societies, mainly examining competition for such economic resources as land, water, and tilling or herding rights, sociological research employing the ecological model has turned to industrial societies and to such economic resources as jobs and capital as well as to political resources such as entitlements and representation. Examples of the latter include Lauwagie's (1982) analysis of Gypsy organization in the United States and Great Britain and Lieberson's (1970) and Olzak's (1982) examinations of Quebec nationalism. (See Banton, 1983, for an extensive general discussion of the role of competition in ethnic relations.)

Ecological theory posits several likely outcomes for ethnic groups as a function of the degree of econo/political inter-ethnic competition: 1) ethnic mobilization—where groups organize along ethnic lines in order to compete for jobs, markets, political influence; 2) ethnic solidarity—where groups close ranks, promoting endogamy in all social spheres (marriage, business, education) and glorifying ethnic uniqueness (seen in celebrations of language, culture, religion); and 3) ethnic antagonism—where groups develop hostilities toward other ethnic groups seen as competitors, with hostilities taking the form of either ideology (racism) or action (pogroms, riots). In all of these cases, group boundaries and individual ethnic identification are strengthened in response to competition. Thus ethnicity waxes and wanes as the degree of competition rises and declines.

The ecological model stresses the situational, flexible nature of ethnic boundaries, links ethnic boundaries to economic production niche boundaries, and identifies inter-ethnic resource competition as the major determinant of several important ethnic processes (mobilization, solidarity, antagonism). As we shall see below, the role of competition in inter-ethnic relations is a shared characteristic of other economic and political models of ethnicity.

The Economic Organization Model

Two themes divide the literature on the relationship of ethnicity to the organization of the economy and the division of labor. The first is generally referred to as "internal colonialism." The second is the "labor market model." The internal colonialism perspective examines the ways in which center exploitation of peripheries enhances ethnic differences. The labor market model focuses more narrowly on the role of ethnicity in labor and commodity markets.

Internal Colonialism

The internal colonialism model attempts to account for the persistence of ethno-regional differences in industrial or industrializing societies where the development of national economies was expected to replace ethnic divisions among the population with unified national identities (Deutsch 1961). The failure of development to eliminate subnationalism, so evident in mobilization among the Welsh, Scottish, Bretons, Catalans, Basques, and Quebecois, led researchers to abandon the search for evidence of integration and assimilation. Instead, internal colonialism researchers sought to account for continued and more often heightened ethnic mobilization by examining patterns of internal exclusion and exploitation. According to the model, many peripheral groups are simply never integrated. Rather, their isolation in peripheral areas is the result of exclusionary policies, and their poverty the result of exploitative programs designed not to develop, but to impoverish peripheral regions.

Hechter's (1971, 1975) analysis of Great Britain outlines the role of peripheral exploitation and subjugation by a dominant, culturally distinct center, and represents the most fully elaborated description of internal colonialism and its impact on ethnic relations. Just as under colonialism, resources and labor residing in geographic peripheries were developed and extracted by a culturally alien, technologically and organizationally superior dominating group. Under internal colonialism, regionally peripheral labor and resources are developed for the enrichment of center groups and interests. The result is an ethnically distinct, economically disadvantaged peripheral population that mobilizes in reaction to exploitation.[3]

One problem with this scenario is its failure to account for the timing of ethnic mobilization. What we see is a culturally distinct group residing in an historically disadvantaged periphery, its resources dwindling, laboring at the command of the center. While we might understand how such a group could remain unassimilated, it is less clear when solidarity would ever be enhanced or when mobilization might occur. Internal colonialism paints a picture of despair, not revolt. This incongruity is more troubling when we examine it in light of social movements' resource mobilization theory which predicts mobilization in the presence, not the absence of resources and organization (McCarthy and Zald 1977, Tilly 1978).

Another troublesome feature of the internal colonialism explanation, a feature shared with the labor market model presented below, is the tendency to view ethnic groups as pre-existing or primordial. As stated above, this view is inconsistent with much evidence[4] of mobilization among new ethnic groups. Both models could easily be made compatible with the view of ethnic boundaries as constructed rather than prior, but as they now stand, they presume the existence of activated ethnic differences.

Labor Market Model

Labor market explanations of ethnic conflict and group formation divide on the issue of labor market segregation. Some researchers emphasize a "cultural division of labor" in which various ethnic groups are segregated into various occupational niches, while others point to the importance of "split labor markets" and intra-niche ethnic competition, where two or more ethnic groups compete for jobs and resources.

The Cultural Division of Labor

The tendency for ethnic groups to cluster in particular occupations or to specialize in particular goods and services has long been the stuff of stereotyping. However, to the extent that networks assist in the acquisition of employment (Granovetter 1974), ethnic ties tend to produce ethnically-linked jobs and markets (Reitz 1982, Cohen 1969). One of the outcomes associated with ethnic group membership, then, can be employment. This is not necessarily an advantage, however. Research demonstrates that there are costs in prestige and income associated with employment in ethnically segregated occupations (Li 1977, Hechter 1978, Tolbert et al. 1980). These liabilities create incentives for ethnic group members to seek a way out of segregated labor markets. And while a culturally divided economy is one where ethnic differences might be expected to be maintained, a desegregated labor market, but one which promotes job competition on the basis of ethnicity, is likely to result in increased ethnic self- and other-awareness.

The Split Labor Market

Bonacich's (1972, 1975, 1979) analysis of "split" labor markets illustrates the process by which the *breakdown* of culturally divided labor markets leads to increased ethnic solidarity, antagonism, and mobilization. The key to understanding the link between desegregation and ethnic mobilization is competition. Employing examples such as the Japanese in California, Chinese in Mississippi, and black Africans in South Africa, Bonacich (1972) shows how the splitting of labor markets along ethnic lines, with the cheaper labor of one group competing with the more costly labor of another group promotes ethnic antagonism between the two groups. A classic example of ethnic antagonism resulting from the splitting of labor markets along ethnic lines, is the use of ethnic scabs to break strikes. Wilson (1978) and Leiberson (1980) report such hostilities directed toward blacks by white strikers in United States northern industries during the nineteenth century.

A comparison of the cultural division of labor and the split labor market arguments reveals a disturbing feature in the labor market model. While the internal colonialism model fails to predict the conditions under which ethnic groups will mobilize or engage in hostile action, the labor market model fails *not* to predict such ethnic phenomena. We find *no* conditions under which ethnic boundaries are not enhanced. For instance, the literature informs us that when labor markets are ethnically segregated, ethnic group membership is an important factor in determining access, and thus ethnic identity and group organization are strengthened. The literature also informs us, however, that the *breakdown* of ethnically segregated labor markets increases inter-ethnic hostility by promoting ethnically-organized job competition, and thus ethnic identity and group organization are strengthened.

Olzak (1983) offers an explanation for this apparent contradiction by pointing out the difference between ethnic solidarity (an *intra*-group process) on the one hand, and ethnic antagonism (an *inter*-group process) on the other. Labor market segregation promotes *intra-ethnic* group organization—a necessary factor in ethnic solidarity. Desegregation promotes *inter-ethnic* group competition—an antecedent to ethnic antagonism. In both cases ethnic boundaries are enhanced and ethnicity is strengthened, however, the mechanisms differ. The two forces combine to produce ethnic mobilization—a process building on and enhancing solidarity, but often resulting from competition and antagonism.

Political Models of Ethnic Processes

The ascendency of the political sector over the cultural, social, and often the economic sectors in modern societies (Bell 1975) is reflected in explanations that emphasize the relationship between the structure and process of politics and ethnic solidarity, antagonism, and mobilization.

Governments tend either to recognize ethnic pluralism in a way that can be noted in political organization and administration or they tend to submerge ethnic differences in favor of the rhetoric and policies of national unity. Switzerland, for instance, with its constitutionally-recognized language diversity and its decentralized, ethnically-organized federated system of decision-making, represents one end of a continuum of ethnic institutionalization. France represents the other end with its constitutionally-asserted national unity and its centralized system of administration.

There is debate among researchers regarding the exact nature of the relationship between ethnic diversity and the political recognition and institutionalization of ethnicity. One side, which I shall call the "political reaction model," argues for the primacy of ethnic differences and sees the institutionalization of ethnicity in national politics simply as a reflection of the need to manage extant ethnic conflict. The other position in the ethnicity/polity debate, which I shall call the "political construction model," argues for exactly the opposite relationship—that the organization of politics can actually produce ethnicity by providing a rationale and incentive for ethnic mobilization. The next two sections present in more detail the two sides in this debate.

The Political Reaction Model

The view of political organization as a strategy for dealing with conflicts arising out of historical linguistic, religious, or cultural divisions among a national population—of politics as a reaction to ethnicity—dominated the primordial and assimilationist models of ethnicity outlined above. While the assimilationist vision of national societies as melting pots has largely been abandoned by social scientists, at least for the present, the primordial model's view of ethnic differences as historically rooted, remains a viable assumption among many students and practitioners of ethnopolitics.

Enloe (1977) and Young (1982) outline several strategies employed by states for dealing with ethnic pluralism. They can be summarized into three categories: assimilation, pluralism, and segregation. While the explicit assimilationist assumptions embedded in the idea of the "nation-state"—sovereign, territorial units containing ethnically homogeneous populations—have lost currency among scholars, Enloe (1977) points out their continued popularity among politicians and administrators in a number of countries, including the United States, Soviet Union, and China.

The pluralist strategy for ethnic management is perhaps best recognized in the body of research referred to as "consociationalism." Lijphart's (1969, 1977) discussion of "consociational democracy" outlines several characteristics of culturally plural democratic states, such as Switzerland, Belgium, Lebanon (until the mid-1970s), the Netherlands, and Austria. They are: 1) clear lines of division among ethnic constituent communities, 2) a balance of power among ethnic constituent communities, 3) leaders who command loyalty representing each ethnic community in, 4) a political system which stresses accommodation and negotiation rather than domination and coercion. Following the "politics of accommodation" (Lijphart 1968) rather than the politics of confrontation, consociationalists represent the interests of their culturally distinct constituencies while simultaneously operating in the interest of unity. Barry (1975) and Steiner and Obler (1975) have criticized Lijphart for presenting more a description of varyingly successful cultural elite cooperation than a theory of stable plural political accommodation.

One key element in that description, however, that points a path toward theory is the notion of proportional representation. The idea is that the composition of representation in governing bodies should mirror the ethnic composition of the electorate. By focusing on ethnic differences as the differences to be represented, and therefore as the important cleavages in the political system, other potential sources of conflict become submerged. Thus, van den Berghe (1981: 188) notes "an essential corollary of ethnic proportionality in CDs (consociational democracies) is the muting of class conflicts. To the extent that ethnic sentiments are politicized, class consciousness is lowered." This observation suggests a rationale for elite emphasis of ethnicity in politics. It also suggests that politics is not so much a simple *reaction* to prior ethnic differences as a mechanism for the *construction* of ethnic differences—a theme that will be developed in the section below.

The third general political strategy for handling ethnic diversity—segregation—is reflected in the current literature on genocide (Kuper 1981) and apartheid (Fredrickson 1981). Here the emphases are on the processes that lead to and result from segregative forms of political reaction. Kuper (1981) outlines several instances of genocidal action locating common themes of intergroup competition and political crisis. Such crises can take the form of post-revolutionary political consolidation (as in the mass expulsion of ethnic Chinese from Vietnam in the late 1970s or the repression of Bahais in Iran in the early 1980s), as well as the search for enemies in times of war (as in the cases of Turkey in World War I, Germany in World War II, and Bangladesh in its secessionist war with Pakistan).

Political reactions to ethnic diversity that result in the often quasi-genocidal policies of segregation, such as forced migration and relocation, are typified in current research on the political treatment of indigenous populations. Banton (1983) points out similarities in the treatment of native peoples (land seizures, relocations, reservations) in a number of countries. Again the explanation centers on intergroup competition, with political policy as the mechanism whereby the dominant group wins. James' (1982, 1985) discussion of the racial categories and associated policies of South African apartheid shows the obvious attractiveness of these policies for controlling competition for land and for providing Afrikaners a source of cheap labor. In addition, James points out the usefulness to those in power of particular sorts of racial desegregation (e.g., "coloureds" whose recent enfranchisement provided the South African regime a veneer of "movement" toward racial equality) and reveals the arbitrariness of racial boundaries, once again suggesting a politically constructed definition of ethnicity, which has consequences for subsequent ethnic identification and group formation.

The Political Construction Model

Those researchers emphasizing the role of political reactions in promoting ethnic conflict and mobilization, tend to stress the importance of prior ethnic diversity, albeit politically recognized, in producing the various patterns of political reaction. In contrast, there has emerged among scholars of ethnic politics a growing recognition of the power of the polity to create new ethnic groups out of extant, but often unorganized ethno-cultural categories (Young 1985), and to promote ethnic awareness and action among formerly mobilized, recently inactive, ethnic groups. The literature suggests four mechanisms whereby political ideology, organization, and policy can create or enhance ethnic identification and group formation.[5]

Nationalist Ideology

Smith (1971) and Connor (1967, 1975) locate the roots of modern ethnic subnationalism in nineteenth-century nationalist ideology, in particular in the "notion that the right to rule is vested in *the people*...ethnically defined people" (Connor 1975: 25). This link between the ideology of national politics and the mobilization of ethnic groups wielding that ideology in the name of subnational independence or autonomy rather than national unity (Smith 1979: 156), represents the first of several ways in which politics constructs or promotes ethnicity.

Ethnicization of the Military

A more planned, political strategy for the strengthening of ethnic differences can be found in Enloe's (1978, 1980) analyses of the role of ethnicity in the composition of militaries. She points out "the almost universal tendency of militaries...to fail to mirror the populations they are intended to protect" (1978: 267). Given the important direct political role played by the military in many of the world's states, this fact of disproportionate military ethnic composition can have great consequences for disproportionate access to power, status, and wealth. Ethnic preferences in the military can promote ethnic identification shifts as in the case of the Sikhs in India (Nayar 1966) or among Tamils in Sri Lanka (Schwartz 1975) and can instigate inter-ethnic antagonism by encouraging competition on the basis of *ethnicity*.

Official Recognition of Ethnic Groups

The official recognition of certain ethnic groups for official purposes is a third way in which politics enhances ethnic identification and group formation. Horowitz (1975: 116) points to the census category as an indicator of the importance of a particular ethnicity. And James (1985) describes the power of political categories to produce "ethnic" groups in South Africa. When special designations involve the allocation of resources (land, educational programs, jobs, housing, financial reparations), the impetus to mobilize increases. Both designated and competing non-designated groups are candidates. Padilla (1982) illustrates the role of politically allocated resource competition in an emerging Latino identity and Greeley (1976) reveals a similar strain in the "white ethnic" movement.

Ethnic Administrative Units

The creation of special administrative units to manage ethnic populations is a fourth way politics produces ethnicity. Enloe (1981) argues that the functioning of government agencies often spotlights political ethnic policies in a way that mobilizes interested constituencies. She cites as examples the United States Immigration and Naturalization Service, arguing that because of its controversial policies "the INS has become a stimulus for Chicano (and other Hispanic group) mobilization" (1981: 133). Similarly, the Bureau of Indian Affairs is the foil against which much American Indian mobilization has occurred (Butler 1978).

The debate between the political reaction and political construction adherents remains unresolved. The power of primordial ethnicity as a lone force in politics, unaugmented by political recognition or resources, seems less compelling in light of the findings of researchers during the 1970s. As Rothschild (1981) points out, while religious, cultural, or linguistic differences can inevitably be found among a population, a "politicization of ethnicity" is required to transform these subpopulations into mobilized ethnic groups contending for political power.

Conclusion

The expansion of the world state system after the Second World War set the stage for much of the ethnic nationalist activity that dominates world politics today. This empirical reality challenged and largely discredited prevailing models of the political development of "nation-states" in political science and political sociology. The subsequent demise of assimilationist/primordial models of ethnicity has become a positive force producing a renaissance in social science theory construction.

While the new models outlined above portray ethnicity as a dynamic emergent force in social, economic, and political life, their emphasis on intra-state political and economic processes combined with the timing of new state proliferation suggests that current ethnic nationalism may be historically specific, unique to this particular period of world history, and ultimately the ephemeral phenomenon it was first conceived. While this remains a possibility, there are several reasons to believe that ethnic nationalism will be more tenacious than such an epochal view suggests.

First, ethnic nationalism, like the state nationalism it challenges, is a difficult notion to delegitimate. The moral unassailability of appeals for self-determination and self-rule serve as testimony to their near status in the modern political consciousness. Even so pervasive and currently compelling an ideology as socialism finds itself continually confronted by subnationalist demands for home rule and finds its programs challenged by the subsequent decentralization of decision-making and resource allocation that results from such local control.

A second reason suggesting a lengthy tenure for ethnic nationalism can be found, ironically, in the growth of supranational organizations linking sovereign states. The proliferation of such organizations as the UN, the EEC, the OAU, SEATO, NATO, ASEAN, and the OAS provide both a rationale and a variety of incentives to subnationalists. The rationale stems from the principles upon which member states' own formation depended: self-determination and independent sovereignty. Such organizations provide constant reaffirmation of these "rights" of nations, and to the extent that ethnonationalists see themselves as "nations," their claims are likewise affirmed. The incentives are similarly built into the organizations themselves. The lowered costs and increased advantages of independent status for an ethnic national group (say, Quebec or Biafra or Wales) in many supranational organizations often make secession an attractive option. For instance, representation and voting rights are generally afforded sovereign states, but not dependent nationality groups (see Nagel and Olzak 1982, for an elaboration of this argument).

Third, while the production of sovereign states has slowed, the same structural and ideological forces remain at large (Wallerstein 1976, 1980), and as it has been argued above, continue to promote subnational mobilization. Whether those economic and political forces will expand the number of independent states to accommodate all groups aspiring to sovereignty is difficult to gauge, particularly since there seems to be a good deal of resistance to dismantling once-erected state boundaries (Young 1976: 66). What is more clear, however, is the ascendancy of cultural pluralism as a political strategy for accommodation within states. Consociationalism, federalism, and devolution may be more the wave of the future than will be Balkanization.

Questions remaining for researchers in the following decades center on the future size and organization of the world state system, the future structure and operation of politics in plural states, the ultimate consequences of the rise of ethnic nationalism for both inter- and intra-state ethnic relations (given the emergence of international pan-ethnic movements and increased competition among ethnic groups enclosed in single states). Since it is virtually impossible for us in the late twentieth century to image a world *not* organized into sovereign states, and given the forces that operate within those states to promote and create ethnic differences, one prediction that can comfortably be made is that the mobilization of ethnicity and its accompanying production of ethos shall remain staple ingredients in world politics.

Notes

1. For a discussion of several processes underway in both new and old states that produce parallel effects on ethnic mobilization, see Nagel and Olzak, 1982.
2. The notion of ethnicity as "new" rather than inherited flies in the face of conventional wisdom, but is more consistent with empirical observations. There are two ways we can conceive of ethnicity as new. First, ethnicity may be *emergent*—as in the case of "Latinos" in the United States (Padilla 1982) or Sikhs in India (Horowitz 1975: 117)—where there is little or no historical identity and where the new ethnic group is a hybrid or amalgam of other language, religious, or kinship units. Or ethnicity may be *resurgent*—as in the case of Quebecois in Canada (Cappon 1978: 327–44) or Palestinians in the Middle East (Plascov 1981: 16–28)—where the group has a history of distinctiveness, but has only recently mobilized.
3. There have been some efforts to extend the notion of "internal colonies" to geographically non-isolated but socio-economically disadvantaged groups, such as blacks or Chicanos in the United States (Blauner 1969, Hurstfield 1978). However, these arguments are essentially labor market explanations and are described in that section below.
4. Some of which are cited above. Other studies showing evidence of newly formed ethnic groups (i.e., those with no history of unity) include Horowitz 1975 (the Tamils of India), Kearney 1967 (the Sinhalese of Pakistan), Nag 1968 (the Naga of India), Kasfir 1979 (the Bakedi and Bagisu of Uganda), Liddle 1970 (the North Tapanuli Batak of Indonesia), and Roff 1975 (the Kadazan of Sabah, Malaysia).
5. A more elaborated discussion of these mechanisms may be found in "The Political Construction of Ethnicity" (Nagel 1984).

Symbolic Dimensions of Linguistic and Ethnocultural Realities[†]

RAYMOND BRETON

In the social climate prevailing in a post-industrial, capitalist society like that of Canada, considerations of collective identity, symbolic interests and behaviour, and social status or honour appear to contribute little to the determination of social organization. The formation of groups, the structuring of their interrelationships, patterns of social inequality, and the functioning of societal institutions seem influenced primarily by material and utilitarian rather than ideal forces and interests. The central lines of conflict among groups and organizations would appear to revolve around the material basis of social life. The growth of that sphere and the distribution of the benefits generated from it seem the basis of the legitimacy of state institutions, and indeed of the entire social system.

Such an impression of society's driving forces can also be obtained from a rapid overview of sociological research in Canada. Indeed, this research seems to reflect how insignificant are matters pertaining to the symbolic-cultural order and the corresponding social agencies and resources.[1] The emphasis seems more on social classes than on status groups.[2] The utilitarian dimension of power relationships and inequalities—both economic and political—seems to receive more attention than the symbolic dimension. The prevailing theoretical approaches or those contending for intellectual dominance in the discipline seem to agree on the centrality of material interests: political economy, neo-Marxism, dependency theories, centre-periphery analysis, conflict theory,[3] and organizational or interorganizational analysis.

[†]"The Production and Allocation of Symbolic Resources: An Analysis of the Linguistic and Ethnocultural Fields in Canada," *Canadian Review of Sociology and Anthropology* 21, 2 (1984): 123–44. This paper was originally presented as the Harry Hawthorne Lecture at the Canadian Sociology and Anthropology Association annual meeting, Vancouver, June 1983.

This slant is also apparent in the recent preoccupation with the role of the state. Much attention is indeed given to the role that state institutions have and continue to play in relation to phenomena such as the accumulation and investment of capital, science and technology, and human capital (including the changing place of women in the socioeconomic structure), and in relation to issues pertaining to the quality of life, but with a focus on its material dimensions—health, housing, and the environment.

Even the study of linguistic and cultural phenomena and especially of the relations among the groups involved has been affected by this "économisme,"[4] although the tendency is perhaps less pronounced in this than in other areas. In this article, I would like to argue that much of society's activities cannot be adequately understood if we over-emphasize the material dimension to the detriment of the symbolic dimension of social organization. This analysis will apply notions and propositions from Weber, analysts of symbolic behaviour, including symbolic interactionists, and from students of status behaviour and politics. First, some of the ways in which the symbolic order has changed will be examined, with a focus on the linguistic and ethnocultural fields. For this purpose, the distinction between the production of symbolic resources and their distribution will be used.[5] Initially, attention will be given to the processes involved in attempting to regenerate the cultural-symbolic capital of the society—to restructure the collective identity and the associated symbolic contents. However, the production of the symbolic order and its transformation entail, almost inevitably, an allocation or re-allocation of social status or recognition among various segments of the society. Accordingly, some of the processes involved in this redistribution and the resistance to it will also be considered.

Second, the role that the state[6] has assumed in these processes will be taken into account. As is well known, a vigorous debate has been going on about the linguistic and ethnocultural fields and government intervention in it. Up until recently, much of the controversy appears to have been over the content of these policies—what should or should not be done in relation to particular issues or problems. By and large, the debate seems to have occurred within a fairly wide consensus as to the necessity and perhaps even the desirability of state involvement in this domain.

Recently, however, a breach appears in that consensus: some critics begin to question or oppose the very idea of state intervention on matters of language and/or ethnicity (e.g., Brotz 1980, Peter 1982, Porter 1975, Roberts and Clifton 1982, Smiley 1980, Vano 1981). Implicitly, if not explicitly, these critics advocate a "laissez-faire" attitude on the part of state institutions in relation to the symbolic order.

This controversy is certainly worthwhile. The debate, however, would benefit considerably from more theory and research on the social forces leading the state to intervene in that field in the first place. Such an analysis, it would seem to me, should precede the formulation of models and hypotheses for the *evaluation* of government policies and programs and their impact. In the discussion that follows, the intention is not to argue whether or not the state should be involved in this area, but rather to consider some of the reasons for its intervention.

I

The formation of societies consists, at one level, in the construction of a symbolic order. This construction entails, first, the definition of a collective identity which, with time, becomes articulated in a system of ideas as to who we are as a people. This identity is represented in the multiplicity of symbols surrounding the rituals of public life, the functioning of institutions, and the public celebration of events, groups and individuals.

The identity component of the symbolic order is important for individual members of the society; it can mobilize their intellectual and emotional energies. This is so because it partly relates to the collective identity shaped by individuals on their own. As symbolic interactionists (e.g., Mead 1934, Blumer 1962, Turner 1968, Strauss 1959, Goffman 1959), social anthropologists (e.g., Cohen 1974b, 1977, Warner 1959), and other theorists (e.g., Duncan 1969, Berger and Luckmann 1966, Gusfield 1981) have argued, there is an interdependence between the individual and collective processes of identity formation. Thus, individuals expect to recognize themselves in public institutions. They expect some consistency between their private identities and the symbolic contents upheld by public authorities, embedded in the societal institutions, and celebrated in public events. Otherwise, individuals feel like social strangers; they feel that the society is not *their* society.

The construction of a symbolic order also entails the shaping of cultural traditions: values and norms on the one hand; customs and ways of doing things on the other. Perhaps the most important component of this cultural way of life is that embedded in the forms and style of public institutions: the form of government and its institutionalized practices; the administration of justice; the school curriculum and the disciplinary methods; the organization of business activities; the conduct of labour-management relations; and so on. The forms and styles of the various institutions also become incorporated in systems of ideas that are symbolically reinforced in laws, official speeches and documents, constitutional provisions and their public discussion, advertisements, and other public relations behaviours.

As in the case of symbols of identity, individuals also expect to recognize themselves in the values and meanings incorporated in the culture of public institutions. They expect some concordance between their own and the public way of life or cultural styles. Gusfield has noted, for example, that law

> provides a reassurance to some that the society is indeed *their* society, its meanings their meanings, and its morality their morality.... The public order is capable of assuring those whose values it reflects that there is a society of consistent values in a culture of logical and morally satisfying meanings. It creates the illusion of cultural dominance (1981: 182).

Finally, I wish to isolate language as a component of the symbolic order, because of its particular significance in multilingual societies. Language, of course, is a means of communication and as such is part of the instrumental culture. But it is also a critical component of the symbolic culture since it constitutes a basis for defining collective identities and life styles (Jackson 1977).

As in the case of identity and culture, members of the society tend to expect a certain degree of congruence between the public language and their own linguistic competence and style. Indeed, in a powerful way, the language used in public affairs and institutions signifies to individuals and groups "that the society is indeed *their* society," and the institutions, their institutions. Language is perhaps the most effective symbolic medium for assuring a mutual reflection of the public world of institutions and the private world of individuals.

These three components of the symbolic order—identity, way of life, and language—are, of course, closely interconnected. They usually reinforce each other. Even though it is possible to distinguish between them analytically, it is frequently impossible to disentangle them empirically. The distinction is nevertheless useful. Public policies, for instance, may address one or the other of these components. In addition, the components may not concord with each other, a situation of tension that may lead to institutional change.

Given the importance of the symbolic order, one can expect its transformation to be resisted in proportion to the magnitude of the perceived change. In fact, frequently such transformations will not be experienced as simple changes, but as disruptions of one's symbolic world of identity and meanings with a resulting sense of alienation. This concept is used here just as it was defined by Nettler: "The 'alienated person' is one who has been estranged from, made unfriendly toward his society and the culture it carries" (1957: 672). For many English-speaking Canadians, the recent changes have brought about a feeling of estrangement from the national society, as earlier changes had done for native peoples and French-speaking Canadians.

The resistance to change is thus quite understandable. And it can be quite intense. It could perhaps be argued that changes in the symbolic order are more strongly resisted than those in the material order since the former involves identities and their social evaluation. This, of course, does not mean that the resistance is irrational. The defence of one's symbolic interests is just as rational as the pursuit and protection of one's material interests. In this connection, it is useful to note du Preez' remarks about the defence of ideologies or, we could say, of any significant element of the symbolic system. He notes that when individuals engage in such a defence

> it is often because they believe that the alternative is chaos, an undoing of themselves as persons, an annihilation of their identity. They preserve the practices of their society because those preserve their identity. The argument that they can remain whatever they are even if society changes is nonsense because the participants see things in terms of their *attachments* to various institutions and practices (1980: 48).

Much of what has been going on in Canada during the recent decades can be profitably described and interpreted from this perspective. Indeed, much of the change has consisted in the restructuring of the symbolic order. These attempts have been varied in content and uneven in impact. They have been initiated by organizations in a variety of institutional sectors: churches, school boards, the media, labour unions, and various associations. Foremost among them were the institutions of the state. These have indeed led the way in this attempted reconstruction of the collective identity, of the system of ideas and symbols, and of the institutional practices that pertain to the linguistic and ethnocultural diversity of our society.

Clearly, the state is not only involved in the economy's management, the pursuit of growth, and the initiation or support of changes found necessary in that sphere. It is also engaged in managing the symbolic system, the protection of its integrity, its enrichment and its adaptation to new circumstances. It is such a process of adaptive change that has been introduced in recent decades in order to better accommodate society's bi-national and multi-cultural composition. Warner (1959) argues that the periodic symbolic activities organized by state and other organizations serve to unify the community as a whole, and that they have an integrative function.[7] His analysis, however, assumes the existence of a symbolic system that expresses the common identity of all segments of society, though such segments may differ in other dimensions. Symbolic activities also serve to link present with past and assure the continuity of the community into the future. The situation in Canada, however, is somewhat different. It involves the creation of new symbolic elements and the transformation of the existing collective identity and its representation. To the extent that this is the case, recent events entail a break with the past and a partly new orientation for the future.

II

Historically, nation building in its symbolic-cultural dimension was oriented toward the construction of a British-type of society in Canada. This was to be reflected in the cultural character of the political, religious, educational, and other public institutions, in the language of society, in the customs, mores, and way of life, and in the symbols used to represent the society and its people. In that sense, English-Canadian nationalism was just as ethnic or cultural as French-Canadian nationalism, although both revealed considerable differences in content. The prevailing normative model called for the coincidence of nation and state.[8] It was unitarian and oriented toward cultural homogeneity. The attempts by other groups such as the Ukrainians and the French to maintain their own language and culture and to build their own subsocieties seemed to threaten the British model of cultural unity sought for in this country.

A tension between a latent unitarian model and the existing cultural diversity has persisted since the Conquest as shown by numerous attempts to impose a common language and numerous conflicts over the control of cultural institutions, especially the educational system and the media, since these constitute the main agencies of symbolic control and socialization.[9]

The process of construction and imposition of a British model of identity and a symbolic system was fairly successful in most parts of Canada. This success is well expressed by Grant:

> Growing up in Ontario, the generation of the 1920s took it for granted that they belonged to a nation. The character of the country was self-

evident. To say it was British was not to deny it was North American. To be a Canadian was to be a unique species of North American. Such alternatives as F.H. Underhill's—"Stop being British if you want to be a nationalist"—seemed obviously ridiculous (1965: 3).

With some variations, the same feeling can be said to have existed among many Canadians growing up in other parts of Canada.

The success was also evident in the process of acculturation. The children and grandchildren of immigrants were being progressively incorporated into a collective identity and an institutional system whose symbolic character was fundamentally British, but regarded as Canadian.

Thus "being Canadian" was in the process of being defined as speaking English within a British-type institutional system. The legitimacy of this symbolic order was becoming established in most segments of the population. There were, of course, exceptions, the case of the French being the most striking. With time, however, and with increasing cultural security, English-Canadian nationalism became somewhat more tolerant and open. As McNaught points out, what he calls the "racial component in the English-speaking view (of nationality) has steadily grown less significant" (1966: 63), and the notion of political nationality (as opposed to cultural nationality) has gained importance. In other words, once the symbolic order was fairly well defined and fairly securely established, cultural pluralism appeared less threatening.[10] The climate was ready for some recognition of that pluralism, except, perhaps, its French component.

Thus confrontations over the symbolic order and over the means for the production and reproduction of that order became less frequent. Even the French community, at least for a while, seemed to have abandoned the fight at the level of public institutions after a number of defeats, particularly in the field of education. (A full analysis of this historical evolution would have to pay systematic attention to differences between the situation in the various parts of the country.)

In the years that followed World War II, numerous changes began— events that, in the 1960s and 1970s, were to challenge and often disrupt this on-its-way-to-becoming consolidated symbolic order. As noted earlier, this consolidation allowed little for a French component. This was so in most parts of Canada and to a significant extent in Québec as well. It was also the case in the national institutions and in particular in the highly visible federal government which, in spite of its cohort of francophone members of Parliament and of cabinet ministers, was largely the government of English Canada, or at least was largely perceived as such by *both* French- and English-speaking Canadians.

These perceptions were documented by the Royal Commission on Bilingualism and Biculturalism.

With the growing awareness of their own collective identity, Québec francophones began to express the fact that they did not recognize themselves in the central political institutions, and indeed in the evolving symbolic order of the entire society. Their intense feeling was that Canadian society was not their society, its institutions not their institutions, its meanings and symbols, not their meanings and symbols. They felt alien or strangers, and in increasing numbers, they wanted out.

Thus, a profound crisis of legitimacy emerged for society's institutions, especially for the state institutions. One of the ways in which institutional elites reacted to this crisis was to attempt to change the symbolic character of the institutions so that the French segment of the population could identify with them. Among the steps taken were the establishment of the Royal Commission which, it is important to note in the present context, was to deal with *bi*lingualism and *bi*culturalism, the Official Languages Act in 1969, the initiation of several programs designed to increase the francophone presence in various institutional domains, and especially in the federal institutions. Numerous changes in the symbols themselves were also introduced: for instance a Canadian Flag was adopted in 1965; Trans-Canada Airlines became Air Canada; the Dominion Bureau of Statistics became Statistics Canada; "O Canada" was proclaimed as the national anthem; stamps were changed; the money was redesigned with more Canadian symbols; and the Constitution was patriated—a Constitution which was called, we must underline, the *British* North America Act. (One could perhaps add the introduction of the metric system as another illustration, since I suspect it was perceived by many as part of the same movement away from a British-modelled symbolic order.)

In short, the state intervened substantially to restructure and reorient the symbolic order, an intervention that has brought about various reactions. Some perceived the changes as a possible enrichment of society's symbolic system and, as a result, of their own symbolic universe. The changes were seen as an opportunity in terms of identity, life style, and cultural capital (Bourdieu and Passeron 1970, Bourdieu 1979). Others have been less positive in their reactions; however, after an initial opposition, have more or less reluctantly accepted change as necessary for national unity or some other such value. Still others have expressed negative reactions ranging from annoyance, resistance, all the way to outright opposition. In these cases, the interventions have been perceived and/or experienced as disruptions of their symbolic universe. They could not identify as easily as they used to with the new system of symbols; they did not feel at ease with the new culture of the public institutions; the new symbolic order was unfamiliar and a source of anxiety.

At the more extreme pole, we find those who saw the changes as an assault on their own identity, institutions, language, and way of life. They perceived the purpose of the interventions to be the dismantling of the institutional forms and customs and of the linguistic practices to which they had been accustomed and which, now, were being progressively replaced by another that was perceived not only as alien, but hostile as well.

For some, these changes no doubt presented a disruption of their career chances or a decreased access to governmental channels. I would argue, however, that most Canadians have remained unaffected in their material interests. For them the disruption was symbolic. First, as my late friend John McDonald pointed out at the time, the main significance of the separatist movement was that it challenged or disturbed the sense of benevolence of English Canadians: "Haven't we been fair in dealing with them?" "If it was not for us, their situation would be even worse." As Peterson Royce notes, "no one appreciates being put in the awkward position of being wrong or appearing to be a bigot" (1982: 200).

Second, it represented a transformation of the symbolic universe such that many could not recognize themselves in the societal institutions anymore. Another group had taken over. "Bilingual Today, French Tomorrow" as Mr. Andrew (1977) stated in his perhaps extreme attempt to express the new cultural-symbolic insecurity of his fellow-Canadians. There was a sense of symbolic loss; indeed, a sense of usurpation of something very important to one's identity.[11]

Viewed from this perspective, many reactions become understandable—reactions which otherwise appear as irrational and purely emotional, if not simply ridiculous. For instance, the complaint that "French is being rammed down our throats" which appears completely misplaced in terms of an instrumental analysis of the Official Languages Act is understandable as a reaction to the symbolic component of the Act. Similarly, for some, French on cereal boxes and on other products is annoying, and even offensive, because it symbolizes the change of the collective identity and of the culture of public institutions. (I am not too sure why the cereal box has itself become a symbol of this transformation. It is perhaps in the morning that we are especially vulnerable to disruptions in our personal life style and that we are correspondingly loath to be reminded, by the innocuous cereal box, of changes taking place in the society-at-large.)

Finally, even among the sympathetic and responsive elements of the population, it generated some uncertainty and therefore cultural anxiety. Are these attempts going to succeed? How will they affect society's character? How can institutions be changed to effectively represent, culturally and symbolically, different collectivities?

The process of symbolic change is a conflictual one: "If culture is being shaped and society being formed as a public entity, then whose culture and whose society it is to be becomes an important counter in political act" (Gusfield 1981: 184). The conflict concerns institutional control of symbolic production and the resulting content of the symbolic-cultural character of the society.[12]

Thus, in attempting to deal with a legitimacy crisis the institutional elites were running the risk of accentuating that very crisis or of generating another. Indeed, restructuring the symbolic order to make it easier for certain social segments to identify with its institutions could alienate and antagonize those accustomed to a sense of cultural dominance, and thus it could put in motion an opposing set of forces that could destroy the new symbolic edifice.

III

There was, of course, much more going on in these transformations. In addition to their implications for restructuring the symbolic order, the institutional interventions also had consequences for the distribution of social status or honour among social groups.

Individuals seek a favourable self-image. This self-image is tied to their social identity which "refers to the individual's knowledge that he belongs to certain social groups together with some emotional and value significance to him of this group membership" (Tajfel 1972b: 292). Moreover, the process whereby individuals seek a positive social identity

> is inextricably a matter of mutual comparisons between groups.... It could be said that there is a process of competition for positive identity, for each group's actions are attempts not at some absolute degree of value but a positively valued differentiation... (Turner 1974: 10).

The competition for a positive social identity occurs along socially defined attributes in a given society. Those attributes or criteria not only pertain to the class position of individuals and groups but also to their status situation. As Weber noted,

> in contrast to the purely economically determined "class situation" we wish to designate as "status situation" every typical component of the life fate of men that is determined by specific, positive or negative,

social estimation of *honor*. This honor may be connected with any quality shared by a plurality... (Gerth and Mills 1958: 186–7).

The status concerns of individuals will therefore bear not only on the actual position of the groups to which they belong relative to that of other groups but also to the community standards and the ways in which they are applied. They will be concerned with the status system and with the means of status attainment. Accordingly, they "will tend to reject as criteria of social status those characteristics not accessible to them and to support those that are."[13] This will be reflected in the reactions of individuals and groups to the institutional policies and practices—those of the state in particular—through which the criteria and standards of social status are established and applied.

Several institutional behaviours are manifestly symbolic: their main purpose is to bestow recognition and honour or to somehow change the existing distribution of social status. Relevant institutional behaviours, however, are not only those that are directly aimed at allocating social status. Some are manifestly instrumental, yet possess a significant impact on the distribution of social honour. Some authors have even argued that the manifest instrumental component is frequently quite secondary for most participants in socio-political and organizational processes and that the manifest content of the issues frequently weighs little in comparison with its implications for the distribution of prestige among participants. March and Olsen, for instance, claim that in organizations "most people... are most of the time less concerned with the content of a decision than they are with eliciting acknowledgment of their importance in the community; (that) participation in the process is a conspicuous certification of status" (March and Olsen 1976: 201). Although this may be an overstatement, it is, in my view, frequently applicable not only in organizations but also in the society-at-large.

Edelman (1964, 1971) also quite convincingly argued that much behaviour of public institutions and authorities and much of the reactions to that behaviour cannot adequately be understood unless attention is given to their implications for the allocation of social honour and recognition. Gusfield underlined the fact that public acts on the part of political groups and elites can be interpreted, at one level, as "ceremonial actions which affect the social status" of those on each side of the issue (1981: 21).

For instance, several institutional interventions mentioned earlier have implications beyond a restructuring of society's symbolic order; they also affect the distribution of social status among linguistic and ethnocultural collectivities in the country. Sometimes this appears intentional; sometimes, however, it is unintended. Correspondingly, reactions to the institutional interventions in the ethnocultural field are, to a considerable extent, reactions to the changing status of one's group relative to other groups. Indeed, I would hypothesize that if we carried out a systematic content analysis of the public debate on issues related to bilingualism and multiculturalism, we would observe that many of its themes and key words concerned relative status, the possible loss of status in the society, the fear of definition as "second class citizens," the disapproval of recognition given to groups out of proportion with their perceived importance, and the perception that one's culture or language is being degraded.[14]

Doubtless the independentist movement in Québec and the nature of the official response to it were generating considerable anxiety among the non-British and non-French groups as to what their status in Canadian society would become. The name of the Royal Commission itself was a symbol generating status anxiety as were several other themes permeating the debate: founding peoples, charter groups, the two-nation society. What was happening was that a collectivity that hitherto had been considered as a minority was in the process of definition as part of the majority—a rather substantial change in the relative status of groups. British-origin Canadians were not assured of an unrivalled position of cultural dominance anymore, and members of other ethnic groups were becoming anxious about the possible accentuation of their minority status.

A re-ranking of status groups was being attempted and, as could be expected, these attempts were generating considerable anxiety and opposition. Status interests were at stake. A conflict existed between those who were attempting, with the assistance of the state, to increase the social valuation of their language and identity and those who were resisting a possible loss, relatively speaking, in official recognition for their own.

A feature of the situation that accentuated the conflict was what Hughes called a "contradiction in status." He suggested "that people carry in their minds a set of expectations concerning the auxiliary traits properly associated with many of the specific positions available in our society" (1945: 354). Among these traits, some are "master status-determining" traits. In Canada, being British, French, or native, constitutes such "master" traits. Hughes also noted that in spite of the high degree of individual mobility and heterogeneity in American society, the "expected characteristics of many favored statuses and positions" remain white, Anglo-Saxon, male, and Protestant (356).[15]

Events in Canada in the last few decades have been challenging those expectations concerning "the auxiliary traits properly associated" with certain public positions. More specifically, a situation was generated in which members of a collectivity considered historically to be of low social status, culturally, technologically and economically inferior and which, in most parts of the country was a small minority[16] were gaining some political power over members of the opposing collectivity. The position of various groups in the status order and the emerging distribution of political power was perceived as diverging, and thus the expectation that the higher status group should run the society was being disturbed.[17]

What complicated this process of change further was that it was taking place on two fronts simultaneously. The restructuring of the collective identity and the redistribution of social recognition were undertaken in Québec as well as on the national scene. The fact that the French-speaking community was split on a number of issues and that the proponents of various views and policies were political opponents is somewhat secondary in the present context. What is critical is that similar processes were going on in these two political arenas. (It should also be noted that the changes undertaken in Québec have, in many ways, been more substantial and have entailed a more dramatic state intervention than is necessary at the federal level.)

In Québec, the restructuring was based on the notion that the French collectivity was a majority. The collective self-conception changed from French Canadians—a minority situation—to Québécois. The state intervened to transform the public environment in terms of that new identity; virtually no public institutions not already conforming with that identity were left untouched.

It should perhaps be mentioned, parenthetically, that the direction of the evolution of this collective identity is far from being clear. Indeed, up until recently, there was close to a one-to-one correspondence between language and ethnicity in French Québec; those of French origin tended to speak French while all others tended to speak English. To the extent that they are successful—as they seem to be to a significant degree—the new social and legal prescriptions will tend to dissociate language from ethnicity. The progressive absorption of people of non-French *origins* into the French-*speaking* community is likely to represent an increasingly serious challenge—a challenge to transform the community's symbolic system and re-define the social construct "Québécois" to be more culturally inclusive. In other words, one could hypothesize that Québec's ethnic nationalism is required to transform itself into a political and territorial nationalism, a transition bound to generate numerous social strains. This transformation of Québec's nationalism would parallel that which British Canadians have been undergoing for several decades.

The changes taking place have also had implications for status distribution among linguistic and ethnocultural groups within Québec. For instance, the English language lost its official status. In the new dispensation, the historical importance of the anglophone community is still recognized, but its status is quite clearly reduced with its minority definition. It may not be regarded in the same light as other minorities, but it is nevertheless seen as a minority.

Of course, many of the specifications of Law 101 have implications for the material interests of the members of the various ethnocultural collectivities in Québec (and perhaps of a small proportion of other Canadians). To a large extent, however, its significance is symbolic. In fact, for most Canadians outside of Québec, it is almost exclusively symbolic. But even for those living in Québec, the symbolic component is considerable. The law, both in its totality and in the clauses that deal specifically with symbols (e.g., signs on commercial establishments), represents changes in the relative status of cultural groups. Its main thrust is to symbolically place one language and identity above the others, to change the ranks they had traditionally occupied.

Finally, it is also useful to consider the multiculturalism policy in this perspective.[18] The main significance of that policy derives from its integral contribution to the reconstruction of the symbolic system and to the redistribution of social status among linguistic and ethnocultural groups in Canadian society. Indeed, it soon became clear that re-shaping the social and institutional identity, customs, and symbols so that members of society's French segment might recognize themselves generated identification and status concerns not only among British-origin Canadians but among the non-British, non-French as well.

Thus, when the policy on multiculturalism was introduced, the non-British, non-French element was not primarily concerned with cultural maintenance. Rather, a status anxiety existed, fear of being defined as second-class citizens, marginal to the identity system that was being established. The minority was resented for what seemed its special status. Thus, the policy responded to the status anxieties voiced with regard to themes like biculturalism, two-nation society, charter groups, and founding peoples. One of its objectives was to affirm symbolically that Canadian society is open to all cultural identities, indicating its recognition of them all, and the implications of cultural equality.

This is the profound meaning of the government statement concerning multiculturalism within a bilingual framework. The frequently quoted portion of the prime minister's statement to the House of Commons in

1971 concerns the implementation of this policy. This is indeed an important part of the statement. In my view, however, more attention should be given to that portion of the statement pertaining to policy objectives and its social context. I would like to quote a few paragraphs from that text:

> A policy of multiculturalism within a bilingual framework commends itself to the government as the most suitable means of assuring the cultural freedom of Canadians. Such a policy should help to break down discriminatory attitudes and cultural jealousies. National unity if it is to mean anything in the deeply personal sense, must be found on confidence in one's own individual identity; out of this can grow respect for that of others and a willingness to share ideas, attitudes and assumptions. A vigorous policy of multiculturalism will help create this initial confidence. It can form the base of a society which is based on fair play for all.
>
> The government will support and encourage the various cultures and ethnic groups that give structure and vitality to our society. They will be encouraged to share their cultural expression and values with other Canadians and to contribute to a richer life for us all (House of Commons Debates 1971b: 8545).

This document is a very interesting piece of data. It seems clear that a main concern of the government pertains to what I have called the cultural-symbolic order of the society. It speaks of "national unity," of "the various cultures and ethnic groups that give structure and vitality to our society," of "a richer life for us all." The image that emerges from the statement is more of cultural fusion than the perpetuation of a multiplicity of different cultures.

Another concern underlying the policy statement is with the status of the various cultural groups: "breaking down jealousies"; "fair play for all"; "respect for (the identity) of others." In fact, one paragraph deals quite explicitly with the proper recognition that the various cultural components of the society should receive:

> In the past, substantial public support has been given largely to the arts and cultural institutions of English-speaking Canada. More recently and largely with the help of the royal commission's earlier recommendations in Volumes I to III, there has been a conscious effort on the government's part to correct any bias against the French language and culture. In the last few months the government has taken steps to provide funds to support cultural-educational centres for native people. The policy I am announcing today accepts the contention of the other cultural communities that they, too, are essential elements in Canada and deserve government assistance in order to contribute to regional and national life in ways that derive from their heritage yet are distinctively Canadian (House of Commons Debates 1971b: 8545–6).

The reader should note the government acceptance of "the contention of the other cultural communities that they, too, are essential elements. . . ." The second concern of the policy pertains to the recognition granted to the various ethnocultural collectivities.

I do not wish to deny that "cultural diversification" is part of the policy. But I would like to suggest that the policy is largely an instrument for re-structuring society's identity system and for managing cultural tensions that arise in the process. By focusing too much on possible policy impact in maintaining (or not maintaining) ethnocultures, we have neglected an important if not central aspect of the policy and its role in transforming society's symbolic component.

This interpretation of multiculturalism's main thrust—both as policy and a social movement—is consistent with the view that ethnicity in urban North America has taken a symbolic or regenerational character (Driedger 1977b). As Gans points out, ethnicity now has "an expressive rather than an instrumental function in people's lives" (1979: 9). It is characterized by the fact that "people are less and less interested in their ethnic cultures and organizations—both sacred and secular—and are instead more concerned with maintaining their ethnic identity . . . and with finding ways of feeling and expressing that identity in suitable ways" (1979: 7). Following this line of reasoning, I would argue that the search for institutional recognition and the competition for status are important means of ethnic expressions of identity—and not only, perhaps not primarily, through various forms of cultural expression.[19] "Groups want to be included in the official history of the society and its pantheon of heroes,"[20] something that in many ways would require a re-writing of Canadian history. They are also watchful of the institutional gestures vis-à-vis other groups and react accordingly (Schneider 1979: 6). "Pluralism involves a sort of jockeying for status and power. It involves a process of invidious comparisons."[21]

Recognition and status are sought in the following areas: from government in its legislation, programs, publications and various symbolic gestures; from universities through special chairs, research centres, conferences, library collections, exhibits; from the public school system through language teaching or in courses and textbook content in areas such as literature and history; from media coverage of events that enhance the group's image or through special programs on aspects of the group's life or culture; from churches through statements concerning the legitimacy of multiculturalism or through activities recognizing or celebrating the sacred and secular dimensions of ethnic identities and cultures.

The pursuit of status also manifests itself in the search for a particular group's participation in the historical formation and evolution of Canadian society or for identifiable contributions to the societal institutions and culture. One increasingly hears, for instance, claims of a "founding people status" on the part of people of different ethnic origins. The arguments presented revolve around the idea that one's group has played a critical if not the main role in settling a particular region, province or community, and in building its institutions. The expectation is that this role should be publicly recognized by society's status-giving institutions.

Conclusion

I have attempted to show that two sets of phenomena must be considered to adequately understand Canada's linguistic and ethnocultural reality and the activities and interventions in that field of various institutions, especially state institutions. These pertain to the structuring of the symbolic component of the social order and to the distribution of social status and recognition among ethnocultural groups.

Such processes can be quite conflictual and emotionally charged. Like class politics, status politics constitute a struggle between contending groups over the distribution of societal resources. In one case, the resources are material; in the other, they are symbolic. Both are equally real. The struggle involves the "certification of one's status" (March and Olsen 1976) as a participant in the socio-political process or the relative decertification of others. It consists of attempts by various groups to acquire "status rights"[22] in particular domains or oppose the claims to such rights on the part of other groups.

The political conflict may be limited to influencing the institutional authorities. In some cases, however, it may concern the control of existing structures and mechanisms for defining the collective identity and the distribution of status. In such instances, the conflict is likely to be more intense. This appears to be central to French participation in the transformation of the symbolic order; it was perceived as overtaking institutional apparatus rather than attempting to influence it.

The changes and attempted changes in the linguistic and ethnocultural fields have involved a complex interaction between the material and symbolic orders—an interaction that could not be adequately considered in this essay. Each sphere has its own relative autonomy, involving distinctive kinds of resources and social processes which are interdependent in the structuring, functioning, and evolution of social organization. Both operate simultaneously in the context of social action.

Several examples of the interdependence between the material and symbolic orders can be observed. For instance, symbolic resources can be used to achieve economic and other utilitarian objectives. They can be used by individuals and groups in competing for economic or political power. Conversely, economic resources can be used in the pursuit of prestige and in the competition that this pursuit entails (Coleman 1969). There are also situations in which the issues at hand involve mutually reinforcing class and status interests. They concord in the sense that the groups in competition or conflict stand to gain or lose on both at the same time. This appears to have been the case with regard to numerous aspects of the federal and Québec language policies. Such situations usually result in more intense conflict because the combination of the two types of interests brings more people into conflict—some primarily because the outcome may affect their businesses or careers, others primarily because the status of their culture or identity is at stake, still others because both sets of interests converge. However, there can also be situations of inconsistency, in which material advantage conflicts with symbolic interests. Minorities frequently face these kinds of situations: they pursue recognition and the development of their symbolic-cultural resources frequently at the cost of considerable material sacrifices, either individually or collectively (see for example Vallee and Shulman 1969).

The pressure for change in the symbolic order and of resistance to attempted changes do not occur randomly; their sources can be located structurally. Specific groups on each side of the conflict could be identified by considering the fact that all segments of society are not equally advantaged (or disadvantaged) in pursuing a positive social identity according to existing institutional arrangements. As indicated, the dominant elements of identity and the prevailing criteria of social status will tend to be rejected by those finding it difficult to compete along those lines, but will be supported by those who are, or anticipate being, on the winning side. For instance, contribution to the construction of Canadian society as a criterion of official recognition and status favours certain groups to the detriment of others. The result is a conflict of status interest between those who feel they can claim a "founding people" status and those who have arrived or established themselves more recently in Canada—the former supporting and the latter rejecting this criterion of status.[23]

In this context the intervention of the state derives some of its significance. Indeed, its intervention frequently modifies the system of opportunities and constraints within which individuals and groups attempt to construct a positive identity or certify their status. State policies can affect—positively or negatively—the strategies and tactics available to members of various ethnocultural groups in their competition for social status (Peterson Royce 1982: 184–94, Lyman and Douglas 1973).

In Canada, the state has always participated in shaping the symbolic order and in managing the relationships among linguistic and cultural groups. This participation has changed over time under the influence of various forces, but it has seldom been absent.[24] Its participation in the symbolic order parallels its involvement in economic management and the relations among various organized or unorganized interests. It is interesting to note that the increasing support in recent times for the view that government should adopt a laissez-faire policy in the ethnocultural field seems to correspond to an increasing claim for less economic intervention.[25]

I would suggest that the argument for state withdrawal from the ethnocultural field is as futile as is that for withdrawal from the economic sphere. Rather, an important task for social scientists is not so much to argue in favour or against state intervention as for an explanation of current involvement. This would entail, for instance, an analysis of the factors that have been shaping state institutions and their relations not only to the economy but to the civil society as well. These include: the emergence of the welfare state;[26] the changing structures for the representation of interests, including the declining role of political parties;[27] the sectoral organization of government activity and decision making; and, the changing conditions for maintaining state legitimacy. It would also require that the critical dimensions of the symbolic order be clarified along with the processes through which it is transformed as a system of collective meanings, the conditions under which the collective identity becomes meaningful for the different segments of the society, and the factors related to the degree of symbolic equality among them.

Another question could be raised about state intervention: what would be the probable consequences of leaving the ethnocultural field and the relations of groups within it open to the forces of the "market." This kind of exercise would perhaps be largely speculative. Yet, it would generate interesting hypotheses for analysing institutional intervention over the last decades, and the possibilities and limits of future interventions.

Finally, it should be noted that although the symbolic order and expressive stratification has been given special attention in this article, it does not imply that other dimensions of the social structure are considered secondary. The cultural-symbolic aspects of intergroup relations should be neither ignored nor presented in some intellectually imperialistic fashion as the most or the only important aspects of that reality. Rather, my argument is that without taking it into account, we will overlook an important dimension of the dynamics of language and ethnicity and of the related institutional policies and practices.

Notes

1. For a discussion of this and related questions, see Ogmundson (1980) and Bell and Tepperman (1979).
2. Even analyses of status groups slip into consideration of material interests. Brandmeyer and Denisoff (1969) note for instance that authors such as Lipset and Hofstadter, in their analysis of conflicts between status groups, actually refer to economic, not status interests (as reflected in the cases they present).
3. Conflict theory is, of course, broader than what is implied here, but it has, in fact, been more extensively applied to economic (classes, occupations, regions) than status groupings.
4. By "Economisme," Bourdieu refers to the inappropriate use of models based on utilitarian interests to explain social phenomena (1975). See also Cohen (1974) for a discussion of such tendencies.
5. This, of course, corresponds to the same broad distinction made in the analysis of economic phenomena. In both areas, the amount and types of resources generated must be considered as well as their distribution among competing groups.
6. The state is not merely the government, far less just the central government. The state is a complex of institutions, including government, but also including the bureaucracy (embodied in the civil service as well as public corporations, central banks, regulatory commissions, etc.), the military, the judiciary, representative assemblies, and (very important for Canada) what Miliband calls the sub-central levels of government, that is, provincial executives, legislatures, and bureaucracies, and municipal institutions (Panitch 1977: 6).
7. See also Warner (1953) and Brody (1982) on the function of symbolic activities for the community.
8. For a discussion of this normative model and of attempts to apply it in contemporary politics, see Young (1976: Chapter 3).
9. Bausenhart notes, for example, that "the suppression of the enemy languages press in September, 1918, may also be seen as the Federal Government's contribution to a movement, which had its beginning in the earlier part of that decade, to establish the supremacy of English in Canada and hence, to abolish bi-lingual schools. This movement spread from the Ontario side of the Québec border to the Rocky Mountains, with the four central provinces ultimately insisting that English be the sole language of instruction in their public school systems. Legislation to this effect reflected the apprehension of the British majority in each of the four provinces about the large number of non-British immigrants living among them" (1972: 42–3).
10. For a discussion of the relation between cultural security and tolerance, see Turner (1974).
11. Weber states that "the development of status is essentially a question of stratification resting upon usurpation. Such usurpation is the normal origin of almost all status honor" (Gerth and Mills 1958: 188).
12. Heinz (1983) presents an interesting analysis of conflict over symbol production between the New Christian Right and groups associated with what he calls secular humanism and liberal Christianity.
13. This statement is taken from comments by Jos Lennards.

14. On the importance of language in symbolic or status inequalities, see Bourdieu (1975).

15. In a very interesting analysis, Kemper (1979) sees the decline in the quality of municipal sources as a result of the reversal in status between providers and consumers of services. Before the decline, providers had generally a lower social status than consumers: the status relation was in concordance with the service relationship. The shift in population toward black and Hispanic resulted in a discrepancy: consumers were now frequently of lower status than the providers. The discrepancy affected the quality of the services.

16. For some English-speaking Canadians, the fact that the French have been conquered is also important in this connection.

17. Morris and Price (1980) present an interesting analysis of English-Canadian images or typifications of French-English relations in Montreal and Toronto and the role they play in a period of change.

18. For an overview and critical examination of the policy, see Burnet (1975c, 1978).

19. The quest for recognizing as opposed to satisfying adaptive needs may be accentuated by the changing socioeconomic and generational background of the population of ethnic collectivities. See, for example, Driedger (1977b), Gans (1979), and Nahirny and Fishman (1965).

20. From a presentation by Vecoli, Canadian Ethnic Studies Association, Thunder Bay, 1983.

21. From the same presentation by Vecoli.

22. "Status rights . . . consist of legitimate normative claims on the behavior of others which constitute advantages—as rewards or resources—for a social position" (Meyer and Roth 1970: 97). On this question, see also Westhues (1976).

23. I am indebted to Jos Lennards for drawing my attention to this element of the situation.

24. Concerning the relative importance of symbolic and material interests Weber notes that "every technological repercussion and economic transformation threatens stratification by status and pushes the class situation into the foreground. Epochs and countries in which the naked class situation is of predominant significance are regularly the periods of technical and economic transformations. And every slowing down of the shifting of economic transformations leads, in due course, to the growth of status structures and makes for a resuscitation of the important role of social honor" (Gerth and Mills 1958: 194).

25. It should be noted that not having a policy (the laissez-faire position) *is* a policy, whether it has been decided upon consciously or not.

26. The notion of the welfare state should be taken in its broadest sense. One of its characteristics is that "it is accepted as a legitimate goal of the political system to intervene through governmental institutions in order to create the conditions under which citizens can pursue their individual goals" (Janowitz 1976: 3).

27. On the transformation of the structures and processes of representations, see for example Meisel (1976), Pross (1982) and Thompson and Stanbury (1979).

Multiculturalism in Canada[†]

JEAN BURNET

In the 1970s the Canadian sociologist S.D. Clark used as the working title of a paper "The Myth of Multiculturalism," although he chose a more anodyne title when he published it. A few years later another sociologist, Karl Peter, entitled a paper, "The Myth of Multiculturalism and Other Political Fables." With all due respect to my colleagues, multiculturalism, as a policy of the federal government and of four provincial governments, is by no means a myth. However, it governs an area of social life in which myths abound. In this article I should like to discuss first the policy and then a few of those myths.

The policy was a long time in coming. The Canadian population has always been ethnically heterogeneous. Even before contacts with Europeans the 250,000 to 300,000 inhabitants of what is now Canada constituted about 50 societies, belonging to a dozen linguistic groups. Some of the societies were nomadic bands of hunters and gatherers; others were highly structured chiefdoms of fishers and cultivators of the soil. In the sixteenth and seventeenth centuries the French entered; in a short time those in the Atlantic region became differentiated from the rest, as Acadians; later, in the nineteenth century, another distinct ethnic group, the Métis, was to emerge as a result of interbreeding between French and Indians. In the eighteenth century the influx of British began, not as one but as several peoples—English, Irish, Scottish, and Welsh—and soon after some Germans and Dutch came. In the latter part of the nineteenth century the area of recruitment of the Canadian population was extended to all of Europe and parts of Asia, and now, particularly since 1967, it includes all of Asia, and Africa and South America as well.

However, official recognition of the diversity of the population as continuing and desirable has been relatively recent. Until the 1960s governmental policy concerning immigration was based upon the principle that those who were admitted into Canadian society should be

[†]"Myths and Multiculturalism," *Canadian Journal of Education* 4, 4 (1979): 43–58. This is a revised version of the original article.

assimilable into the dominant British and French ethnic groups. Even policy regarding native peoples was dominated by that principle: it was aimed at isolation and gradual assimilation.

The immigration policy bore hardest upon those peoples who were considered unassimilable. They included peoples physically different from the dominant groups, and it is unnecessary to repeat the history, now widely considered to have been shameful, of overt and covert exclusionary measures directed against Chinese, Japanese, South Asians, and blacks. As late as the 1950s one federal minister of immigration after another had to defend regulations on allegedly scientific grounds that most natural and social scientists regarded as nonsensical; for example, the restrictions on black immigration were said to have been imposed because it had been "scientifically proven" that blacks could not endure cold climates. The Jews were also considered unassimilable, and Abella and Troper (1982) have related how Canada drew the line even at admitting Jewish refugees from Nazism during the 1930s.

It is true that from the 1920s on—and the 1920s was the decade of the Chinese Immigration Act, excluding from Canada all Chinese except university students, merchants, Canadian-born Chinese returning from abroad, and diplomatic personnel—there was much talk of the Canadian mosaic. Speakers and writers indefatigably praised the situation in which ethnic groups could retain their distinctiveness and yet be Canadian, in contrast to the American melting pot as they conceived it. They vied with each other in proposing visual and gustatory metaphors such as "flower garden," "salad," and "stew" for the Canadian situation. In 1965 Porter could say that the mosaic was the country's most cherished value.

But beyond rhetoric singularly little support was given by either federal or provincial governments to groups that wanted to maintain their old world heritages. Cultural agencies, with niggardly funding, could afford little attention to any groups other than the British, French, and natives. Private broadcasting in languages other than English and French was strictly regulated, and permitted only when it could be justified in terms of "integration"; the public corporation, the CBC, recognized only English and French and, in its Northern Service, native languages. In the public schools teaching in languages other than English and French, including Indian and Inuit languages, was proscribed, and even the teaching of modern languages was not greatly encouraged.

The turn-about took place in the 1960s. It was during that decade that relations between English Canadians and French Canadians, or rather that substantial portion of French Canadians who now began to identify themselves increasingly as Québécois, reached the critical stage out of which they have not yet passed—"the greatest crisis in [Canadian] history," said the Royal Commission on Bilingualism and Biculturalism in 1965. At the time ethnic movements were occurring everywhere in the world, and in many cases were leading to the birth of new nations. The germs of nationalism had been incubating in Quebec for a long time. Now, with a high degree of urbanization and industrialization and a rising educational level in the population, they broke out. The death of Maurice Duplessis, the Quiet Revolution of Jean Lesage, the hatching of several separatist movements, and the flaring up of terrorism from 1963 to 1970 were a few of the events of the time.

The federal government's response to the situation was the setting up in 1963 of the Royal Commission on Bilingualism and Biculturalism. The essence of its mandate was "to inquire into and report upon the existing state of bilingualism and biculturalism in Canada and to recommend what steps should be taken to develop the Canadian confederation on the basis of an equal partnership between the two founding races" (Royal Commission on Bilingualism and Biculturalism 1967: 173). It carried out a massive research program, and made numerous recommendations concerning linguistic policy, education, the world of work, and the federal capital.

The Native Peoples also had been touched by urbanization and industrialization. The economic developments of the postwar period had broken through their isolation. Some of them moved to urban communities, and others found industry moving north into their ancestral lands. At the same time, the technological revolution in communication made them aware as never before of what was happening elsewhere. "Red Power" began to be talked about.

That the government did not establish a royal commission in this case, but rather a committee of anthropologists to report on natives who had Indian status and thus were of special concern to government and possibly to anthropologists also, reflects the degree to which the native peoples were still set apart from the rest of Canadian society. The Hawthorn-Tremblay report (1966, 1967), monumental as it was, dealt with only about a quarter of the Indian, Inuit, and Métis people, and not at all with the small but fast-growing number of urban dwellers among the Native Peoples.

As for those not British, French, or Native in origin, the Royal Commission on Bilingualism and Biculturalism was enjoined to take into account "the contribution made by the other ethnic groups to the cultural enrichment of Canada and the measures that should be taken to safeguard that contribution" (Royal Commission on Bilingualism and Biculturalism 1967: 173). Further, two of the ten commissioners, J.B. Rudnyckyj and Paul Wyczynski, were Slavic post-World War II immigrants to Canada. Nonetheless, the first intention of the Commission was to deal with the other ethnic groups only as they affected English-French relations, and to fulfil its mandate in a literal, if limited fashion by having members of eight groups write essays on the contributions of those groups to the cultural enrichment of Canada. However, the briefs submitted to the Commission and the discussions at public and private hearings, sometimes highly charged, revealed that there was a host of ethnic interest groups eager to win recognition and financial support from the government. In the end, the Commission devoted Book 4 of its *Report* to the other ethnic groups, presenting an account based on a small amount of research devoted to other ethnic groups, data accumulated as a by-product of the examination of the status of the English and French, and other miscellaneous materials. They also made sixteen recommendations and numerous suggestions.

Book 4 of the *Report of the Royal Commission on Bilingualism and Biculturalism* appeared in March 1970. On October 8, 1971, the Prime Minister announced the federal government's response, which was to accept all those recommendations directed to federal departments and agencies and to proclaim a policy of multiculturalism within a bilingual framework. The government pledged to provide support for such a policy in four ways:

First, resources permitting, the government will seek to assist all Canadian cultural groups that have demonstrated a desire and effort to continue to develop a capacity to grow and contribute to Canada, and a clear need for assistance, the small and weak groups no less than the strong and highly organized.

Second, the government will assist members of all cultural groups to overcome cultural barriers to full participation in Canadian society.

Third, the government will promote creative encounters and interchange among all Canadian cultural groups in the interests of national unity.

Fourth, the government will continue to assist immigrants to acquire at least one of Canada's official languages in order to become full participants in Canadian society (House of Commons Debates 1971a).

The policy of multiculturalism within a bilingual framework, at first intended to apply to "other ethnic groups," has increasingly over the last fourteen years come to apply to all ethnic groups, and thus to all Canadians. For example, under the policy, research and teaching concerning the Native Peoples, the British Isles groups, and the French-

Canadian groups, as well as the other ethnic groups, have been encouraged, although less advantage has been taken of the policy by these groups (with the exception of the Scots) than by others. The charter member groups have of course other resources; they also probably have a tendency still to consider the term "ethnic" as pejorative (Burnet 1975a).

It is sometimes considered that, having stated the policy, the government forgot about it except at election times. However, that is far from true: multiculturalism has not been simply a campaign slogan of the Liberal party. There has been since 1972 a minister of state responsible for multiculturalism. The Canadian Consultative Council on Multiculturalism (now the Canadian Multiculturalism Council) was established in 1973, composed of more than 100 representatives of various ethnic groups, to advise the minister; it has held several national conferences, has had regular regional and national meetings, and has made many recommendations to government (Canadian Consultative Council on Multiculturalism 1973, 1977). The Multiculturalism Directorate, within the Department of the Secretary of State, has carried on liaison activities with ethnic communities and with the ethnic press; initiated and developed studies and research, including studies of the non-official languages (O'Bryan, Reitz, and Kuplowska 1976) and of attitudes towards multiculturalism (Berry, Kalin, and Taylor 1976) and a series of histories of ethnic groups (Adachi 1976, Anderson and Higgs 1976, Radecki 1976, Reid 1976, Abu-Laban 1980, Chimbos 1980, Loken 1980, Lupul 1982, Dreisziger 1982, Rasporich 1982, Wickberg 1982, Aun 1985, Buchignani and Indra 1985); assisted the Canadian Ethnic Studies Association to develop as a full-fledged learned society with two regular publications; sponsored activities in the performing and the visual arts; assisted in programs aimed at retention of non-official languages, and given grants for a vast array of other projects. The budget allotted to multiculturalism, although by no means large, has been increased in times of fiscal restraint. The federal cultural agencies such as the National Film Board, the National Museums of Canada, the National Library, the Public Archives, the Canadian Radio-Television and Telecommunications Commission and the Canadian Broadcasting Corporation, and the Canada Council have also contributed to the implementing of the policy of multiculturalism, as have other directorates and branches of the Department of the Secretary of State and other government departments (Multiculturalism and the Government of Canada 1978).

That other parties than the Liberals subscribed to the policy is indicated by their favourable reception of it in the House, by the retention of the policy by the Progressive Conservatives in 1979–80 and after September 1984, and by the fact that the provinces of Ontario, Manitoba, Saskatchewan, and Alberta have in their turn proclaimed policies of multiculturalism. Saskatchewan in 1974 passed the Saskatchewan Multicultural Act, Alberta in 1984 a Cultural Heritage Act. None of the provincial governments involved was Liberal. It is difficult to guess the extent to which the adoption of the federal policy influenced the provinces. However, since the schools are seen as having a key role to play in many of the programs of multiculturalism, and education is under provincial jurisdiction, provincial initiatives are an essential part of any picture. These have involved such measures as appointment of advisory committees or councils on multiculturalism, their members drawn from the province's ethnic groups; conferences, including conferences on curriculum; publications, including multicultural history projects, ethnocultural directories, multiculturalism; grants for various ethnic or multicultural projects; and expansion in the schools of the use of non-official languages as languages of instruction and of the teaching of non-official languages as subjects, expansion of the teaching of various cultures, and introduction of multiculturalism as a topic into curricula.

The policy then is no myth, but it does have defects and ambiguities. Let me single out three of them. First, the name itself implies something that is hardly possible: that many cultures can be maintained in Canada. In fact, except for such isolated groups as the Hutterites, no ethnic group brings a total culture to Canada, and none can maintain intact what it brings under the impact of the new environment, social as well as geographical. It is ethnic identity that can and does persist, and selected cultural patterns as symbolic expressions of that identity. The attempt to maintain cultures has led some groups to protest against such measures aimed at promoting "creative encounters and interchange" as multicultural centres, since cultural maintenance depends on isolation. Second, the policy as proclaimed takes insufficient regard of the special problems and interests of those members of ethnic groups (in some ethnic groups a small proportion of the whole, in others virtually all) who are new arrivals in Canada. The reason is not only the divergence of interest between the Canadian-born, whose concern is for persistence, and the immigrants, whose concern is for adjustment; it is also the administrative division of labour in the federal structure, which puts immigration under one federal ministry and multiculturalism under another. It is probable that the immigrants belonging to the visible minorities are particularly disadvantaged by this inadequacy of the policy (Burnet 1975b). Third, while the aim of the policy can be neatly expressed as being equality, equality among ethnic groups in Canada is by no means easy to interpret. What various people concerned with the administration of the policy envisage as desirable is not clear (Burnet 1978). But whatever its imperfections the policy exists, if not, as W.W. Isajiw (1978) has pointed out, as public philosophy, at least as part of government policy.

In the discussions of multiculturalism and in the research carried out under the policy, there are, however, many myths. It is worth considering them because the myths are themselves valuable indices of group organization and functioning. It is also worth recognizing them as myths, and not accepting them as accurate portrayals of historical or contemporary situations, which should be studied in themselves.

Those of us who grew up in Canada before World War II learned certain myths as we passed through the schools. We learned that, after the Viking visits to Canadian coasts, it was John Cabot of Bristol who first explored the eastern seaboard, followed after a time by Jacques Cartier, and that Cabot and Cartier were only the first of a number of English, Scottish, and French explorers who eventually extended knowledge of the territory that is now Canada from the east to the Pacific, and from the Great Lakes to the Arctic. The explorers opened the way for settlers, again French and British: Louis Hébert and his successors in New France; United Empire Loyalists and American frontiersmen in the Maritime provinces and Ontario; British from the homeland, eastern Canada, and the United States in the west and the far west. True, others came also, particularly to the prairies, and these, with few exceptions, were welcomed, to settle the vast lands in peace and security under the guarantees of British justice, fair play, and freedom. The mosaic was an expression of British benevolence: it caught admirably the vision of Sir Wilfrid Laurier: "I want the marble to remain the marble; the granite to remain the granite; the oak to remain the oak; and out of all these elements I would build a nation great among the nations of the world."

Recently, however, the myths of the prewar period have been discredited, and new myths have appeared, related to the policy of multiculturalism. They may be regarded as corrective of the earlier myths. They are, however, little more factual.

One myth that has become apparent as more and more groups have come to write their history as Canadians is the myth of early arrival. Many claim that their ancestors were among the first explorers to sail along Canadian shores, set foot on Canadian soil, or even settle here. The Chinese, for example, have tales of Buddhist monks who drifted from China in their junks and landed on the west coast in the fifth and sixth centuries, the Greeks of seamen who came in the eighteenth century, and the Ukrainians of Cossacks who came with the Russians and the Dane Bering, also in the eighteenth century. On the east coast, while the arrival of the Scandinavians as long ago as 1000 A.D. is authenticated, Scots, Irish, Germans, and Portuguese are among those said either to have been on board the Viking ships or to have followed soon after. A Pole, Janz Kolna, is said to have discovered Labrador in 1476 (Kos-Rabcewicz-Zubkowski 1966: 12); and a revision of place-names has been demanded to record that John Cabot was really Italian Giovanni Caboto. As for early settlers, the Chinese claim a settlement near the present site of Vancouver in 499 A.D., and the Russians, Ukrainians, Poles, and Byelorussians all claim that their ethnic fellows were among the de Meuron and Watteville soldiers who took part in the War of 1812, some of whom settled either in Upper Canada or in the Red River colony.

However, the tales of early exploration and early settlement are hard to substantiate. Many seem to belong to legend rather than historical fact. Also, since the implication is often that a particular culture has long Canadian roots, it needs to be said that many of the first settlers of whom we know brought with them little of the culture of their homelands. Either they were mercenary soldiers whose culture was of the army camp, or they were individuals whose adventurous lives had already exposed them to the French or British culture and the French or English language of those among whom came to live.

The interesting things about the myth of early arrival are its frequency and its relation to other myths by which people and institutions attempt to give themselves the respectability of long lineage. The tendency to consider that to have been here for a long time is to have certain rights has probably been accentuated by the use made of antiquity by Canadians of French and British origins. The phrase "two founding peoples" in the terms of reference of the Royal Commission on Bilingualism and Biculturalism (I translate from the French version of the terms; the use of the word "races" in the English version creates problems I wish to avoid) was intended to refer to more than time in Canada; it can, however, and often is interpreted as referring simply to time, since on that level it can be challenged.

It is also notable that the common estimate of the proportion of the population that is of other ethnic origins than British, French, and

Native is one-third. Since the French Canadians also estimate their strength as one-third, this leaves the British and the Native groups as the remaining third. The myth of the thirds has existed for at least twenty years. It has been expressed almost routinely in speeches by politicians, including the successive ministers responsible for multiculturalism.

The first thing that must be said concerning this myth is that the exact ethnic composition of Canadian society is not known. An ethnic group is made up of those who share a feeling of peoplehood (Gordon 1978: 106–7). It is thus not definable in objective terms: there is always some self-selection involved. Further, it is now recognized that ethnic identity is not as fixed as it once was, or once was thought to be: intermarriage is only one of the factors creating possibilities for choice. The Canadian census tries to use ethnic origin, defined as the ethnic or cultural group to which a person or his ancestor belonged on coming to this continent, as an objective index of the ethnic composition of the population. But even ethnic origin categories are subject to many contingencies, not the least of which are the wording of census questions, the number and order of listed categories, and the manner of collection of the census data (Kralt 1978).

As late as the 1971 census, the proportion of the Canadian population that was not British, French, or Native in ethnic origin was much closer to one-quarter than one-third; it was, in fact, 25.5 percent. In the 1981 census, where for the first time multiple origins as well as single origins were recorded, the proportion of the population claiming either a single non-British, non-French, non-Native origin or a multiple origin in which there was a non-British, non-French, or non-Native component had risen almost to 30 percent; the proportion claiming either a single other origin or a multiple origin in which there was no British, French, or Native origin was 24.7 percent. It may, of course, be argued that in claiming to be a third of the population those of other origins are simply anticipating a little, since they are the component of the population that has been steadily increasing for more than a century. However, in terms of ethnic identity it may well be the group that appears to be dwindling, the English-Canadian group, that is increasing, through the process of assimilation. To the degree that language is an index of assimilation, and it is only a crude one, it is worth noting that by 1981 English was the mother tongue of 61 percent and the language most often spoken at home of 68 percent of the population.

In discussing those of other origins as a third of the population, another myth developed, that of common bonds among the members of the other ethnic groups, or sometimes common bonds among all the minorities, the French Canadians, the Amerindians, and the other ethnic groups. Both forms of this myth were prevalent in the 1960s. The first was introduced by Senator Paul Yusyk when he attempted to forge a Third Force; his efforts resulted in little, however. The latter form was expressed on such occasions as tours of the West by prominent Quebec politicians; the tours also bore little fruit in agreements between French Canadians and spokesmen for other ethnic groups.

In fact, it may be questioned whether common bonds exist. The other ethnic groups vary in many respects, among them numbers, region of concentration, time of arrival, occupational, income, and educational distribution, physical characteristics, relations with their homeland, degree of ethnic awareness, and capacity for collective action. Moreover, there are among them memories of old wars and antagonisms. Indeed, even the members of a single ethnic group are usually highly differentiated, especially if some of them have lived in Canada for a long time. As for the French Canadians, they seem unaware of many of the ethnic distinctions that exist among those they lump together as English Canadians, and of any comparison between their claims and those of other ethnic groups. Likewise, the Native Peoples are convinced of the uniqueness of their situation and their rights. Hence, while temporary coalitions of ethnic groups concerning specific issues such as immigration policy may occur, no Third Force is likely to emerge.

It may be asked in what circumstances ethnic groups, singly or together, tend to estimate their strength as much greater or much less than the corresponding ethnic origin categories in the census. One circumstance is, of course, the writing of briefs to the government. It is assumed that the force of such briefs varies directly with the number of potential votes that they represent. It was probably on this assumption that associations representing one particular ethnic group in a certain province prepared their briefs to the Royal Commission on Bilingualism and Biculturalism. The related ethnic origin category was 11 percent of the population of the province, yet in their briefs the associations argued ingeniously that they should be looked upon as speaking for 25 percent, 50 percent, and, if I recall correctly, even 75 percent of the population. Another circumstance might well be the rise of members of the ethnic group in the social and economic hierarchy and the prominence of some of them. In recent years the upward mobility of Canadian-born members of many non-British groups and the entrance of highly skilled and well-educated immigrants belonging to other groups has probably created a feeling of being numerous.

Another current myth replaces the myth of British benevolence with the myth of British villainy and of unremitting oppression of other ethnic groups by those of British origin. Racial and ethnic prejudice and discrimination, it holds, are peculiarly Anglo-Saxon or Anglo-Celtic—peculiarly WASPish, as many say who would allow no other ethnic epithet than WASP to cross their lips. The English Canadians have created institutions that since they are built on British models and require the use of the English language put others at a disadvantage; in addition, they have exclusionary attitudes—"Anglo-Saxon arrogance"—in all spheres of private and public life. Hence, continues the myth, until those not of British origin attained the numbers and strength to wrest a measure of recognition, they were universally despised, ignored, and discriminated against. Those others were themselves, of course, not arrogant or exclusionary, and at least relatively free from prejudice.

This myth has emerged as historians have begun to explore the nativism of Canadian immigration policy and Canadian attitudes to other ethnic groups, and to write the histories of ethnic groups in Canada. They have been shocked as they have found editorial writers and politicians applying ethnic epithets and other derogatory terms to the other ethnic groups, and as they have explored violent incidents involving racial and ethnic groups. The historians treading these new paths are young; some of them are immigrants to Canada. They tend to project what they discover in documentary sources to the whole Canadian population, and to picture all Anglo-Celts as in all situations anti-foreign, anti-Catholic, and racist (Palmer 1976).

Illustrations of the myth abound particularly in Manitoba, Saskatchewan, and Alberta, where those of non-British, non-French, and non-Native origins constituted 45 percent of the population according to the 1971 census, and those with an "other" component 48 percent in 1981. It was expressed in two charming National Film Board films shown on television on the two Sunday evenings immediately preceding Christmas in 1978. The first, "Teach Me to Dance," was set in western Canada in 1919. It concerned two girls of 11 or 12 years of age—Lesia, who was Ukrainian, and English-Canadian Sarah. Lesia, tormented by the class bully (whose name was MacIntyre), exclaimed in Ukrainian, and had to write on the blackboard two hundred times, "I must not speak Ukrainian in school." She also was being made to learn to recite a bombastic poem about the British Empire. Meanwhile her father had been refused credit by English Canadians "with vinegar for blood." Sarah, visiting

Lesia's home, was delighted by a Ukrainian dance and asked to learn it. She proposed to the teacher that she and Lesia perform it at the Christmas concert. The teacher rather dubiously consented but on the night of the concert Sarah's father forbade her to dance. The bittersweet ending of the film showed Sarah visiting Lesia in the barn the next day and dancing with her. The second film, shown on Christmas Eve, was "Raisins and Almonds." It also was set in the west, about 10 years later, and it concerned a somewhat younger girl. She, a member of the only Jewish family in town, was at the age of 7 the town's outstanding elocutionist. As such she was invited, as she had been twice before, to participate in a church's Christmas concert. She was reluctant, since Santa Claus had in previous years brought gifts for all the other children but none for her, but she was persuaded by her parents to accept the invitation. This time the child received a gift, a doll, which she later discovered to be one of her own, outfitted with new clothes by her mother. Incidentally, according to Fredelle Bruser Maynard's memoir on which the film was based, the town was largely Scandinavian, and the church was Lutheran; however, the film leaves the impression that it was English Canadians who were so thoughtless as not to provide a gift for a small visitor at Christmas (Maynard 1973).

The second film was autobiographical; perhaps the first was also. But to give pride of place on national television to the two films, one centering on an ethnic group that does not celebrate Christmas and the other on a group, part of which does not celebrate it on December 25, and both having as theme the callousness of English Canadians to members of other ethnic groups, and young children at that, is to lift such incidents out of the status of occasional occurrences to mythic proportions.

The same myth was expressed by Sonia Cipywnyk of the Faculty of Education at the University of Saskatchewan, in a paper in which she said she was eschewing the role of academic and telling it as it was (1978). She wrote:

> For the ethnic child of my father's and my generation, school could be and often was, a painful place. Everything valued by one's parents, everything that made up one's after-school life, was feared, misunderstood, occasionally ridiculed, and always subtly undermined. Everything associated with the most significant landmarks of human existence, everything that was most sacred, most poignant, most satisfying—all of that was somehow second or third rate.
>
> The Canadian—and in my day that meant the English—way meant keeping a stiff upper lip, suppressing one's emotions, doing things "properly," and, above all, shedding one's ethnicity as if it were an outer

skin one could unzip and leave behind like a cocoon and, in the process, become a standard Canadian Monarch butterfly. It meant singing "Rule Britannia," "There'll Always Be an England," "In Days of Yore," and "God Save the King" every day during morning exercises. Teachers of United Empire Loyalist stock from southern Ontario were imported to make sure that all this was done "properly." "O Canada" was sung, too, but the message was clear and simple—Canadian = English.

Yet some scepticism is in order. Without questioning the British influence on social structures, including schools, and the "overwhelmingly British and French cultural perspective within most curricula" (Werner et al.: 55), one may ask whether this was how it was or how it felt. It is hard to believe that no English-Canadian teachers in the West acted on the precept that pride in one's background and confidence in oneself were prerequisites of learning. My teachers in small-town Ontario did; and high school teachers in ethnically heterogeneous areas of Toronto described devising projects to enhance their students' knowledge of and appreciation for their ethnic background long before the term "multiculturalism" was current. Presumably, teachers in the West were on the average younger, less experienced, and more mobile than those in central Canada; presumably also they were indoctrinated, during whatever short training they underwent—John Diefenbaker's instruction in pedagogy at Normal School lasted an hour (1978)—with the importance of assimilating the non-British among whom they were to work. Yet there are at least a few indications that they did not all fear, misunderstand, ridicule, and undermine the values of their pupils of non-British origin. John Charyk, in his trilogy about rural schools, tells of a teacher of British origin who profited from his time in a western school district settled by Scandinavians to learn to speak, read, and write Norwegian and Swedish (1977: 206), and Gabrielle Roy, an extraordinarily gifted one-time teacher in the West, reveals in *Ces enfants de ma vie* (1977) an exquisite sensitivity to the values and traditions of the parents of her pupils.

The fact that neither Roy nor Charyk, a long-time teacher in east-central Alberta, was, like Sonia Cipywnyk's teachers, U.E. Loyalist from Ontario perhaps should be underlined. Young people born or bred or both on the prairies were not long in replacing the school teachers from the Maritime provinces and from Ontario in western schools, and from an early time they included young people of non-British origins. Presumably they generally served areas in which people of their own ethnic background were concentrated, though Ukrainian Canadian John Charyk did not. Certainly there were schools in the Slavic belt and the German belt in which it was children of British origin who were made to feel that they were outsiders, since although English was the language of the classroom, Ukrainian or Polish or German was the language of the playground, and since it was not the English Canadians who set the standards for school lunches and manners of dressing but the Central Europeans. I interviewed a colleague whose sister and she had been the only Canadians of British origin in such a school in Saskatchewan in the 1930s and 1940s, and when I asked how the traditions of her Slavic neighbours had been regarded, her answer was prompt: "They taught us how to live." She went on to explain that, far from despising the heritage of the Ukrainians and Poles, her father had learned from them how to construct barn and house and her mother how to provide an adequate diet under Saskatchewan conditions.

This is not to deny that school was a painful place for the child of non-British origin. But there were also other reasons than the values of the school system and the attitudes of teachers and fellow-students for the pain. One reason the children of non-British origin shared with their classmates of British origin; the almost inevitable gap opens as children grow up between them and their parents. The other exacerbated that gap; the difference in social and geographical environment between Europe and the Canadian West, which made the values, beliefs, and customs brought from the old land less than completely appropriate in the new.

The warmth, generosity, and openness of others as compared to English Canadians may also not have been universal. Readers of Rudy Wiebe's *Peace Shall Destroy Many* (1962) will recall that in this novel the Russian Mennonites were anything but accepting of the Indians and halfbreeds who lived near them. Those who are familiar with *Raisins and Almonds* (Maynard 1973) know that the small Jewish child whose Christmases were bitter, joined with two Norwegian Canadian friends in tormenting the Chinese keeper of a candy store; so much, by the way, for the myth that young children do not discriminate. It is easy to regard all of the intolerance and discrimination that is now being revealed to be part of Canadian history as being English Canadian, or WASPish. Perhaps it is too easy.

A particularly widespread and thoroughly accepted part of the myth of unremitting oppression of those not of British origin is the concept of the vertical mosaic. As stated by Porter (1965), this is a product of a British conspiracy. Recently Darroch (1979), Reitz (1980), and others have presented data and argument that throw strong doubt on the vertical mosaic. They have shown that neither the measured occupational dissimilarity between ethnic groups nor the inequality in occupational ranks of immigrant groups is very great or very stable. Further, the situation in the United States is not more open.

It is important to question the myth of oppression by those of British origin because denigration of Canadians of British origin is no firmer basis for multiculturalism than denigration of other Canadians. If we are to understand one another, we must forgo the pleasure of regarding some ethnic groups as more virtuous than others, and look instead in a detached way at the kinds of things people—all people—do in various situations. We have it on the authority of two distinguished sociologists, E.T. Thompson and E.C. Hughes (1958: 3), that "nothing is so devastatingly equalitarian as detachment."

What is the point of calling attention to the myths concerning ethnicity in Canadian society? In the first place, it is to indicate how little still is known about the Canadian population, how much historians and social scientists have yet to do to increase our knowledge of our society, and particularly of its ethnic dimension. Canadians have neglected their past, and have left much of the study of their present to outsiders. Usually they have excused themselves by referring to the country's youth, but a centenarian is hardly young in a world where so many new nations have come into being in the last 50 or 60 years. It is hardly appropriate now simply to substitute myth for myth as society changes. It is time for historian and sociologist to deepen our knowledge of our past and of our present, and to depict it not in *images d'Epinal*, but in all its shadings.

In the second place, the myths themselves should be recognized and studied. They are not an accurate picture of how it was, but they tell how it seemed to some people, or how some people wanted or want it to be presented. The myths shaped and shape today behaviour and attitudes, in ways by no means irrelevant for social cohesion. Thus they too are important, if we are to understand what we were and what we are.

part II

Ethnic demography and ecology

Growth and Distribution of Canada's Ethnic Populations, 1871–1981 [†]

WARREN E. KALBACH

The Canadian government, through its periodic national censuses, has collected data for over a century which have significance for the social, economic, and political development of the country's regional populations and communities. The consistent inclusion of questions in the census dealing with the ethnic and cultural origins, and other characteristics of individuals permanently residing in Canada has resulted in an impressive accumulation of information concerning the nature of Canadian society. It is possible not only to examine the country's social, economic, and demographic structure, but also to determine the relative contributions made to this structure through migration and the natural increase of Canada's diverse ethnic and cultural groups. The analysis of the growth and distribution of Canada's population presented in this paper focuses on two of these basic data series (country of birth and ethnic origins), which have particular importance for the understanding of the cultural fabric of Canadian society. Such trends provide a general perspective from which to view the other papers in this volume.

Population Growth
The Foreign-born Population

The growth and composition of Canada's population varied considerably following Confederation in 1867. In slightly more than a hundred years, Canada's population increased from 3.7 million to 24.3 million. The average annual rate of growth has varied in response to fluctuations in fertility rates and immigration flows. During the 1930s the growth rate was as low as 1.0 percent compared to almost 3 percent during the

†This article has not been previously published.

first decade of the twentieth century when heavy immigration coincided with relatively high levels of fertility. The significance of immigration for Canada, in addition to its contribution to population size, is reflected in its effects on the native-born and foreign-born proportions. However, even though Canada was initially settled by immigrants and immigration continues to be one of its major sources of growth, its contribution has never exceeded that of natural increase in the years following Confederation. Since 1871, the proportion foreign-born in Canada has never exceeded the 22 percent level which was achieved between 1911 and 1941. The size of the foreign-born population continues to reflect the varying significance of Canada's fertility and immigration levels. With the collapse of the "baby boom" and continuation of fairly high levels of immigration, the foreign-born proportion has increased only slightly. The history of Canada's population growth, immigration, and changes in size of its foreign-born population since 1871 is summarized in Table 1. Note that with the exception of the 1930s, the foreign-born population always increased in numbers during each decade since 1871, but its rate of growth has not always kept pace with that of the native-born.

Children of the Foreign-born

Data on the foreign-born alone do not reveal the full extent of their contribution to the growth of the national population. Children born in Canada to foreign-born residents are generally included with all native-born persons in census publications, so that it is not possible to estimate their direct contribution to total growth. Only twice in recent decades have data been collected on the nativity of the parents that would permit an examination of the generational components and their relative sizes. These data, from the 1931 and 1971 censuses, identifying three generational groupings of the population, are shown in Table 2.

It is apparent that the foreign-born make an additional and rather significant contribution to the population in the form of second-generation Canadians. In 1931, their children made up approximately one-quarter of the population, whereas the two groups combined comprised almost one-half of the total. While the numbers of first- and second-generation Canadians increased from 4.7 million in 1931 to 7.1 in 1971, their combined relative size actually declined to 33 percent during this period. Nevertheless, in both years the total contribution of the foreign-born to the nation's population was actually more than twice as much as it would have been had their children not been taken into consideration. Unfortunately, the question on nativity of parents was dropped from the 1981 census so that no estimate of the change in their

Table 1
Population Increase, Immigration, and the Foreign-born Population: Canada, 1871–81 to 1971–81

Decade	Population			Immigration		Foreign-born	
	Total Population[a] ('000)	Percent Decade Increase (%)	Annual Rate of Population Increase (%)	Number of Immigrants ('000)	Percent of Average Decade Population (%)	Total Foreign-born ('000)	Percent Foreign-born (%)
1871–1881	3,689	17.2	1.6	353	8.8	602	16.7
1881–1891	4,325	11.8	1.1	903	19.7	603	13.9
1891–1901	4,833	11.1	1.1	326	6.4	644	13.3
1901–1911	5,371	34.2	2.9	1,759	28.0	700	13.0
1911–1921	7,207	21.9	2.0	1,612	20.2	1,587	22.0
1921–1931	8,788	18.1	1.7	1,203	12.6	1,956	22.3
1931–1941	10,377	10.9	1.0	150	1.4	2,308	22.2
1941–1951	11,507	21.7	1.7	548	4.4	2,010	17.5
1951–1961	14,009	30.2	2.6	1,543	9.6	2,060	14.7
1961–1971	18,238	18.3	1.7	1,429	7.2	2,844	15.6
1971–1981	21,569	12.9	1.1	1,447	6.3	3,296	15.3
1981–	24,343	—	—	—	—	3,919	16.1

Source: Dominion Bureau of Statistics, *Censuses of Canada, 1851 to 1961*; Statistics Canada, *1971 Census of Canada* (Ottawa: Information Canada); *1981 Census of Canada* (Ottawa: Minister of Supply and Services Canada [Catalogue 95-941]), Table 1; Employment and Immigration Canada, *Immigration Statistics, 1983* (Ottawa: Minister of Supply and Services Canada, 1985a); W.E. Kalbach, *The Effect of Immigration on Population, The Canadian Immigration and Population Study* (Department of Manpower and Immigration, Ottawa: Information Canada, 1974), Tables 1.1 and 2.6.

[a] Population at the beginning of the decade.

proportionate share of the total population can be made for the 1971–1981 decade. However, in view of the slight increase in the proportion foreign-born in Canada during this period, it is possible that the proportion second-generation also increased slightly.

Table 2
Population by Generations: Canada, 1931, 1971, and 1981

	1931		1971		1981	
Generation[a]	Number	Percent	Number	Percent	Number[c]	Percent
Foreign-born: 1st generation	2,234,600	21.6	3,177,200	14.7	3,919,252	16.1
Native-born: 2nd generation	8,125,100	78.4	18,391,100	85.3	20,423,929	83.9
	2,509,500	24.2	3,986,700	18.5	—	—
3rd[b] generation	5,615,600	54.2	14,404,400	66.8	—	—
Total:	10,359,700	100.0	21,568,300	100.0	24,343,181	100.0

Source: Dominion Bureau of Statistics, *1931 Census of Canada* (Ottawa: The Queen's Printer), Vol. III, Table 27, and Vol. IV, Table 15; Statistics Canada, *1971 Census of Canada*, Bulletin 1.3–6 (Ottawa: Information Canada, 1974), Table 46; *1981 Census of Canada*, Catalogue 95–941 (Vol. 3 – Profile Series B, 1983), Table 1.

[a] Generations are defined as follows: 1st generation are the foreign-born with foreign-born parents; 2nd generation are the native-born with one or both parents foreign-born; 3rd and subsequent generations are the native-born with native-born parents. The foreign-born also include some who were born outside Canada to native-born parents, of which there were 69,500 in 1931, 118,300 in 1971, and approximately 40,000 in 1981. The question for "birthplace of parents" was not included in the 1981 Census.

[b] The 1931 total excludes 17,136 persons for whom nativity of parents was not stated.

[c] Estimates of numbers of foreign- and native-born based on the Canada total of 24,343,181 from the 100% enumeration census schedule.

Ethnic Populations[1]

The French were the first to establish a foothold in the New World now called Canada. Even after the British secured political control after the Seven Years' War, the majority of the population was still French-speaking. Not until the emigration of British Empire Loyalists from the American colonies after the American Revolution were the British able to achieve numerical superiority in addition to the political control they had won earlier. By the time of Confederation, just under two-thirds, or

60.5 percent, of the population were of British origins, while almost one-third, or 31.3 percent, were French. The remaining population was predominately German, with some Dutch and a scattering of Scandinavians, Russians, and Italians.

The British have managed to maintain their numerical dominance throughout the century; yet, on the other hand, the population of French origin has continued to be the single largest homogeneous cultural group in Canada. On only two occasions have the numbers of French been exceeded by another relatively homogeneous group. In 1921, and again in 1971, the English outnumbered the French. But, in 1981 changed census procedures permitted multiple ethnic responses, making it impossible to develop any reliable estimates that would be comparable with those based on earlier censuses. Of those reporting a single ethnic origin, 6,439,000 were reported to be of French origin, compared to 6,109,000 of English origin. Determining which of the two was actually the largest at the time of the 1981 census, in terms comparable to estimates from earlier censuses, would depend upon the procedures used to allocate those reporting multiple origins. However inconvenient the loss of comparability may be for the analysis of historical trends, the information on multiple origins collected by the 1981 census will provide new insights into the changing nature of Canadian society. In any event, the inherent difficulties in obtaining both valid and reliable data on ethnic origins of individuals from censuses of populations make it advisable to use considerable caution in the interpretation of these data.[2]

The more detailed ethnic composition of the British Isles origin group, shown in Table 3, underscores the greater heterogeneity of the British vis-à-vis the French. According to these data, the Irish tended to have numerical superiority over the English until 1901. But, after the heavy influx of immigrants during the early twentieth century, they were exceeded by both the English and the Scottish. Perhaps the other most significant aspect of this particular period of Canadian history was the rising prominence of the "other" ethnic populations in the Canadian mosaic. In 1871, the British accounted for about two-thirds of the population. Since that time, their proportion has declined rather consistently over the years to about 40 percent in 1981. The French component of the population was much more stable during this period, nevertheless it also declined from about 31 percent in 1871 to approximately 27 percent in 1981. All of the other ethnic populations combined increased from a negligible 8 percent to a third of the total population.

The predominance of the Germans and Dutch in this residual group of "other" ethnic populations prior to the 1900s has already been mentioned. With the opening of the prairies for settlement, and the events in

Table 3
Population[a] of British Isles, French, and Other Selected Origins:
Canada, Selected Years, 1871–1971

Ethnic Group	1871[b]	1881	1901	1921	1941	1961	1971
Total[c]	3,486	4,325	5,371	8,788	11,507	18,238	21,568
British Isles	2,111	2,549	3,063	4,869	5,716	7,997	9,624
English	706	881	1,261	2,545	2,968	4,195	6,246
Irish	846	957	989	1,108	1,268	1,753	1,581
Scottish	550	700	800	1,174	1,404	1,902	1,720
Other	8	10	13	42	76	146	86
French	1,083	1,299	1,649	2,453	3,483	5,540	6,180
Other							
European	240	299	458	1,247	2,044	4,117	4,960
Austrian, n.o.s.	—	—	11	108	38	107	42
Belgian	—	—	3	20	30	61	51
Czech and Slovak	—	—	—	9	43	73	82
Finnish[d]	—	—	3	21	42	59	59
German	203	254	311	295	465	1,050	1,317
Greek	—	—	—	6	12	56	124
Hungarian[e]	—	—	2	13	55	126	132
Italian	1	2	11	67	113	450	731
Jewish	—	1	16	126	170	173	297
Lithuanian	—	—	—	2	8	28	25
Netherlands	30	30	34	118	213	430	426
Polish	—	—	6	53	167	324	316
Romanian[f]	—	—	—	13	25	44	27
Russian[g]	1	1	20	100	84	119	64
Scandinavian	2	5	31	167	245	387	385
Ukrainian	—	—	6	107	306	473	581
Yugoslav	—	—	—	4	21	69	105
Other	4	6	5	18	10	88	195
Asiatic	—	4	24	66	74	122	286
Chinese	—	4	17	40	35	58	119
Japanese	—	—	5	16	23	29	37
Other	—	—	2	10	16	34	129
Other[h]	52	174	177	153	190	463	519
Native People	—	—	—	114	126	220	313
Blacks	—	—	—	18	22	32	34
Other	—	—	—	21	42	210	172

Source: Dominion Bureau of Statistics, *1961 Census of Canada*, Bulletin 7:1–6
(Ottawa: The Queen's Printer, 1966), Table 1 and Table I; Statistics Canada, *1971 Census
of Canada*, Bulletin 1.3–2 (Ottawa: Information Canada, 1973), Table 1; D. Kubat and D.
Thornton, *A Statistical Profile of Canadian Society* (Toronto: McGraw-Hill Ryerson Ltd.,
1974), Table f–10.

[a] Numbers rounded to the nearest 1,000. [b] Four original provinces only. [c] Excludes
Newfoundland prior to 1951. [d] Includes Estonian prior to 1951. [e] Includes Lithuanian
and Moravian in 1901 and 1911. [f] Includes Bulgarian in 1901 and 1911. [g] Includes
Finnish and Polish in 1871 and 1881. [h] Includes "not stated" prior to 1971. In 1971 "not
stated" cases were computer assigned.

Table 4
Population by Selected Ethnic Origins[1]: Canada, 1981

Ethnic Origin	Number
British	9,674,245
French	6,439,100
Multiple (British and French)	1,522,075
Other European	
Austrian	40,630
Balkan	129,075
Baltic	50,300
Belgian and Luxembourg	43,000
Czech and Slovak	67,695
Dutch	408,240
Finnish	52,315
German	1,142,365
Greek	154,365
Magyar	116,390
Italian	747,970
Jewish	264,025
Polish	254,485
Portuguese	188,105
Romanian	22,485
Russian	49,435
Scandinavian	282,795
Spanish	53,540
Swiss	29,805
Ukrainian	529,615
Asian/African	
African	45,215
Armenian	21,155
Asian Arab	60,140
Chinese	289,245
Indo-Chinese	43,725
Indo-Pakistani	121,445
Japanese	40,995
North African Arab	10,545
Pacific Island	155,290
West Asian	10,055
Other	
Latin American	117,555
Native People	413,380
Other Single Origins	176,160
Other Multiple Origins[2]	316,540
Total Population[3]	24,083,500

Source: 1981 *Census of Canada.*

Note: Totals may not equal the sum of components due to rounding. [1]The 1981 Census is the first to accept more than one ethnic origin for an individual. Therefore, this table includes counts of single and multiple origins. [2]Includes multiple origins of European, Jewish, and other origins not included elsewhere and multiple origins of Native People and British, French, European, Jewish, or Other Origins. [3]Excludes inmates.

Europe leading up to the First World War and its aftermath, the numbers of eastern and southern Europeans in the Canadian population began to increase significantly. However, of the two previously mentioned, only the Germans have consistently maintained their relative numerical position, and are still the largest ethnic origin population in Canada after the British and the French.

In 1911, the Ukrainians, Scandinavians, and Dutch were the next largest ethnic populations after the Germans. After World War II and the resumption of immigration, further changes in their relative sizes occurred. Note in Table 3 that the Dutch surpassed the Scandinavians between 1941 and 1961, while the Italian origin population exceeded the Ukrainians between 1961 and 1971.

Because changes in procedures for the 1981 census of Canada affected the comparability of its data with earlier censuses, the most recent information on Canada's ethnic populations has been presented separately in Table 4. These data clearly show that a number of Asian and other non-European ethnic populations surpassed many of the older European ethnic populations. The most notable case is the population of Chinese origin. In addition, and for the first time, the census has provided an estimate of the extent of ethnic mixing that has occurred in Canadian society through intermarriage. The proportion reporting multiple origins at the time of the 1981 census was approximately 8 percent, with combinations of British and French with each other as well as others comprising the largest portion of this group. This is not unexpected considering that the British and French have been numerically and culturally dominant for so much of Canada's history.

Components of Population Change

Fertility, Immigration, and Population Growth

The actual levels of fertility for the decades following Confederation, and through the first twenty years of the twentieth century, are still subject to considerable debate. Nevertheless, whichever estimates are taken as most correct, it is clear that births have had, and continue to have, greater significance for population growth in Canada than immigration. For the decade of heaviest immigration, i.e., 1901–11, births exceeded immigrants by over 380,000. In fact, for every decade since Confederation, fertility measured in numbers of births has consistently exceeded the reported numbers of immigrants. Figure 1 shows the relative contribution made by natural increase (i.e., births minus deaths) and net migration to the interdecade increase in Canada's population between 1871 and 1981. Between 1901 and 1931, and for the four decades following 1941, additions to the population through natural increase were supplemented by positive net migration. For the first three decades of Confederation, and the Depression decade of 1931–41, the full contribution of natural increase to Canada's growth was inhibited by a negative net migration. The relative contribution made by natural increase and net migration has obviously varied significantly since Confederation. For the two "peak" growth periods, i.e., 1901–11 and 1951–61, net migration accounted for 44 percent of the former decade's growth, but only 26 percent of the latter baby boom decade's increase. The postwar surge in immigration was clearly overshadowed by the excess of births over deaths during the baby boom years.

Figure 1
Components of Population Change: Canada, 1871–81 to 1971–81

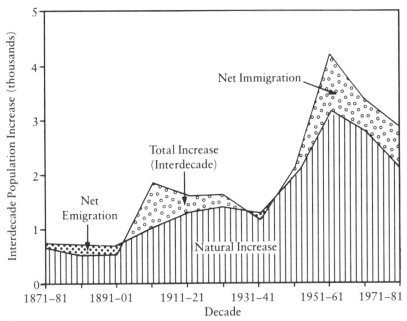

Source: Department of Employment and Immigration, *Immigration 1984* (Ottawa: Minister of Supply and Services Canada).

The effective contribution to population growth by births is mitigated by the number of deaths; and, similarly, the direct effects of arriving immigrants are reduced in proportion to the number of emigrants who leave the country. While the later component is extremely difficult to estimate accurately, data from the census, immigration records, and vital statistics show that the net gain from natural increase during the 1901–11 decade exceeded net immigration by at least 220,000. Estimates for other decades consistently show the greater contribution of natural increase over net immigration. For certain single years, the significance of net immigration has occasionally increased dramatically, but for the years following the Second World War, its net effect never reached 50 percent of the annual population increase. In 1951, an estimated net immigration of 184,000 accounted for 41 percent of the population increase for that year. The highest net immigration, which occurred in 1956, and amounted to 200,000, contributed somewhat less, or 38 percent, to that year's growth; and, in 1966, an estimated 131,000 net immigrants contributed 36 percent of that year's increase. At no time during the postwar period did net immigration ever achieve the distinction of contributing the major share of the country's growth.[3]

Fertility, Immigration, and Ethnic Composition

As fertility and immigration both contribute to numerical changes in the population, they can also effect its ethnic composition. Ethnic differences in fertility can cause the native-born component of some groups to increase more rapidly than others, while shifts in the source countries for immigrants will affect the ethnic composition of the foreign-born whether levels of immigration are rising or falling. Of the two, differences in fertility would most likely produce the greatest effects on the ethnic composition of the native-born population. While changes in the character of the immigrant stream can produce significant shifts in the ethnic composition of the foreign-born in a relatively short period of time, the effects are greatly reduced when the foreign-born are combined with the native-born population, because of their relatively small size compared to the latter population. Similarly, whatever the fertility differentials might be among the foreign-born by ethnic origins, the impact of the annual cohorts of births contributed to the native-born population by the foreign-born would be relatively slight.

It is a well-established fact that the French have maintained their relative position in Canada through high fertility rather than through dependence upon immigration, as has been the case for the British origins group. Data collected as recently as 1981 show that the fertility of married women is still generally higher for those of French origin than those belonging to most other ethnic groups. The few exceptions are to be found among younger married women under 25 years of age, and women from some Protestant groups (e.g., Hutterites, Mennonites, Mormons, etc.).[4]

Following the postwar baby boom, fertility levels resumed their downward trend for the nation as a whole; rates have been falling faster in Quebec than elsewhere since 1957. By 1968, Quebec had the lowest crude birth rate of any province in Canada. In addition, Quebec was the only province whose gross reproduction rate (GRR) had fallen below 1.0 by 1970, a level somewhat below that required for population replacement.[5] By 1981, the fertility of French-Canadian women, still in their childbearing years, was close to the lowest levels reported for any ethnic population.[6]

For obvious reasons, these trends have caused alarm among Quebec politicians and others concerned with the province's future. To the extent that Quebec can neither reverse the present trend in fertility nor succeed in attracting French-speaking immigrants, it will have to pursue more drastic measures to preserve the French-Canadian culture and language. Concerns about Quebec's demographic future are now being expressed in the form of legislation aimed at restricting access to English language schools as well as restricting the use of English throughout the province.[7]

Changes in the source countries of arriving immigrants have been the primary reason for the continuing decline in the proportion of the British-origin population in Canada following Confederation. The arrival of large numbers of immigrants from other western and northern European countries had never been regarded as a problem by those of British origins because of their general cultural similarity. However, the influx of "new" immigrants from central, eastern, and southern Europe during the early 1900s became the cause of growing concern among the "old" immigrants, who felt that immigration from non-traditional source areas would have deleterious effects on the established Canadian way of life.

Between 1926 and 1966, the proportion of immigrants of northern and western European origins, including British, declined significantly, as did the proportion of central and eastern European origins. In contrast, the relative numbers of immigrants of southern and southeastern European origins increased during this period, especially after World War II. While the latter group comprised only 4.5 percent of all immigrants coming to Canada between 1926 and 1946, their proportion jumped to 15 percent during the immediate postwar period, and then doubled to 30 percent for the 1956–66 period. Immigrants of Asian origins, while still relatively small in numbers, also showed significant increases. From less than 1 percent before the war, they increased to 6.5 percent during this same period. These data are summarized in Table 5a.

Table 5a

Origins of Immigrants Arriving in Canada: 1926–66
Immigration by Ethnic-Origin Groups: 1926–45, 1946–55, and
1956–66

Ethnic-Origin Group	1926–45	1946–55	1955–66
British Isles	47.8	34.1	32.9
Northwestern European	24.4	30.2	20.7
Central and East European	19.1	15.1	7.7
Southeastern and South European	4.5	15.3	29.9
Jewish	3.4	3.5	2.2
Asian and Other Origins	0.8	1.7	6.5
Total: Percent	100.0	100.0	100.0
Number	950,944	1,222,318	1,476,444

Source: Department of Manpower and Immigration, *Annual Immigration Reports*; Royal Commission on Bilingualism and Biculturalism, *The Cultural Contribution of the Other Ethnic Groups, Book IV* (Ottawa: The Queen's Printer, 1970), Table A-1; and, W.E. Kalbach, *The Effect of Immigration on Population, The Immigration and Population Study* (Department of Manpower and Immigration, Ottawa: Information Canada, 1974), Table 2.1.

Table 5b

Origins of Immigrants Arriving in Canada: 1966–80
Immigration by Last Country of Permanent Residence: 1966–70,
1971–75, and 1976–80

Country of Last Permanent Residence	1966–70	1971–75	1976–80
Britain and Rep. of Ireland	25.2	16.4	14.1
United States of America	11.4	14.3	9.9
Northern and Western Europe	15.8	6.8	6.8
Central and Eastern Europe	1.8	1.4	2.3
Southern and Southeastern Europe	22.8	15.6	8.8
Israel	0.8	0.6	0.9
Australia and Europe, n.e.s.	2.6	1.7	1.4
Asia			
South, S.E., and East Asia	9.4	20.7	31.7
Middle East and North Africa	2.1	2.3	4.8
All Others	8.1	20.2	19.3
Total: Percent	100.0	100.0	100.0
Number	910,837	834,452	605,869

Source: Canada Manpower and Immigration, *Immigration Statistics*, for years 1966–1976; Employment and Immigration Canada, *Immigration Statistics*, for years 1977–1980 (Ottawa: Minister of Supplies and Services).

Ethnic-origin data were not collected after 1966, but parallel trends can be seen in data for "country of last permanent residence" which were also collected during the same postwar years, and are still collected by the Department of Employment and Immigration. These data, presented in Table 5b for the fifteen-year period 1966–80, clearly show the rapidly changing character of Canada's most recent immigrants.

The proportions of arriving immigrants from the British Isles and other northern and western European countries have continued to show significant declines. While those from southeastern and southern Europe had shown spectacular gains up to the 1955–66 period, their proportion of immigrant arrivals declined rapidly since then. Probably the most significant of these recent changes has been the spectacular increase in the proportions of immigrants coming from Asian and other non-European countries. As recently as the 1966–70 period, only 19.6 percent of arriving immigrants had come from non-European source countries. As the data in Table 5b clearly show, this proportion increased dramatically to 43.2 percent during the 1971–75 period, and to over half, or 56 percent, for 1976–80.

A better picture of the changing ethnic mix of arriving immigrants can be obtained by examining the lists of leading source countries presented in Table 6. The shift to non-European source countries is very clear. The effects of these changes on the ethnic composition of the foreign-born population will, of course, be dependent on variations in immigration levels. For the years shown, the small number of arriving immigrants in 1984 would have produced the least effect, while the 1951 immigration of close to 200,000 would have had a considerably greater impact. Of course, a continuation of the shift to non-European source countries, in the long run, will significantly alter the character of both the first and second generations of Canadians.

Much of the shift to non-European source countries in recent decades, apparent in Tables 5 and 6, can be attributed to the elimination of restrictions based on racial and ethnic origins and to the contrasts in economic conditions which had developed between the traditional source countries and many of the third world countries, vis-à-vis the state of the Canadian economy. Faced with a commitment to maintain a non-discriminatory policy during a period of rising demand for emigration in many non-European countries, the government was compelled to review and revise its policies and regulations in order to develop a more objective method of regulating immigration in relation to its national requirements.

The government's Green Paper on immigration and population in 1974, provided the arguments and the rationale for the various regulations made by the government under the authority of the old 1952

Table 6
The Leading Source Countries of Immigrants: Selected Years

1951	1960	1968	1976	1984
Britain	Italy	Britain	Britain	Vietnam
Germany	Britain	United States	United States	Hong Kong
Italy	United States	Italy	Hong Kong	United States
Netherlands	Germany	Germany	Jamaica	India
Poland	Netherlands	Hong Kong	Lebanon	Britain
France	Portugal	France	India	Poland
United States	Greece	Austria	Philippines	Philippines
Belgium	France	Greece	Portugal	El Salvador
Yugoslavia	Poland	Portugal	Italy	Jamaica
Denmark	Austria	Yugoslavia	Guyana	China

Source: Department of Manpower and Immigration, *The Immigration Program, Vol. 2, A Report of the Canadian Immigration and Population Study* (Ottawa: Information Canada, 1974), Table 3.3, p. 84; *1976 Immigration Statistics*, Table 3; and Employment and Immigration Canada, *Annual Report to Parliament on Future Immigration Levels, 1985* (Ottawa: Minister of Supply and Services Canada, 1985b), Statistical Appendix.

Immigration Act, including the introduction of the more objective "point" system in 1967 for determining eligibility for admission of unsponsored or independent workers.[8] The Green Paper also led to the overhauling of the existing immigration laws and regulations and ultimately to the introduction of a new Immigration Act in 1976. The new act explicitly prohibits discrimination on the grounds of race, national or ethnic origin, colour, religion, or sex. It emphasizes the importance of family reunification, fulfilment of international obligations regarding refugees and displaced persons, and the need to tailor the selection of immigrants to the country's economic needs while fulfilling appropriate demographic goals established through consultation with the provinces and other appropriate parties.[9]

The Immigration Act of 1976 established, for the first time in Canada, the basis for a general quota system that would permit better control over the numbers of immigrants admitted to Canada. The new act requires the government to lay before Parliament, prior to each calendar year, its report specifying the numbers of immigrants it "deems it appropriate to admit" and "the manner in which demographic considerations have been taken into account in determining that number."[10] The admission of unsponsored or independent workers was greatly restricted during the period following the enactment of the new Immigration Act as the economy remained depressed and the country continued to be plagued by high levels of unemployment. Continuing annual reviews of immigration by the new Conservative government generally have been consistent with the "short-term" goals of their predecessors which were primarily concerned with restricting admissions of workers during periods of high unemployment. However, the need to justify their recommended annual intake of immigrants in terms of demographic considerations, has succeeded in bringing new problems to the attention of the government that would be a consequence of permitting only minimal immigration while fertility levels in Canada continue at below replacement levels. The nature of these problems would seem to be sufficiently serious to warrant ameliorative action on the part of government. The fact that the Minister of Immigration recommended increases in immigration levels for 1986 and 1987, albeit modest ones, represents a major change in immigration policy with significant consequences for both the volume and character of future immigration to Canada.

Population Distribution

Regional Patterns
The Foreign-born: 1901–1981

The patterns of residential location exhibited by immigrants, like their growth rate, have been uneven through this period of Canadian history. The heavy immigration of the early twentieth century coincided with the opening and settlement of the prairies, and the foreign-born concentrated heavily in this western region. The proportion of the foreign-born locating in the prairie provinces doubled in the first decade, and it was not until after 1921, with continuing immigration and a shift in the pattern of settlement to other areas, that their heavy concentration in the prairies began to show signs of erosion. In Table 7, it is evident that by 1961 the distribution of foreign-born had almost returned to what it had been at the beginning of the century. The life cycle of the early settlers seems to have been almost completed. They have raised their families, and many of those who have not already passed on have moved away from their farms in retirement. By 1981, more than half of all the foreign-born remaining in Canada were located in Ontario. Quebec and British Columbia were the only other major regions to show net gains in their relative share of foreign-born over this total eighty-year period. In contrast, the Atlantic provinces, the Yukon, the Northwest Territories, and the prairie provinces all experienced relative declines, but only in the prairies, the Yukon, and Northwest Territories did the *number* of foreign-born actually experience a decline (this occurred only between 1961 and 1971). During the subsequent, and most recent decade, all areas had again recorded increases in their total populations.

Table 7
Percent of Population Foreign-born: Canada's Regions, 1901–1981

Region	1901	1911	1921	1931	1941	1951[a]	1961	1971	1981
Atlantic Provinces	6.7	3.6	3.4	3.0	3.2	2.7	2.3	2.2	2.1
Quebec	12.7	9.2	9.7	10.9	11.1	11.1	13.6	14.2	13.6
Ontario	46.3	32.0	32.8	34.9	36.3	41.2	47.6	51.8	52.4
Prairie Provinces	20.3	40.8	40.7	37.3	34.2	28.4	21.4	16.5	15.4
British Columbia	11.3	14.1	13.3	13.8	15.1	16.5	14.9	15.1	16.3
Yukon and N.W.T.	2.7	0.3	0.1	0.1	0.1	0.1	0.2	0.1	0.2
Total:									
Percent	100.0	100.0	100.0	100.0	100.0	100.0	100.0	99.9	100.0
Number ('000)	700	1,587	1,956	2,308	2,019	2,060	2,844	3,296	3,919[b]

Source: Censuses of Canada, 1901 to 1981.
[a] Newfoundland not included prior to 1951.
[b] Estimates of total and foreign-born populations, from the 20% sample, reported as 24,083,500 and 3,867,160 respectively.

Native-born Generation

Prior to World War II there was still a very clear east-west distinction in the balance between first-generation Canadians and their children, and the third and subsequent generations of native-born population with native-born parentage.[11] Quebec and the eastern provinces were dominated by the latter generations. In no case did the foreign-born and their children amount to more than 20 percent. While Ontario's population was almost evenly divided, the western provinces were almost as dominated by the combined first and second generations as Quebec and the eastern provinces were by the third and subsequent generations. Alberta and British Columbia both had the highest proportion of first and second generations combined of 80 percent while Saskatchewan and Manitoba had 76 and 74 percent respectively.

By 1971, the picture had changed radically in the West as a result of the aging of the foreign-born, changing migration patterns, and the high postwar fertility of the native-born. A majority of every province's population, except British Columbia, were native-born of native-born parentage. Even in British Columbia, with 53 percent of its population still first or second generation, its decline from 80 percent in 1931 was both significant and consistent with the overall trend. Ontario's combined first and second generations declined from 51 to 44 percent during the forty-year period 1931–1971, in spite of the heavy influx of postwar immigrants to that province. The balance changed very little in Quebec, and both Quebec and Ontario were somewhat unique in that, unlike the other provinces, their first and second generations were relatively the same size—reflecting, no doubt, the lower fertility of the more recent foreign-born who had settled in these areas. The proportions of third and latter generations in the populations of the Atlantic provinces increased, with only Nova Scotia failing to exceed 90 percent by 1971. The significance of these changes in generational composition of the population would appear to be different for the Atlantic provinces than for the western part of the country. In the first case, where there is a high proportion of British origins, a continuing decline in the foreign-born component and their descendents could work to strengthen the culture of the dominant group. In the latter case, the same trend would tend to reduce the ethnic distinctiveness of those non-British origin groups that had settled in Canada's west.

During the most recent intercensal period, the proportion foreign-born in Canada's population actually increased by about 10 percent from 14.7 in 1971 to 16.1 percent in 1981.[12] Ontario experienced the only "above average" increase, reflecting among other things, Ontario's continuing attraction as a prime destination for arriving immigrants. The three prairie provinces were the only provinces to record declines, while all the remaining provinces experienced relative small increases of approximately 1 percent or less. The continuing declines in the prairies would more likely reflect the aging of their foreign-born, while increases in their relative numbers in the East would tend to be a reflection of the passing of the postwar baby boom and dramatically lower levels of fertility that have characterized the numerically dominant native-born during the most recent decades.

Ethnic Populations

The population of French descent in Canada has compensated, in part, for its smaller size by maintaining a singularly high degree of regional concentration. Had they been more evenly distributed throughout Canada, they would not have been able to achieve the numerical dominance in any one region that they have in Quebec today. In 1981, slightly more than three-fourths of Canada's population of French origin lived in Quebec, where they comprised 80 percent of the province's population. Those of British origin, more generally dispersed, numerically dominated the French in every province outside of Quebec. Yet, only in Nova Scotia, Prince Edward Island, and Newfoundland could one find proportions of British nearly as high, or higher, than the concentration of French in Quebec. Of these, only Newfoundland, could be considered to be more British than Quebec is French. In 1981, 92 percent reported British origins only, while another 2.6 percent reported multiple British and Other origins. Only 2.7 percent were of French origin, while the remaining 2.5 percent were of other origins. The other European origins have tended to be more highly concentrated in the provinces west of Ontario, with the notable exception of the Italians and Jews. The former are highly concentrated in Ontario, while the latter are found in disproportionately greater numbers in Quebec, Ontario, and Manitoba. Asians, whether considering the combined group as a whole, or the Chinese separately, are most concentrated in British Columbia, but are also found in above average numbers in Alberta and Ontario.

Very little detail was provided on the ethnic composition of the population in 1901. Nevertheless, the data in Table 8 still permit an examination of changes in the relative concentrations of the three major groupings of ethnic origins that have occurred over a period of eighty years as a result of differential rates of natural increase and the net effects of both internal and international migration. The net effects of the population dynamics during this period, while not dramatic, have been an increase in the relative concentration of those of French origin in New Brunswick and Quebec, as well as for the population of British origins in both the Atlantic Provinces and the three most western provinces. For the remaining combined population of all other origins, its degree of relative concentration declined significantly in the western provinces, and to a lesser extent in several of the Atlantic provinces while increasing in Ontario, Quebec, and in Prince Edward Island. However, with respect to the latter two provinces, the "other" origins are still underrepresented to a considerable degree. Another manifestation of these long-term trends is the increasing ethnic diversity which has characterized all of the provinces' populations, except Quebec, during the most recent intercensal decade, 1971–1981.

Overall, there do not seem to be any startling shifts in the relative concentrations of the major ethnic origin groups in Canada's major regions. The basic pattern of the geographical ethnic mosaic would seem to have been laid down fairly early in Canada's history by the two founding groups, and their relatively large size would tend to resist the effects of rapid shifts caused by recent migrants responding to the increased opportunities found in Canada's largest metropolitan centres. In the long run, however, the tendency for more rapid industrial and economic development to occur in central Canada and in the far West (and North) can be expected to continue to channel the more recent immigrants, as well as internal migrants of differing origins, into these areas. If this is in fact the case, Canada's ethnic patterns will, in time, shift accordingly.

Table 8
Percentage Composition of the Population by Ethnic Origins for Province of Residence: Canada, 1901 and 1981

Ethnic Origin	Total	Nfld.	P.E.I.	N.S.	N.B.	Que.	Ont.	Man.	Sask.	Alta.	B.C.	Yukon	N.W.T.
1901													
British	57.0	..	85.1	78.1	71.7	17.6	79.3	64.4	43.9	47.8	59.6	39.2	0.5
French	30.7	..	13.4	9.8	24.2	80.2	7.3	6.3	2.9	6.2	2.6	6.5	0.2
Other	12.3	..	1.5	12.1	4.1	2.2	13.4	29.3	53.2	46.0	37.8	54.3	99.3
Total	100.0	100.0	100.0	100.0	100.0	100.0	100.0	100.0	100.0	100.0	100.0	100.0	100.0
1981													
British	40.2	92.2	77.0	72.5	53.5	7.7	52.6	36.9	38.3	43.5	51.0	43.6	22.4
French	26.7	2.7	12.2	8.5	36.4	80.2	7.7	7.3	4.9	5.1	3.4	4.7	3.9
Multiple (Br. & Fr.)	6.3	2.6	6.9	7.9	5.5	1.8	7.9	7.1	7.8	9.6	9.1	10.7	4.4
Other European													
German	4.7	0.3	0.7	3.9	0.9	0.5	4.4	10.7	16.9	10.5	6.9	5.6	2.5
Dutch	1.7	0.1	1.1	1.6	0.6	0.1	2.2	3.3	1.8	2.9	2.7	1.7	0.7
Scandinavian	1.2	0.1	0.2	0.3	0.3	0.1	0.5	2.5	4.5	3.5	3.1	3.2	1.3
Polish	1.1	--	0.1	0.3	0.1	0.3	1.4	2.8	1.9	1.7	0.9	0.8	0.5
Russian	0.2	--				--	0.1	0.4	0.7	0.3	0.7	0.2	0.2
Ukrainian	2.2	-	0.1	0.2	0.1	0.2	1.6	9.8	8.0	6.2	2.3	2.8	1.3
Italian	3.1	0.1	0.4	0.2	2.6	5.7	0.9	0.3	1.2	1.2	1.9	0.4	0.5
Portuguese	0.8	--		0.1	--	0.4	1.5	0.8	0.1	0.3	0.6	--	0.1
Jewish	1.1	0.1	0.1	0.2	0.1	1.4	1.5	1.5	0.2	0.4	0.5	0.1	0.1
Multiple (Eur. & Oth.)	1.0	0.1	0.1	0.6	0.2	0.2	1.0	2.3	2.5	2.2	1.5	1.7	0.7
Asiatic	2.5	0.3	0.2	0.4	0.2	0.6	3.1	2.5	1.0	3.2	3.7	1.4	0.7
Other													
Black[a]	0.1	--	--	0.3	--	0.1	0.2	0.1	--	0.1	0.1	--	-
Latin American	0.5	--	--	0.1	--	0.4	0.9	0.4	0.1	0.3	0.2	--	0.1
Native People	1.7	0.6	0.4	0.8	0.7	0.7	0.1	5.9	5.7	2.7	2.4	14.8	55.6
Mult. (Native & Oth.)	0.3	0.2	0.2	0.2	0.1	0.1	0.3	0.6	0.5	0.5	0.7	2.7	2.4
All Other	4.6	0.6	0.7	1.8	0.9	2.6	6.5	4.2	4.8	5.7	5.3	5.3	2.6
Total	100.0	100.0	100.0	100.0	100.0	100.0	100.0	100.0	100.0	100.0	100.0	100.0	100.0

SOURCE: Statistics Canada, *1981 Census of Canada*, Catalogue 92–911 (Ottawa: Minister of Supply and Services, February, 1984), Table 1; Dominion Bureau of Statistics, *1961 Census of Canada*, Bulletin 7:1–6 (Ottawa: The Queen's Printer, 1966), Tables 1, 2, 3.
a Includes African Black, Canadian Black, and Other Black.   -- Less than 0.05   - Nil or zero   .. Figures not available

The Rural-Urban Shift

Since Confederation the rural-urban distribution of Canada's population has almost completely reversed itself. In 1871, eight out of every ten persons lived in rural areas. By 1981, only 24 percent were still classified as rural. Urbanization continued throughout the entire period at a steady pace, and by 1921 the population was almost evenly divided between rural and urban areas. The surprising fact is that the heavy influx of immigrants to the prairies in the first decade of the twentieth century did not slow the process at all. The rural population did increase by over half a million at this time, but the urban population grew by one and a quarter million, causing the proportion of the population that was rural to decline from 63 to 55 percent.

The Foreign-born Population

The settlement of agricultural lands in the West, at a time of heavy immigration, suggests that the foreign-born would be found in the rural areas in disproportionately larger numbers. While this may have been the case during the early decades of Confederation, by 1921 a larger proportion of the foreign-born than the native-born were to be found in urban areas. The results of subsequent censuses show that this has not only continued to be the case, but also that the difference between the native- and foreign-born has continued to increase. In 1921, the proportion of foreign-born residing in urban areas was 56 percent, compared to 48 percent for the native-born. Sixty years later, the proportions for the foreign- and native-born were 89 and 73 percent respectively.

Not only have the foreign-born urbanized to a greater extent than those born in Canada, but they have also shown a greater preference for the larger urban centres. In 1981, while 47 percent of the native-born were located in urban places of 100,000 or more, 74 percent of the foreign-born were similarly located.[13]

Urbanization of Ethnic Populations

Historically, some ethnic populations have been persistently urban in their settlement patterns, while others have remained entrenched in rural areas. As early as Confederation, two-thirds of the population of Jewish origins resided in urban areas, and by 1981 almost all, or 99 percent, were urban residents. At the other extreme are such ethnoreligious groups as the Hutterites, who have always lived in rural colonies in Canada, and the native Indians, who have generally found themselves on the outside of the white man's municipal boundaries. In 1981, little more than one-third, or 36 percent, of the native people were living in urban areas.

From the data presented in Table 9, it is clear that the two founding groups have charted a course between the extremes mentioned. Those of British origins have generally been more urbanized than the French, but the two groups have been slowly converging over the years as the nation itself has become more urbanized. In 1971, for the first time, both the British and French origin populations showed equal proportions, or 76 percent, living in urban areas. During the following decade, a reversal of the historical long-term trend of continuing urbanization took place, slightly reducing the levels for the British and French origins to 74 and 73 percent respectively. There is considerable variation among the remaining ethnic groups. The population of Italian origin, for example, has been steadily approaching the high level of urbanization that has historically characterized the Jewish population in Canada. Among the other ethnic groups not included in Table 9, only the Dutch can be characterized by a disproportionately low number of urban residents, while the Ukrainians are now slightly above the average for Canada as a whole.

Table 9
Percent Urban[a] for Selected Ethnic-Origin Populations: Canada, 1871–1981

| | | | Ethnic Origin | | | | |
Year	Total	British	French	German	Italian	Jewish	Nat. People
1871	19.6	22.3	18.8	11.1	53.5	67.2	1.7
1881	25.7	28.8	23.1	16.4	61.3	79.5	0.6
1901	37.5	41.8	33.7	28.0	65.4	94.2	5.1
1911	45.4	50.4	40.9	33.5	69.8	94.0	3.7
1921	49.5	53.7	47.7	33.2	79.3	95.7	3.7
1931	53.7	57.5	54.0	36.9	81.6	96.5	3.9
1941	54.3	58.3	54.9	36.4	80.9	96.0	3.6
1951	61.6	65.7	59.9	44.2	88.1	98.7	6.7
1961	69.6	71.2	68.2	61.8	94.7	98.8	12.9
1971	76.2	75.9	75.9	68.8	96.6	98.8	30.1
1981	75.6	74.5	73.3	68.3	94.9	98.5	36.4

Source: Censuses of Canada, 1871–1981.
[a] Definition of "urban" is that in effect at the time of the particular census.

Not unexpectedly, the non-Europeans, as well as some new European groups, which have been immigrating to Canada in increasing numbers in recent years, have been settling almost exclusively in urban areas. At the time of the 1981 census, 98 percent of the Chinese lived in urban areas, as well as 96 percent of the Indo-Pakistanis. The proportions for most Asian groups were in the 90's. The Portuguese, too, are almost totally urban, with 97 percent enumerated in urban areas. In addition to these more recent immigrant groups, the population reporting multiple origins also showed a predisposition towards urban residence with between 77 and 88 percent living in cities.

Additional data on residence for selected urban size categories do not change the overall picture materially with respect to propensities for urban settlement. But, the data in Table 10 do show significant variations in ethnic preferences for residence in the larger metropolitan areas. With the exception of those of Jewish and Italian origins, and such recent arrivals as the Portuguese, Greeks, and Spanish, most of the major European origin groups, including the French and British, show rather low propensities for settlement in the larger urban centres with populations over 500,000. By contrast, the picture is quite different for the

Table 10
Selected Ethnic-Origin Populations by Urban Size Groups: Canada, 1981

| Ethnic Origin | Urban Size Group | | | |
| | 500,000 | 100,000–499,999 | 1,000–99,999 | Total Urban |
		(%)		
British	34.9	12.5	27.1	74.5
French	40.9	6.9	25.5	73.3
German	30.1	13.8	24.4	68.3
Ukrainian	44.3	11.9	19.9	76.1
Italian	74.4	10.9	9.6	94.9
Jewish	92.1	3.6	2.8	98.5
Greek	84.4	7.4	6.1	97.9
Portuguese	75.6	10.2	10.8	96.6
Spanish	82.9	5.6	7.5	96.0
Chinese	82.2	7.0	8.8	98.0
Indo-Pakistani	75.4	6.9	13.5	95.8
Indo-Chinese	64.5	10.5	21.0	96.0
Japanese	73.7	3.3	14.6	91.6
West Asian	77.4	12.2	6.4	96.0

Source: Statistics Canada, *1981 Census,* Catalogue 92–911 (Ottawa: Minister of Supply and Services Canada, 1984), Table 2.

more recent non-European immigrants who have shown a decided preference for Canada's urban centres of over 100,000, and especially those over 500,000. The changing ethnic composition of Canadian immigration since the 1960s, and the increasing concentration of non-Europeans in the largest urban centres, are contributing to an increase in the ethnic diversity of Canada's population, both nationally and regionally, as well as affecting the nature of its urban neighbourhoods.

Residential Segregation in Metropolitan Areas

It should not be forgotten that the urbanization of Canada's population was proceeding at a rapid rate at the same time the prairies were being settled. Many of the factors underlying the settlement and persistence of ethnic bloc communities in the West would also have relevance for the appearance and persistence of ethnic neighbourhoods and communities in the larger metropolitan areas.[14] Strong feelings of ethnic and cultural identity, the desire to maintain ethnic languages, the need for specialized ethnic related services and institutional support, and variations in the socioeconomic status of arriving immigrant groups all contributed to the emergence of ethnic residential concentrations and communities in the larger urban centres in much the same manner as they had for those settling in the more rural areas.[15]

Recent research has also shown that such ecological factors as city size, recency of immigration, and the relative timing of arrival of the various groups have independently contributed to variations in the degree of residential segregation that have been observed for Canada's various ethnic populations. The size of an ethnic group, relative to the culturally dominant group, has also been shown to be a major explanatory factor accounting for the emergence of ethnic institutions and the visibility and persistence of ethnic communities within Canada's urban areas.[16]

According to early urban theorists, the dynamic factor underlying the spatial differentiation of urban populations was economic competition.[17] As the entrance status of most immigrants arriving in North America during the late nineteenth century and early twentieth century was relatively low, the ethnic ghettos and neighbourhoods that formed in central areas of the large cities were seen to be the natural consequence of the forces of competition operating in the urban setting. As the immigrants established themselves and improved their social and economic position in the community, they were expected to move away from the crowded low income core areas and towards higher status suburban areas, their places being taken by more recent arrivals. In the process, they were expected to generally disperse throughout the community. Residence in the centrally located ethnic neighbourhoods of the city was seen only as a transitory phenomenon that would diminish as immigrant groups became more economically integrated and socially assimilated into the dominant society.

Canada's ethnically diverse urban populations show significant variations in their propensities for residential segregation. Although there is some evidence of an overall decline in the degree of residential segregation between 1951 and 1961,[18] there has been no indication of any significant change in subsequent decades.[19] Most of the Canadian studies have been fairly consistent in showing a stable hierarchical pattern of tendencies for residential segregation by ethnic origins similar to those evident in Table 11.[20] Those of Jewish origin continue to be one of the most highly residentially segregated groups, while the culturally and numerically dominant British origins, i.e., the English, Irish, and Scottish, are the most widely dispersed relative to the other ethnic origins.

Table 11
Indexes of Residential Segregation[a] for Selected Ethnic Origins in Montreal, Toronto, Winnipeg, and Vancouver Census Metropolitan Areas, 1981

| Ethnic Origin | Census Metropolitan Areas | | | |
	Montreal	Toronto	Winnipeg	Vancouver
English	44.9	18.5	16.0	13.0
Irish	32.6	16.7	17.0	10.2
Scottish	47.1	17.7	18.0	11.6
French	47.4	19.6	37.8	20.2
Dutch	56.5	31.5	23.4	23.6
German	41.0	18.5	19.8	15.9
Polish	43.0	37.1	28.1	19.9
Ukrainian	47.2	32.6	27.8	15.9
Jewish	82.8	72.6	71.8	54.0
Italian	54.6	49.8	32.4	42.0
Portuguese	58.9	62.1	67.5	57.4
Chinese	60.0	45.3	45.3	50.9
Indo-Pakistani	62.7	43.6	59.3	39.4

Source: Statistics Canada special tabulations, 1981 Census.
[a] The Index of Segregation is a measure of the degree of dissimilarity between the residential distributions of a specific ethnic (origin) population and the remaining combined (ethnic-origin) populations. The index of 54.6 for Italians in Montreal means that 54.6 percent of the Italian-origin population would have to move to another census tract before their residential distribution would be the same as that for the remaining population.

Western, northern, and some central Europeans show only moderately greater tendencies for segregation than the British while higher propensities to segregate are characteristic of eastern and southern Europeans, as well as non-Europeans. While the hierarchical order appears to be stable for Canada's largest urban cities, the data in Table 11 also show a noticeable regional variation in the levels of ethnic segregation. Differences in residential distribution tend to be highest in Montreal, one of the older and larger cities in the East, and lowest among the younger and more rapidly growing cities of the West.

Conditions in a rapidly growing urbanizing society, experiencing high levels of population and social mobility and rising levels of education, have generally been thought to be favourable for rapid integration and assimilation of immigrants. To the extent that this is true, ethnic residential segregation should decline as the socioeconomic status of immigrants or their children improve. Analysis of the 1971 census data, which provided information on the generation status of individuals, supported the assimilation hypothesis for some groups; and shed new light on the nature of the relationship between socioeconomic status and residential segregation.[21]

In the Toronto Census Metropolitan Area, the assimilation pattern of diminishing residential segregation through successive generations appears valid for the British and French and some of the older northern and western European immigrant groups. However, the same claim cannot be made for all of the smaller or the more recent immigrants; nor, does it seem to be valid for any of the ethnic groups in Montreal where the dominant cultural context for immigrants is French, rather than British, as in Toronto. For the French in Montreal, the third-plus generations exhibited the greater degree of segregation, while the British showed higher levels of residential segregation for both first and the third-plus generations. Residential segregation patterns for the total populations of Italian and Jewish origins are shown in Figure 2 to illustrate the nature of the ethnic mosaic for several of the larger minority immigrant groups within the French-Canadian community.

Overall, educational status was negatively associated with residential segregation in Montreal, but not in Toronto where segregation was minimal for the intermediate educational status group. Segregation patterns were not uniformly consistent for all ethnic populations. Only when residential segregation was examined by educational status within generation groups did the curvilinear nature of the relationship come into sharper focus for the majority of ethnic groups in Toronto. It is becoming increasingly clear that in Canada, at least, socioeconomic

Figure 2
Patterns of Residential Concentration for Populations of Jewish and Italian Ethnic and Cultural Origins: Montreal Census Metropolitan Area, 1981

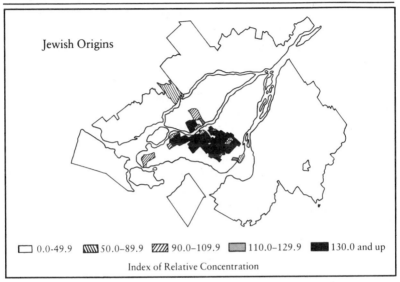

Jewish Origins

☐ 0.0–49.9 ▨ 50.0–89.9 ▨ 90.0–109.9 ▨ 110.0–129.9 ■ 130.0 and up

Index of Relative Concentration

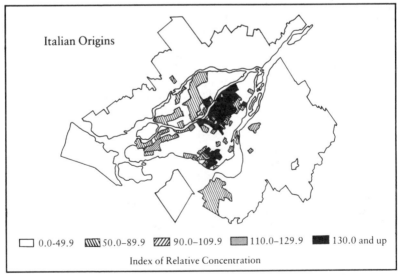

Italian Origins

☐ 0.0–49.9 ▨ 50.0–89.9 ▨ 90.0–109.9 ▨ 110.0–129.9 ■ 130.0 and up

Index of Relative Concentration

Source: 1981 Census of Canada.

Credit: Population Research Lab, Erindale College, University of Toronto.

status by itself is insufficient to account for ethnic differences in residential segregation. Its importance clearly varies for different ethnic origins as does the importance of cultural factors. In addition, the size of different ethnic populations as well as their generational composition in relation to the dominant ethnic population, are factors which must be taken into account in attempting to explain the nature of the Canadian ethnic mosaic. For most groups, a continuing influx of foreign-born immigrants would appear to be a necessary condition for future cultural survival. Under present conditions, most of those who must rely solely on natural increase to maintain their numbers will continue to face a losing battle. Even those who do succeed in keeping their fertility levels above replacement levels will still have to find ways of strengthening their ethnic commitment and identity to overcome the normal loss through intergenerational attrition. In short, Canada will survive as a multicultural society only to the extent that it succeeds in maintaining a significant inflow of immigrants to compensate for the inability of its native-born population to replace itself.

Notes

1. Data on ethnic populations in this paper are based on the "ethnic origin" question included in the Canadian Census. The data are not necessarily indicative of the individual's ethnic identity or the strength of his feelings about his identity or identification with an ethnic community. Prior to the 1981 Census of Canada, the census attempted to establish the respondent's ethnic or cultural background, by asking "to which ethnic or cultural group do you, or your ancestor, on the male side belong on first coming to this continent?" The 1981 census dropped the reference to "the male side" and left it up to the respondent to choose the appropriate side in cases of ethnic intermarriage. Also, for the first time, the census accepted "multiple origin" responses and published data for the most frequently occurring combinations.

2. The problems associated with the collection and interpretation of ethnic-origin data have long been recognized. Unexplained deviations from long-term trends or other apparent anomalies in the data should alert the reader, or user, of ethnic-origin or other census data to possible problems. For example, in Table 3, the rather large increase in the population of Jewish origins between 1961 and 1971 is largely the result of changes in the 1971 Census editing procedures. Specifically, individuals who reported their religion as Jewish were automatically included in the Jewish ethnic-origin population regardless of the origin reported. Other changes in the census schedules and enumeration procedures may partly account for the larger than expected increase in numbers of English origin and declines in the other British Isles origin groups. More recently, in the 1981 Census of Canada, the decision to permit multiple responses to the ethnic

origin question, in addition to dropping the reference to "the male side" of the respondent's ancestry, has seriously affected the comparability of the 1981 ethnic origin data with respect to earlier censuses. For this reason, and because of the increasing number of immigrants coming from non-European countries, the 1981 census data are presented separately in Table 4, rather than inviting invalid comparisons for some groups by including them in the historical series presented in Table 3. These and other problems are discussed in the "Introduction" to Volume 1, Part 3, of the *1971 Census of Canada*; and, W.O. Boxhill, *A User's Guide to 1981 Census Data on Ethnic Origins*, Statistics Canada, Catalogue 99–949 Occasional (Ottawa: Minister of Supply and Services, 1986).

3. W.E. Kalbach, *The Effect of Immigration on Population*, The Canadian Immigration and Population Study (Department of Manpower and Immigration, Ottawa: Information Canada, 1974), Table 3.2; and, Employment and Immigration Canada, *1983 Immigration Statistics* (Ottawa: Minister of Supply and Services Canada, 1985a), Table 1.

4. Jacques Henripin, *Trends and Factors of Fertility in Canada*, 1961 Census Monograph (Ottawa: Information Canada, 1972), Table 6.11; Statistics Canada, *1981 Census of Canada*, Catalogue 92–906 (Ottawa: Minister of Supply and Services Canada, 1983), Tables 10 and 11.

5. Statistics Canada, *Vital Statistics, 1971*, Volume 1 (Ottawa: Information Canada, 1974), Tables 5 and 10.

6. Statistics Canada, *1981 Census of Canada*, Catalogue 92–906, Table 10.

7. See Quebec's Bill 101 for legislation designed to limit access to schooling in the English language for children with non-English mother tongues.

8. Department of Manpower and Immigration, *The Green Paper on Immigration*, Volumes I–IV, The Canadian Immigration and Population Study (Ottawa: Information Canada, 1974).

9. Canada, The House of Commons, Bill C-24, Part I, Section 3, 2nd Session, Thirtieth Parliament, 25–26 Elizabeth II, 1976–77.

10. Canada, Bill C-24, Part I–pt.7.

11. Dominion Bureau of Statistics, *1931 Census of Canada* (Ottawa: Queen's Printer), Vol. III, Table 27, and Vol.IV, Table 15; Statistics Canada, *1971 Census of Canada*, Bulletin 1.3–6 (Ottawa: Information Canada, 1974), Table 46.

12. Statistics Canada, *1981 Census of Canada*, Catalogue 95–941 (Ottawa: Minister of Supply and Services, 1983), Table 1.

13. Statistics Canada, *1981 Census of Canada*, Catalogue 92–913 (Ottawa: Minister of Supply and Services, 1984), Tables 2A and 2B.

14. Leo Driedger and G. Church, "Residential Segregation and Institutional Completeness: A Comparison of Ethnic Minorities," *The Canadian Review of Sociology and Anthropology* 11 (1): 30–52.

15. Leo Driedger, "Maintenance of Urban Ethnic Boundaries: The French in St. Boniface," *The Sociological Quarterly* 20 (Winter 1979): 89–108.

16. T.R. Balakrishnan, "Ethnic Residential Segregation in the Metropolitan Areas of Canada," *Canadian Journal of Sociology* 1(4): 481–497.

17. E.W. Burgess, "The Growth of the City: An Introduction to a Research Project," in *The City*, edited by R.E. Park, E.W. Burgess, and R.E. McKenzie (Chicago: University of Chicago Press), pp. 47–62.

18. Balakrishnan, "Ethnic Residential Segregation."

19. T.R. Balakrishnan, "Changing Patterns in Ethnic Residential Segregation in the Metropolitan Areas of Canada," *The Canadian Review of Sociology and Anthropology* 19 (1): 92–110; and T.R. Balakrishnan and J. Kralt, "Residential Concentration of Ethnic/Visible Minority Groups in the Metropolitan Areas of Montreal, Toronto and Vancouver" (Paper presented at the 81st Biennial Conference of the Canadian Ethnic Studies Association, Montreal, Oct. 16–19, 1985). See also this volume.

20. A.G. Darroch and W.G. Marston, "Ethnic Differentiation: Ecological Aspects of a Multidimensional Approach," *International Migration Review* 4 (Fall 1969): 71–95; A.H. Richmond, *Ethnic Residential Segregation in Metropolitan Toronto* (Research report, Survey Research Centre, York University, 1972); W.E. Kalbach, "Ethnic Residential Segregation and Its Significance for the Individual in an Urban Setting" (Research Paper #124, Centre for Urban and Community Studies, University of Toronto, July 1981).

21. A.H. Richmond and W.E. Kalbach, *Factors in the Adjustment of Immigrants and their Descendants*, Statistics Canada Census Analytical Study (Ottawa: Ministry of Supply and Services Canada, 1980), pp. 183–201.

Patterns of Urban Ethnicity[†]

A. GORDON DARROCH AND
WILFRED G. MARSTON

Introduction

In this paper we formulate a conceptual linkage between three disparate orientations in recent urban analysis. These are 1) the ethnic assimilation-pluralism debate, especially in light of the apparent renaissance of ethnic identity and the persistence of ethnic stratification in urban areas; 2) the surprising persistence of ethnic residential segregation and concentration; and 3) the renewed interest in the theoretical importance of demographic parameters as factors in the social organization of urban life in general and ethnic subcultures in particular. We base our discussions on a wide, though selective, literature drawn from urban research in the United States and Canada. We reformulate links between the basic demographic parameters (both the absolute and the relative size of urban populations and subgroups) and ethnic residential patterns on the one hand and the persistence, or indeed, "emergence" of ethnic communities and forms of ethnic stratification on the other. Specifically, we draw on several recent contributions to the analysis of urban ethnicity to formulate a model in which specific patterns of *interaction* between urban size and the relative size and the residential patterns of the ethnic groups and key conditions giving rise to processes that sustain urban ethnic pluralism and stratification. In the course of the discussion, we 1) distinguish between the understanding of precipitating conditions and social processes and indicate how the two are complementary in an integrated analysis of urban ethnicity; 2) discuss the main conceptual

†"Patterns of Urban Ethnicity: Toward a Revised Ecological Model," in *Urbanism and Urbanization: Views, Aspects and Dimensions*, edited by Noel Iverson (Leiden, The Netherlands: E.J. Brill, 1984). This is a revised version of the original chapter.

developments regarding each of the three orientations; 3) present an outline of an analytic model linking them; and 4) in conclusion, attempt to indicate the primary areas for future conceptualization and research.

Ethnic Assimilation and Pluralism

Sociological interest in ethnic relations has been dominated by attention to the assimilation process, or by concern with apparent circumstantial limitations of the process. Conventionally, assimilation has been taken to be virtually inevitable in the course of urbanization and industrialization. Thus, it has been thought that under the homogenizing influence of these two forces, ethnic minorities must increasingly conform to and adopt the cultural standards of dominant populations and integrate into the social structure of a wider "modern" society. One version of this thesis, of course, is the classical ecological view employed by Park (1926) and Wirth (1938) in terms of the "natural history" of ethnic and race relations, passing from isolation through the stages of competition and conflict to eventual accommodation and assimilation. Both the original formulation and various neo-ecological theories have been taken to task for their conceptual simplicity and unrepentant determinism (Etzioni 1959, Reitz 1980). Though in many respects the critique of the original Chicago School is warranted, the focus on its particularly explicit claims may have served to distract attention from a much wider theoretical limitation in the study of urban ethnicity. For it is increasingly realized, though only recently argued, that the assumption of an "eventual" assimilation of ethnic minorities is a premise of virtually every major classical theory which informs current sociology— American liberal-functionalist (Metzger 1979), Weberian and Marxist (Lockwood 1970). The consequence of this rare theoretic convergence for the study of ethnicity in an urban world has been cogently put by Parkin (1979: 32). "Thus, one of the less welcome legacies bequeathed by the classical writers to contemporary social theory has been to render it theoretically unprepared to deal with the renaissance of ethnic identity and conflict in the very heartlands of western capitalism."

Though the dominant emphasis has been on ethnic and racial assimilation as a trend in urban society, alternative interpretations of persistent forms which ethnic relations might take have continued to be offered. The earlier interpretations tended to emphasize the limits of assimilation; for example, the dissolving of all but basic religious differences between Protestant, Catholic and Jew in the U.S. (Herberg 1955, Gordon 1964), or the persistence of immigrant attachments and "entrance statuses" in the face of wider integrative forces toward individual achievement and mobility (Porter 1965). Broadly speaking, the theoretical character of these statements might be called ambivalent functionalism. On the one hand, they took ethnicity to be a residual form of pluralism—a leftover of the past, and a barrier to the full incorporation of individuals in competitive, market societies. In Metzger's words (1971: 635), "this tradition of sociological theory views ethnicity as a survival of primary, quasi-tribal loyalties, which can only have a dysfunctional place in the achievement-oriented rationalized, and impersonal social relationships of the modern, industrial-bureaucratic order." On the other hand, these views were also explicitly Durkheimian in their analysis of the social and political value of limited, ethnic-religious pluralism. In this context, aspects of the work of Gordon, Eisenstadt and Porter are mirrored in Etzioni's (1959) early and very explicit claim that ethnic pluralism had important functions in preserving and stabilizing American society. The functions of ethnic groups are, he reasoned,

> comparable to those of occupational groups, professional associations and voluntary associations in general. They are sources of the pluralism which is the basis of an open, democratic society. They are the sources of consolidation of competing centers of power, which is a vital condition for the maintenance of the democratic process. Moreover, ethnic groups, which cut across other social groups—most important of which are social classes—are an important factor for maintaining the solidarity of American society and avoiding class consciousness and class conflict (260).[1]

More recently, there has been a greatly revived interest in urban ethnic pluralism, as well as in other forms of ethnic community life and consciousness, especially nationalist and separatist movements. In part, the revival may be a response to the paucity of conceptual inspiration we have had at hand for dealing with ethnic questions, but it is also a response to several related factors of urban life that simply fly in the face of assimilationist premises. In U.S. cities there are the persistent inequalities between black and white populations; there is the rise of black consciousness as a social and political force (Taylor 1979), and the persistence, indeed, "emergence" of white ethnic and Hispanic communities (Glazer and Moynihan 1975, Grebler 1970). In Canada, there has been a comparable though distinct form of urban ethnic visibility (Richmond 1972, Driedger 1977b), especially as selective immigration continues and as political policies and programs in support of official "multiculturalism" have found wide acceptance (Berry et al. 1977). It should likewise be noted that this persistent and, in some cases, "emergent" ethnicity is again considered a significant factor limiting the development of class consciousness and class antagonism (Lopreato and Hazelrigg 1972, Parkin 1979).[2]

It is clear, then, that ethnicity continues to serve as a powerful basis of social differentiation and it is by no means confined to racial differentiation in urban areas of the United States. Indeed, as Parkin (1979: 33) argues, "Ethnic conflict would now appear to be as normal a feature of advanced industrial societies as class conflict, even though its theoretical treatment is still at a relatively primitive stage." As if to exemplify the point, Berry (1973: 61) speaks of the "ethnic factor" in Chicago:

> Race and ethnicity now dominate the public life of Chicago. Chicago's residential patterns, neighborhood schools, shops, community newspapers, hospitals, old-age homes, cemeteries, savings and loan associations, charitable, fraternal, and cultural organizations attest to the role of ethnicity in culture and politics. Public decisions affecting home ownership, schools, public housing, police, shopkeepers, allocation of state and federal funds are increasingly perceived in terms of nationality groups and racial group attachments. Ethnicity defines interest groups in the city, and is rewarded and encouraged by the politicians and established institutions.

While the ethnic factor is no doubt stronger in Chicago (and New York, Montreal and Toronto) than in smaller urban areas, ethnicity is increasingly recognized as being a much more prominent force in the life of most urban areas than has generally been acknowledged by sociologists.

Definitions and Conceptual Issues

One factor indicating the relatively primitive stage of ethnic theory is the inconsistency in the use of basis concepts. The term "ethnicity" itself has quite widely varying definitions and usages. Some, like Porter (1975) and Greeley (1974), consider ethnicity necessarily to mean some expression of "primordial" sentiments—a semi-gemeinschaft collectivity based on real or fictive notions of descent (Greeley 1974: 108). This view of ethnicity as an essentially ascribed and immutable characteristic of persons tends, we shall argue, to reinforce an assimilationist perspective in which ascriptive characteristics must lose their salience in the historic movement to rationalistic, achievement-oriented societies.[3]

On the other hand, a number of recent contributions have treated ethnicity more as a socially constructed identity than merely as an ascribed trait with continuing salience. This is the defining characteristic of the work that emphasizes "emergent ethnicity": ethnic affiliations can be best understood, not as tendencies inherited from a common past, but as social responses to specific social and economic circumstances, opportunities and limitations (Yancey et al. 1976: 400). If one takes this point of view seriously, as we do, then it also follows that the conventional distinction between "ascribed" and "achieved" characteristics is certainly less clear than it once seemed, if not entirely inappropriate.

There are also the difficulties alluded to above in the use of the terms "assimilation" and "pluralism." The analytic problem arises first in failing to distinguish a variety of meanings or levels of reference to the notion of assimilation, or conversely, of pluralism. The assimilation-pluralism distinction is multidimensional; moreover, the relationships *among* the dimensions entail different social processes. Specifically, it is possible for some or perhaps all of the members of an ethnic population to ignore their putative ethnic identity and/or to have it ignored by others, in any number of specific social situations, but not in others. Following Gordon's (1964) terminology it is clearly possible for some groups to be culturally assimilated, but not structurally assimilated. That is, the members of the group may conform to the basic values and norms of the society and participate fully in the essential institutional structure of the society. On the other hand, members of the group may have no sustained primary relationships with members of the host society or of a dominant population—that is, relationships in social networks, clubs, cliques and so forth—hence, the lack of structural assimilation.[4] In Gordon's view, structural assimilation is a necessary and sufficient condition for the elimination of ethnic status or identity as a significant basis of social differentiation. Thus, sharing the main assumptions of assimilationist theory, Gordon reasoned that structural assimilation is the "critical barrier" separating minority groups and the host society.

Ethnic Residential Patterns

There is a second focus of urban research which we believe requires revised conceptualization in order to bear fruitfully on the question of contemporary urban, ethnic pluralism. This is the longstanding tradition on the analysis of urban ethnic and racial residential patterns.

The analysis of residential patterns has been a prominent, though very largely a separate, field of study in urban ethnic and racial relations. It has been pursued as an extension of the theoretical and methodological lead of the Chicago school (Park 1950, Hawley 1950, Lieberson 1963, Duncan and Lieberson 1959). However, studies of assimilation or pluralism in the wider cultural and structural sense have often given only passing consideration to residential patterns, for example, by treating the persistence of residential segregation as an *indicator* of pluralism (or of "failed assimilation"), or as a contingent condition mirroring more fundamental social processes (see, for example, Gordon 1964, Metzger 1971, note especially the criticism of Gordon's influential work by Kantrowitz 1973 in this respect). This peripheral position of residential patterns in the larger analysis of ethnicity is evident in the fact that most textbooks on Race and Ethnic Relations give only passing, if any, attention to ethnic residential segregation.

Of course, urban ecologists share part of the blame for this less-than-central position of residential patterns in the study of ethnicity. For the most part, the description of trends and patterns of residential segregation has been taken as a sufficient research focus, it being acknowledged that this does, however, leave open the question of the actual processes that produce the segregation, not to mention the question of its social consequences (cf. Darroch and Marston 1971, Farley 1977). To be sure, most studies begin by referring to such classic statements as Park's (1926), to the effect that spatial relations are so frequently correlated with social relations that the spatial may be taken as an index of social patterns; or to Hawley's (1944: 674) view that, "Redistribution of a minority group in the same territorial pattern as that of the majority group results in a dissipation of subordinate status and an assimilation of the subjugated group into the social structure." But, by and large, these analytical statements are employed to justify the measurement of segregation trends and patterns rather than to serve as a starting point for further theoretical or empirical analysis. Thus, these studies have provided a wealth of descriptive information on segregation trends and patterns, but they frequently stop short of exploring the ways in which these trends and patterns influence inter- and intra-ethnic relations or ethnic stratification and conflict.

Despite this apparent conceptual hesitation, recent literature has revealed a resurgence of interest in the importance of spatial parameters for social organization, an interest pursued at several levels of analysis, ranging from interpersonal relations to institutional functions (cf. Hall 1966, Ebbesen et al. 1976). More directly significant for urban sociology is the fact that a growing number of studies document the wider social impact of spatial patterns of urban ethnic life, though they do not attempt to place them in a more complex interpretive framework. For example, Lieberson's (1963) well known study found that the ability to speak English, American citizenship, and occupational improvement were positively linked to reductions in residential segregation for white ethnic groups in ten U.S. cities. Roof (1972) demonstrated that for southern U.S. cities, at least, segregation directly affects educational inequality, which in turn affects occupational inequality and income inequality. Steger (1973) has indicated how residential segregation clearly stifles income opportunities for blacks. He estimated that the total cost of income opportunity deprivation resulting from residential segregation exceeds ten billion dollars annually in the United States. Drawing on such studies Marston and Van Valey (1979) have argued that the residential segregation of ethnic and racial groups is alone probably sufficient to prevent any significant structural assimilation, in Gordon's (1964) terms noted above. Other studies have indicated that physical distance and social isolation encourage the institutionalization of inequalities in such key realms as education and social services (McEntire 1960, Williams 1964).

Empirical studies of the relation of urban ethnic segregation to ethnic subcultural life are particularly scarce. For a North American city as a whole, in fact, there is only one study of which we are aware. It warrants some comment. Following a provocative analysis by Breton (1964) of the effect of ethnic "institutional completeness"[5] on ethnic identity, Driedger and Church (1974) and Driedger (1978) present strong empirical evidence that residential segregation is a condition of the maintenance of institutional completeness, in which services required by members of an ethnic group are provided by the ethnic community itself, given its spatial boundedness.

Driedger and Church discovered that the French in Winnipeg were strongly tied to their community, staunch supporters of their own institutions, and also highly segregated residentially. Moreover, as the extent of their residential segregation increased over time, the French maintained ethnic isolation in the original areas of institutional concentration and, as well, kept their residential mobility within the original settlement area.

The Scandinavians, on the other hand, never developed an isolated pattern of residence and traditionally maintained few ethnically based religious, educational and other institutions. The Jews, while moving out of their original areas of concentration into the suburbs, re-established their religious and cultural institutions in their new residential location. In other words, their upward social mobility gave rise to inter-neighborhood geographic mobility, but residential segregation and institutional completeness were re-established in the new suburban neighborhood(s).

In a later study of Winnipeg, Driedger (1978) concluded that "the urban French community by means of residential segregation, with limited out mobility, has maintained a French culture within a fairly complete ethnic institutional framework" (1978: 193). In contrast to this experience, he observed that the Ukrainians are beginning to move out of their original neighborhoods and the strength of their institutional completeness is weakening. Moreover, the Poles, who were never a heavily concentrated population, had correspondingly never developed a high level of institutional completeness in Winnipeg.

The comparative interethnic analysis undertaken by Driedger and his colleagues is unique, but several other recent works have taken a similarly fresh look at the relation of spatial boundaries to ethnic community life. Suttles' (1968) ethnographic study of the social significance of territory and neighborhood in slum areas, to which we referred above, has led to an impressive reconsideration of the significance of spatial patterns in the "social construction of communities" (1972). Further, several authors have begun to review studies of urban ethnicity in a new light, arguing that common structural conditions form an essential foundation for the maintenance of white ethnic identities and communities in urban areas (Yancey et al. 1976). The most significant feature of the latter studies is the insistence on the structural basis of ethnicity, which is itself understood to be a cultural formation. The approach challenges the assimilationist implications of most prior theory and research.

In the following analysis we attempt to formulate a model which draws together the implications of an analysis of residential patterns as they limit interethnic relations and, simultaneously, as a key structural condition giving rise to the formation and maintenance of urban ethnic subcultures. The development of such a model, however, requires some consideration of the basic spatial conditions of urban areas and ethnic communities as well as of the problems of their measurement. We discuss the measurement problem briefly and only insofar as it is essential to a specification of the issues at hand.

Residential Patterns: Segregation vs. Concentration

It is our contention that failure to solve the problem of measurement has been one of the central limitations in the analysis of residential patterns as a structural condition of urban life. The most common measures of residential patterns—measures of residential "segregation"—simply fail to capture aspects of the spatial patterns which may be *most* important in influencing ethnic relations and community formation.

Traditionally, residential segregation has been taken to mean the difference in the distribution of two ethnic groups, or of other groups, throughout an urban area. A high level of residential segregation implies that most members of a given ethnic group live in neighborhoods inhabited predominantly by members of that group only. By contrast, a low level of residential segregation implies that most members of a given ethnic group live in neighborhoods that contain a high percentage of members from another or other ethnic groups.

Most studies of residential segregation employ an "index of dissimilarity" as a measure of the degree of residential separation between two groups; for example, between ethnic minorities and a majority group, between ethnic minorities or between two occupational or other status groups (see Duncan and Duncan 1955 or Taeuber and Taeuber 1965 for a discussion of the strengths and weaknesses of this measure). The index is a summary measure of the degree of residential separation between two groups over an entire urban area. It does not however reflect either the pattern of separation or the location tendencies of either group. Take, for example, the following hypothetical cases, examples in which the shaded areas represent an entirely black population of a city, the blank areas an entirely white population.

Figure 1
Comparison of Ethnic Patterns in Two Cities

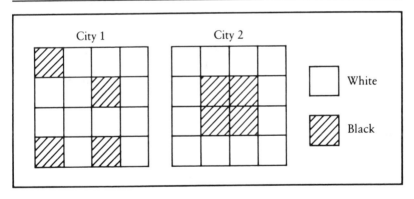

In both cases the segregation index between blacks and whites is at its maximum, since there are no subareas containing both blacks and whites. Clearly, though, city 1 represents a "scattered" pattern and city 2 represents a "concentrated" pattern. The differences are of considerable sociological interest. For example, *ceteris parabus*, the probability of physical contact and, hence, of sustained social contact between blacks and whites is greater in the first case. Moreover, a concentrated pattern, especially for relatively large ethnic groups, makes possible the establishment of institutions, services and stores that cater primarily to that group. Of course, this is exactly the kind of "institutional completeness" which may be essential for sustaining the boundaries of ethnic or racial communities.

Our discussion of measurement only touches the several issues raised in the methodological literature, but we wish to draw attention to the likelihood that one feature of residential patterning missed by conventional measures may be of particular significance in the context of the revival of interest in urban ethnic pluralism. We shall argue in the following section that the aspect of residential patterning most critical to an understanding of the structural basis of urban ethnic pluralism is the extent to which an ethnic group is *concentrated* in sufficient numbers, say, to "dominate" the life of a neighborhood.

Demographic Parameters of Urban Ethnicity

In much of contemporary sociology, the stature of demographic parameters parallels that of spatial parameters. Variables such as sheer size, relative size of subpopulations, and population composition have been treated peripherally, in that they are typically considered as "useful background information." It hasn't always been that way. In the nineteenth century and early in this century, demographic parameters were central to several notable accounts of the nature of social life (Durkheim 1955, Simmel 1950, Park 1926, Wirth 1938). In recent decades such parameters have been largely dismissed as too obvious, too simplistic, or perhaps even as nonsociological, at least in the predominant interpretations of urban life (Gans 1962).[6]

Again, however, there appears to be a resurgence of sociological interest in the potential explanatory power of demographic parameters, as there has been in ethnic pluralism itself. This interest is seen in studies of small groups (Steiner 1972, Tucker and Friedman 1972, Shaw 1976), of formal organizations (Blau 1970, Mayhew et al. 1972); of communities (Fischer 1975, 1976, Kasarda 1974) and of societies (Kasarda 1974, Nolan 1979). The theoretical formulations of Fischer (1975, 1976) and Blau (1970, 1977) are of particular relevance to our proposed model.

Fischer has offered an imaginative reconsideration of the role that demographic factors play in a "subcultural theory of urbanism." His analysis provides a framework for a specification of the ways in which demographic variables affect processes of pluralism and forms of ethnic conflict. Fischer's arguments provide the basis for our development of a more complete model of urban ethnic pluralism.

The main purpose of Fischer's revisionist theory is to account for the unique character of large urban areas, specifically in terms of their capacity to generate forms of unconventional behavior—deviance, innovation, political dissidence, and so forth. While unconventional behavior represents the central focus of his overall argument, its relevance to urban ethnicity is both direct and compelling. In fact, it is precisely the maintenance of ethnic subcultures that Fischer finds most persuasive as an exemplification of his theory.

Fischer's central argument is deceptively simple. Most generally, he contends "that urbanism independently affects social life..." (1976: 35). Fischer uses the term "urbanism" rather idiosyncratically to refer to urban size and density. More commonly the term "urbanization" would be used, but Fischer makes a very specific analytic argument that size and density have independent effects on other aspects of urban life. Specifically, his subcultural theory of urbanism contends that the foremost social consequence of increasing urban size is the promotion of diverse subcultures. Thus people in large urban areas live in meaningful social worlds and, "These worlds are inhabited by persons who share relatively distinctive traits (like ethnicity and occupation), who tend to interact especially with one another, and who manifest a relatively distinct set of beliefs and behaviors" (1976: 36; it should be noted that Fischer uses the terms *subculture* and *social world* interchangeably).

Fischer (1976: 37) argues that there are two basic ways in which large urban size produces the urban mosaic of "little social worlds":

1) Large communities attract migrants from wider areas than do small towns, migrants who bring with them a great variety of cultural backgrounds, and thus contribute to the formation of a diverse set of social worlds. 2) Large size produces... structural differentiation—occupational specialization, the rise of specialized institutions, and of special interest groups. To each of these structural units are usually attached subcultures.... In these ways, urbanism generates a variety of social worlds.

The impact of urban population concentration goes beyond the creation of distinct social worlds or subcultures. Fischer argues that large urban areas also tend systematically to "intensify" these social worlds through two powerful processes. The first process is based on the attainment of *critical mass*, that is, "a population size large enough to permit what would otherwise be only a small group of individuals to become a vital, active subculture" (1976: 37). The relevance of critical mass to urban ethnicity is made abundantly clear in the following passage:

Sufficient numbers allow them to support institutions—clubs, newspapers, and specialized stores, for example, that serve the group; allow them to have a visible and affirmed identity, to act together in their own behalf, and to interact extensively with each other (Fischer 1976: 37).

The second process of subcultural intensification results from contact between subcultures which are enhanced by the other demographic condition of urbanism, *density*.

> People in different social worlds often do touch.... But in doing so, they sometimes rub against one another to recoil, with sparks flying upward. Whether the encounter is between blacks and Irish, hardhats and hippies, or town and gown, people from one subculture often find people in another subculture threatening, offensive, or both. A common reaction is to embrace one's own social world all the more firmly, thus contributing to its further intensification (Fischer 1976: 38).

Though his analysis presents a model of the bases of urban pluralism, Fischer acknowledges that the impact of urbanism is by no means unidirectional. He is fully aware of the forces inherent in increased size, diversity, and, at least by implication, density, that encourage increased interethnic contact and perhaps even assimilation. A major way in which ethnic identity and intensity may be undermined in large urban areas is through the growth of *alternative* bases of association such as subcultures founded on occupation, life style or special interests. The tension between such countervailing forces is a central feature of Fischer's analysis, and sets it apart from conventional assimilationist views:

> These subcultures attract individuals' allegiance and modify the values of ethnic groups. Yet, at the same time, the urban effect of larger numbers within ethnic groups and the subcultural opposition among them should have the same vitalizing effects for ethnic groups that they do for other subcultures. We should expect, therefore, to observe both processes—weakening and strengthening—and see them working against each other (1976: 128).

The significance of demographic parameters is further supported by two observations recently put forward by Peter Blau. The first statement (1970) amounts to a specification of Fischer's theory and the second (1977) lends substantial reinforcement to it. In considering the implications of the size of formal organizations, Blau noted that as organizations increase in size (number of employees) they routinely become more structurally differentiated—vertically, horizontally, and territorially. However, and more significantly, the increase in structural differentiation does not "keep pace" (increases at a declining rate) with the increase in overall organizational size; thus the number of employees per unit of the organization also increases with organizational size.

While to our knowledge there is as yet no empirical support for it, we believe it is useful to apply this same principle to the relationship between increasing urban size and ethnic diversity. Blau's perspective, like Fischer's, is analytic, focusing on social structural tendencies resulting from essentially demographic conditions. Thus, it is entirely plausible that as urban areas increase in size (number of residents) the number of identifiable ethnic groups also increases, but, in general, at a rate which is lower than the rate of population growth. Consequently, larger urban areas not only have more ethnic groups, but the population of each ethnic group also tends to be larger than in smaller urban areas. The application of Blau's argument to urban areas clarifies Fischer's argument that urban size itself creates diversity and in turn tends to produce the "critical mass" of given ethnic (or other) groups within the urban area.

Blau's other work (1977) adds support to Fischer's theory. Specifically, he addresses the question of which groups have higher rates of intergroup associations than others and why they do. At an entirely structural level of analysis, he argues,

> the arithmetic properties of groups imply the theorem that in the relation between any two groups, the rate of intergroup associations of the smaller group exceeds that of the larger. This first theorem applies to three forms of associations and all their specific manifestations: 1) the proportion intermarried (or having another exclusive association as mutual best friends) in the smaller group exceeds that in the larger; 2) the mean number of intergroup associates in the smaller group exceeds that in the larger; 3) the mean amount of time spent in intergroup association is greater for the smaller than for the larger group (1977: 35).

Blau means by intergroup relations, of course, ties *between* groups. Conversely, then, the argument parallels Fischer's view that a small ethnic group is more likely to experience weakened ties *among* the members of the ethnic group than is a large ethnic group. We take these specifications of the demographic conditions of urban ethnicity as a point of departure for proposing a model of the ecological bases of urban ethnic pluralism which integrates both spatial and demographic considerations.

A Model of Urban Ethnic Pluralism: Ecological Conditions

A review of the issues regarding spatial and demographic aspects of urban ethnicity strongly suggests that both sets of parameters have similar, if not identical, effects on ethnic pluralism. For example, we argued that ethnic residential patterns, especially residential concentration, directly contributes to the development and maintenance of ethnic subcultures characterized by institutional completeness. In Fischer's theory, it is increasing size and diversity which give rise to a "critical mass" of individuals of a given ethnicity and directly contribute to the "intensification" of ethnic subcultures. By "intensification" Fischer refers to the strength of subcultural beliefs, values, norms and customs (1975: 1325).

For the most part, these apparently parallel processes generating urban ethnicity have been dealt with separately. On the one hand, studies of ethnic residential segregation have rarely considered the impact of urban size, diversity or critical mass, especially as they may interact with segregation in affecting the nature of urban ethnic communities.[7] On the other hand, Fischer does not explicitly consider the possibility that the impact of urbanism on ethnic patterns may be significantly mediated by residential patterning.

Our proposed model of the basic processes involved takes urban size itself and the "critical mass" of ethnic groups as related in the manner which Fischer and Blau suggest. We argue further that the separate and joint effects of size and mass on the intensity of ethnic pluralism or, in the case of any given group, on the strength of ethnic identity and density of ethnic networks, are significantly mediated by ethnic residential patterning. Specifically, we have taken residential concentrations of ethnic populations to be the primary intervening variable in a process in which the demographic parameters affect ethnic pluralism, that is, affect both the numbers of ethnic subcultures and their "intensity," to use Fischer's term again. Since we have already argued that both the "critical mass" of an ethnic population and residential concentrations have their major impact on ethnic subcultures, by way of sustaining the institutional completeness of the ethnic community, the latter too should be entered into the model as a separate intervening and mediating factor. In schematic form, the model may be presented as shown in Figure 2.

If we ignore for the moment the residential concentration variable and read straight across the model, it follows Fischer's essential argument. That is, as urban areas increase in population so too do the number of ethnic groups (structural differentiation). Following Blau, we suggest that the rate at which the number of ethnic groups increases does not in general keep pace with the rate of growth of the urban population. Thus, as urban areas grow the number of residents within each ethnic group also tends to increase. In turn this increases the possibility of one or more ethnic groups attaining a population size we have called a "critical

Figure 2

Model Showing the Relationship Between Ethnic Residential Concentration and Five Other Variables

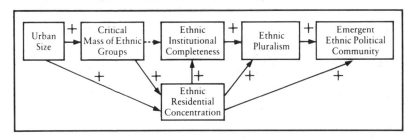

mass." It is a feature of both Fischer's and our model that the lower limit of this critical mass remains unspecified, though presumably not unspecifiable.

In turn, a precondition of a full complement of ethnic institutions is some critical mass of ethnic group members who can avail themselves of these services and functions. Institutional completeness, therefore, greatly facilitates the development and maintenance of intense ethnic subcultures, in that it encourages the context within which social interactions, both secondary and primary, are confined to the ethnic group itself. Finally, to the extent that an ethnic group has developed a subculture within which identification and social interaction are primarily internal to the group, it is significantly easier to mobilize a political constituency, for example, that views issues and problems along ethnic lines. In a later discussion we trace some of the possible implications of ethnic mobilization for ethnic stratification.

Urban size and critical mass would contribute significantly less to institutional completeness and in turn to ethnic pluralism than is suggested above when an ethnic group is so residentially dispersed throughout the urban area that in any given neighborhood its members do not make up a majority of the population. This situation would arise from either of the following two processes: 1) ethnic group members selected housing primarily on the basis of socioeconomic factors, with ethnicity playing no role at all, or 2) ethnic group members tended to select housing on the basis of their ethnic affiliation, but these housing areas were "scattered" throughout the urban area. In the latter case ethnic group members might be "concentrated" in a number of small pockets, but each pocket would tend to be too small to facilitate the maintenance of ethnic institutions and dense social networks confined to the ethnic neighborhood.

Thus the model we present (Figure 2) indicates that the residential concentration of ethnic populations seems most likely to be a key structural variable which, in effect, intensifies or heightens the relations between the initial demographic preconditions of ethnic pluralism and the several aspects of the ethnic communities themselves, including their institutional base, the intensity of their relations and identities and eventually the possibilities of their social and political mobilization. The model indicates, by a dashed arrow, that Fischer's proposed direct effect of the critical mass of a subgroup on the intensification of subgroup life may be entirely or primarily mediated by the role of residential concentrations. His original model perhaps subsumes such intermediary conditions under the general notions of intensification; we have given a detailed justification for the specification.

The model may be viewed in another light. We may consider the size of ethnic subgroups as a variable, rather than as a question of some minimum threshold, as conveyed by the concept of "critical mass." In this case, the implications for ethnic pluralism are surprisingly informative, even in the most simple situations created by the interaction of just two of the variables, ethnic group size and ethnic residential patterns. The simple cross-tabulation of the two is shown below, where the difference between large and small populations refers to populations above and below the threshold defined as a "critical mass," and the distinction between a scattered and concentrated pattern is consistent with the distinction drawn earlier.

Figure 3
A Simple Interaction Model of Ethnic Pluralism

| | Residential Pattern | |
Ethnic Size	Scattered	Concentrated
Small	1	2
Large	3	4

The social implications of Case 1 are straightforward. A relatively small ethnic group, residentially distributed in a scattered pattern, has both demographic and spatial conditions working against it with regard to resisting pressures toward assimilation. In this situation there would be limited chances of developing and maintaining ethnically bounded services and functions because of the lack of 1) critical mass and 2) a territorially concentrated population. Moreover it is likely that the rate of interethnic contact at both the secondary and primary levels would be relatively high in this situation. Ethnic identities may still be sustained, but in the absence of ethnic neighborhoods and the subcultural life they nurture.

Case 2 represents a situation where demographic and spatial parameters affect ethnicity in opposing ways. On the one hand, the relatively small size operates to encourage assimilation and discourage subcultural intensity. On the other hand, the concentrated residential pattern provides the setting for maintaining multiple ethnic institutions which counter assimilation pressures. A basic question about such concentration is whether or not there are sufficient numbers of the ethnic group to "dominate" the neighborhood in its institutional makeup, that is, to have it become socially recognized as a neighborhood with a particular ethnic character. For example, a study of the city of Flint, Michigan (Marston and Zinn 1979), revealed that both Arab and Hispanic populations tended to be concentrated in a few areas, but never sufficiently to make up the majority, or even to give the areas a predominately Arab or Hispanic character.

Case 3 is perhaps the most interesting in the sense that it might be possible to compare the impact of differing residential patterns for one ethnic group in a single urban area. We might expect in the case of a relatively large ethnic population which tends to be scattered throughout an urban area that at least one of the neighborhoods would contain a fairly large concentration of that group. This would typically be the original settlement area in the inner city and the one which many ethnic group members left to take up residence in a more scattered pattern throughout the rest of the urban area. In other words, this case compares the effects upon ethnicity of social life in a neighborhood composed almost entirely of persons of the same ethnic origin with social life in an ethnically heterogeneous neighborhood. There has been some research with respect to the sense of alienation among blacks in America which makes such a comparison, but with conflicting results to date. In some cases, blacks tend to be less alienated and have less of a sense of powerlessness in a virtually all-black ghetto than in racially mixed areas (Wilson 1971), and in others just the reverse pattern was found (Bullough 1967, Kapsis 1979). To our knowledge, no attempt has been made to assess the extent to which the location of ethnic enclaves within an urban area results in assimilation and/or pluralist tendencies. The present model of the interaction of ethnic group size and residential patterning provides a framework for research and a clear set of hypotheses.

Case 4 represents the classic situation of the development and maintenance of urban ethnic pluralism, or from a somewhat different perspective, it represents the ideal situation for "emergent" ethnicity. Here we have both demographic and spatial parameters favoring the development of ethnic pluralism. It represents the situation in which the necessary *critical* mass is *residentially concentrated* so that a given ethnic group simply has the opportunity to exercise a dominant influence upon the way of life in a residential area. Yancey et al. (1976: 392) have made the same point in suggesting that the "ecological" structure of cities is a catalyst in the social definition and maintenance of urban ethnicity. The strength of ethnic networks and the frequency of ethnic interaction, they argue, are enhanced by common occupational positions, residential concentration and stability under which ethnic identity and interaction may be maintained, in our view, but they are conditions that enhance the sense of ethnic community boundary and salience in everyday life.

The model we have discussed also specifies that the size of urban areas is a prior condition affecting the form of the interaction between the size of an ethnic population and its residential concentration, and their consequences for ethnic pluralism. In this we follow Fischer (1976). Clearly it would be possible to try to specify various forms of this complex association; for example, what are the consequences one could expect in cases of relatively small ethnic populations which tend to be residentially scattered in large metropolitan areas, in comparison to similar ethnic groups in smaller cities and towns? On the other hand, if these small ethnic groups were quite highly concentrated residentially, would this tend to minimize the differences, in their effect upon ethnicity, between large and small urban environments? These complex interactions, even if considered *ceteris parabus*, as we have done throughout, would have to take into account Fischer's convincing argument that urbanization entails essentially countervailing forces.

Ethnicity as a Social Process: Widening the Focus of Future Research

Thus far, we have emphasized how the particular interactions of population size and spatial patterns channel and limit ethnic relations and, in some cases, are critical in determining in part the nature of urban ethnic pluralism. It is an emphasis that is evident in the work of Fischer and of Blau, on which we drew, and such a "conditioning" effect was the clear orientation of earlier ecological theory. On the other hand, several recent reconsiderations of the genesis and maintenance of urban ethnicity allude to another, distinct aspect of these processes which warrants explication. Several of these analyses indicate that, especially under conditions where a critical mass of an ethnic population is also residentially concentrated (Case 4 in the above schema), ethnic identities, social networks and institutions are likely to be created. That is, the analyses point to the processes whereby ethnicity is "socially constructed" under these particularly propitious conditions or, at least, reformulated and reinterpreted (Singer 1962, Yancey et al. 1976, Taylor 1979).

It is worth noting, however, that even in the more sophisticated treatments of ethnic "ethnogenesis" or "emergent ethnicity," accounts of the effects of structual conditions are largely expressed in terms which suggest their impact is direct, impersonal and aggregative. This follows the conventional forms of expression which structural and demographic analyses take. Specifically, to cite two of the most important studies again, it is argued that ethnicity "is *crystallised* under conditions which reinforce the maintenance of kinship and friendship networks" (Yancey et al. 1976: 302, emphasis added) and that "Residential concentration *fosters* a variety of formal and informal associations to satisfy the needs of those so concentrated" (Taylor 1979: 1409, emphasis added). The language itself is a shorthand account, we might say, in which the actual processes of "crystallization" and "fostering" are taken for granted. In so doing, the analyses raise, but leave unresolved, the question of how the forms of social order are actually achieved or created by the "actors" in question. This question calls for an analysis of actual social processes.

Ethnicity as a Social Process

The treatment of ethnicity in recent works tends strongly to challenge the conventional notion of ethnic characteristics as attributes of individuals, and it reveals as well a shift towards the notion of ethnicity as a variable. In this respect the conventional assumptions of assimilationist theory in urban society are challenged. We shall argue that both of these aspects of revised ethnic theory lead to a further conceptual clarification, in which ethnicity itself may be understood as a *social process*. We indicate some of the implications of this form of analysis and provide one specific example, the case of urban ethnic stratification.

As we noted above, the predominant explanations of urban ethnicity are based heavily on assumptions about the inevitability of assimilation. Such assumptions tend to be taken for granted when ethnicity is seen as a more or less static attribute of individuals—that is, as a set of ascriptive characteristics. There is an implicit contrast involved, of course, and a familiar one, between the primordial and given quality of so-called "ascribed" attributes and statuses and the seemingly optional and open quality of "achieved" ones. The contrast has been exaggerated.[8] Consider, for example, the various forms of "passing" which can be resorted to by members of minority ethnic and racial groups or the frequency with which ethnic identities or behavioral patterns are situationally invoked, being relevant on some occasions and clearly irrelevant or perhaps detrimental on others. Ethnicity, it seems is an adaptable and transitional phenomenon, either as a personal identity or as a social label.

Parallelling their sensitivity to the "emergent" nature of urban ethnicity, recent accounts tend more or less to recognize this socially constructed and managed nature of urban ethnicity. Glazer and Moynihan (1970), for example, interpret ethnicity as a primary basis for the formation of political interest groups in American society. Taking a largely social-psychological approach, Greeley (1974) argues that ethnicity is a form of resistance to the anomic and rationalized conditions of urban society.[9] According to these interpretations ethnic identities are largely "made" in the New World urban context, and are responses to the specific conditions met there. The raw material, of course, is some racial, linguistic or cultural differentia, but ethnicity does not issue from the Old World "prefabricated" as a changeless social category.

Thus, the revival of interest in urban ethnicity has led to an examination of the particular processes that contribute to variation in the form and strength of ethnic affiliations and practices. Specifically, the focus of analysis has shifted from a primary concern with the expected demise of ethnicity to interest in the variations in social conditions which give rise to ethnic pluralism. The contexts of urban ethnicity range for example, from closely bounded communities, with mainly local patterns of interaction and high institutional density or completeness, to the other extreme of residentially dispersed groups maintaining their affiliations through widely cast family and social networks (Kosa 1956, Etzioni 1959, Reitz 1980). Several authors have drawn attention to the conceptual implications of this shift in focus. The study of ethnic pluralism under variant circumstances, they note, means that we must treat ethnicity as a continuous variable, rather than as an inherent attribute of persons (Cohen 1974a, Yancey et al. 1976).

The notion of ethnicity as a variable is clearly a step toward a more complete analysis of ethnic pluralism. Yet we think it harbors further implications which should be made clear. We argue that treating ethnicity as a variable also implies it must be conceived of as a *social process* in itself. Again the fusion of conditional and contextual analysis is implied in the present redefinition. To regard ethnicity as a social process is to go beyond examining variations in its forms and underlying conditions at any point in time; it means that we consider also its historical dimensions. For urban ethnicity not only varies from one situational context to another, but ebbs and flows in individual experience, through the phases of individual life cycles, and in the collective realities of social and economic relations.

To reiterate, in common usage, ethnicity conveys a sense of fixed membership by virtue of "inherited" attributes, whether cultural or physical. In the present analysis of the social implications of ethnicity, however, it is seen as an experience that happens, not once and for all, but in the context of changing structural conditions and intergroup relations. It must, therefore, be seen as a set of ongoing relationships sustained by particular institutional arrangements. Some of the central implications of understanding ethnicity as an ongoing historical process are drawn in Metzger's (1971: 644) discussion of the consequences of abandoning the conventional assumptions of assimilationist theory. They are again two sides of the same coin. The break from conventional theory, he argues, "will make it possible for sociologists to reaffirm that minority-majority relations are in fact group relations and not merely relations between prejudiced and victimized individuals. As such, they are implicated in the struggle for power and privilege in the society, and the theory of collective behavior and political sociology may be more pertinent to understanding them than the theory of social mobility and assimilation," and it "will make it possible to study the forces...which facilitate or hinder assimilation or, conversely, the forces which generate the sense of ethnic and racial identity even within the homogenizing confines of modern society."

Urban Ethnic Pluralism and Ethnic Stratification

Several of the recent contributions to a revised analysis of urban ethnicity have noted a particular convergence of conditions which seem to underlie the heightening of ethnic consciousness and community. These studies tend to suggest that urban ethnic subcultures are most intense when patterns of ethnic stratification become associated, on the one hand, with ethnic residential concentrations, and on the other, with a high dependence on local ethnic institutions and services, that is, with ethnic institutional completeness. We suggest, in fact, that this work points to a critical intersection of three structural conditions essential to the formation and maintenance of urban neighborhoods in which there are strong ethnic networks and commitments. The intersection seems to occur when historical patterns of ethnic subordination and domination are framed by the residential concentration of ethnic populations and coincident ethnic institutional completeness. At the extreme, of course, these conditions characterize a totally "ghetto-ized" population. Hershberg (1973) and Taylor (1979), for example, make exactly this triangulation of social and economic subordination, residential concentration and local institutional density central to their interpretation of the roots of urban black consciousness in this century in the U.S. We have already noted that Fischer's (1975: 1325) abstract model of the basis of urban subcultural "intensity" requires, in his terms, two "independently sufficient" processes. The first relates the critical mass of a (residentially concentrated) population to its institutional completeness and the second entails, in effect, the political and personal consequences of urban stratification, that is, subtle, often invidious comparisons among groups and sharper conflicts of a potentially violent kind (1975: 1327).

Finally, we can note again that one of the few detailed empirical studies (Driedger and Church 1974; also see Driedger 1977b) that has compared patterns of urban ethnic pluralism with assimilation indicates that the conjunction of residential concentration and institutional completeness was the distinguishing characteristic of the French and the Jewish communities of Winnipeg, Manitoba, which enabled them, over time, to sustain distinct ethnic boundaries. Although the point is largely taken for granted in the original analysis, it is of central importance that it was members of precisely these two groups who had experienced the greatest degree of ethnic discrimination as well as class and status deprivation.

The question arises, then, if a particular convergence of structural conditions does indeed "foster" relatively intense ethnic communities, what exactly are the social processes involved? Again, we try to bridge structural and processual analyses, at least as an exemplification of the kind of analysis which can fruitfully be pursued.

An analysis of the relationship of ethnic stratification to ethnic community life begins with a question of the relative visibility, to the ordinary members of an ethnic population, of inequality in the wider society. As in any analysis of class and stratification, this question of the "transparency" of the structures of inequality is one which relates larger institutional patterns to peoples' perceptions and consciousness in everyday life. Specifically, one of the important consequences of the association of ethnic residential concentration and ethnic institutional density in urban areas is that together they form exactly the sort of social prism through which economic and political inequalities among ethnic groups are made recognizable to the groups' members. The visibility of shared fate is, thus, more readily interpreted in specifically ethnic, subcultural terms. For a more dispersed and less cohesive group, ethnic discrimination and stratification are much more likely to be interpreted as individual problems of "adjustment," rather than as political and social issues bound to the status and class position of the ethnic community.

If the visibility of ethnic stratification is magnified for residentially concentrated urban ethnic communities, then reciprocal relations also are likely, we argue, in which ethnic experiences and identities become potentially active forces in the maintenance and alteration of the forms of urban stratification. We shall try to indicate briefly how such an analysis can be pursued.

An important contribution to this discussion emerges in the recent revival of interest in Weber's analysis of ethnicity and the processes of "social closure" (Weber 1968, Neuwirth 1967, Hechter 1974 and 1976, Breton 1979). As Parkin (1979: 44) expressed it, "By social closure Weber means the process by which social collectivities seek to maximize rewards by restricting access to resources and opportunities to a limited circle of eligibles." Ethnic heritage is only one of any number of possible bases for justifying forms of exclusion, but clearly, like sex, it is a prime candidate to serve such a "gatekeeping" purpose (Neuwirth 1967: 150–51). It is important, too, that closure strategies are not the prerogative of dominant groups, since there are a variety of reactive strategies which excluded groups of varying status may initiate as ways of attempting to ursurp some additional benefits in competitive, market circumstances (Parkin 1979: Ch.5). In the context of urban ethnicity, then, the concept of closure is of value in considering the ways in which patterns of ethnic residential and institutional concentration become systematic means of maintaining an order of ethnic stratification.

The role of residential patterns may be especially significant in urban areas where the forces leading toward social homogenization and individual assimilation are undoubtedly powerful. A number of well-known examples of urban processes in which spatial concentrations may serve as a critical condition of closure and exclusion may be cited. The flight of middle-class whites to suburban residences for reasons of sustaining social and educational separation is one; the highly selective location of subsidized housing in cities and the changing locational patterns of industrial and manufacturing employment are others.[10]

As we noted above, however, the manner in which concentrations of ethnic populations and institutions may operate as a particularly effective means of social closure is not limited to the question of sustaining dominance. Social closure as practiced by subordinate groups is a means both of defense and "mobility," that is, as a political means of increasing its members' access to the resources and opportunities of the larger society. A clear example of this is the relationship between ethnic neighborhood concentration and an "ethnic voice" or block voting in local government. In addition, residential concentration often produces a strategic population which is readily amenable to mobilization—a factor of some importance, especially with regard to ethnic conflict. It is suggested, in fact, that their residential dispersal might actually be detrimental to the interests of ethnic populations. It would weaken an ethnic minority's opportunity for political socialization and reduce the powerful political force that a large and residentially concentrated ethnic population represents. This argument is also applicable to the experience of blacks in urban areas in the United States.

Of course, the significance of the relationship between the political mobilization and territorial concentration of ethnic populations has been made explicit with reference to regional concentrations of ethnic communities. It is often recognized that ethnic political organizations and social movements have territorial boundaries as an essential condition of their effective formation—the Basques, the Quebecois and the Celts bear sufficient witness (Lieberson 1972, Hechter 1976). We suggest that urban residential concentrations are an important social analog of these regional patterns. Such visible and socially acknowledged residential neighborhoods carry well-understood implications in the field of urban politics, whether with regard to organizing the vote-forming protective residents' associations or containing the potential explosiveness of the ghetto.

Conclusion

We have tried to formulate a model that specifies the most salient consequences of demographic and spatial parameters for urban ethnic pluralism. We have argued that there are clear advantages in including both kinds of parameters in a single analysis. While both demographic and spatial features of urban areas clearly exert some independent influence on ethnic groups, we contend that consideration of the interaction between them provides a more powerful framework within which to assess the basic structural conditions underlying urban ethnic pluralism. In short, the model emphasizes the significance of ethnic residential *concentration* rather than the more common notion of segregation, and it emphasizes as a key variable the "institutional completeness" engendered by such concentration. We reject conventional assumptions about the inevitability of ethnic assimilation as a result of industrialization and urbanization. We suggest that it is precisely the interaction of urban size, ethnic group size and residential and institutional patterns that affects the balance of processes leading toward individual assimilation or, alternatively, toward the maintenance of distinct ethnic communities and intense ethnic identities. This balance has to be understood in terms of several different forms or levels of assimilation and ethnic relations. Finally, we indicate how explanations of the effects of demographic and residential patterns on urban ethnicity might be united with explanations of urban ethnic stratification and politics.

Notes

1. Although Durkheim's (1955) emphasis was on trade and professional associations, hardly a more direct summary could have been given of his view of the essential role of various social groups mediating between individual and state in the preservation of dispersed power and individual liberty.
2. For the purpose of our discussion, we consider both racial and national origin groups to be *forms of ethnic groups*. In so doing we adopt a common, though not exclusive, usage. Milton Gordon's (1964: 27–8) influential statement illustrates our usage.
   > When I use the term "ethnic group" then, . . . I shall mean by it any group which is defined or set off by race, religion, or national origin, or some combination of these categories. I do not mean to imply that these three concepts mean the same thing. They do not. . . . However, all of these categories have a common social psychological referent, in that all of them serve to create, through historical circumstances, a sense of peoplehood for [the] groups. . . ."

   Thus, he takes the core meaning of ethnic identity to be the sense that,
   > These are the "people" of my ancestors, therefore they are my people and they will be the people of my children and their children.

   Like other recent analyses of the conditions underlying "emergent ethnicity" (Yancey et al. 1976) and "black ethnicity" (Taylor 1979) in urban areas, our analysis focuses on the common structural and historical conditions generating community formation among members of urban national origin and racial groups. The context of our usage in this chapter will make the point of view clear.

3. Greeley (1974) is well known for resisting this theoretical implication despite his insistence on ethnicity as a "primordial" sentiment.
4. Gordon also recognized five other potential distinctions of types of assimilation—marital, identificational, attitude receptional (absence of prejudice), behavioral receptional (absence of discrimination) and civic (absence of conflict). But he did assume that structural assimilation was the key process; once it had taken place, the other forms of assimilation would follow suit. In this sense the other forms were treated as residual or subsumed under structural assimilation.
5. Institutional completeness at its extreme would mean that ethnic group members "would never have to make use of native institutions for the satisfaction of any of their needs, such as education, work, food and clothing, medical care, or social assistance" (Breton 1964: 194).
6. One notable exception to the relegation of demographic parameters to the "background" involves macro-theories of racial/ethnic relations which incorporate such factors as the relative size of minority populations as a central independent variable in accounting for both discrimination and socioeconomic inequalities. Influenced by the theoretical formulations of Williams (1974) and Allport (1954), a number of researchers have found that the larger the relative size of a minority, 1) the greater the degree of discrimination against the minority (Blalock 1956, 1967) and 2) the greater the majority-minority disparities in income and occupational status (Blalock 1967, Brown and Fuguitt 1972, Turner 1951, Frisbie and Neidert 1977). In a similar vein, Karnig (1979) found that city size is significantly and favorably associated with over twenty measures of black economic, political, and cultural development.
7. Some descriptive studies of racial residential segregation which have controlled for urban size and the relative size of the black population demonstrate that segregation is higher in larger urban areas and where blacks make up a higher percentage of the total population (cf. Van Valey et al. 1978). These conclusions are qualified to the extent that the only measure of residential patterning was a measure of segregation (dissimilarity index), which does not control for the relative size of the minority populations or reflect other aspects of urban patterns, as noted above.

   To our knowledge, the only study that directly addresses the interaction of demographic and spatial parameters with respect to ethnicity is Balakrishnan's (1976) analysis of ethnic residential segregation in urban Canada. He considered the impact of urban size, ethnic diversity, and ethnic group size on the level of ethnic residential segregation for the sixteen metropolitan areas in Canada. He found segregation to be positively correlated with total population size and with the percent of the total population which was non-British and, to a lesser extent, with the size of the ethnic group itself. However, a measure of ethnic diversity, per se, was not significantly associated with segregation levels. Although this study invites further analysis, it also employs the conventional measure of residential segregation and, hence, may not capture important aspects of residential patterning.
8. We draw directly on Parkin's (1979: 70–1) brief but cogent criticism of the conventional usages of the terms. Parkin's entire discussion of ethnicity and class theory is very illuminating.

9. Even in the case of Greeley or of Fischer, for that matter, when ethnicity is explicitly defined as group membership determined by descent, there is a focus primarily on its variability and the situational nature of its significance. Fischer explicitly notes the complementarity of the intrinsic character of ethnic identity with its socially constructed nature (1976: 1330–32).

10. An emphasis on the implications of spatial concentrations and boundaries for processes of maintaining ethnic stratification corresponds with the common observation that ethnic *group* differences in measures of income and social status frequently correlate strongly with measures of ethnic residential dissimilarity, while individual differences in socioeconomic status statistically account for little residential segregation (Darroch and Marston 1972; also see Guest and Weed 1976, for a different but complementary view).

Segregation of Visible Minorities in Montreal, Toronto, and Vancouver[†]

T. R. BALAKRISHNAN AND JOHN KRALT

The ethnic composition of the Canadian population has become more heterogeneous in recent decades. To a considerable extent this is due to the nature of immigration in the postwar years, especially since the early 1960s. Asian, Caribbean, and other Third World immigration to Canada has increased substantially while immigration from traditional countries of origin such as the United Kingdom, Netherlands, and others in Western Europe has decreased. Immigration from certain Southern Europe countries such as Portugal, Italy, and Greece has also increased. Refugees from Eastern Europe have further added to the ethnic plurality of Canadian society. One result of the changes in immigration patterns is the increase in the proportion of visible minorities in Canada.

An equally significant trend is the concentration of visible minority groups in the larger cities of Canada. While in the earlier days distribution of new immigrants had been more spread out with many settling in rural areas to start farming, the recent immigrants, especially those belonging to the visible minority groups, have settled in the larger cities of Toronto, Montreal, and Vancouver.

The changing nature of the ethnic population, mainly of the visible minorities, their concentration patterns and their socioeconomic and demographic profile has important consequences for the Canadian society at large, and is the focus of this paper.

The definition of a visible minority group in a multicultural society such as Canada is difficult to outline and will naturally be subject to criticism. Secretary of State for Multiculturalism has tentatively defined ten groups as visible minorities, including: Blacks, Indo-Pakistanis,

---

†This article has not been previously published. It was originally presented at the Canadian Ethnic Studies Association conference, Montreal, 1985.

Chinese, Indo-Chinese, Japanese, Koreans, Ethnic Philippinos, Pacific Islanders, Lebanese, and Arabic. For the purpose of this study we will include only the three largest groups, Blacks, Indo-Pakistanis, and Chinese, each with populations of more than 100,000 in Canada. Other visible minority groups are too small to enable meaningful statistical analysis especially when using census tract data.

The number of ethnic groups coded in the 1981 census is more than 100, with the analysis of these groups complicated due to the reporting of multiple responses. The visible minority groups form only a small subset of all the groups. Though our primary concern is with visible minority groups, we will include the British and French charter groups and a few other minority groups in our study of ethnic concentration. Comparison of ethnic groups is important.

The main objectives of this paper are to:

a) identify and describe the extent and patterns of residential concentration of visible minority groups in the census metropolitan areas of Montreal, Toronto, and Vancouver;

b) examine the similarities and dissimilarities among the visible minority and selected other ethnic groups in their residential concentrations; and

c) investigate the possible causes for the existence and differences in the residential concentrations of various ethnic groups by examining such correlated data as period of immigration and language facility.

This study should also provide comparisons with the earlier studies done using 1961 and 1971 census data, though fraught with problems of changes in definition and categorization. Multiple responses to ethnic background (while making the 1981 ethnic data much richer) greatly increased the methodological difficulties. The special tabulations done for this paper, are however, a significant improvement over the published 1981 census statistics especially when dealing with visible minorities.

Theoretical Considerations

Residential concentration of any ethnic group may be the result of voluntary or involuntary causes. Proponents of voluntary segregation sometimes referred to as the "cultural proximity model," argue that persons of the same ethnic ancestry may choose to live in proximity so that social interaction can be maximized and group norms and values can be maintained (Driedger and Church 1974, Balakrishnan 1982). Ethnic groups may voluntarily promote residential segregation to maintain identity. Size and concentration may enable an ethnic group to establish traditions such as ethnic clubs, churches, language newspapers, and specialty stores, all of which require a threshold population. We hypothesize that over time, ethnic groups will assimilate the cultural traits of the wider society and consequently residential segregation will decrease, as the needs for cultural proximity lessen. Some support for this assimilation hypothesis was found in a study of residential segregation in the Canadian metropolitan areas during 1951–1961, as there was a noticeable decrease (Balakrishnan 1976). However, a later study using 1961–1971 segregation indices did not show a decrease but a slight increase (Balakrishnan 1982). While voluntary segregation and subsequent assimilation into the mainstream of Canadian society may be true for some European immigrants, some researchers hypothesize that it may not hold for visible immigrants from Asia, Africa, and the Americas (see for example Kalbach 1981).

In contrast, involuntary segregation is largely the result of discrimination against the ethnic group, forcing them to concentrate in a limited number of areas. Access to housing, and various social institutions may be limited due to prejudice, resulting in involuntary residential concentration of visible minorities. This is typical of non-white segregation in the United States (Taeuber and Taeuber 1965, Taeuber 1970).

Two different hypotheses have been advanced and tested in recent research for the observed patterns and changes in residential segregation. First, the social class hypothesis, states that ethnic segregation is mainly due to social class differences among the ethnic groups. Ethnic groups vary in social class due to reasons such as educational background, language facility, and recency of immigration among others. Ethnic segregation may be no more than one facet of social class segregation. Residential concentration of social classes may reflect the unequal resources of the classes which may reduce the choice of residential location for the lower classes. If this hypothesis is true, residential segregation by ethnic groups should decrease over time, as ethnic groups become more mobile and become similar in their class structure. This social mobility and assimilation approach has been tested in many studies in the U.S. and to a limited extent in Canada. However, it has been found that even when social class is controlled, ethnic segregation remains significant (Darroch and Marston 1971, Kantrowitz 1973).

The second hypothesis, which has been called the social distance hypothesis, states that ethnic residential segregation is basically due to social distance between the ethnic groups. A few Canadian studies have measured social distance between the ethnic groups in Canada and found them to be similar to those found in the U.S. (Driedger and Peters 1977, Pineo 1977). In Pineo's study a measure of "social standing" was developed and the visible minorities formed the bottom of this scale. Two studies in the metropolitan areas of Canada for the years 1961 and 1971 found that residential segregation increased with social distance. Asians who had the highest social distance from the Western Europe groups were the most segregated (Balakrishnan 1976, 1982).[1] Others have also found that visible minorities are residentially concentrated due to systemic racial discrimination (Kalbach 1981). A number of studies of the black population in the U.S. clearly show that social distance is far more important than social class in their residential concentration (Taeuber and Taeuber 1965, Massey 1979, 1981).[2]

In addition to the foregoing hypotheses of the influence of social class and social distance on ethnic segregation, we will look at the relationship of ethnic group size, and such factors as recency of immigration and official language facility and concentration patterns.

Since this paper depends on available census data, and not on indepth survey information specifically collected to assess the reasons for residential location and perceptions and experience of discrimination, testing of the hypotheses has to be indirect. However, this study will still provide a profile of ethnic/visible minorities who are concentrated and causal relationships can be inferred.

Data

The basic data used are the 1981 census statistics for the census tracts of the three metropolitan areas of Montreal, Toronto, and Vancouver. The detailed distribution of the ethnic population in each census tract was obtained from Statistics Canada in machine readable form. Multiple responses were allowed in the 1981 census. While they enrich the data in their usefulness, they also create methodological problems. Other researchers have examined this problem extensively (Kralt, internal document 1983). For this study the ethnic groups will be restricted to the following ten groups:

British only (single responses)
French only (single responses)
German-Austrian (single and multiple responses)
Italian (single and multiple responses)
Jewish (single and multiple responses)
Greek (single and multiple responses)
Portuguese (single and multiple responses)
Black and Caribbean
Indo-Pakistani
Chinese.

British and French are the dominant origins in Canada, and as such are worth investigating as reference groups for the others. Eighty-seven percent of the British and 90 percent of the French gave only a single response in the 1981 Canadian census. For practical consideration of mutual exclusiveness, only those who gave single responses for British or French are included in this study.

For the Jewish and the three European groups of Italian, Greek, and Portuguese, the single responses varied from 85 to 96 percent. However, all responses are included as the absolute numbers of multiple responses for these groups were small. A cursory examination of settlement patterns suggested no major differences between those who gave single or multiple responses. For German-Austrian the single response rate varies from 62 percent in Toronto to 69 percent in Montreal. The classification criteria for the three visible minority groups were more complicated. They included an examination of place of birth, religion, and home language in addition to the ethnicity reported before a definitive ethnic status is assigned (Kralt, internal document 1983).

About two-thirds of the visible minorities in Canada live in the three largest metropolitan areas of Montreal, Toronto, and Vancouver. About the same proportion of others, such as Jews, Greeks, Italians, and Portuguese also live in these areas. Of the groups examined here, only the German-Austrian group and the British and French are more dispersed. Since our unit of analysis is the census tract it is reasonable to concentrate the study on these cities as they have enough census tracts to enable a statistical analysis.

The population distribution by the selected ethnic groups for the three metropolitan areas is presented in Table 1. The "French only" ethnic group in Montreal make up 65.0 percent of the metropolitan population, and including "British only" add up to 76.3 percent. In Toronto and Vancouver these two charter groups form only about half the population, making these two cities more ethnically diverse than Montreal. The three visible minority groups of Black and Caribbean, Indo-Pakistani, and Chinese are 3.0 percent of Montreal's, 9.9 percent of Toronto's, and 10.4 percent of Vancouver's populations. The patterns of residential concentration vary considerably. The German-Austrian group is proportionately more concentrated in Vancouver and less in Montreal. Jews form more than 3 percent of the population in Montreal and Toronto, but less than 1 percent in Vancouver. Italians are concentrated more in Toronto, where they form almost 10 percent of the metropolitan population, while in Montreal they are 5.5 percent and in Vancouver only 2.4 percent. Among the visible minority groups, Blacks and Caribbeans comprise 4.2 percent of Toronto's population, but only 1.8 percent of Montreal's and 0.6 percent of Vancouver's populations. Chinese are heavily represented in Vancouver, but make up only 0.6 percent of Montreal's population. To the extent that size is a factor in residential segregation, these very different distribution patterns should have some influence on intercity variations of ethnic concentrations.

Table 1
Population Distribution by Selected Ethnic Groups for Metropolitan Montreal, Toronto, and Vancouver, 1981

Ethnic Group	Montreal		Toronto		Vancouver	
	Popu-lation	% of Total	Popu-lation	% of Total	Popu-lation	% of Total
British Only	318,965	11.3	1,390,055	46.4	612,185	48.3
French Only	1,837,980	65.0	74,755	2.5	36,830	2.9
German-Austrian	24,275	0.9	89,845	3.0	78,620	6.2
Jewish	89,520	3.2	109,340	3.6	11,470	0.9
Italian	156,605	5.5	297,265	9.9	30,680	2.4
Greek	48,185	1.7	64,970	2.2	6,240	0.5
Portuguese	23,235	0.8	88,895	3.0	7,965	0.6
Black and Caribbean	51,165	1.8	126,295	4.2	7,210	0.6
Indo-Pakistani	16,275	0.6	79,095	2.6	37,540	3.0
Chinese	17,910	0.6	91,510	3.1	85,760	6.8
Total Metropolitan Area Population	2,828,420	100.0	2,998,885	100.0	1,268,185	100.0
Number of Census Tracts	665		608		246	

Ethnic Concentration

Before constructing summary measures of concentration for the various ethnic groups for the three cities, it may be useful to get a descriptive picture of the extent of concentration. Census tracts in each of the metropolitan areas were arranged in decreasing order of ethnic population, so that cumulative proportions of the population could be calculated. Table 2 shows the extent of concentration, by examining the proportion of tracts in which 50 percent and 90 percent of an ethnic group population is found.

Table 2
Percentage of Census Tracts in Which 50 and 90 Percent of Ethnic Group Populations Are Concentrated

Ethnic Group	Montreal 50%	Montreal 90%	Toronto 50%	Toronto 90%	Vancouver 50%	Vancouver 90%
British Only	13.1	53.2	29.9	73.6	35.0	78.5
French Only	25.6	69.0	25.7	69.7	26.0	72.4
German-Austrian	13.4	47.5	26.3	70.1	30.5	75.2
Jewish	2.3	9.5	3.3	18.8	7.7	36.2
Italian	7.9	38.8	11.3	48.0	10.2	56.5
Greek	3.0	24.3	11.0	46.2	9.8	40.2
Portuguese	6.6	32.3	4.1	33.7	6.1	29.3
Black and Caribbean	11.4	44.1	14.3	52.0	21.1	56.1
Indo-Pakistani	7.4	28.7	11.8	48.2	16.3	55.7
Chinese	7.2	28.7	10.2	47.5	11.4	47.2
Total Number of Census Tracts	665		608		246	

French in Toronto and Vancouver, though they form less than 3 percent of the total population are not concentrated at all. As a matter of fact they are as dispersed as the British majority group. Seventy percent of the tracts need to be covered before 90 percent of the French population are included. The same is true of the German-Austrians, who are as dispersed as the British and French.

Jews are by far the most concentrated minority group in Canada. In Montreal, half of the Jewish population is found in 2.3 percent of the census tracts and 90 percent in less than 10 percent of the tracts. In Toronto and Vancouver they are also heavily segregated, though to a slightly lesser extent. Fifty percent of the Jewish population is found in 3.3 percent of the tracts in Toronto and 7.7 percent in Vancouver. Jews are concentrated even more than the visible minorities and they reach record levels similiar to black concentrations found in the large U.S. cities. The fact that Jews are not a visible minority and do not belong to lower socioeconomic classes, points to the need to look at additional causes for high segregation.

The three Southern European groups—Italian, Greek, and Portuguese—are concentrated far more than the British and the French. They are also slightly more concentrated than the visible minority groups. Fifty percent of the Greeks in Montreal reside in 3.0 percent of the census tracts. Fifty percent of the Portuguese live in 6.6 percent of the tracts in Montreal, 4.1 percent of the tracts in Toronto, and 6.1 percent in Vancouver. Italians are slightly less concentrated than the Greeks or the Portuguese. This may be partly a statistical artifact as there are many more Italians than Greeks or Portuguese.

The visible minority groups are most segregated in Montreal, slightly less in Toronto, and still less in Vancouver. There are not many differences between the three. Blacks and Caribbeans are the least segregated and Chinese the most, with the Indo-Pakistanis in between. But the differences are not significant. Fifty percent of the Black and Caribbean population live in 11.4 percent of the tracts in Montreal, 14.3 percent of the tracts in Toronto, and 21.1 percent of the tracts in Vancouver. The fact that the visible minority groups are far less concentrated than the Jewish population as well as the Southern Europeans was unanticipated. It calls the social distance hypothesis into serious question; other explanations must be found.

Another way of looking at ethnic segregation is to see what proportion of the city does not contain any particular ethnic group. The higher this proportion, the greater the chance that the general population will seldom come into contact with the ethnic group in question. Table 3 shows the number of census tracts in which there is no specified ethnic group and the total population of these tracts. In more than half of the tracts in Montreal (where 53 percent of the city's population live) there is not a single Jewish resident. This is almost true for the Indo-Pakistanis and Chinese as well. About a third of the Montreal area does not have any Greek, or Portuguese either; about an eighth of Montreal does not have a Black or Caribbean resident. Italians and German-Austrians are found in most areas. In Toronto, Jews and Portuguese are the only two groups which are not found in a sixth of the tracts. In Vancouver, Jews, Greeks, and Portuguese are most segregated, taking into account proportion of tracts with none.

"Ethnic neighbourhoods" in the central cities of the three metropolitan areas are shown in Figures 1 to 3. Only those minorities for whom a contiguous number of census tracts of heavy concentration can be identified are presented in these figures. Isolated tracts with more than the average proportion of an ethnic population are not shown and overlaps have been avoided. Thus the figures are only crude indicators of neighbourhoods. In Montreal, the population in the Jewish neighbourhood is 70 percent Jewish (Figure 1). Heavy concentration of Greeks (about half of the population of the tracts) can also be identified.

Table 3
Number of Census Tracts and Their Population in Which There Is No Ethnic Group

Ethnic Group	Montreal		Toronto		Vancouver	
	Number of Tracts	CMA Pop. in the Tracts (%)	Number of Tracts	CMA Pop. in the Tracts (%)	Number of Tracts	CMA Pop. in the Tracts (%)
British Only	3	0.3	3	0.0	1	0.0
French Only	5	0.8	9	0.2	1	0.1
German-Austrian	120	10.5	11	0.1	1	0.1
Jewish	370	53.0	147	19.1	57	17.6
Italian	43	2.6	16	0.4	4	0.4
Greek	256	32.2	83	9.0	80	26.2
Portuguese	263	36.1	117	13.0	102	36.8
Black and Caribbean	112	12.2	31	1.7	40	12.6
Indo-Pakistani	335	44.9	70	6.9	14	3.7
Chinese	332	45.2	67	6.6	12	2.9
Total	665	100.0	608	100.0	246	100.0

Though they form a smaller proportion, clear neighbourhoods can be delineated for the Portuguese and Chinese and to a lesser extent for the Italians as well. Neighbourhoods cannot be identified for the Indo-Pakistani or Black-Caribbean groups.

In Toronto, neighbourhoods (where more than 50 percent belong to a particular ethnic group) can be identified for Jews, Portuguese, and Italians (Figure 2). Heavy concentrations can also be found among the Chinese and Greeks. However, as in Montreal, no clear neighbourhoods could be constructed for the Indo-Pakistanis or Black-Caribbeans.

In Vancouver, neighbourhoods where more than half of the same ethnic origin (excluding British) exist only for the Chinese, although neighbourhoods can be clearly identified at lower levels of concentration for Greeks, Jews, Italians, Portuguese, and Indo-Pakistanis (Figure 3).

French neighbourhoods do not exist either in Toronto or Vancouver. Though concentrations of British can be found in Montreal, a British neighbourhood cannot be identified, probably because of the sizeable number of British in Montreal.

Two summary measures are constructed to investigate concentration of the minority groups. The first one is derived from concentration

Figure 1
Ethnic Concentrations in Montreal: 1981

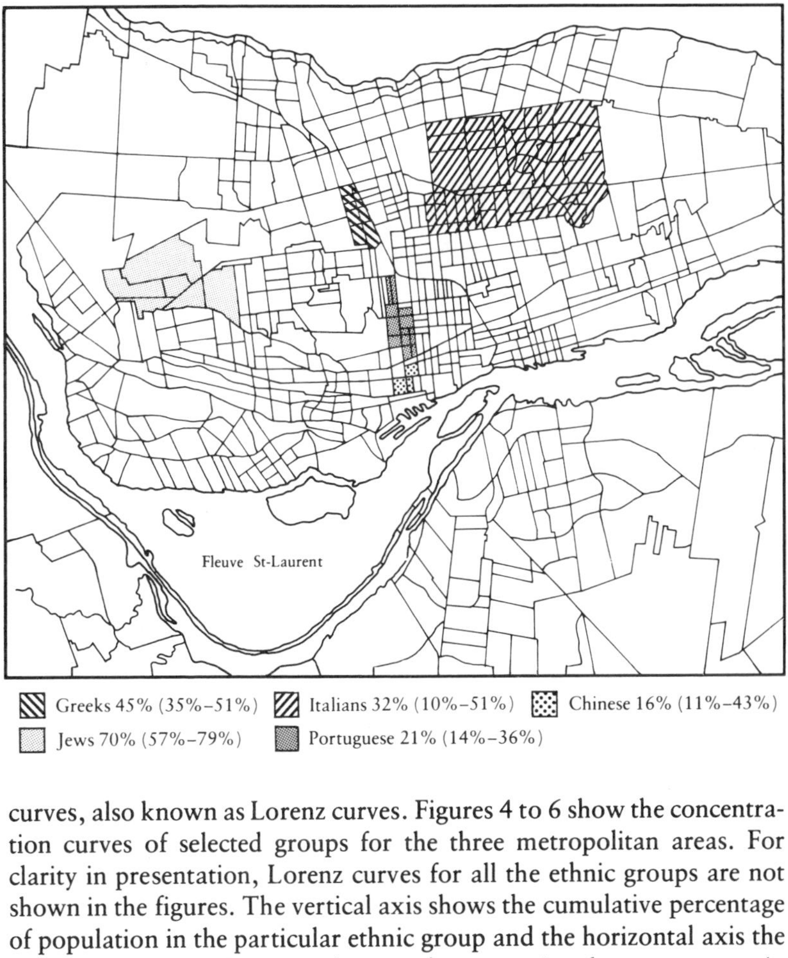
Fleuve St-Laurent
Greeks 45% (35%–51%)
Italians 32% (10%–51%)
Chinese 16% (11%–43%)
Jews 70% (57%–79%)
Portuguese 21% (14%–36%)

curves, also known as Lorenz curves. Figures 4 to 6 show the concentration curves of selected groups for the three metropolitan areas. For clarity in presentation, Lorenz curves for all the ethnic groups are not shown in the figures. The vertical axis shows the cumulative percentage of population in the particular ethnic group and the horizontal axis the percentage of nonethnic population, after arranging the census tracts in decreasing order of ethnic population. A curve that coincides with the diagonal line indicates that the ethnic population is distributed the same way as the rest of the population, implying no concentration. The farther the curve is from the diagonal, the greater the concentration. In all the cities, Jews and Portuguese show the highest concentrations. In Montreal, the British show medium concentration and surprisingly, the Black-Caribbean group show lower concentration than the other

Figure 2
Ethnic Concentrations in Toronto: 1981

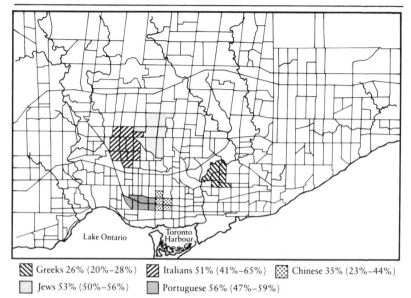

Greeks 26% (20%–28%)   Italians 51% (41%–65%)   Chinese 35% (23%–44%)
Jews 53% (50%–56%)   Portuguese 56% (47%–59%)

Figure 3
Ethnic Concentrations in Vancouver: 1981

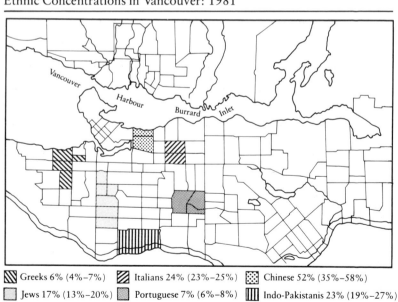

Greeks 6% (4%–7%)   Italians 24% (23%–25%)   Chinese 52% (35%–58%)
Jews 17% (13%–20%)   Portuguese 7% (6%–8%)   Indo-Pakistanis 23% (19%–27%)

groups. In Toronto, the Chinese and Black-Caribbeans show medium levels of concentration and the French practically no concentration at all. In Vancouver, the Chinese and Indo-Pakistanis show medium concentration and the German-Austrian group the lowest level of concentration. The Gini Index is the ratio of the area between the curve and the diagonal to the area of the triangle above the diagonal line. Thus the range for the index is 0 to 1, indicating no concentration or complete concentration (no other population resides in those areas where the particular ethnic group is found).

Figure 4
Concentration Curves for Selected Minority Groups: Montreal, 1981

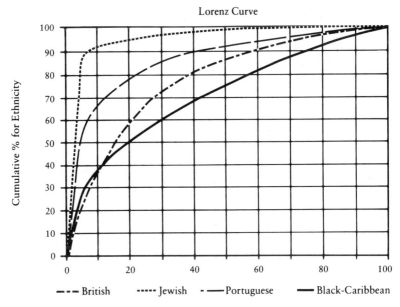

The second index used here is the more commonly known Index of Dissimilarity. This index is the sum of either the positive or negative differences between the proportional distributions of two ethnic populations. The index ranges from zero to unity, indicating complete similarity or dissimilarity between the residential distributions of the two ethnic populations. For each ethnic group in this study two types of indices of dissimilarity are calculated, one of that group from everybody else and the other of each group from every other group. Table 4 shows the Gini indices and the indices of dissimilarity of each of the ten ethnic groups from the rest of the population. Though the Gini Index and the Index of

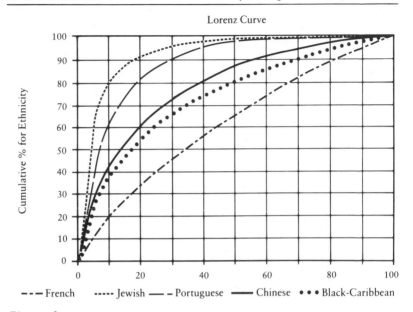

Figure 5
Concentration Curves for Selected Minority Groups: Toronto, 1981

Lorenz Curve

Cumulative % for Ethnicity

--- French   ····· Jewish   — — Portuguese   —— Chinese   • • • Black-Caribbean

Figure 6
Concentration Curves for Selected Minority Groups: Vancouver, 1981

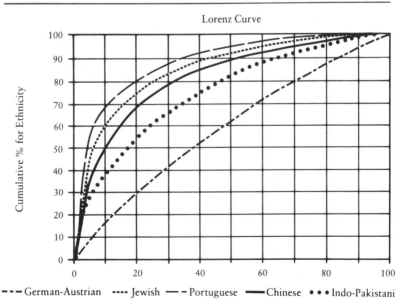

Lorenz Curve

Cumulative % for Ethnicity

--- German-Austrian   ···· Jewish   — — Portuguese   —— Chinese   • • • Indo-Pakistani

Dissimilarity are two conceptually different measures, one measuring concentration and the other segregation with different formulae for their construction, they are highly correlated. The correlation between the Gini Index and the Index of Dissimilarity when we take the ten groups and the three metropolitan areas together is an astonishingly high 0.98. Thus for all practical purposes, it does not make any difference as to which index is used.

Table 4
Indices of Dissimilarity of Each Ethnic Group From All Other Groups and Gini Indices of Concentration

Ethnic Group	Montreal		Toronto		Vancouver	
	Index of Dissimilarity	Gini Index	Index of Dissimilarity	Gini Index	Index of Dissimilarity	Gini Index
British Only	.459	.539	.261	.229	.176	.145
French Only	.472	.460	.198	.220	.210	.249
German-Austrian	.409	.504	.192	.205	.157	.174
Jewish	.832	.931	.740	.867	.562	.715
Italian	.565	.689	.506	.627	.448	.566
Greek	.658	.823	.461	.589	.480	.643
Portuguese	.603	.763	.633	.777	.589	.752
Black and Caribbean	.463	.582	.376	.474	.325	.419
Indo-Pakistani	.579	.712	.401	.520	.379	.496
Chinese	.595	.738	.447	.577	.502	.622
Mean	.564	.674	.422	.509	.382	.478

The indices are high in Montreal for all the ethnic/visible minority groups. Earlier studies have all shown high segregation in Montreal in comparison to the rest of the metropolitan areas in Canada (Balakrishnan 1976, 1982). Obviously the ability to speak French plays a large part in the residential location in Montreal. Language facility among the ethnic groups varies a great deal depending on date of immigration, place of origin, etc. Generally the indices are lowest for the British only, French only, and German-Austrian groups. British in Toronto and Vancouver form amost half the population and hence cannot have a large index due to the way the indices are calculated. This is however not true in the case of the French, who form only a small proportion of the population. In spite of their small number, the French are dispersed widely in the metropolitan areas of Toronto and Vancouver.

The highest indices of concentration are found among the Jews. In Montreal, the index of dissimilarity for Jews is .832 and the Gini index of concentration .931, far higher than for any other group. These indices are very similar to what are found for Blacks in the large U.S. cities. Though they are somewhat lower in Toronto and Vancouver, the indices are still much higher for Jews than for the other groups, the index of dissimilarity being .740 in Toronto and .562 in Vancouver. Next to the Jews, Greeks are most segregated in Montreal with an index of dissimilarity of .658 and a Gini index of .823. This is not surprising as we have already found that 50 percent of the Greeks are concentrated in 3 percent of the census tracts in Montreal. Other groups of Italians, Portuguese, and the three visible minorities have about the same levels of segregation, except the Black and Caribbean group, which has an index of dissimilarity of only .463. The Black and Caribbean group in Montreal is a mix of Haitians, other Black-Caribbeans, and French Africans who are to some extent different in cultural background and language facility, resulting in a greater dispersion than would be expected otherwise.

In Toronto, the indices are lower than in Montreal, but their relative positions are practically the same. British, French, and German-Austrian have very low indices, around .200. A noticeable difference from Montreal is that the Jews and the three Southern European groups have higher indices of dissimilarity and Gini indices than the visible minority groups. For example, the index of dissimilarity for the Portuguese in Toronto is .633, while it is only .376 for the Black and Caribbean group, and .401 for Indo-Pakistanis. We need to look at factors such as English language facility and period of immigration in trying to explain these differences in the levels of segregation.

Among the visible minority groups, the Chinese are the most segregated with an index of dissimilarity of .595 in Montreal, .447 in Toronto, and .502 in Vancouver. The Indo-Pakistanis rank next followed by the Blacks and Caribbeans.

Segregation Between the Ethnic Groups

Indices of dissimilarity between pairs of ethnic groups are presented in Table 5 for the three metropolitan areas. Again all the indices are higher in Montreal than in Toronto or Vancouver. However, the pattern of segregation is remarkably similar in the three cities. The index of dissimilarity between German-Austrian and British is very low in all the cities (.294 in Montreal, .157 in Toronto, and .151 in Vancouver). Outside of the unique case of Montreal, the index between British and French is also quite low (.181 in Toronto and .209 in Vancouver).

Table 5

Indices of Dissimilarity Between Ethnic/Visible Minority Groups in Montreal, Toronto, and Vancouver—1981

MONTREAL

	British Only	French Only	German-Austrian	Jewish	Italian	Greek	Portuguese	Black and Caribbean	Indo-Pakistani	Chinese
British Only	---									
French Only	.532	---								
German-Austrian	.294	.511	---							
Jewish	.737	.892	.723	---						
Italian	.663	.584	.678	.890	---					
Greek	.675	.736	.634	.704	.757	---				
Portuguese	.732	.624	.728	.883	.676	.715	---			
Black-Caribbean	.525	.547	.566	.743	.478	.642	.643	---		
Indo-Pakistani	.472	.691	.493	.733	.735	.613	.745	.524	---	
Chinese	.564	.697	.604	.716	.706	.597	.659	.539	.500	---

TORONTO

	British Only	French Only	German-Austrian	Jewish	Italian	Greek	Portuguese	Black and Caribbean	Indo-Pakistani	Chinese
British Only	---									
French Only	.181	---								
German-Austrian	.157	.243	---							
Jewish	.749	.757	.738	---						
Italian	.541	.544	.535	.817	---					
Greek	.502	.504	.528	.791	.560	---				
Portuguese	.666	.652	.676	.885	.620	.680	---			
Black-Caribbean	.416	.382	.452	.787	.491	.484	.654	---		
Indo-Pakistani	.441	.414	.466	.798	.522	.523	.654	.293	---	
Chinese	.479	.464	.505	.733	.635	.471	.675	.461	.469	---

VANCOUVER

	British Only	French Only	German-Austrian	Jewish	Italian	Greek	Portuguese	Black and Caribbean	Indo-Pakistani	Chinese
British Only	---									
French Only	.209	---								
German-Austrian	.151	.223	---							
Jewish	.557	.612	.597	---						
Italian	.488	.504	.492	.730	---					
Greek	.507	.546	.532	.546	.599	---				
Portuguese	.647	.647	.629	.803	.516	.668	---			
Black-Caribbean	.338	.334	.343	.602	.542	.590	.640	---		
Indo-Pakistani	.432	.435	.383	.673	.492	.583	.534	.462	---	
Chinese	.547	.574	.525	.641	.423	.565	.414	.542	.428	---

Segregation of Visible Minorities 153

The groups of British, French, and German-Austrians have lower indices of dissimilarity with the visible minority groups than with the Italians, Greeks, Portuguese, or Jews. The indices are in the range of .334 to .466 in Toronto and Vancouver with Black-Caribbean and Indo-Pakistani groups, while they are in the range of .504 to .757 with the Southern European groups and the Jews, throwing doubt on the social distance hypothesis of residential segregation. This is not to deny the existence of social distance among the ethnic groups, which is well documented (Pineo 1977). The social distance between the Northwestern European groups and the visible minorities is much greater than between Southern European and Northwestern European groups or between Jews and British or French. What is more likely is that, voluntary segregation among the ethnic groups which increases the advantages of cultural proximity clearly operates more in the case of Jews, Greeks, Portuguese, and Italians. We hope to study in detail the influence of language facility and immigration patterns in the last two decades on residential segregation. Both Black-Caribbean and Indo-Pakistani immigrants are more fluent in English or French than the recent Portuguese or Greek immigrants. In the long run these factors will be less important, and we would expect residential segregation of Southern European groups to lower, while the visible minorities may continue to face discrimination in housing, and hence residential segregation due to greater social distance. It is also possible that whatever the reasons, certain ethnic groups retain their ethnic identity and develop stronger community ties such as the Jews and Southern European groups. This fact is not so evident among the visible minority groups of Blacks and Caribbeans or Indo-Pakistanis, which definitely needs statistical documentation by investigating the ethnic institutions prevalent in the various minority communities.

Social Class and Segregation

The social class hypothesis of residential segregation says that the lower classes are more likely to be segregated because their socioeconomic status restricts them to the poorer areas of the city which are often found near the core. They do not have the resources and hence the option to choose among a number of residential areas in a city. As a corollary, recent immigrants who are often in the lower socioeconomic levels are more concentrated, and as they improve their status and get more assimilated in the society, their segregation will decrease. Without special tabulations for small areas by ethnic background and socioeconomic characteristics, we cannot directly test this hypothesis. However we can look at the overall status of neighbourhoods in which particular ethnic minorities are found concentrated and indirectly test the hypothesis. Census tracts where the percentage of an ethnic population is found to be greater than the percentage in the metropolitan area as a whole were identified as areas of concentration. Table 6 presents the mean socioeconomic indices (SES) of those tracts so identified for each ethnic group in the three metropolitan areas. The SES index for each census tract was constructed taking into account the proportion in the higher occupations, proportion with high school education among adults, and proportion with family income above $20,000 in 1981. This index was computed for each census tract in all the tracted metropolitan areas in Canada and standardized to a distribution with a mean of 50 and a standard deviation of 10. In Montreal, the percentage of the British population is more than the city percentage in 185 of the 665 census tracts, and the mean SES index of these tracts is 52.1. In contrast, the mean SES index of the 383 tracts in which the French are overrepresented is only 43.9. Jews live in areas with the highest SES index of 56.5, which to a considerable extent is due to their own higher status. Italians, Portuguese, and Black-Caribbeans live in the poorer neighbourhoods with an SES index in the range of 42 to 44. Relative positions of the various ethnic groups are not too different in Toronto and Vancouver, except for one or two exceptions. The French in Toronto and Vancouver live in higher SES areas than they do in Montreal. Jewish areas in Toronto had the highest SES index of 58.1. British and German-Austrians also live in areas with a higher SES level than the other minority groups. As in Montreal, the lowest SES index was associated with the Portuguese neighbourhoods, with a mean index of only 44.0. Italian neighbourhoods were only slightly higher at 46.2. The areas where the visible minorities were overrepresented were higher in Toronto with a mean index varying between 48.3 and 50.8. In Vancouver also, Jewish areas had the highest SES index of 56.4 and the Portuguese the lowest at 48.1.

The preceding analysis of the SES index of areas by ethnic minority overrepresentation shows that the extent of concentration has little relationship to the SES level of the areas. Though admittedly a crude measure, it shows that Jews who are highly segregated have high SES and Portuguese who are highly segregated have low SES. Similarly, French who are least segregated in Montreal have a low SES, but higher SES in the other cities where they are well dispersed. Only with more extensive analysis, especially by socioeconomic characteristics of groups who live in concentrated areas and outside the concentrated areas, can we really make firm conclusions between social class and segregation patterns.

Conclusion

This is a preliminary study of selected ethnic and visible minority group concentrations in the metropolitan areas of Montreal, Toronto, and Vancouver. We found that considerable residential segregation exists not only among the visible minorities but also among many other minorities from Southern Europe as well as the Jews.

A somewhat surprising finding was the lower levels of segregation among the visible minority groups in comparison to the minority groups from Southern Europe and the Jews. The authors assumed that race with its associated high social distance, supported by many studies, would show higher residential segregation. By and large this was not found to be true. We may speculate on the possible reasons which future studies will have to document. Official language facility (French in Montreal and English in Toronto and Vancouver) may influence the decision to settle in certain areas of the city. Indo-Pakistanis, Black-Caribbeans, and Chinese, especially from Hong Kong and Taiwan, are often more proficient in English compared to Southern European groups of Portuguese, Greek, or Italian, at least at the time when they arrive in Canada. The high segregation in Montreal for almost all the minority groups may be due to the fact that many of them are not fluent in French. A particular reason for the relatively low concentration of Black-Caribbean groups in Montreal may be due to the fact that they comprise a diversity of French-speaking Haitians, Blacks from French West Africa, and English-speaking Blacks from the United States, Africa, and the Caribbean. This heterogeneity among the black population (country of origin and language use), may be a cause for the lower level of residential concentration. Although difficult to do with 1981 census data, this hypothesis could be tested by an analysis of specific black populations.

Another hypothesis to explain the greater concentration found among the Greek, Portuguese, Italian, and Jewish populations in comparison to the visible minority groups, is that they are more homogeneous in their cultural background and probably participate more in ethnic activities. In other words, their institutional completeness is higher. Indo-Pakistanis, for example come from a wide variety of backgrounds, including mother tongue, religion, food and dress, and other cultural traits. The same is true of the black population. Particular religious customs can also promote residential concentration. In the case of the

Jews, their high concentration around the synagogues, is probably due to the tradition of walking to the synagogues on the Sabbath.

For most of the groups, it appears that period of immigration plays a major part in where the groups are concentrated. If we examine the Italian ethnic group, the group on our map which has resided in Canada the longest, a very high percentage are immigrants, i.e., born outside Canada. Given the nature of the society where many of these immigrants have originated, it would be strange if there were not residential concentration.

We hypothesize that in the long run, segregation that can be attributed to factors such as official language facility, recency of immigration, and cultural background will decrease as integration into the host society increases and class differences by ethnicity decrease. It will be interesting to see whether social distance, based especially on race and visible minorities, will continue. If it does, visible minorities will have a harder time integrating into Canadian society and will hence be more residentially segregated than other groups.

Segregation is a complex factor of social differentiation in both social class and social distance but in other factors such as language facility, cultural background, and recency of immigration as well. Our data and analysis have shown that simple explanations are far from satisfactory. For many ethnic groups, residential concentration is also a function of size, at least when geographic measures such as census tracts are used to determine the extent of concentration. Census statistics reveal patterns of concentration but do not help us very much in understanding the causes behind those patterns. Sample surveys using an indepth questionnaire may provide important information on why and how the choice of residential location is made.

Notes

1. In comparing 1961 and 1971 data to those of 1981, the reader is cautioned to keep in mind that the sizes of the visible minority population have increased dramatically between 1971 and 1981. As a result, many of the findings based on pre-1981 census data may not be applicable by 1981.
2. There is some question whether the American experience can be applied to Canada. For example, visible minorities do not usually make up the same percent of a Canadian city's population as Blacks do in the United States.

Bilingualism and Multiculturalism: A National Reading[†]

REGINALD W. BIBBY

It is well recognized that the Canadian government's official response to the cultural diversity of the country has involved two pivotal policies. The first is bilingualism, the second multiculturalism. While both policies technically have their sources in the 1960s and the Royal Commission on Bilingualism and Biculturalism, they reflect the age-old national quest for unity in the face of diversity.

Bilingualism represents a response to the precarious reality of two dominant national groups co-existing within Canada. The official resolution is the declaration that the country has not one but two founding peoples. Consequently, to be a Canadian is to be proficient in English, French, or both languages. Nothing less than the official recognition of their right to be Canadians in their own languages would have been acceptable to either Anglophones or Francophones. Since the passing of the Official Languages Act, linguistic duality has been enshrined.

Multiculturalism is the official response to a further Canadian reality—the existence of a large number of cultural groups besides those of British and French ancestry. Essentially a pluralistic solution taking on a "mosaic" form, it stands in contrast to the assimilationist, "melting pot" ideal, frequently associated with the United States. The multicultural posture of the federal government became explicit in 1974 with the establishing of a multiculturalism program within the Secretary of State. The Prime Minister at the time, Pierre Trudeau, said this in making the announcement:

†This article has not been previously published. The research was sponsored, in part, by grants from the Social Sciences and Humanities Research Council of Canada.

A policy of multiculturalism within a bilingual framework commends itself to the Government as the most suitable means of assuring the cultural freedom of Canadians (*Corpus Almanac of Canada*, Ottawa, 1974).

At the federal government level, then, Canada's cultural diversity is officially acknowledged and encouraged. One Canada, two languages, and many cultures, complete with acceptance and respect of differences, comprise the national ideals.

Since the mid-1970s, the author has been monitoring the extent to which the bilingual and multicultural ideals have been accepted by Canadians from British Columbia to Newfoundland. The method has been a series of national mail surveys conducted in 1975, 1980, and 1985. The surveys involve highly representative samples of approximately 1,200 Canadians, with accuracy levels of about plus or minus 4 percentage points, 19 times in 20. Of considerable importance, the surveys have dealt with a wide range of subject material, with intergroup relations only one of the topics involved. Consequently, there has been no detectable bias in either a positive or negative direction for virtually any one theme, including, of course, government policies concerning language and cultural groups. What follows is a brief overview of some of the major pertinent findings.

Bilingualism

As of 1985, just under 60 percent of Canadians endorse the country having two official languages (see Table 1). This represents a modest increase from 49 percent in 1975 and 55 percent in 1980. At the same time, one-third of Canadians continue to maintain that English alone should be the country's official language.

In every region, there have been slight increases in the favouring of bilingualism since the 1970s. However, almost two decades after the federal government passed the Official Languages Act, slightly less than 1 in 2 Canadians outside of Quebec agree with the policy. The endorsement levels range from a high of about 50 percent in Ontario and the Atlantic region, through 41 percent in B.C., to a low of 36 percent on the Prairies. Indeed, a majority of Canadians west of Ontario continue to favour "English only." At the same time, a modest move in the bilingual direction has been taking place over the past decade (B.C. 37 percent to 41 percent, Prairies 28 percent to 35 percent). Nevertheless, since 1980, only minimal progress in "selling bilingualism" outside of Quebec is evident (45 percent to 46 percent). Quebec, with the apparent passing of

Table 1
Endorsing of Bilingualism by Region: 1985, 1980, 1975; by Age and
Education: 1985 (%)

	English and French	English Only
Nationally		
1985	57	33
1980	55	36
1975	49	37
British Columbia		
1985	41	49
1980	44	45
1975	37	50
Prairies		
1985	36	50
1980	36	57
1975	28	64
Ontario		
1985	51	40
1980	51	45
1975	47	42
Atlantic		
1985	49	36
1980	38	44
1975	45	45
Outside Quebec		
1985	46	43
1980	45	48
1975	41	49
Quebec		
1985	91	3
1980	83	4
1975	71	7
1985		
18–34	60	27
35–54	57	34
55 +	53	41
Degree or more	72	20
HS – Some PS	61	32
Less than HS	48	40

separatist tendencies, has increasingly backed bilingualism over the decade.

The tendency to endorse bilingualism is somewhat more common among younger people, and is particularly more prevalent among better educated Canadians. These findings suggest that, with the passage of time, bilingualism will continue to know a slow, but steadily increasing level of acceptance.

Multiculturalism
Mosaic vs. Melting Pot

In the latest of the surveys, Canadians were presented with a sketch of the "mosaic" and "melting pot" models and asked for their preference. Close to 6 in 10 say they favour the "mosaic" model for the country, while just under 3 in 10 prefer the "melting pot" idea. Most of the remainder indicate no preference, with a small number suggesting other policies (see Table 2).

Table 2
Preference for Mosaic vs. Melting Pot Models: 1985 (%)

	Mosaic	Melting Pot	No Pref.	Other	Totals
Nationally	56	27	13	4	100
British Columbia	53	35	11	1	100
Prairies	58	32	6	4	100
Ontario	58	29	9	4	100
Quebec	58	16	21	5	100
Atlantic	49	29	21	1	100
18–34	61	20	15	4	100
35–54	53	31	12	4	100
55 +	54	33	11	2	100
Degree or more	70	17	6	7	100
HS – PS	53	29	15	3	100
Less than HS	41	37	20	2	100

The "mosaic" idea is favoured by close to the same proportion of people in each of the country's five regions, with the "melting pot" model least popular in Quebec. As with bilingualism, the mosaic receives slightly more support from younger people, with its endorsement increasing markedly with education.

Perceived Prevalence of Discrimination

Although Canadians endorse the "mosaic" ideal, approximately 60 percent continue as in 1980 to acknowledge that discrimination against racial or cultural groups exists in their communities (see Table 3). Nationally, there has been a slight increase in the perception that things are "getting better" (20 percent in 1985 vs. 15 percent in 1980). Regionally, British Columbians are more likely than others to feel that discrimination exists, but is neither better nor worse than in the past; Prairie respondents to see the situation as deteriorating somewhat; Quebec to assert that things are getting better; and Ontario (41 percent) and particularly Atlantic (55 percent) respondents to maintain that discrimination has never been a serious problem. Generally speaking, younger Canadians, and those with higher levels of education, are more likely than others to see discrimination as existing, and being eradicated very slowly.

Beyond the mere perception of discrimination, however, the national surveys have attempted to probe attitudes toward racial and cultural minorities over time—attitudes that may have implications for behaviour in the form of discrimination.

French-English Relations

In 1975, 21 percent of Canadians viewed French-English relations as a "very serious" problem. That figure has now dropped to 13 percent—16 percent in Quebec, 12 percent outside of Quebec (see Table 4).

The proportion of people outside of Quebec who think French Canadians have too much power has also declined slightly from 43 percent to 37 percent during the 1975–85 period.

Perception of excessive French-Canadian power has decreased only mildly since 1975, and appears to have actually increased somewhat on the Prairies since 1980. The perception of "too much" French-Canadian power differs little by age, but is somewhat less common among Canadians with a university education.

Within Quebec, on the other hand, the proportion feeling Quebec has insufficient power in the nation's affairs has decreased from 70 percent in 1975 to 53 percent as of 1985.

Indo-Pakistanis

Since 1980, there has been a 6 percent decrease in the proportion of Canadians who say they feel uneasy in the presence of East Indians and Pakistanis (23 percent to 17 percent), with most of this decrease occurring outside of western Canada (see Table 5). The B.C. level now is

Table 3

Perception of Discrimination by Region: 1985, 1980*; by Age and Education: 1985 (%)

"Do you feel that any racial or cultural groups in your community are discriminated against?"

	Yes, and Getting Worse	Yes, But Getting Better	Yes, But No Change	No, Was Problem in Past	No, and Never A Problem	Totals
Nationally						
1985	11	20	28	9	32	100
1980	14	15	26	9	36	100
British Columbia						
1985	11	17	41	5	26	100
1980	22	14	35	8	21	100
Prairies						
1985	20	13	30	8	29	100
1980	13	8	32	7	39	100
Ontario						
1985	9	17	25	8	41	100
1980	16	12	21	7	44	100
Quebec						
1985	9	31	28	13	19	100
1980	11	27	26	14	22	100
Atlantic						
1985	4	14	16	11	55	100
1980	3	12	22	6	57	100
1985						
18–34	10	16	38	7	29	100
35–54	13	22	24	7	34	100
55 +	8	23	14	16	39	100
Degree or more	14	27	31	7	21	100
HS – PS	8	17	30	10	35	100
Less than HS	12	17	12	11	48	100

*Item not included in the 1975 survey.

Table 4

French-English Relations by Region: 1985, 1980, 1975; by Age and Education: 1985 (%)

	Constitute a Very Serious Problem	French Canadians' Power in National Life: Too Much	Too Little
Nationally			
1985	13	29	21
1980	23	28	21
1975	21	32	27
British Columbia			
1985	13	39	6
1980	13	44	12
1975	14	44	9
Prairies			
1985	15	49	10
1980	20	37	10
1975	21	59	7
Ontario			
1985	11	30	9
1980	17	32	9
1975	12	36	10
Atlantic			
1985	10	36	15
1980	17	32	7
1975	15	40	12
Outside Quebec			
1985	12	37	10
1980	17	35	9
1975	15	43	10
Quebec			
1985	16	5	53
1980	39	7	55
1975	37	5	70
1985			
18–34	13	26	25
35–54	11	31	18
55 +	14	30	18
Degree or more	11	21	21
HS – PS	16	32	20
Less than HS	7	32	24

Table 5

Inclination to Feel At Ease With Various Groups by Region: 1985, 1980, 1975; by Age and Education: 1985

	Indo/Pak.	Can. Ind.	Jew	Black	Oriental
	\% Indicating "At Ease"				
Nationally					
1985	83	90	91	88	91
1980	77	86	93	89	91
1975	**	87	91	84	86
British Columbia					
1985	83	98	98	93	98
1980	85	92	95	95	95
1975	**	87	93	88	92
Prairies					
1985	78	88	87	84	88
1980	77	82	96	89	95
1975	**	78	93	81	83
Ontario					
1985	83	93	93	91	93
1980	73	89	96	91	92
1975	**	88	93	81	88
Quebec					
1985	86	87	87	86	86
1980	79	82	89	84	85
1975	**	92	88	88	84
Atlantic					
1985	84	92	92	85	91
1980	81	85	90	85	88
1975	**	88	94	83	84
1985					
18–34	82	89	90	88	91
35–54	86	94	92	90	93
55 +	80	88	91	86	87
Degree or more	88	93	94	92	94
HS – PS	82	90	91	88	91
Less than HS	77	84	86	82	82

**Item not included in the 1975 survey.

similar to Ontario, Quebec, and the Atlantic region, whereas the Prairie level of uneasiness (22 percent) is marginally highest.

The perception that Indo-Pakistanis have too much power in the country has decreased mildly since 1980 (see Table 6). Once again, the change in perception has been from Ontario eastward. In B.C. and Alberta, the sense of excessive power has become somewhat more prevalent between 1980 and 1985. Since the 1970s, disapproval of Indo-Pakistanis marrying Whites has dropped markedly—from 42 percent to 28 percent (see Table 7). Generally speaking, negative attitudes toward these Asian groups are somewhat more common among older and less well-educated Canadians than others.

Canadian Indians

Some 90 percent of Canadians—almost the same proportion as in 1975 and 1980—continue to say they feel comfortable around Canadian Indians. Over the past decade there has been an increase in such sentiments in all regions except Quebec, where the level has remained close to 90 percent (see Table 5). There has, however, been a rise since 1980 (from 6 percent to 22 percent) in the proportion of those who feel Indians have excessive power in the country's affairs, particularly in the West. At the same time, some 50 percent of Canadians continue to maintain that native people have too little power in the nation's affairs. With respect to intermarriage, 25 percent of Canadians were opposed to Indians marrying Whites in 1975; that figure has now fallen to 16 percent. Regional variations in attitudes toward native people tend to be minor, but are slightly more negative on the Prairies. Age and education are not consistently related to positive or negative attitudes, suggesting the importance of additional factors.

Jews

The 1980s have been seen by many as a time of accelerated anti-Semitism. However, the surveys give limited support to such an impression. The proportion of Canadians who claim they "feel at ease" with Jews has remained steady since 1975, at just over 90 percent. There has been a noticeable decrease—from 28 percent to 14 percent to 11 percent—in the perception that Jews have too much power. In addition, opposition to Jews marrying Protestants and Catholics has declined marginally from about 21 percent in 1975 to a current 17 percent. To the extent anti-Jewish sentiments exist, they differ very little by region of the country—with the exception of a marginal increase in negative feelings on the Prairies since 1980. Negative feelings for the population as a

Table 6
Perception of National Power of Various Groups by Region: 1985, 1980, 1975; by Age and Education: 1985

	% Indicating Have "Too Much Power"				
	Indo/Pak.	Can. Ind.	Jew	Black	Oriental
Nationally					
1985	14	22	11	5	7
1980	16	6	14	**	**
1975	**	7	28	**	**
British Columbia					
1985	21	22	2	1	4
1980	15	4	7	**	**
1975	**	9	18	**	**
Prairies					
1985	27	29	16	7	13
1980	14	11	8	**	**
1975	**	16	20	**	**
Ontario					
1985	14	8	12	6	8
1980	22	2	12	**	**
1975	**	4	23	**	**
Quebec					
1985	2	2	11	3	3
1980	6	6	22	**	**
1975	**	4	46	**	**
Atlantic					
1985	15	15	11	8	11
1980	20	12	13	**	**
1975	**	14	20	**	**
1985					
18–34	13	16	8	4	9
35–54	10	11	13	5	4
55 +	20	8	14	6	9
Degree or more	8	8	9	2	4
HS – PS	15	14	12	6	8
Less than HS	20	12	15	7	13

**Item not included in the 1975 survey.

Table 7

Attitudes Toward Intermarriage by Region: 1985, 1980, 1975; by Age and Education: 1985

	% Disapproving						
	White Black	White Indo/Pak.	White Oriental	White Can. Ind.	Prot. Jew	Jew Cath.	Prot. Cath.
Nationally							
1985	28	28	23	16	16	18	11
1980	37	34	26	20	17	20	12
1975	43	42	34	25	20	22	14
British Columbia							
1985	15	17	11	11	11	12	12
1980	19	22	13	15	12	18	11
1975	30	33	21	19	17	18	13
Prairies							
1985	25	28	21	17	16	18	18
1980	39	38	29	29	18	22	16
1975	44	44	39	34	25	27	19
Ontario							
1985	30	29	23	13	13	14	14
1980	44	42	30	19	15	17	8
1975	48	46	36	26	16	20	10
Quebec							
1985	29	27	24	16	21	24	14
1980	28	24	21	17	17	19	12
1975	36	36	31	20	23	21	15
Atlantic							
1985	37	36	34	31	24	27	27
1980	52	40	34	27	25	31	21
1975	59	50	46	37	23	31	15
1985							
18–34	13	15	10	7	8	11	16
35–54	27	25	22	16	15	15	10
55 +	56	53	46	33	33	36	22
Degree or more	16	14	12	7	14	16	7
HS – PS	29	29	24	18	15	17	10
Less than HS	52	52	44	29	30	34	24

whole are somewhat more prevalent among older people, and among those with less education.

Blacks and Orientals

Approximately 90 percent of Canadians say they feel at ease with Blacks and Orientals. Only about 5 percent see either group as having "too much power." Opposition to intermarriage has declined since 1975 from 43 percent to 28 percent for Blacks and 34 percent to 23 percent for Orientals (see Tables 5, 6, and 7). Regional differences in attitudes toward either group are fairly small. However, there is a tendency for British Columbians to express the most positive sentiments. People on the Prairies have seemingly become slightly more negative toward members of these two groups since 1980. Attitudes concerning Blacks and Orientals differ somewhat by education, but negligibly by age, except for intermarriage, where the relationship is negative.

Conclusion

These findings indicate that bilingualism is gradually becoming accepted across the country. Yet, the process is fairly slow, with receptivity particularly cold in western Canada. Differences by age and education, however, suggest that the level of acceptance will continue to increase with time.

In theory, the multicultural ideal is endorsed by a majority of people in every region of the country. However, about 60 percent acknowledge that discrimination continues to exist in their communities. Still, one-third of these people think things are getting better, and there are some signs that such may be the case. The surveys reveal that there has been a mild softening of attitudes on the part of both Anglophones and Francophones. Slightly less negative views of Indo-Pakistanis, Natives, Jews, Blacks, and Orientals also seem apparent.

This is not to say that racist and ethnocentric attitudes have been relegated to history. On the contrary, the surveys document their ongoing presence. The Prairies, for example, appear to have regressed slightly since 1980—perhaps in part reflecting anxiety associated with the region's economic downturn.

Yet the news concerning policy realization is far from all bad. Canada may still be a long way away from full cultural and racial harmony. But in the post-1969 years since bilingualism and multiculturalism were officially enshrined, in the midst of frequent charges of rising racism and intergroup conflict, the situation shows signs of steadily improving. The mosaic is becoming more than a myth.

part III

Ethnic identity and solidarity

Theoretical Frameworks in the Study of Ethnic Identity[†]

ARNOLD DASHEFSKY

There seems to be both academic and political recognition of a resurgence of interest in ethnicity and ethnic identity. Witness the rise of black and other ethnic study programs and U.S. Congressional passage of a bill on Ethnic Heritage Studies. (For a general explanation of the reasons for this interest see Glazer and Moynihan 1970.) Despite the fact that sociologists, psychologists, and anthropologists have been studying ethnic identity before it came into fashion, there is, nevertheless, a good deal of confusion as to the nature of ethnic identity. (For some conceptual clarification see Dashefsky 1972.) In part, this may be due to the different theoretical biases to which researchers in these disciplines adhere. It is the intention of this paper to develop the distinctions among several theoretical frameworks that have been utilized to study ethnic identity with the goal of highlighting the different facets of identity each examines. In this way some order may be introduced that might lead to a broadly conceived cross-disciplinary social psychology of ethnicity.

In his book *The Structure of Scientific Revolutions* (1962) Thomas Kuhn noted that unlike the various physical and natural sciences wherein one paradigm predominates for each, in the social sciences several competing theoretical frameworks are present. This means that in sociology or social psychology no one theoretical position is the basis for most research. Rather the whole body of theory and research can be organized within several schools. What holds all of the works together in each school of thought is a broad set of assumptions about human behavior. These shared assumptions define the nature of the theoretical

[†]"Theoretical Frameworks in the Study of Ethnic Groups: Toward a Social Psychology of Ethnicity," *Ethnicity* 2 (1975): 10–18. This is a revised version of a seminar paper presented at the annual meeting of the American Sociological Association, New Orleans, August 1972. The author wishes to thank Joseph Zygmunt for his very helpful comments on an earlier draft of this paper.

orientation; but they may not be equated with a theory, which is a logically interrelated set of assumptions, definitions, and propositions that explain some aspect of reality.

The theoretical frameworks that have been employed to conceptualize and operationalize the nature of being ethnic have emerged from sociology and psychology. This is not to say that all studies of ethnic identity have been derived from a clearly recognizable theoretical position. Many have not; but when they have, such studies have generally drawn on at least one of four frameworks: sociocultural, interactionist, group dynamicist, and psychoanalytic.

We may classify these four theoretical orientations along two axes as shown in Table 1: their ontology (theory of reality) and their methodology. On the ontological axis one can classify a theoretical orientation according to its emphasis on the extent to which the individual's behavior is best understood as part of a larger whole (macro-) or best understood apart from it (micro-). On the methodological axis one can classify a theoretical framework on the basis of its reliance on the more sociological methods of the field study, survey research, or sociohistorical analysis or on the more psychological methods of experimental or clinical studies.

In the upper left cell the *sociocultural* orientation represents a macro-sociological approach in which identity is studied in relationship to social structure and culture. In the lower left cell the *interactionist* approach may be viewed as micro-sociological in which identity is viewed in relationship to the mediating symbols in social relationships. In the upper right cell the *group dynamicist* position is seen as a macro-psychological approach in which identity is studied in relation to the group context.[1] The fourth cell represents a micro-psychological approach embodied in the *behaviorist* (and reinforcement) tradition in which identity is explained in terms of reinforced responses to stimuli. Nevertheless, there is little research on ethnicity in this framework because of the difficulty of studying ethnicity a) in the laboratory and b) in terms of the mechanistic stimulus-response model, both of which are fundamental assumptions in this tradition. Rather, the fourth alternative I shall deal with is the *psychoanalytic* perspective, which also represents a macro-psychological viewpoint in that ethnic identity is explained in relationship to unconscious processes that transcend the physiological functioning of the human body and shape the entire personality structure.[2]

The classifications in Table 1 are useful not in the sense that rigid boundaries exist separating these theoretical frameworks, but as a

Table 1
Theoretical Orientations in the Social Psychology of Ethnicity

| | | Methodology | |
		Sociology	Psychology
Ontology	Macro-	Sociocultural	Group Dynamicist
			Psychoanalytic
	Micro-	Interactionist	Behaviorist

heuristic device for separating out the alternative assumptions of each. Indeed, we may see the mutual influences of these positions along the axes of either a shared ontology or a shared methodology. For example, along the ontological axis the interactionist position was an attempt to rebut the mechanistic image of human beings of the behaviorist position and thereby created the impetus for a new methodology; along the methodological axis the group dynamicists went beyond the behaviorist experimentation with dogs to that of primate and human subjects and in the course of doing so developed a new ontology.

For each of these four frameworks the major *assumptions* will be set forth and an *illustration* of the treatment of ethnic identity will be briefly discussed. An examination of the original works cited in the illustrations will be helpful in following the points raised.

Sociocultural

Assumptions

The sociocultural framework represents a macro-sociological approach to the issue of ethnic identity. Among its major assumptions are the following:

A1. An individual's behavior occurs in the context of ongoing social and cultural systems.

A2. The social system defines the relationship among individuals (or social structure), and the cultural system defines the mutual expectations individuals share (or normative structure).

From these assumptions we can derive at least two propositions:

P1. Human behavior may be understood as the result of cumulated historical experiences that have shaped the social and cultural systems.

P2. The study of human behavior in the context of social and cultural systems reduces the importance of studying attitudes, perceptions, and self-conceptions on the individual and interpersonal levels.

Illustration

Gordon, particularly in his discussion of *The Subsociety and the Subculture* (1964: 19–30), reviews the historical origins of ethnicity and ethnic identity. From the Pleistocene hunter to the ancient Assyrian to the medieval European serf to the contemporary American, the individual tended to respond to the question "Who are you?" in terms of membership in a certain people. Such a discussion of ethnic identity by Gordon points to the significance of viewing the humans as a product of their cultural (and historical) experience (A1, P1). Moreover, Gordon's designation of his discussion as dealing with the subsociety and the subculture illustrates the importance in the sociocultural framework of dealing with culture and society as fundamental units (A2, P2). Furthermore, Gordon's reference to the *expectations* for being a Protestant, Catholic, or a Jew in American society indicates the significance of the analysis of the normative structure for understanding ethnic identity (A2).

Gordon's study of the extent of assimilation, relying on a sociocultural perspective and utilizing in part a sociohistorical analysis, parallels the more social psychological concern with ethnic identity. Gordon emphasizes the degree of assimilation of ethnic group members and the nature of their *social identity*, i.e., the extent to which individuals are categorized by others as members of an ethnic group (or age or occupational categories, etc.).

Interactionist

Assumptions

Rose (1962) has attempted to formalize the major assumptions and derived propositions in the interactionist approach. Among the assumptions he has postulated are the following:

A1. The humans live in a symbolic world.

A2. The humans are stimulated and stimulate others through symbols.

A3. The humans learn through symbolic communication the expectations for their behavior.

A4. Symbols and their meanings and values frequently occur in complex clusters such as roles which guide the individual's behavior.

A5. The humans ability to think permits an assessment of their course of action.

From these assumptions Rose derives two propositions:

P1. Humans can predict each other's behavior and adjust their own behavior about their predictions.

P2. Humans define themselves in relationship to other persons and situations.

Illustration

The discussion of "Group Identification and the Minority Community" by Rose and Rose (1965: 247–52) offers several points of illustration of the major assumptions of the interactionist perspective as they are applied to the study of ethnic identity. The Roses focus on the ethnic group as a minority and emphasize the point that minority group members must "consider themselves" to be a minority. We remember that human beings define themselves in relationship to others (P2). Furthermore, a high sense of group identification involves giving "great weight to its common understandings." Here we see the importance of shared symbols and their meanings and values (A4) for shaping ethnic identity. These two points reveal the interactionist approach to ethnic identity as conceptualized in terms of *group identification*, which is associated with a parallel *self-conception* (i.e., the organized set of attitudes one holds about oneself). In addition, the importance of communication is noted in the role of the minority religious institutions, newspapers, and schools and the use of in-group words and allusions, all of which symbolically reinforce identification to the ethnic minority community (A3) and tend to produce the parallel self-conception.

No one article, however, can adequately portray all of the nuances of a particular theoretical perspective. Rose and Rose, for example, omitted references to the interpersonal sources of group identification, e.g., family and peers, although they stressed the intergroup aspect.

Group Dynamicist

Assumptions

The group dynamicists represent a macro-sociological approach to the study of ethnic identity. Their main assumptions are the following:

A1. Individual's organization of their perceptual world is dependent on the surrounding stimuli.

A2. The surrounding stimuli include the physical and social environments.

A3. The study of human behavior involves an examination of the forces operating in a given moment.

Deutsch and Krauss (1965: 16–17) have developed some propositions which may be viewed as deriving from the above:

P1. "In organized social interactions, some of the patterns of interaction will remain invariant despite replacement of the individuals participating in the interaction."

P2. "The meaning of the behavior of individuals will be very much influenced by their perceived social role and by the perceived social context or frame of reference in which it occurs."

P3. "Social relations involve the relations of at least two people and, as such, are not completely predictable from knowledge of the isolated individuals."

Illustration

Allport, in his discussion of the "Formation of In-groups" (1958: 27–46), presents the implications of the group dynamicist orientation for the study of prejudice and in so doing indicates the bearing of that approach on the study of ethnic identity. Indeed, *in-group loyalty* (or ethnic group identification) is built up as the individual learns about out-group hostility (or prejudice). This discussion reflects the group dynamicist position in several ways. The description of the botanist whose sympathies and antipathies vary according to how he defines his relation to others suggests that social relations cannot be predicted from knowledge of the isolated individual (P3). The varying perceptions of two Americans with respect to the national in-group suggests that persons' organization of their perception depends on what stimuli (s)he chooses to perceive (A1). The discussion of the relationship between reference group and in-group as it bears on the "self-hating" black person suggests that in order to understand a person's behavior both the perceived social role (drawn from the reference group) and the perceived social context (dependent on the in-group) have to be taken into account (P2). Finally, the conceptualization of in-group loyalties into concentric circles suggests that each loyalty is a kind of force field pulling the individual to it and that the attractions may vary at different times (A3).

It is important to note that Allport was merely summarizing the position of the group dynamicists with respect to prejudice and ethnic identity. He tends to hold to a more individual rather than collective approach that stresses personality formation and development. Nevertheless, his statement is one of the best summaries available. Indeed, Allport points out one of the weaknesses of the group dynamicist position: It fails to provide a developmental approach to the study of ethnic identity. Rather than dealing with the socialization of ethnic persons, it focuses on attitude formation and change in the context of the forces operating in a given moment. Moreover, it seems to link outgroup hostility (i.e., prejudice) and in-group loyalty (i.e., ethnic identification) as in direct relationship. Such a conceptualization may apply more to those in a population who may be described as possessing an "authoritarian personality" and a penchant for polarizing relationships into "it's us or them." Actually, individuals are able to harmonize to some extent ethnic solidarity without excessive prejudice toward the outgroup. As Allport suggests, however, it is not a frequent occurrence; but it is possible.

Psychoanalytic

Assumptions

The psychoanalytic approach rests upon several fundamental assumptions initially set forth by Sigmund Freud. Among the more important ones are the following:

A1. Sexual instincts or drives (including love and affection) underlie human behavior.

A2. The human personality is rooted in the dialectic between the id (individual) and the superego (society), which is synthesized in the ego as outcome.

A3. Sexual pleasure is found in different zones of the body in varying stages of the development of the human organism.

A4. Human beings engage in unconscious mental activity.

Among the many propositions derived from these assumptions two stand out:

P1. The inner dynamics or psychodynamics resulting from the sexual drives of the human being manifest themselves in terms of specific attitudes and behavior.

P2. Adult characteristics depend on the previous psychosexual development of the human being.

Illustration

Erikson in his discussion of "Race and the Wider Identity" (1968: 295–320) presents a psychoanalytic approach to the study of ethnic identity. For Erikson (1963) identity or *ego identity* refers to the psychological core of what the individual means to himself or herself. It is primarily an unconscious phenomenon that results from a series of childhood identifications and passes through a crisis period in adolescence. His discussion of the inferiority feelings and self-hate that black people feel as victims of racism and the defense mechanisms they rely on suggests the importance of understanding the psychodynamics of the personality (P1). Furthermore, the emphasis on the role of the parents (the mother being primary) on the subsequent development of identity points to the importance of the developmental stages through which the child must pass in order to become an adult (P2). As a final illustration, Erikson's attack on the "Who am I?" view of identity associated with the work of sociologists Kuhn and McPartland (1954) suggests his concern with the need to understand identity in terms of unconscious forces rather than on the level of conscious thinking and speaking (A4).

It is Erikson's view in *Identity Youth and Crisis* (1968) that the unfolding structuring of identity is built up through a series of inner conflicts in varying stages of the life cycle from infancy to old age. Identity, however, is crystallized through a set of crises during adolescence which reflect each of the inner conflicts previously experienced or subsequently to be experienced in various stages of the life cycle. It is this recognition of the ongoing nature of socialization which at one and the same time represents a departure from Freud and an affinity for the sociological position. Despite these insights the difficulty as with psychoanalytic works in general is to establish the truth by empirical test rather than by persuasive example.

Summary and Implications

It has been noted in other contexts (e.g., Van den Berghe 1967) that the study of ethnic relations lacks sufficient theoretical integration. In this paper we suggest that the study of ethnic identity may rely on one of at least four theoretical frameworks for its point of departure: sociocultural, interactionist, group dynamicist, and psychoanalytic. For each of these frameworks the major assumptions and derived propositions were set forth and an illustrative example of the treatment of ethnic identity was discussed.

The examination of these theoretical frameworks should be amplified by reference to specific substantive studies.[3] Future study should link the more common emphasis on substantive and/or applied concerns to the particular theoretical framework. In this way, the examination of diverse ethnic identities may be integrated into the larger body of theory, thereby further developing a social psychology of ethnicity.

Notes

1. Both the group dynamicist and sociocultural traditions represent macro-approaches. They both share the point of view that to understand the individual's behavior one has to look at the larger system in which behavior is enmeshed.

Nevertheless, while the socioculturalists stress the role of historical experiences, the group dynamicists ignore them.

2. In this sense the psychodynamic processes represent the unit of analysis and the larger whole refers to the body. In its more socially anchored neo-Freudian formulation the individual is the unit of analysis and the societal or group context represents the larger whole. In this connection it is interesting to note that the anthropological perspective on ethnic identity derives from the psychoanalytic and sociocultural approaches, frequently in a fused form as in the case of Kardiner and Ovesey's *The Mark of Oppression* (1951). Perhaps, this is testimony to the essentially macro-approach of the psychoanalytic perspective which facilitates its convergence with the sociocultural framework.

3. In the sociocultural approach, see, e.g., Silberman (1964: 109–22) on blacks; McFee (1968: 1096–1103) and Bushnell (1968: 1108–16) on Indians. In the interactionist approach, see, e.g., Farris and Brymer (1970: 411–25) on Chicanos; Dashefsky and Shapiro (1974) and Sartre (1948) on Jews. In the group dynamicist approach see, e.g., Lewin (1948: 148–58) on Jews. In the psychoanalytic approach see, e.g., Grier and Cobbs (1968) and Fanon (1967) on blacks. There is an abundance of data on Afro-Americans and Jewish Americans with respect to ethnic identity, but much less data appear available for other ethnic groups. Recently more studies on ethnic identity have appeared on the more oppressed ethnic groups, e.g., Mexican-Americans, Puerto Rican-Americans, and Native-Americans; and little has appeared on Euro-American ethnic groups, e.g., Italian-Americans, Polish-Americans, and Greek-Americans. Certainly the question of ethnic identity may be more salient for the former, but it may still be a relevant issue for the latter.

Indian Cultural Diversity[†]

JOHN A. PRICE

Culture is a category of behavior which includes a material, a social, an ideological, and a communications dimension. *Material culture* is observable in the physical products, tools, and constructions of humans, such as food, shelter, and clothing. *Social culture* is directly observable only in the fleeting interactions between humans, but because these interactions are so repetitive and predictive we say they are institutionalized in economics, politics, kinship, and so forth. *Ideological culture* is observable in the meanings and emotions that are conveyed through speech, writing, gestures, and arts. *Communications culture* is the learned patterns of speech, writing, gestures, and arts as media or carrier systems for meanings and emotions. We speak of small units of culture as *culture traits*.

In order to work with common baselines of cultures in comparative studies, we try to reconstruct what the Indian cultures were like prior to European influence; this is the *prehistoric* period. Following this is the *protohistoric* period, which describes the transition from European influence to written description. During this period, a few European explorers, along with trade goods and horses, traveled among the Native peoples before the Natives had been extensively described. The *ethnographic present* refers to the period during which a culture is initially described; it also refers to the grammatical use of the present tense for historical description, as in "the Blackfoot hunt buffalo on horseback." In this paper we focus on prehistoric Indian culture.

Prehistory: Early Cultural Evolution

Humans entered the New World about 29,000 years ago, coming from Siberia by way of large river valleys in Alaska and Canada that were more often ice free in a time of nearly continent wide ice sheets. A site

†*Indians of Canada: Cultural Dynamics* (Scarborough, Ontario: Prentice-Hall Canada Inc., 1975), pp. 37–54. This is a revised version of the original chapter.

near Old Crow River in the Yukon dates to 23–27,000 B.C. In association with the bones of now extinct woolly elephants called mammoths, the archaeologists found butchery tools and what appears to be a skin scraper made by cutting serrations at the tip of a caribou shinbone. The addition of stone projectile points to the ends of wooden spears seems to come into widespread use after about 13,000 B.C., after the Yukon-Mackenzie Corridor opened up permanently through the glaciers. Then mammoth hunters thrived in the Great Plains east of the Rocky Mountains.

Between 6–3,000 B.C. there was an *altithermal*, a period that was warmer and drier than today; most of the glaciers melted, and over 100 species of large animals died out, probably in part due to the overkill by the rising population of hunters. With the rise of human populations and the decline in the species of mammals, North American culture underwent a fundamental shift, away from the Paleolithic concentration on hunting large mammals toward the Mesolithic culture's broadened and intensified use of all available food resources in each environmental niche. Hunting continued, but it expanded to include smaller mammals and birds and in some environments was even largely replaced by such foods as fish, shellfish, and wild rice. Cultures adapted more to the local environments and there was a lot of environmentally related inventiveness: in new forms of housing (igloos, tipis, wigwams, longhouses, and cedar plank houses); clothing; and transportation (sleds, toboggans, kayaks, birchbark canoes, the round coracle boat in the Plains, and the dugout cedar canoes of British Columbia).

The Archaic is a late Mesolithic culture (about 5–1,000 B.C.) that is characterized by ground stone axes to cut wood, a few copper artifacts, and village cemeteries. The northern Shield Archaic extended from the Maritimes across northern Quebec and Ontario to the Keewatin District of the Northwest Territories and is characterized by hunting caribou, moose, and wild fowl. This seems to be the ancestral culture to people like the Cree, Montagnais, Naskapi, and Micmac. The Laurentian Archaic in southern Ontario, Quebec, New York, and Vermont hunted deer, elk, beaver, and bear. They used the spear thrower, did a lot of fishing, and used many forest plants. They had cemeteries where they covered the bodies with red ochre and placed burial goods with the body. The Ojibwa, with traits like wild rice gathering, were close to the Laurentian Archaic when they were first described by European explorers.

The Arctic Small Tool tradition (3–1,000 B.C.) is the first far northern form of the Mesolithic; whale, walrus, seal, and caribou hunters were evident above the tree line. A more distinctly Inuit culture developed in northern Alaska about 1,000 B.C. and spread along the Canadian coasts and into Greenland, Labrador, and Newfoundland, aided in its spread by the development of fine skin-covered boats, the small hunting kayak, and the large umiak. The Inuit had tailored clothing, snow goggles, semi-subterranean houses, oil lamps, and ground slate and ivory tools. By the time of the widespread Thule Inuit of A.D. 1,000, there were sleds drawn by dogs, harpoons with sealskin floats, sinew-backed bows, the man's crooked knife and the woman's semilunar knife, and the tambourine drum.

The subarctic site of Klo-kut at a caribou crossing point on the Porcupine River in the Yukon shows 1,500 years of Dene-like culture, ancestral to the current Dene-speaking peoples of the region, such as Kutchin, Tutchone, and Hare. There is continuity in semi-subterranean houses, serrated and stemmed stone arrowpoints, barbed bone and arrowheads, fish spears, some copper projectile points and knives, and birchbark baskets. Broad similarities across the subarctic include snow-shoes, toboggans, canoes, shamanism, bear ceremonialism, fishing weirs, and game drives.

In southern Canada there are three regions where Native societies evolved beyond the level of the simple hunting *band* society with its small, semi-nomadic groups, egalitarian politics, and sharing economics. The more advanced societies were in southern Ontario and Quebec with the agricultural Iroquoian-speaking *tribes*; along the British Columbia coast with its fishing tribes and *chiefdoms*; and then, using horses introduced into the Americas by the Spaniards, the tribal level buffalo hunters of the Plains, such as the Blackfoot of Alberta.

Agriculture was first brought into Canada a little prior to A.D. 600, in the Grand River area of southern Ontario, probably by the Princess Point people who seem to be the ancestors of the Neutral, Petun, and Huron. They had stone platform pipes, ceramics, small circular burial mounds, and blade flake tools. They seemed to have farmed the river mud flats as part of an annual migratory round of hunting, fishing, and plant gathering. By about A.D. 800 corn farming in upland areas was a significant subsistence activity. Beans and squash were added to the farming after about A.D. 1,400 and made a major contribution to nutrition.

An increasing localization of pottery techniques and motifs indicates that the women potters stayed in their home villages, an early sign of the matrilocal postmarital residence that led to the matrilineal kinship structure of the Iroquoian-speaking societies. Eventually large villages were built, up to ten acres with rows of multi-family, quonset-shaped longhouses. The villages had defensive features, indicating extensive warfare, such as a surrounding palisade ring of high upright logs. After A.D. 1,400 the Hurons generally withdrew from the Toronto area and formed a defensive concentration in the Midland area between Lakes Huron, Couchiching, and Simcoe.

While the Iroquoian peoples achieved a *tribal* level of evolution (pan-tribal politics and religion, reciprocal economics, large permanent villages, etc.), several Pacific coast societies went even farther and developed to the *chiefdom* level (centralized politics and religion, redistributive economics, elaborate social ranking with slavery, elaborate music and fine arts, etc.). In a worldwide context these west coast cultures were the most unusual in Canada, since chiefdoms were based on fishing, rather than agriculture.

The history of the 54 Native languages of Canada adds another dimension to our understanding of Canadian Native heritage. Beothuk in Newfoundland, Kutenai in southeast B.C., and Haida on the Queen Charlotte Islands seem to be "isolates"—languages with relationships to other languages that are so ancient, in the order of several thousand years, that we cannot trace the connections. Two are on large islands and the third in a mountainous area where enclaves of physical isolation kept these groups somewhat culturally isolated. Tlingit of northern B.C. is probably a distant member of the Dene phylum that occupies the western subarctic of the Yukon, northern B.C., and southern Northwest Territories.

Tsimshian in northern coastal B.C. might be related to the Penutian languages of Oregon, California, and Mexico. Then the Wakashan and Salishan families of languages are probably related to each other when we go back far enough in time, in a Mosan phylum of languages. B.C. is linguistically and culturally the most diversified and historically complex province in Canada in prehistoric times because of the wealth of its riverine and marine resources and its ecological diversity.

Inuktitut is a relatively recent arrival into Canada, only about 3,000 years ago, and it is related to the Eskimo, Aleut, and Chukotan languages of Alaska and Siberia. The ancient and widespread family of the eastern Subarctic hunters is Algonquian while the Iroquoian languages seem to have spread just in the last 1,400 years into southern Ontario and Quebec with the population expansion that agriculture allowed. Having briefly reviewed prehistoric cultural evolution in Canada, let us turn next to examining some prehistoric cultural traits and areas.

Prehistoric Cultural Traits

Some broadly defined traits are universal, such as the use of language, telling of origin stories, living in families, prohibiting incest, gift giving, and holding funeral rites. With more-limited definitions there are traits that correspond to limited historical and ecological areas, such as continents or *cultural areas*, large zones of similar cultures. Aboriginal Canada was not an integrated area: its culture areas overlapped with Alaska, Greenland, and the U.S. There is no unique single trait common to all aboriginal Canadian Indians, though the area had a large proportion of the world's remaining simple hunting band societies at the time of the ethnographic present. The universal traits are particularly those that have survived from an early common historical horizon, and that can persist into new ecological settings and be retained through changes with the evolution of culture. Some of the obvious universals are tools such as stone knives and bows and arrows. There are also social and religious traits that come from an early time horizon and were universally still practised at the time of ethnographic description.

Food

Deadfalls, pitfalls, and snares were in use. Land mammals were occasionally hunted by driving them into water, or, in the Plains, over cliffs or into compounds. Long fences of wood (piles of stones in the Arctic) were occasionally used in driving game. Except for the Blackfoot and Gros Ventres, who did little fishing, all societies had composite fishhooks, fish spears (leisters), gill nets, seines, and fish weirs.

Meat was everywhere dried in smoke or over a fire, though there was little fuel for this in the Arctic. Stone boiling (briefly putting fire-heated stones in a water container) was in use, except in the Arctic for lack of fuel and in Iroquoia where pottery was used. The earth oven was a general western trait. The use of milling stones with a lateral grinding movement was virtually absent, but pounding foods with a stone or wood mortar and pestle was common. Salt was not intentionally gathered or eaten in any Native Canadian society though it was used in many other North American societies. Though never important as a food, dogs were eaten ceremonially in the Pacific, Plains, and Iroquoia and even specially fattened for eating in Iroquoia.

Constructions and Crafts

Hide coverings were used for houses in the Arctic, Subarctic, and Plains; bark in the Subarctic, Iroquoia; and both bark and wood planks in the Pacific. In the east, the conical-tent foundations usually had three poles; and, from the Blackfoot westward, four poles. Defensive palisades were built around villages in both Iroquoia and the Pacific, and the historic Plains adopted the circular arrangement of tents in their camps in part for defence. Iroquoia and the Pacific had multi-family houses and wooden sitting platforms.

All areas had snowshoes. Toboggans were widely used except in the Pacific, but the sled was used only in the Arctic. All had boats: finely tailored hide-covered canoes in the Arctic; bark canoes in the Subarctic and Iroquoia; a bowl-shaped, hide-covered thing called the bull boat or coracle in the Plains; and the great dugout wood canoes of the Pacific.

Clothing was made of skins, finely tailored in the Arctic and semi-tailored elsewhere, except in the Pacific where robes were woven of twisted cedar bark. Twisted and woven fur strip robes were also used, except in the Arctic and Plains where large skins were plentiful. Women usually made all the clothing. They first dressed the skins by scraping, then usually used mashed brains to soften the skins. The Inuit and some Pacific societies soaked sea mammal hides in urine to remove the excess grease. Soft and continuous-soled moccasins were used, except in a few Inuit societies. The moccasin with a separate hard sole was also used in the Arctic and Plains. Only women made basketry and it was made everywhere except in the Plains. Porcupine quill decoration was common, except in the Arctic and Pacific. Tattooing was in use in the Arctic, western Subarctic, and Pacific.

Rituals and Entertainments

All had life crisis ceremonies for birth, puberty, marriage, and death. A girl's puberty ceremony began at her first menstruation. The first large game killed by a boy was treated ceremonially and often given away to people from outside the household. The dead were placed on platforms or in trees in one form of disposal, except in the Arctic where there are no trees. First-fruits rites were held each year for the first game or fish or plants harvested. Bears were everywhere treated with special ceremony when they were killed. All societies used shamanistic curing and divination techniques. All enjoyed water vapor sweating. Bear ceremonialism, shamanism, and water vapor sweating are all boreal traits that are found in the northern parts of Europe and Asia, as well as North America.

All had dancing, drumming, singing, and story telling. The North American Natives were unusual in the world in the extent of their gambling, particularly with hand games in which one side hides small marked and unmarked objects made of wood or bone, and the other side guesses the location of the marked object. Dice games were popular, as was story telling with string figures. Tobacco was probably aboriginal only in southern Canada, particularly Iroquoia, Plains, and Plateau; and had more ceremonial uses than are found today.

Prehistoric Cultural Areas

The Arctic and Subarctic areas tend to run east-west while the Iroquoia, Plains, Plateau, and Pacific areas all run north-south. All areas are cut by the U.S.-Canada border and the majority of the Plains and Plateau areas are on the U.S. side. The Arctic is an unusual culture area in that it had such a severe climate for humans that it was occupied very late in human history and by only one society, the Inuit, who are relatively homogeneous. Inuit culture extends along the coastlines from the eastern tip of Siberia through northern Alaska and Canada, to Greenland. Thus the Inuit today live under the administration of the U.S.S.R., the U.S., Canada, and Greenland, a protectorate of Denmark.

The Subarctic is the largest area, stretching from interior Alaska across the Yukon and Northwest Territories through northern Ontario and Quebec, to the Atlantic provinces. It is an area of boreal forests with long, cold winters. The population densities here were very low and the pattern of life was a semi-nomadic round of hunting and fishing within a territory by small groups. The major items of material culture usually use hide or bark.

Iroquoia is a sub-area of the agricultural eastern woodlands, where there was some hunting and fishing, but Natives depended primarily on corn, beans, and squash. They made bark canoes and covered their "longhouses" with bark. They made pottery and lived a fairly sedentary life in large, well-defended villages.

Canada has only the northern tip of the Plains, a large zone that extends along the east flank of the Rocky Mountains and into the flat grasslands from southern Alberta and Saskatchewan to Texas. The major food was buffalo, which was hunted on foot by small bands much like the Subarctic hunting of caribou, until the Europeans introduced the horse. Then there was a very rapid diffusion of new traits and the evolution of a new culture in the Plains. The material culture then focused on horses and the buffalo.

Figure 1
Prehistoric Cultural Areas

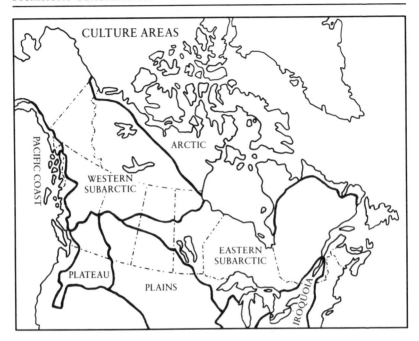

CULTURE AREAS

ARCTIC

PACIFIC COAST

WESTERN SUBARCTIC

EASTERN SUBARCTIC

PLATEAU

PLAINS

IROQUOIA

The Plateau area of the western mountains has been called a foraging area because of the pattern there of gathering a very diverse mix of plant, fish, and animal foods. The Plateau people turned to small and scattered food sources. However, in the Canadian portion of the Plateau there was a strong orientation toward fishing the headwaters of the Fraser, Thompson, and Columbia Rivers.

The Pacific is an area of indented coastlines with fiords and steep mountains, heavy rainfall, a mild climate, dense forests, and abundant fish. The population was the largest and most sedentary of any of the culture areas. Salmon was the principal food, taken particularly in runs in the spring and summer by means of traps or weirs in the rivers. The technology made wide use of the straight-grained cedar wood for canoes, plank houses, boxes, dishes, and carvings. Cedar bark was twisted and woven into mats and robes. Finer artistic weaving used the hair of mountain goats and domestic dogs. The social organization included social grading that could be classified as ranging from nobles to commoners and slaves. This social gradation was organized through the kinship system and validation ceremonies we call potlatches.

The population density estimates in Table 1 were taken from Driver (1969: map 6). A more conservative but fairly reliable source on aboriginal populations is Kroeber (1934). His material includes the following estimates for Canada and the adjacent areas (see Table 2). The northern densities of 1–2 per 100 square kilometers are among the lowest in the world while the Pacific densities are high for fishing societies.

Table 1
Culture Area Traits

	Arctic	Subarctic	Iroquoia	Plains	Pacific
Population per 100 square km	0–10	0–60	25–150	10–60	25–375 +
Level of Evolution	bands	bands	tribes	tribes	chiefdoms
Language Families	Eskimo-Aleut	Athapascan Algonquian Beothuk	Iroquoian	Algonquian Athapascan Siouan	Tlingit Haida Tsimshian Wakashan Salish
Major Cooking	stone lamp toasting	roast	soups in pottery	roast	smoked fish
Houses: Winter	igloo	earth lodge	bark longhouse	hide tipi	plank house
Summer	hide tent	bark/hide wigwam	bark wigwam	hide tipi	mat lodge
Transportation	kayak umiak sled	bark canoe toboggan	bark canoe toboggan	travois	dugout canoe
Intergroup Conflicts	rare feuds	rare feuds	warfare with torture	horse and scalp raids	raids with slavery

If estimates are made about Canada proper then about 60,000 have to be taken from the total for those living in the U.S. However, Kroeber tended to underestimate the early effects of White diseases. For example, my estimate for Iroquoia is 56,000, or 32 per cent more than Kroeber's. Thus, the aboriginal population of Canada was probably somewhat over 300,000.

Table 2
Population Densities by Area

	Population	Territory (100 km²)	Density
Arctic	30,900	15,057	2
Subarctic—Micmac, Abnaki	7,300	3,285	2
—Ojibwa, Ottawa, Algonkin	37,300	5,188	7
—Cree, Montagnais, Naskapi	23,000	25,677	1
—Athapascan	33,930	38,944	1
Iroquoia	42,500	4,421	10
Plains	50,500	13,978	4
Plateau	47,650	6,600	7
Pacific—Salish	23,700	725	33
—Wakashan, Bella Coola	17,300	594	29
—Tlingit, Haida, Tsimshian, Haisla	28,100	1,666	17
Totals	342,180	155,079	2.2

Social Institutional Evolution

Just as we use such broad ecological types as Arctic, Subarctic, and Plains, we find that broad evolutionary categories are useful. When thoughts about evolution were quite different in the nineteenth century, people used the typology of primitive, barbaric, and civilized. These terms became too loaded in favor of complex societies and were used pejoratively against the simpler societies, on many mistaken assumptions about human nature. As we needed more neutral terms and we needed to make finer distinctions, the terms band, tribe, chiefdom, and state came into use.

The *band*, the simplest category of society, had hunting and gathering food production, a sharing kind of economics, and a style of leadership based on common residence and divisions of labor by sex, age, and ability. Indian women specialized in gathering and processing plants, so we have them to thank for the Neolithic Revolution through the domestication of plants and probably for the invention of a broad range of domestic equipment such as basketry, pottery, and the mortar and pestle. We have the men to thank for our heritage of hunting, warfare, religion, and politics.

The *tribe* developed economic, social, and political ties that are broader in scope than those of bands. Sharing continues to predominate in the intimate sectors of life, such as the household, but the calculations of reciprocity are developed as a basis of economic distribution beyond such spheres. Impersonal trade develops. Lineal kinship groups and other "pan-tribal sodalities" create social ties beyond the residential communities and give political cohesion to the society. Most tribal societies of the world were horticulturalists, with simple hand gardening, but the tribal level was also achieved by some fishing and pastoral societies.

Table 3
A Model of the Evolution of Social Institutions

Stage	Economic Production	Economic Distribution	Political	Religious
State	Agriculture	Administration and markets	Laws and bureaucracy	Priesthoods
Chiefdom	Horticulture, pastoralism, or fishing	Redistribution	Chieftainship	Public dramas
Tribe	"	Reciprocity	Pan-tribal sodalities	Religious societies
Band	Hunting, gathering	Sharing	Residential and task leaders	Curing Food increase

At a more advanced level there develops a central integration of economic, social, political, and religious factors. This is referred to as a *chiefdom* because there is usually a chief and some kind of administrating group that serves as an integrating center to tax and redistribute goods and services and to organize feasts, warfare, major religious ceremonies, and long-distance trade. Chiefdoms typically have elaborate social ranking and a class system, often with some slavery; well developed arts, in part because some people are allowed to specialize as artists; pageantry; and so forth. Beyond the chiefdom the *state* level was achieved with intensive agriculture, a centrally administered economy with markets, a legal structure with a large scale bureaucracy, and priestly (full-time specialists) religions that support the ideology of the state.

These stages are not seen as stable entities, but only as arbitrary slices made on a continuum. Just as we make arbitrary criteria to define where one ecological zone ends and the next begins, we need conventional terms to talk about different degrees of evolutionary complexity. I find it occasionally useful to add the intermediate terms of band-tribe, tribe-chiefdom, and chiefdom-state for a total of seven evolutionary types. A scalogram of sequential traits is an even better description of our current systems model of evolutionary processes.

Carneiro (1968) developed a scale of fifty traits in a rough evolutionary sequence across one-hundred societies around the world. This yields a fairly discrete model of the systematic changes that occur with the expansion in energy available, population growth, political centralization, economic specialization and exchange, and so forth. In Table 4 I have abstracted out the Canadian societies in the sample and made some corrections. The time level is the ethnographic present. There is an element of interpretation in determining the presence or absence of a trait, but we have some precision in our definitions. For example, gift exchange and some sporadic trade exist between individuals in different communities in all societies, but "trade between communities" means some form of regular trade network.

Kinship Systems

Kinship generally is more important in primitive societies than in modern societies, and the studies of kinship have been seen as important to understanding the structure of primitive society. It is a more personal kind of society in which kinfolk are more important in living groups, work groups, and marriage arrangements.

Native people were generally tolerant of diverse kinds of marriage arrangements. For example, *fraternal polyandry*, by which two or more brothers married the same woman, occurred on rare occasions in most societies. For example, if an older brother was hurt and unable to hunt, his younger brother might move in to do the hunting for the household and become a second husband. *Monogamy* was the most common form of marriage and the exclusive form in the Iroquoian societies. *Polygyny*, having more than one wife, occurred in more than 20 per cent of the marriages in ethnographic present times only in the tribal and chiefdom societies of the west. *Sororal polygyny*, by which a man marries two or more sisters, was by far the most common form of plural marriage.

Where a couple live after marriage would be usually determined by economic advantage. In band societies there is a need for flexibility to move where game herds shift, and postmarital residence is usually *bilocal* (in either the husband's or the wife's camp), or *neolocal* (a new camp). In

Table 4
Scalogram of 17 Traits in 9 Societies

Trait	Naskapi	Inuit	Kaska	Ojibwa (Chippewa)	Gros Ventres	Blackfoot	Salish (Clallam)	Iroquois	Kwakiutl
Leader bestows land, slaves or rank									X
Special deference to leaders									X
Full-time craft specialists									X
Supra-provincial organization								X	X
Full-time retainers for leaders									X
Death penalty decreed								X	X
Full-time political leader								X	X
Judicial process								X	X
Neolithic food level					X	X	X	X	X
Craft specialization						X	X	X	X
Significant status differences						X	X	X	X
Communities of 100 or more				X	X	X	X	X	X
Peace-keeping machinery					X	X	X	X	X
Social segments above family			X	X	X	X	X	X	X
Formal political leadership					X	X	X	X	X
Trade between communities				X			X	X	X
Special religious practitioners	X	X	X	X	X	X	X	X	X
Levels	Band	Band	Band	Band-Tribe	Tribe	Tribe	Tribe-Chiefdom	Tribe-Chiefdom	Chiefdom
Traits	1	1	2	4	6	8	9	13	17

Source: Carneiro 1968, with corrections.

farming tribes, such as the Huron, the women produce the bulk of the food and men move into the wife's community, a *matrilocal* pattern. If physical strength or the cooperation of men is emphasized in tribal or chiefdom subsistence economics, then the postmarital residence pattern is usually *patrilocal*, moving into the husband's community.

Mode of postmarital residence seems to be the primary determinant of ideological concepts about descent. If people live with *either* of their parent's kinfolk, or set up a new household, they tend to develop a *bilateral* descent system, an ideology, common to both the Inuit and the modern Canadians, that they equally descended from both sides. If children routinely grow up in an environment dominated by the mother's relatives then a *matrilineal* descent system evolves. Following the ideology of descent, and coordinated with it, is the development of lineal social groups (*lineages*, and a collection of related lineages making a *clan*), lineal inheritance, lineal patterning of marriages, and lineal patterning of kinship terminology. Historical and other influences do sometimes mix up the patterns, so that for example one occasionally finds lineal groups in a society with an ideology of bilateral descent. The most common chain of events seems to be 1) sex roles in subsistence, 2) postmarital residence patterns, 3) ideology of descent, 4) a variety of coordinated kinship forms.

Kinship terminologies (the terms of reference one uses for one's relatives) are internally systematic. This is because there is a correlation between terms and behaviors. Terms are related to a society's social rules respecting incest prohibition, marriage eligibility and preferences, where a married couple will live, reckoning descent, inheritance, and succession to offices and titles. The distinctions between several systems show up in just the terms for what Canadians call aunts, uncles, and cousins. However, since these concepts are so foreign to Canadians, they are difficult for us to understand.

The first comparative study of kinship systems was that of Lewis Henry Morgan, published in 1870 as *Systems of Consanguinity and Affinity of the Human Family*. In the process of studying Iroquois customs he found that they classified kinship relations quite differently from Europeans. They had a *unilineal* system while the European systems are bilateral, tracing descent in both the mother's and father's line. The Iroquois system is female-oriented, while the Europeans are male-oriented; the Iroquois have a *matri*-lineal system while the Europeans tend toward the *patri*-lineal—for instance, they carry on the father's name rather than the mother's name. The centers of matrilineal organization in Canada were the Iroquoians in the east and the Tsimshian and certain neighboring western Dene, such as the Haida, Tlingit, and Kaska. Morgan was also impressed by the fact that the Ojibwa, who were just north of the Iroquoians, had a system that was unilineal like the Iroquois, but it was patrilineal. The rest of the Canadian societies tended to be loosely bilateral in descent.

The *Iroquois* system occurs in many places in the world where the mother is lumped together with her sister and the father with his brother. It bifurcates the parents into their different lineages and merges those of the siblings of the same sex within the two sides. Thus in a bifurcate merging system there is one term for both mother and mother's sister and one term for father and father's brother. The mother's sister behaves somewhat the same as the biological mother so they are covered by the same words. Parallel-cousins, mother's sister's children, are within one's own lineage so they are called brother and sister. Mother's brother's daughter and father's sister's daughter have special terms. They are cross-cousins, in that one crosses from one sex to another in the parental generation in order to trace the kinship connection. The category is important in strongly lineal societies because it is definitely in a different lineage, and is therefore a marriageable category, often a preferred one because it is otherwise socially close. Among the Haida and the Kaska the preferred marriage was between a man and his mother's brother's daughter—a cross-cousin marriage.

Crow is also a bifurcate merging system when the focus is on uncles and aunts, but it is more specific than Iroquois when the focus is on cousin terms. It makes fine distinctions between members of one's own descent group, and broad, lumping categories of the relatives of the parent who is not in one's own descent group. It equates the same-sex members of the in-marrying parent's descent group regardless of generation. Thus, there is lumping across the generations. Iroquois is simply unilineal and can go either way. Both the matrilineal Iroquoians (Huron, Petun, Neutral, and Iroquois) and the patrilineal Ojibwa (as well as the bilateral Cree) used Iroquois cousin terminology. The Ojibwa were only weakly patrilineal. Crow is used in *strongly matrilineal* descent groups.

For example, in the matrilineal Crow system a man's brother's children are referred to by the same terms as his own children: son and daughter. His maternal cross-cousins—mother's brother's children—are also called son and daughter though they are in his own generation. None of these "children" are in his lineage. His parallel cousins are called brother and sister. His paternal cross-cousins, father's sister's children, are called father and father's sister. The only Crow systems in Canada were in the matrilineal block in the northwest: Haida, Tlingit, Tahltan, and Kaska. All these are Dene-speaking peoples.

Another possible system is called Hawaiian. This is a generational, extremely lumping, system associated with bilateral descent. There were Hawaiian systems of cousin terminology in the western groups, such as

Salish, Nootka, Kwakiutl, Carrier, Sekani, Slave, Beaver, and Gros Ventre. Blackfoot had a mixture of Iroquois and Hawaiian elements.

Most Canadians and people of European descent use a system that has such general terms as uncle and aunt that it does not tell whether one is referring to one's mother's or father's side; and terms such as cousin, which ignore both the lineal side and the sex. The technical term for this kind of bilateral terminology is *Eskimo*. This is a simple system in that the main distinction is between lineals (one's parents, grandparents, children, and grandparents) and collaterals (everyone else—aunts, uncles, brothers, sisters, nieces, and nephews). This type of system is found in societies that de-emphasize lineages and typically lack clans. These are societies that emphasize the nuclear family and have no strict rule about where a married couple will live. The simplest *and* the most complex tend to have Eskimo kinship terminology while the intermediate societies tend to have lineal systems.

Table 5
Kinship Traits by Case Studies

	Inuit	Cree	Huron	Blackfoot	Kwakiutl
Polygamy	rare	rare	none	common	common
Postmarital Residence	bilocal	patrilocal	matrilocal	patrilocal	patrilocal
Descent	bilateral	bilateral	matrilineal	bilateral	patrilineal
Lineal Groups	none	none	clans	none	clans
Cousin Terms	Eskimo	Iroquois	Iroquois	Iroquois-Hawaiian	Hawaiian
Aunt Terms	Eskimo	bifurcate-collateral	bifurcate-merging	bifurcate-merging	lineal

In Canada such simple societies as the Inuit, Micmac, Malecite, and Kutenai used Eskimo terminology. However, there are exceptions. Simple societies such as the Ojibwa and Kaska developed lineal features, apparently more because of the diffusion of influences from adjacent societies than from internal structural evolution. We also find relatively complex societies such as the Salish with bilateral descent, Hawaiian cousin terminology; yet they have patrilineal clans. Lineal descent and the appropriate terminology seems to have evolved independently in many cultural traditions around the world, primarily because of patterns of unilocal postmarital residence, lineage work groups, lineage inheritance, and so forth. It did not evolve in all traditions and there were secondary borrowings of lineal ideas and practices between societies. Morgan's early problem of explaining the differences between European, Iroquois, and Ojibwa systems of kinship can only be resolved by a comparative analysis of cultural dynamics.

Conclusion

The specific evolutionary, environmental, and historical heritages of the various Native peoples of Canada have made their adaptations to Canadian society as different from each other as the differences we see in other Canadians. Micmacs, Mohawks, Inuit, and Nootka are at least as different from each other as Canadians with Greek, French, English, and Swedish heritages are different from each other. Canadians will not really understand contemporary Native peoples until we know the differences between Micmacs and Nootka as well as we know the differences between Greeks and Swedes.

The Development of Ideologies in Quebec[†]

MARCEL RIOUX

Historic Outline

In order to understand the recent evolution of ideologies in Quebec, it is necessary to establish where this period fits in the historical context. What ideas did the Quebecois, that is, the Francophone majority, have of themselves and their society? What goals did they, as a group, have and what means did they advocate for attaining them? The interpretation of ideologies proposed here will take two centuries of history into account and will, therefore, necessarily be schematic.

When can we begin to speak of an ideology for the Quebecois? Usually, as soon as a group has proved itself to be a distinct group and a strong enough "we" has been formed to oppose other "we's," individuals appear who define the situation and who clearly explain this collective consciousness. Under the French regime, it seems that the other group, which Canadiens were beginning to oppose, was still too close to them for the birth of an ideology. Canadiens had a feeling of nonidentity toward French metropolitans, but this feeling was not yet used as an explicit concept.

Conquered in 1760, ruined by the war, deprived of their elites, the Quebec peasants spent their first forty years under English domination just surviving and a new elite slowly emerged from their ranks which assumed the function of defining the Quebec community and represent-

†Gerald Gold and Marc-Adelard Tremblay, eds., *Communities and Culture in French Canada* (Toronto: Holt, Rinehart and Winston, 1973). Excerpted from *Revue de l'Institut de Sociologie* 1 (1968): 95–124.

ing it politically. This new Francophone bourgeoisie, made up of people from the liberal professions, was to oppose the mercantile class which, in turn, was to represent the Anglophone minority. This social class made up of the liberal professions took it upon itself to define the Quebec nation: this brings us to our first ideology. Fernand Ouellet wrote that, with the appearance of a national consciousness at the heart of the bourgeoisie, its political vocation was greatly strengthened. From that time on, it no longer defended its class interests or proposed abstract values as far as the people were concerned; it represented the nation and its essential attributes. In 1810, Craig wrote:

> In truth, it seems to be their desire to be considered as forming a separate nation. The *Canadien* nation is their constant expression....[1]

What is the relationship between this bourgeoisie and the people? Fernand Dumont gives the following explanation:

> The fact that this bourgeoisie was, at first, accepted by the people as their natural spokesman is clear, and can be explained, we feel, quite easily. As sons of the people, its members kept the essential attitudes of the peasantry from which they came.[2]

From the turn of the century to the 1830s, this new bourgeoisie got on well with the clergy; both groups had approximately the same views about Canadiens. But soon a division occurred in the Legislative Assembly: "with Papineau, the dream of an autonomous French-Canadian Republic began to take form."[3] The period known as the romantic period in French Canada was to finish badly: the Insurrection in 1837–38 was soon checked. The Church was seen more and more frequently by many of the bourgeoisie elite as an ally of the colonizers. When the Church, with Monseigneur Lartigue as spokesman, condemned the Insurrection, it realized that its directives were not well received in the Montreal region. Monseigneur Lartigue's intervention aroused anger which was expressed through popular demonstrations and violently anticlerical articles in patriotic newspapers. In Montreal, where 1200 *patriotes* paraded in front of the Saint-Jacques Cathedral during Vespers, it was said that the pastoral letter would hasten the "revolution," and in Chambly, three men left the church while the letter was being read. They formed a group to welcome Monseigneur Bourget and the clergy after Mass with cries of "Down with the movement!" and "Vive Papineau!" Elsewhere, priests were treated to the singing of the *Marseillaise* and the *Libera*.[4] In 1834, Papineau had already chastised the Church:

This Act [Quebec Act, 1774] retained all the rights, privileges and power of the clergy (although these advantages are better preserved through the confidence, religious persuasion, and conviction of the people), because it was fast losing its temporal authority with them as far as determining their ideas and opinions was concerned. The clergy eagerly welcomed this Act, took up the government's cause, and, ignoring that of the people, found it good because it was advantageous.[5]

Thus it can be seen that the first ideology of Quebec was formulated by a secular elite who defined Quebec as a nation. Independence was the aim of this nation. In an epilogue to the results of the Insurrection, Etienne Parent, a journalist, wrote in 1839:

There were people, and we were among them, who thought that with the backing and the favour of England, the French Canadians could flatter themselves for having retained and spread their nationality in such a way as to form an independent nation afterwards . . . .[6]

As Fernand Dumont writes:

The Insurrection marks the failure in a sort of spasm of agony of this first attempt to define the situation and the future of the French-Canadian nation.[7]

The Rise of the Ideology of Conservation

The secular bourgeoisie which dominated the Assembly from 1820–1840 acted like a national bourgeoisie and took upon itself the task of defining the Quebec community and its future. It did not cause a great stir among the people who were afraid of the liberalism, anticlericalism, and anti-British ideas of the *patriotes*. On the whole, the clergy remained faithful to the British Crown. Derbyshire, who was an envoy from Durham, "also reported the noteworthy observation of the Abbé Ducharme, *curé* of Sainte-Thérèse":

It was the educated men, the doctors, notaries, and lawyers, who were at the head of the rebellion and were the great seducers of the people, and he seemed to derive from it an argument against educating the lower orders.[8]

That is why, once the Rebellion had been suppressed and its leaders had fled, the clergy could regain its control over the people, with the aid of the British powers. The British, with Governor Durham as their spokesman, became aware of the prevailing situation in Quebec.

Durham stated that he had come to Canada thinking he would find a conflict between the people and the executive, but instead, he had found

...two nations warring in the bosom of a single state: I found a struggle, not of principles, but of races.... The national feud forces itself on the very senses, irresistibly and palpably, as the origin or essence of every dispute which divides the community; we discover that dissensions, which appear to have another origin, are but forms of this constant and all-pervading quarrel: and that every contest is one of French and English in the outset, or becomes so ere it has run its course.[9]

Durham's solution was simple: he proposed the assimilation of Lower Canada, which was largely Francophone, with Upper Canada, which was mainly Anglophone.

I entertain no doubt of the national character which must be given to Lower Canada; it must be that of the British Empire; that of the majority of British America; that of the great race which must, in the lapse of no long period of time, be predominant over the whole North American Continent. Without effecting the change so rapidly or roughly as to shock the feelings and trample on the welfare of the existing generation, it must henceforth be the first and steady purpose of the British Government to establish an English population, with English laws and language, in this Province, and to trust its government to none but a decidedly English Legislature.[10]

Durham added:

I should indeed be surprised if the more reflecting part of the French Canadians entertain at present any hope of continuing to preserve their nationality. Much as they struggle against it, it is obvious that the process of assimilation to English habits is already commencing. The English language is gaining ground, as the language of the rich and of the employers of labour naturally will.[11]

It is hard to be more explicit.

The Durham Report and the Act of Union which followed the Insurrection, mark a very important turning point in the history of Quebec. It was not until the late 1950s, more than a hundred years later, that there appeared an equally important period, from an ideological point of view. We cannot overemphasize this period. Quebec's professional bourgeoisie was descended from the peasantry and had defended the traditional form of culture which had developed in Quebec since the Conquest. Was this, however, through choice or necessity? Being the ruling class of a people who were dominated politically, economically, and socially, the liberal bourgeoisie was obliged to defend what existed, and what existed was a people that the Conquest had relegated to agriculture. There is nothing to indicate that the Quebecois chose to defend the traditional form of economy they practised. It was the dialectic of the situation which gave it momentum. These people that the liberal bourgeoisie wanted to lead to independence, "with the support and favour of England," were, for the time being, poor illiterate farmers. By opposing the dominators and the Anglophone mercantile class which represents it, the national bourgeoisie defended a way of life imposed on it since the Conquest and the failure of the Insurrection. There is nothing to lead us to believe that it was this way of life that they had defended. Above all, the liberal bourgeoisie was defending the right of the Quebec people to live as a total society. Papineau and his followers were insisting on the liberty of a majority group, which had been conquered militarily, economically, and politically by a minority.

However, everything changed after the 1840s. Despair beset even the most committed Quebecois. It was no longer a question of leading the people to independence, but of fighting against assimilation and Anglicization. With backing from Durham, the clergy became the main spokesman for the Quebec people; they no longer proclaimed an ideology of independence, but one of conservation. From the point of view of the ideology held in the first few decades of the nineteenth century, the new ideology they were expounding marks a tragic contraction. Sensing quite well that they were to become a minority, the Quebecois no longer sought to become an independent society, but strove to preserve their culture. The Quebec group was no longer a nation that had one day to obtain its independence, but an ethnic group with a particular culture (religion, language, customs); this culture would have to be preserved as a sacred heritage. Durham accused the Quebecois of having no history or literature; they had to prove to him that they had a past and that it was great—to such an extent that the period to be glorified by those who defined the situation was to become the past. The English soon realized that it was necessary to divide the Quebecois, both along the St. Lawrence, and later in Acadia, in order to establish a viable state that the English could control at will. Lord Elgin knew this well when he wrote:

> I believe that the problem of how to govern Canada would be solved if the French would split into a Liberal and a Conservative Party and join the Upper Canadian parties bearing the corresponding names. The great difficulty hitherto has been that a Conservative Government has meant Government of Upper Canadians which is intolerable to the French—and a Radical Government a Government of the French which is no less hateful to the British.... The national element would be merged in the political if the split to which I refer was accomplished.[12]

Dumont writes:

> Politics will become a ground on which politicians will periodically defend their nationality; but it will only be one area among others for formulating nationalist ideologies.[13]

The arrival of responsible government enabled the elite in the liberal professions to find employment and to acquire a certain vertical mobility in administration and business. Georges-Etienne Cartier, a businessman and politician, is one of the first examples of a type of Quebecois who was to profit from the new regime. He took part in the 1837 Insurrection, but as Wade writes:

> ...he took no part in the second rising, having perhaps been led by his lifelong Sulpician friends to see that the clergy was right in condemning opposition to the constituted authorities, a view which he later recognized as "the only one that offered some chance of salvation for the French Canadians."[14]

With the backing of this same clergy, he and his party were to win all the elections in Quebec until the end of the century. Conservatism was triumphant. Some young people from the cities went to settle in the country, in the heart of traditional society. Gérin-Lajoie's novel, *Jean Rivard*, well explains this glorification of the earth. In 1849, the author wrote in his diary:

> I have returned to my project of going to live in the country as soon as possible.... Oh, if only I were a farmer!... He does not become rich by beggaring others, as lawyers, doctors, and merchants sometimes do. He draws his wealth from the earth: his is the state most natural to man. Farmers form the least egotistical and most virtuous class of the population. But this class has need of educated men who can serve its interests. The educated farmer has all the leisure necessary to do good; he can serve as guide to his neighbors, counsel the ignorant, sustain the weak, and defend him against the rapacity of the speculator. The enlightened and virtuous farmer is to my mind the best type of man.[15]

Several novels from this period were constructed around the theme of fidelity to agriculture and ancestral values. These romantic works, as well as historical studies, were to propagate the ideology of conservation that the petite-bourgeoisie and the Church were systematically building up. The historian Michel Brunet wrote:

> From then on, the Canadian Church enjoyed a freedom it had not possessed since 1760. Without being fully aware of it, it benefited from the establishment of ministerial responsibility and a new climate of religious tolerance among the Protestant elite in Great Britain and English Canada.... From 1840 to 1865, the Canadian episcopacy directed a Catholic counter-reform. This was necessary. Free thought had made considerable progress among the lay ruling classes and the population in general had become accustomed to neglecting its religious duties.... The clergy led a vigilant fight against the last representatives of liberal thought. Some of the Institut canadien and all of the anticlericals who remained faithful to the revolutionary romanticism of the decade of 1830 continued to voice their opposition but they no longer influenced the bulk of the population.[16]

The Church profited from the liberty that the English were according them as a reward for their loyalist attitude during the Insurrection, and strove to get the people under their influence again. This thoroughly succeeded. From that time on, the Church fulfilled for the nation the role that it had filled for many minority groups: that of compensation. The minority should not be saddened by its existing situation because the rewards would come much later. If the Quebecois were to realize themselves fully, to become what they really are, it was out of the question to imitate the material successes of the English. It mattered little that they were conquered and poor, because they had a providential mission to accomplish in North America: to evangelize and civilize the continent. National history, particularly in the person of Garneau, helped the Church greatly to build the new ideology of conservation. Nourished by Voltaire and de Raynal, Garneau advocated prudence and fidelity to traditions. He wrote:

> For us, part of our strength comes from our traditions; let us not separate ourselves from these as we change them gradually. We find good examples to follow in the history of our own mother country. Without laying claim to a similar destiny, our wisdom and our strong unity will greatly ease the difficulties of our situation and will arouse the interest of nations and make our cause appear more sacred to them.[17]

The "Catholic reaction,"[18] in the words of Father Léon Pouliot, s.j., took several years to sweep away all that remained of anticlericalism in Quebec. The greatest battle that the clergy had to wage was against the Institut canadien,[19] several members of which were free thinkers. Auguste Viatte describes this struggle as follows:

> A final battle remained to be waged. Quebec is evolving. Montreal is becoming inflexible. The Institut canadien is firing red cannon balls and Mgr. Bourget wishes to stop them. Starting in 1857, a priest destroyed 1500 "indexed" volumes at the Rolland Library, among which were the complete works of Lamartine, including *Jocelyn* and *Chute d'un ange*. In 1858, the Bishop also required the Institut to commit its manuscripts to flames.

Arthur Buies fought a final battle with his *Lanterne*.

> In vain, he peddled his own journal. The depots refused him and the last number appeared in 1869. At this time, Garneau died and Crémazie was in flight; an era was ending; the spring rains that follow so prolonged a drought will disturb the fertility of the soil and will bring about a change in the climate.[20]

Buies resisted until 1869; the "Catholic reaction" had by then had many years to do its work and for the bulk of the population to have been taken into the hands of the Church.

It seems best to follow Dumont's interpretation that the predominance the Church acquired was achieved with the consent of

> ...leaders, even nonbelievers, who could not help but recognize that religion was an essential factor in social solidarity and a fundamental element in the differentiation of the French-Canadian nation from that of the English.[21]

The federation of the territories of British North America and the British North America Act, which should have been the constitutional document that consecrated this federation, was bound to accentuate what was embryonic in the Durham Report and in the Act of Union. In 1840, the Act which united English Upper Canada and French Lower Canada was supposed to have the result, in the spirit of Durham and the English lawmakers, of rapidly Anglicizing Lower Canada. It had done nothing. But with Confederation, that is, with the union of all British territories in North America (Upper Canada, Lower Canada, New Brunswick, Nova Scotia, and Prince Edward Island), the assimilation process appeared to be unavoidable. As a minority in this new political formation, the Quebecois again strengthened their ideology of defence and conservation. Although the Quebecois remained the majority in Lower Canada, they were no longer the majority in Canada as a whole. Even inside Quebec, where they represented nearly 75 percent of the population of nearly a million inhabitants, their economic and social position no longer corresponded to their numerical importance. The large cities, such as Montreal and Quebec, had just acquired a Francophone majority. But the English dominated commerce, industry, and finance. Thus even within Quebec, English and Canadiens were opposed to each other on all points: the Canadiens, rural and poor, were Catholics and French in their linguistic tradition; the English, urban and better off economically, were Protestants.

Although the period of Confederation marked a great economic boom in Canada, there was also a profound economic malaise in Quebec which was shown by a massive emigration to the United States. The Canadian economy was being displaced toward southern Ontario and the Quebecois were seeking work in New England. To counter this emigration, the clerical elite and the petite-bourgeoisie began a vast movement of colonization and a return to the land. Quebec followed in detail its ideology of conservation which forced it to remain within its borders:

> ...relatively sheltered from Anglo-Saxon influences, it (Lower Canada) is entirely taken up with the preservation of its personality which it wishes to keep immutable by time and space, in a sealed vase.[22]

An increasingly accentuated rift developed with France. In 1871, the year of the Commune, Mgr. Raymond wrote:

> The capital of France, centre of these uprisings and of this filth, does not seem to me as more than a soiled land, like that of Babylon or Sodom, and as such calling for the vengeance of heaven.[23]

Gradually the theory of the two Frances was built up. Thomas Chapais gave it most explicit formulation:

> There are now two Frances, radical France and conservative France, the infidel France and Catholic France, the France that blasphemes and the France that prays. Our France is this second one.[24]

This distancing from France was not compensated for by any rapprochement with the English in Canada.

In the decade of 1880, the Riel affair again seemed to harden the relations between Quebec and Canada. When Laurier, a Quebecois, became Prime Minister of Canada from 1896 to 1911, it seemed to mark a truce in the struggle between the two groups: he was elected as much by Quebec as by Canada.

During Laurier's term of office, the Quebec economy experienced an accelerated growth. Although the movement toward industrialization was mostly directed from the outside and activated in Quebec by the Anglophone element, it is possible to date the first decades of this century as those of radical transformation which the traditional lifestyle of the Quebecois had to go through. And it was from the perspective of the problem of the worker that Quebec first faced the consequences of its massive industrialization.[25] There, as elsewhere, the ideology of conservation played a strong role. To prevent the Quebecois from joining international unions, the clergy strongly encouraged the founding of Catholic unions that would protect them from the religious neutrality of the Americans.

In 1911, when Laurier left the government after fifteen years in power, Quebec had changed extensively. In 1871 Quebec was 77 percent rural, but forty years later, it was half urban. Because of its industrial and commercial development, Montreal had attracted many rural people who increased the ranks of labourers and salaried workers. The Anglophone minority continued to hold the wealth and the industrial and financial power. Already, at that time, the Quebecois writer Errol Bouchette earnestly advised his compatriots to invest in industry rather than land; for him, the future of Quebec was in industry rather than agriculture. Bouchette stated with bitterness that a Francophone population of 1,293,000 inhabitants sent only 722 students to university, whereas the English in Quebec sent 1358 for a population of 196,000. Only twenty-seven Francophone students were preparing for scientific careers, whereas there were 250 such students among the Anglophones in Quebec.

Viatte wrote:

> About 1890, one would believe that Canadien literature (Quebecois) was going to die. Conformism becomes conservatism and any type of new wave is censured. The critics deplored in vain "this quasi-inability to produce which results from language difficulties, the absence of graduate schools, the scarcity of books, the general indifference to any question that is a bit enlightened, political chicanery to the death, and from the progressive invasion of the American spirit."[26]

A few years later, in the first decade of the twentieth century, the Literary School of Montreal aroused great hopes. But it was necessary to wait forty more years before the movement really had any momentum.

The encounter between Francophones and Anglophones that was evident during the Boer War in 1899, when the Quebecois refused to participate in an imperialist struggle, continued during the Great War of 1914–18. The question of the Ontario separate schools again aggravated the conflict between Quebec and the rest of Canada. In the Legislative Assembly in Quebec, a deputy minister presented a bill aimed at the withdrawal of Quebec from Confederation; the debates lasted for many days. In the end, the deputy withdrew his bill, the Prime Minister of Quebec, Lomer Gouin, declared himself against withdrawal from Confederation, invoking the fate of the Francophone minorities in Canada and the impossibility for Quebec alone to ensure her economic survival. It was during this period that Henri Bourassa, the grandson of Louis-Joseph Papineau, the leader of the 1837 Insurrection, became the champion of a type of pan-Canadian nationalism. Bourassa pleaded for an international policy that was Canadian and no longer British. Toward 1917, facing the facts as he saw them from the turn of events— conscription for overseas service, persecutions of the Francophone minorites in Ontario—he turned to the study of religious problems and published a book, *Le Pape, arbitre de la paix*, and arranged a big conference on "Language, Guardian of the Faith." His influence on generations of Quebecois was profound and explains certain positions of traditional nationalists who today still gravitate around *Le Devoir* and *Action Nationale*.

During the early post-War years, Quebec continued to industrialize at an accelerated pace. The United States increasingly expanded its economic and cultural hold on Quebec. In 1921, the Francophone population of Canada reached its lowest level ever—27.9 percent. For the first time in history the urban population of Quebec, 56.01 percent, was greater than the rural population. Montreal had 618,506 inhabitants of whom 63.9 percent were Francophones. Many important industrial centres were developing: Three Rivers, Hull, Shawinigan, Grand'Mère, Chicoutimi, La Tuque. The national resources of Quebec continued to be exploited by foreigners. The lack of capital and technicians further accentuated the domination of the country. In the 1930s, a separatist movement arose which was directly descended from the traditional nationalist movement. The War came to put an end to this movement. Not that the conflict between Francophones and Anglophones was mitigated; as in 1899 and in 1914–18, the majority of the Francophone population of Quebec opposed sending troops overseas. The movement of industrialization and urbanization that was produced by the Second World War was bound to lay the ground for lively days ahead.

A Characterization of Quebecois Ideologies 1945–1985

We shall use the definition of a global ideology that was developed in the first part of these remarks to describe and characterize the ideologies of Quebec since 1945. In summary, a global ideology is a plan for living which is proposed to a society by one of its subgroups and which aims at expressing the total consciousness of the society and sharing its definition of the situation with the whole of the society. In a complex society, the conflict of ideologies expresses above all the conflict of subgroups which are competing for the majority's acceptance of their theory of society and, ultimately, to govern that society.

The Ideology of Conservation

When the Second World War broke out in 1939, the dominant ideology in Quebec was the ideology of conservation that had begun to develop in the second half of the nineteenth century. The majority of those in Quebec who had taken it upon themselves to define the nation and who had directed collective action had rallied to this ideology. For about one-hundred years, the ideology of conservation had been dominant, and the clergy and many of the liberal professions had been its champions. This does not imply that this was the only definition of Quebec that had existed during this century, but other definitions did not gain the favour of the public and did not guide the behaviour of the majority of Quebecois. The clergy and the liberal professions were at leisure to disseminate their ideology since they controlled, for all practical purposes, most of the information media, houses of learning, books, and textbooks. It is also necessary to add that the Quebecois also live in another political entity, that of Canada as a whole, they could and can, if necessary, forget the fact that they are Quebecois and participate in the ideology of Canada. The Quebecois can physically or otherwise escape their nationality and live as though they were Canadians or North Americans. Ideological conflicts cannot be produced for this precise reason. In addition, during all this time national education remained in the hands of the clergy, which was thus able to propagate and impose its own definition of the Quebecois group. How does one characterize this ideology? It defined the Quebecois group as the bearer of a culture, that is, as a group with an edifying history which became a minority in the nineteenth century and whose task it is to preserve this heritage it had received from its ancestors and which it must transmit intact to its descendants. This heritage is essentially composed of the Catholic religion, the French language, and an indeterminate number of traditions and customs. The privileged time of this ideology has passed. At the time when it was worked out, the Quebecois were becoming a minority and risking assimilation. It was to be expected that this ideology therefore idealized the traits of Quebec society in the second half of the nineteenth century when it was effectively Catholic, French speaking, agricultural, and traditional. Threatened with assimilation, this type of society and its principal characteristics were not supposed to change. Thus, it had to be rationalized and justified. This culture was not only that of the Quebecois, but the best culture that had ever existed. This ideology took hold over the years; from the end of the nineteenth century, it was transmitted almost intact to the beginning of the Second World War.

The Laval University sociologist Gérald Fortin has analysed the contents of *l'Action française*, later called *l'Action Nationale*, one of the principal reviews that transmitted this ideology over the course of years. His analysis extends from its appearance in 1917 until 1953[27] and brings out the principal themes of this ideology of conservation. It phrases the merits of the French language, the Catholic religion, the spiritual culture, the national history, rural life, and the family; it warns of the dangers of English imperialism, industrialization, urbanization, and the means of mass communication; it preaches about buying Quebecois and respect for the two cultures and the Francophone minorities. In the decade 1945–53, he writes, an interest in economic and social questions is growing and the question of the worker appears in the review. Fortin writes:

If the ends and the means of the ideology are considered, it may be seen that the goals have not changed; they have been more strongly confirmed as new interpretations of the situation have been worked out. [28]

The Ideology of Contestation and Recoupment

After the Second World War, the ideology of conservation was seriously disputed by another stratum of the population: union leaders, intellectuals, journalists, artists, students, and some members of the liberal professions. It is obvious that this form of contestation had its historical antecedents; it can, in many respects, be linked to the liberal tradition. This certainly does not question the fact that Quebec possessed a culture that is different from that of the rest of Canada, the principal elements of which must be preserved but, according to this ideology, the culture must be brought up-to-date. The ideological movement which arose during the Second World War was above all a movement of reaction against the old ideology of conservation. That is, its negative aspect, which opposed the old, was the most nebulous and almost always remained implicit.

It can be said that the ideology and old power structure in Quebec were becoming anachronistic in face of the demographic, economic, and social changes that Quebec went through between 1939 and 1945. Its irrationality was obvious. If, for convenience, we consider the decade between 1939 and 1950, it is noticeable, according to the study by Faucher and Lamontagne, that the labour force in Quebec doubled:

> This increase, in absolute terms, is equal to the growth witnessed during the whole century ending in 1939.... During the period under review, the rate of industrialization in Quebec has been higher than that of Canada as a whole. Since 1939, in volume terms, output of manufacturing industries rose by 92 percent in Quebec and by 88 percent in Canada, while new investment in manufacturing increased by 181 percent in this province and by only 154 percent in the whole country. [29]

Nathan Keyfitz, in his work, shows the movement of the population of Quebec from agriculture to industry:

> During the war and post-war years, the population in agriculture in the province of Quebec dropped from 252,000 to 188,000, a decline of 64,000. This decline more than counterbalanced the steady rise that had been shown from 1901, and hence the surprising result that, although the province of Quebec is almost three times as great in population in 1951 as it was in 1901, it contains fewer men in agriculture. The increase in non-agricultural industry is shown in every one of the thirteen main occupational groups, except fishing and trapping which, like farming, declined sharply. The rise from 79,000 to 237,000 in manufacturing occupations is especially conspicuous. [30]

Thus it appears that Quebec has undergone more important changes on a larger scale during the decade of 1939–49 than in any other decade of its history, except those of the Conquest and the Insurrection. The ideology of conservation which had survived all the other waves of industrialization and urbanization could not successfully resist the last. It must be added that this ideology, which had been dominant for so many years, had largely become inoperative on the level of everyday life. It continued to guide the general policies of the nation, but it no longer directed the behaviour of the more dynamic Quebecois who kept to themselves or withdrew into small groups which worked within other frames of reference. The patriotic societies continued to defend French-Canadian culture (our religion, our language, and our traditions) while the majority of individuals shared a number of core images concerning their nation; others were ideologically integrated into other North American societies, particularly into Canada.

The dispute of this ideology began in the post-War years. Clearly the sociologists and economists in the Faculty of Social Science at Laval University formed the most coherent centre for dispute at the end of the 1940s and during the 1950s. This group adopted reviews, *Cité Libre* is the most obvious example, and movements such as the Canadian Institute for Public Affairs (L'Institut Canadien des Affaires Publiques), which brought together intellectuals, professors, union leaders, journalists, and liberal politicians. Drawing their inspiration from the analyses of economists and sociologists from the Quebecois milieu and from their knowledge of other Western democracies, these movements and individuals undertook the systematic criticism of the ideology of conservation as well as of Quebecois culture.

Some writers have said that the 1950s was a decade when social problems were dealt with, that is, when the problems of the workers were recognized. These so-called social themes were even introduced into the pages of *Action Nationale*, which, as we have seen, had long been one of the most representative spokesmen of the ideology of conservation. Already by 1949, the reverberations that were provoked by the asbestos strike had brought about a realization that Quebec was no longer a traditional society living principally from agriculture, but a society in which the majority of citizens were salaried workers; a few years later, it was said that Quebec society was experiencing a slow proletarianization.

It is quite evident that in criticizing the ideology of conservation and Quebec culture in general, opponents had to criticize not only ideas, values, behaviour, and institutions, but also those groups and individ-

uals who, according to them, were responsible for the global orientations that were influencing the direction Quebec was taking. Quite
clearly this was a way of getting at the clergy who had always been
responsible for national education in Quebec. Open discussions on
education, religion, and the traditional interpretation of our history date
from these years. There was bound to be criticism of Quebec Catholi-
cism and those who had narrowed, particularized, and "Quebecisized"
its content. This fact is well expressed by Maurice Tremblay:

> Through this attitude of fierce defence against Protestant influences and
> French modernism, the Church has no doubt succeeded in keeping
> French-Canadian culture entirely Catholic; unfortunately, it must be
> recognized that this has been, to a great extent, at the expense of a
> narrow sterile dogmatism and an authoritarianism rooted in conserva-
> tism. On the whole, this French-Canadian Catholicism thus appears to
> us to be a canned Catholicism, at the rear guard of the radical changes
> the world is demanding of Christianity.... We have here an example of
> this narrow and unproductive ultramontanism that the Church has
> made its right arm in a general policy of conservation and defence of
> French-Canadian Christianity.

This Church has always sided with the traditional society for which it
has been largely responsible, and has wished to preserve itself in the
North American world which is repudiating and overtaking it in every
respect. Tremblay further says:

> In effect, in a general manner the Church in French Canada tends to
> run against the increasing industrialization and urbanization, to main-
> tain the structures and lifestyles of a rural civilization that it can domi-
> nate and guide in its own ideal of a religious and Christian life for
> which it has an obvious nostalgia.[31]

The other power that was strongly attacked by this group who were
trying to define the situation throughout this period, is the political
power that was embedded in Quebec from 1936 until 1960[32] through the
Union Nationale and its leader Maurice Duplessis. Relying on the
population, this party put into practice the ideology of conservation that
had been perpetuated in Quebec for many decades.

Acting completely pragmatically and distrusting intellectuals and
idealogues, Duplessis implemented the most conservative policies in the
name of autonomy and of coarse peasant good sense. In the best vein of
traditional conservatism, he carried out a form of personal politics in
which everyone knew each other and the prince granted his largesse to
the good (those who voted for him) and left the wicked to sink (counties
and regions which had shown some opposition). This manner of admin-
istering Quebec was as anachronistic as the ideology which inspired it. It
included many characteristics of preindustrial society which tallied

exactly with those of the ideology of conservation that had been developed expressly to ensure the preservation of the traditional society which Quebec had been in the middle of the nineteenth century.

The liberal opposition which was made up of partisans of the Liberal Party—and other opponents—took fifteen years to defeat these two powers, political and ideological, which were grafted together and worked shoulder to shoulder to rally a majority of electors. The traditionalists leaned on the two fundamental characteristics of the Quebec situation: the fact that the Quebecois have their own identity that clearly distinguishes them from other North American groups, and a second conviction which is a corollary of the first, the fact that they have remained a people whose culture is still traditional while living in a society that is largely industrialized and urbanized. In conclusion, the ideological opposition prior to 1960 wished to fill the gap that had formed between Quebec culture (ideas, values, symbols, attitudes, motivations) and Quebec society (technology, economy, urbanization, industrialization). This gap between culture and society in Quebec produced a global gap between Quebec and other North American countries. It can be said that those who opposed the regime (ideology and power) in Quebec during the period 1945–60, not only supported an ideology of contestation but also an ideology of recoupment.

In criticizing the delay experienced by Quebec in almost every aspect of human activity, the opponents have above all criticized the elites whom they held responsible for such a state of affairs. What did the new ideologists want for Quebec? What type of society did they want Quebec to become? It is necessary here, from the perspective of the analysis of ideologies, to make certain distinctions. It seems that the critical and negative part of this phase has been the most encouraged, the most systematic, and by far the most varied; this is easily explained. The ideology of conservation and the political powers had idealized Quebec culture to such an extent that it became an urgent necessity for opponents to deflate the balloons that had been blown up over decades. According to those in power, Quebec had the best educational system, the purest religion, the language closest to that of the Louis-fourteenth era, and the most humanist traditions. On top of that was grafted a messianism which wished to make the rest of the world participate in these cultural treasures. According to the opinion that has been attributed to Duplessis, the Quebecois had become improved Frenchmen. It is not surprising that the first task of the post-War opponents was to criticize what Quebec had become and to compare the miserable reality to the fantasmagorias of the elites.

The opponents agreed relatively well over what they opposed, but they were not united in a similar manner over the positive objectives that they laid down for the society which they wished to construct. Furthermore, it seems that when mobilized by combat, they submitted to the rule of force and most of them did not question themselves about the positive aspect of their ideology. Opposition to the regime had brought together many individuals and groups who came from very different backgrounds: Catholic and progressive syndicalists, Catholic action leaders, Catholic and progressive intellectuals, members of the Liberal parties of Quebec and of Canada, and students from various disciplines. It would not be exaggerated to say that because of the history of Quebec and its political and intellectual climate, the only other model of society which the protestors could recognize as comparable was that of other North American societies. The majority of them wanted Quebec to become a liberal democracy, like Washington or Ottawa. Some of them had been influenced by European currents of thought, particularly French, for example, the review *Esprit*, but, for the majority it was the Ottawa model that consciously or unconsciously prevailed. During this period, a number of professors and students from the Faculty of Social Science at Laval University openly sided with Ottawa. The most typical example is that of Maurice Lamontagne[33] who was to rally to Ottawa after 1954. Three of the principal leaders of the post-War opposition movement, Marchand, Pelletier, and Trudeau were to join Lamontagne several years later. Others such as Sauvé and Pepin[34] also entered the Canadian government. Although many opposed the Ottawa regime during the 1950s, it is clear, after the fact, that their preferences unconsciously lay here and that the positive aspect of their ideology was largely drawn from the model of the liberal democracy. We have tried to find articles from this period which expressed the positive aspect of the ideology of contestation. They are very rare. One of the few that we have found is that of Lamontagne to which we will return later.

From the point of view of the global ideologism of Quebec, that which we have taken here, we have laid out three principal ideologies: the ideology of conservation which was dominant for a century and which largely remained intact at the end of the War; the ideology of recoupment toward which most of the opposition of the 1950s would turn; the third, the ideology of development and participation, does not appear to have crystallized until the end of the 1950s. In Hegelian terms, a period of affirmation can be seen in the first ideology, in the second, the negation of the first, and, in the third, the negation of the negation.

The Ideology of Development and Participation

If we examine carefully the issues of *Cité Libre,* an organ of opinion which led the most systematic and coherent fight against the ideology of conservation, it will be seen that this was really a review of contestation against Duplessis, the clergy, the educational system, and many other subjects, but it never developed the positive aspect of its ideology in a systematic manner. At the outset, in 1950 and until the beginning of 1960, it fought against the ideology of conservation; beginning with the 1960s, it began to run up against the third ideology; it was only in 1964 that Pierre Elliott Trudeau wrote what seemed to be the most positive statement that the review ever published: "Pour une politique fonction-nelle." We would like now to characterize this third ideology which *Cité Libre* set itself against in the 1960s.

The ideology of recoupment largely contributed to the discrediting of traditional power elites and the ideology of conservation; essentially, it has directed its criticisms against the Quebecois themselves as a group; that is, it has been concerned with internal criticism. If one could schematize the thoughts of the principal spokesmen of this ideology, they do not seem to cast doubt on the fundamental postulate of the ideology of conservation, that Quebec forms a culture, that is, an ethnic group which possesses certain characteristics of language, religion, and tradi-tions that distinguish it from other ethnic groups in Canada or the North American continent. If Quebec is behind compared to other ethnic groups, it is because of its elites which have misled it into the paths of conservatism, nationalism, chauvinism, and messianism. They now want this ethnic group to acquire a more open culture and ideology and integrate itself into Canadian society: according to Lamontagne, it is a question of a clear integration into Confederation. We thus see that this ideology of recoupment retains, for the most part, the essence of the ideology of conservation in that Quebec possesses a distinct culture and that it must accommodate itself to being implicated with Canada. The essential difference between conservation and recovery lies in the type of culture that Quebec should have. The first ideology is directed toward the past; the second is resolutely turned toward the present; it demands that Quebec culture be brought up-to-date and that it be reflected in the rest of Canada.

The third ideology also retains certain elements of the ideology of conservation in that it recognizes that Quebec possesses a different culture from other North American groups. Together with the ideology of recoupment, it recognizes that the elites of the past have perverted this heritage, that this culture and the ideology of conservation have become anachronistic, and that Quebec must move smoothly into the twentieth century. It recognizes that the lag between the social structure of Quebec and its culture must be filled. But the resemblance with the other ideologies ends there. It reaches back across the years to rejoin the first ideology of Quebec, before Confederation and even before Union. Quebec is not only a culture, that is, an ethnic group which possesses certain differences of language, religion, and traditions, but is a society that must be self-determined and gain its own independence. Now, because this ideology is set in the second half of the twentieth century and because Quebec has become an industrial society, it must, as any other industrial society, control its economy and polity. For the holders of this ideology, there can, therefore, be no question that Quebec should integrate itself with other societies such as Canada.

How do we explain the birth and development of this ideology? It could be suggested with some justification that it is written into the line of our traditional ideologies. But that is not the complete answer. The adherents of the two ideologies do not come from the same strata of society. The traditional nationalists or the liberals of the ideology of recoupment do not seem to have become, for the most part, partisans of the third and most recent ideology. Other groups in the population who have become active since 1960, workers, members of co-operatives, white-collar workers, teachers, civil servants, and students are the most active contributors to the development and diffusion of this ideology. It is true that there are several strata of the population who were already beginning to make their presence felt in the ideology of recoupment, but other strata have become more important and others, such as the newly unionized, are tending to subscribe, often implicitly, to this new definition of Quebec society.

In a phenomenon as diffuse as the birth of a new ideology, it is difficult to follow all the stages precisely. The criticism to which Quebec society has been submitted since the end of the last War has not happened without heart-rendering anguish and profound disequilibrium in a population which traditionally "was in quiet possession of the truth." The most firmly established truths, the most diffused myths, were attacked by more and more individuals and subgroups. Finally, in 1960, what has rapidly become known as the Quiet Revolution began and the time came to change the ideological climate of Quebec in a global manner. From the point of view that we are taking here, that is, of an ideology concerned with the theory that groups advance of their own accord, it is certain that one of the first effects of 1960 and the reforms that followed was to reaffirm the image that many Quebecois held of themselves and their society. One did not willingly boast about being a Quebecois during the dark years. To dethrone Duplessis, it was necessary to attack and to denounce all those teachers, politicians, and professional elites who were responsible for the fact that Quebec was the only feudal state "north of the Rio Grande." The day that more and more Quebecois realized that they could collectively escape from their rut, was the day that they acquired a taste for change and began to redefine themselves, set new goals for themselves, and seek the means to reach them. The ideology of recoupment, which wished to bring Quebec onto an equal footing with the rest of North America, served as a generator of many new policies and reforms. Now, in the same way as in the sixties it was a problem for the people of Quebec to progress to another stage of thinking and development, so the means available to do this and the direction that this reform should take could not be the same as those which had been used many decades ago by the Anglo-Saxon democracies of North America—the societies to which Quebec was catching up.

There had previously been independentist movements during the Duplessis regime. Although the new generation of independentists admitted almost all the critics who had been opposed to the state of Quebec society, they went further than the *Cité Libre* criticism and asked whether many of the problems of Quebec did not come from the fact that it had always been a dominated society; this explained the narrowing of their culture, their economic inferiority, and their morbid fear of losing their identity. They were thus exposing themselves to external criticism. And because on a worldwide scale there was increasing talk of decolonization and of national liberation, these terms quickly came to be used and new goals were set for the collective action of the Quebecois. From the beginning, however, these new movements split into two major factions: those who, like the Alliance Laurentienne, on the whole accepted the definition of the Quebecois group that the ideology of conservation had established; and those who, like Raoul Roy's *Revue Socialiste*, began to give another definition of the Quebec nation. The first more traditional group placed itself in the line of ideological choices that Quebec had known for decades; the second group was to define the ideology of development and participation which will now be discussed in greater detail.

On account of the homogeneity of the Quebecois and their culture (setting aside the Anglophone minority), the political options of Quebec since Confederation and the frame of reference of all political parties has always oscillated between certain more or less rightist tendencies. However, a considerable consensus has always existed between liberals and conservatives on the principal political options. It was striking to note that in the recent past, the differences between the partisans of the Union Nationale and of the Liberal Party were quite minimal. The *Journal des Débats* of the Quebec Legislative Assembly gave the impression of a group whose ideas were interchangeable, who shared the same values. Often the only difference that separated them was the width of the corridor between the party in power and the opposition. Their differences were in tendencies rather than in doctrine. It is only recently that a more important cleavage has appeared betweeen the left and the right. This phenomenon is so new in Quebec that at first it was said that these terms had no place in the political vocabulary of the nation since they did not correspond to any reality. Referring only to the members of the Assembly, it is quite evident that these terms do not mean very much. But with the third ideology which has appeared in the past few years, the terms right and left are beginning to refer to an increasingly clearly marked reality. Certainly, on the one hand, the Quebecois have not reinvented socialism, Marxism, self-management, state planning, or participatory democracy, but, on the other hand, it is also evident that the logic of the present situation has motivated them to take inspiration from these ideas to resolve problems that are demanding their attention in a very real way. It seems certain that it is above all the ideas of decolonization and national liberation that have awakened echoes among those who were troubled over the destiny and future of their nation. The phenomena of decolonization and of national liberation, which could be found in many nations of the world during the fifties, brought with them ideas of the good life and the good society, of the role of the economy, and of social classes, which were the same as those in the nineteenth century when the bourgeois classes of most Western nations undertook their national revolutions. Thus all these ideas finally reached a small part of Quebec youth who became aware that they could be applied to their own situation. But in explaining the development of ideologies in Quebec the influence of an international convergence must not be exaggerated; it is rather a case of a primarily local aid to phenomena that are the outcome of several decades of history. It must not be forgotten that the three ideologies are superimposed on each other and that they possess characteristics creating a chain of which the links are closely interrelated. The radical falling out of the third ideology is to a large extent developing away from a common understanding about Quebec society.

What precisely is this third ideology? It could be said that the three Quebecois ideologies are not mutually distinguishable and that there is no question, as some could believe, of a seesaw game between political parties. Let us first say that the distinguishing characteristic of the ideology of conservation is to consider the Quebecois group as a cultural minority within Canada; this group is largely centred in Quebec but has offshoots in other provinces. All these groups constitute the bearers of the French-Canadian culture (religion, language, and traditions) that must be preserved and transmitted as intact as possible over the generations. The ideology of recoupment also considers the French Canadians as a minority group spread across the country who must modernize their culture throughout that nation; this is a modern version of the ideology of conservation. There is here a difference between conservatives and liberals: the first want more autonomy for Quebec to ensure the conservation of its culture; the second want Quebec to become more integrated into Canada in order to profit from the advantages of the modern state while still preserving and enriching its culture and allowing it to spread across Canada.

The third ideology seems to be the most radical and from the beginning it was more strongly differentiated from the first two than these are differentiated from each other. It breaks from the other two by defining the Quebecois Francophone group not only as a culture but as a modern industrial society which has been dominated economically and politically by the rest of Canada; it ceases to speak of French Canadians and speaks of Quebecois. For most of the people holding this ideology the minorities outside Quebec participate in French-Canadian culture but not in Quebec society. Of primary importance is that the Quebec nation be saved and liberated. This ideology is in accord with the ideology of recoupment in its fight against the ideology of conservation and in thinking that Quebecois culture must be modernized but not necessarily taking North American societies as models. In effect, the greatest mutation that this ideology represents in comparison with the others is that it develops a different idea of man and society in general, and of Quebecois in society in particular. It is here that we return to the Quiet Revolution and the international context in which it came into being.

Not only did the ideology of recoupment borrow its model of a good society from Canadian society, but it can also be said that the ideology of conservation was largely inspired by the same source. These two ideologies, one of which was dominant for many years and the other, long in a minority position, established itself after the Second World War, have both developed a kind of symbiosis with the dominant culture. It can be said that they borrowed from it their dominant ideas on the subject of life in society; that is, according to these ideologies, of a more or less developed capitalism which, however, fitted well with the philosophy of American society. The ideology of conservation has preserved or acquired some concepts derived from certain social encyclicals and from certain rightist dictatorships (Spain, Portugal) but, at its base, the model remained that of the so-called liberal democracies. In the 1950s nothing could predict that the upsetting of the Duplessis regime would result in this third ideology. Observers predicted that the ideology of recoupment, shared by the members of the Liberal Party, would become predominant and would take over from the ideology of conservation. But it happened otherwise.

But the independentist movements which had begun to arise again at the end of the fifties did much to attract attention to the idea of domination of one society by another. Still for many it was the question of political independence that was to facilitate the cultural expansion of Quebec. But the logic of the Quiet Revolution as carried out by the liberals must not be underestimated. Not only did their slogan of *Maîtres chez nous* contribute to the reinvigoration of Quebec and the Quebecois in their own eyes, but it also contributed to the launching of reform in the two major problem areas of Quebec both on the national level and on the economic level. It has also helped to link these two objectives which have tended to exclude each other: the national objectives remaining the prerogative of the right and the socio-economic objectives being traditionally those of the left. The task of catching up was initiated through a modern civil service, extensive reforms in education, nationalization of electricity, the S.G.F., conseil d'orientation économique, régime de rentes, caisse de dépôt et de placement, and the B.A.E.Q. The Liberals, through their dynamism, succeeded in interesting large sections of the population in their reforms (educators, civil servants, students, and underdeveloped regions), and kindling among them the desire to participate in this Quiet Revolution.

From an ideological point of view, challenging society and its myth quickly made the Quebecois aware that far from having built their society in its final form in the nineteenth century, it still remained to be built. Part of the population quickly came to see Quebec as a developing nation which not only removed them from their past conservatism but also diffentiated them from other North American societies. This is another characteristic that brought them closer to colonized countries on the road to liberation and development. However, as opposed to countries that had developed in the nineteenth century and in the first decades of the twentieth century, the nations of today which are in the first phases of industrialization, or, like Quebec, are behind in relation to highly industrialized countries, have many models of development at their disposal. Even the concept of development no longer has the exclusive economic meaning that it acquired at the time of the triumph of capitalism. Not able or not desiring to entrust the problem of developing society to industrial entrepreneurs or financiers, the nations which are today on the path to development or who consider themselves to have already achieved it, must count on the state and on their whole population in order to reach their objectives.

In Quebec there are many intellectuals, youth, members of unions and co-operatives, and social activists who have realized that for the Quebecois to attain their desire of becoming *maître chez eux*, there must be planned socio-economic development and the establishment of a participatory democracy. The underdevelopment of Quebec, the relative homogeneity of the population, the exacerbation of national opinion, and the shallow roots of liberal democracy in Quebec have all encouraged the diffusion throughout the population of ideas of development and of participation. The powerful Quebec labour movement and the entry of new strata of the population into the unions give this ideology of development and participation great potential.

Must it be added that these ideologies are presently being disputed? Nothing definite has been achieved and there does not seem to be any way of predicting which of the three ideologies will become dominant in the near future. This should soon develop into a struggle between the two most recent ideologies, that of recoupment and that of participation.

René Lévesque and the Quebecois Party sought to build the separatist dream, but now the Liberals are again in power.

Notes

1. F. Ouellet, *Histoire économique et sociale du Québec, 1760–1850* (Paris: Fides, 1966), p. 210.
2. F. Dumont, "Idéologie et conscience historique dans la société canadienne-française du XIX siècle," manuscript, 1965, p. 11.
3. Dumont, "Idéologie," p. 16.
4. M. Wade, *The French Canadians, 1760–1945*, vol. 1 (London: Macmillan, 1967), p. 192.
5. T. Chapais, "Cours d'histoire du Canada" in *The French Canadians*, vol. 4 (London: Macmillan, 1967), p. 27.
6. G. Filteau, *Histoire des Patriotes*, vol. 13 (Montréal: 1942), pp. 243–44.

7. Dumont, "Idéologie," p. 18.
8. Wade, *The French Canadians*, p. 186.
9. Wade, *The French Canadians*, p. 197.
10. Wade, *The French Canadians*, p. 208.
11. Wade, *The French Canadians*, p. 212.
12. Wade, *The French Canadians*, p. 252.
13. Dumont, "Idéologie," p. 31.
14. Wade, *The French Canadians*, p. 311.
15. Louvigny de Montigny, *Antoine Gérin-Lajoie* (Toronto: 1849), p. 13.
16. Michel Brunet, "Trois dominantes de la pensée canadienne-française," *Ecrits du Canada français* 3 (1957): 98–100.
17. F. S. Garneau, *Histoire du Canada* (1852), pp. 401–2.
18. Léon Pouliot, *La réaction catholique de Montréal, 1840–1841* (Montréal: 1942).
19. The Institut canadien was founded in 1844 and brought together young Canadiens who were interested in arts and sciences. This association, with its liberal spirit, came into conflict with the clergy until its dissolution in about 1878.
20. Auguste Viatte, *Histoire littéraire de l'Amérique française* (Quebec: Presses universitaires Laval, 1954), pp. 95–8.
21. Dumont, "Idéologie."
22. Viatte, *Histoire littéraire*, p. 99.
23. Mgr. Raymond, *Revue canadienne* (January 1, 1871): 38.
24. Thomas Chapais, *Discours et conférences* (Québec: 1908), p. 39
25. Louis Maheu has written his thesis on this problem (Département de Sociologie, Université de Montréal, 1966).
26. Viatte, *Histoire littéraire*, p. 133.
27. Gérald Fortin, "An Analysis of the Ideology of French-Canadian Nationalist Magazines: 1917–1954," manuscript, Cornell University, 1956.
28. Fortin, "An Analysis," p. 205.
29. A. Faucher and M. Lamontagne, in *French-Canadian Society*, vol. 1, edited by M. Rioux and Y. Martin (Toronto: McClelland and Stewart, 1964), p. 267.
30. Nathan Keyfitz, "Population Problems," in *French Canadian Society*, vol. 1, edited by M. Rioux and Y. Martin (Toronto: McClelland and Stewart, 1964), p. 227.
31. Maurice Tremblay, "La pensée sociale au Canada français," manuscript, 1950, pp. 33 and 36.
32. With an interruption for the War years, 1939–1944.
33. He was to become a minister in the Pearson government.
34. These five men were then ministers in the Pearson government.

Finding Identity: Separation, Integration, Assimilation, or Marginality?[†]

JOHN W. BERRY

Individuals who live in culturally plural societies are likely to differ in the way that they wish to become involved with other persons and groups in the society. These varying preferences are termed *acculturation attitudes*. In this article we present a conceptualization of four varieties of these attitudes, and examine their roles in the lives of groups of native people, French Canadians, and Korean, Portuguese, and Hungarian immigrants in Canada.

By culturally plural societies, we mean those in which more than one cultural or ethnic group is represented in the population, and for which there is some likelihood that they will be able to maintain themselves into the future. In such a situation, a process of acculturation is likely to exist, so that the individuals and groups in contact will influence each other, inducing some degree of change in each other's way of life and individual behaviour (Berry 1980a).

The Issues

Acculturation takes place when two groups "come into continuous first-hand contact, with subsequent changes in the original culture patterns of either or both groups" (Redfield 1955: 149). In plural societies such

[†]This article has not been previously published. The author has been working in recent years on issues of psychological acculturation in Canada, primarily with immigrant groups. Earlier participants in this general project worked with native people; the contributions of Liz Sommerlad, Bob Annis, and Tom Mawhinney are evident in this paper. Much of the recent empirical work has been carried out by Uichol Kim, Sue Power, Marta Young, and Merridee Bujaki; their work is gratefully acknowledged. An earlier version of this paper was presented at the Canadian Ethnic Studies Association conference, Montreal, 1985.

group contact is a fundamental feature of social life, and the study of how groups change as a result has been a central focus of research in ethnic studies. In addition to this focus on groups, from a psychological point of view there is a parallel phenomenon of *psychological acculturation* in which individuals may change in a number of ways. These changes may involve personal values and habits (dress, eating), beliefs (religion, political ideology), social relationships (marriage, clubs), and identity (as belonging to one's heritage group or to the new society).

These two levels of acculturation (the collective group level, and the individual psychological level) are important to keep in mind when carrying out research because not every individual participates in the acculturation experience of his group in exactly the same way. We cannot assume that because the group generally acculturates in a particular way (for example by converting to a new religion) that each individual wants to do so, or indeed eventually does so. That is, there are likely to be individual differences in how a person participates in the acculturation process, and these need to be taken into account if we are to understand the phenomena of psychological acculturation.

Previous studies of how individuals orient themselves to acculturation have generally been carried out within two distinct research traditions: modernization and ethnic group relations. In the first of these traditions, research has usually been concerned with how an individual changes in psychological characteristics (such as beliefs, values, personality, and abilities) along a dimension running between "traditionalism" to "modernism." In a critical review of this field (Berry 1980b), one of the problems noted was that there is an underlying assumption that all individuals who are experiencing acculturation move along this modernization dimension from a more or less standard condition of traditionalism (involving low education, subsistence economic roles, minimal political participation, etc.) to a more or less common end point of modernity (involving education, differentiated economic roles, greater participation in civic life, etc.). Such a unidimensional view of personal change implies that there will be increased psychological homogeneity both within and across acculturating societies. However, such increased uniformity is not evident in the literature; indeed, many novel social and psychological phenomena emerge during acculturation, including new social (political and religious) movements, new attitudes and abilities, and so on. Undoubtedly, some changes occur along this single dimension, but much of it does not, and a more complex conceptualization is needed that will allow for the appearance of these novel phenomena.

The second research tradition has been concerned with relationships among the ethnic and cultural groups that are in contact during acculturation. Much of this work has taken place with a focus on the groups themselves (usually within the disciplines of sociology and anthropology), while some has also focused on the individual; psychological studies of individual attitudes and prejudices (e.g., Berry, Kalin, and Taylor 1977) abound in the field. The central issues here are the extent to which individuals prefer their own and other groups, seek to have or avoid contact with these groups, and generally are accepting, or not, of social and psychological differences they come across in their daily lives. This research tradition has not typically attended to the dynamic or change aspects of acculturation; instead, single "snapshots" of ethnic attitudes and prejudices are taken at a single point in time, disregarding the continuous contact and changes that take place over the course of acculturation.

A Conceptual Framework

These two attitudinal domains have been merged in a model of attitudes toward acculturation (Berry 1984a). The model is based upon the observation that in plural societies, individuals and groups must confront two important issues. One pertains to the maintenance and development of one's ethnic distinctiveness in society, deciding whether or not ingroup cultural identity and customs are of value and should be retained (cf. traditional-modern attitudes). The other issue involves the desirability of inter-ethnic contact, deciding whether positive relations with the larger society are of value and to be sought (cf. ethnic attitudes).

A framework has been developed (see Figure 1) that attempts to capture both these domains, while at the same time avoiding the problems that were noted previously. The framework can be employed at four levels of analysis: at the first level, it can help in the identification of national policies that are being pursued in plural societies; at the second, goals of particular ethnic groups can be identified; the third is the attitudes held by people generally toward how others should be involved with the larger society; and the fourth is the attitudes held by members of particular ethnic groups toward how they wish themselves to acculturate. The first two are at the collective or group level of analysis, while the latter two focus on individual preferences. In this article we are mainly concerned with the last of these, where they are referred to as *acculturation attitudes*.

The two dimensions of the framework represent continuous (rather than dichotomous) preferences or values. For example, with respect to the first issue, that of the maintenance of cultural identity and practices, orientations can vary from full-scale maintenance to complete loss, rather than the simple "yes" or "no" provided in the framework. Similarly, for the second issue, that of having contact and relationships with other groups, orientations can vary from full daily involvement through to a complete turning away from any involvement at all with other groups. Thus, while recognizing the continuous nature of these two dimensions, it is convenient for conceptual purposes to provide dichotomous ("yes" or "no") responses to them. When this is done, the fourfold typology is generated, and these are termed *assimilation*, *integration*, *separation*, and *marginalization*.[1]

When the first question is answered "no," and the second is answered "yes," the assimilation option is defined, namely, relinquishing one's cultural identity and moving into the larger society. This can take place by way of absorption of a nondominant group into an established dominant group, or it can be by way of the merging of many groups to form a new society, as in the "melting pot" concept. In a detailed analysis of this form of acculturation, Gordon (1964) distinguishes a number of subvarieties or processes; most important among these are *cultural or behavioural assimilation*, in which collective and individual behaviours become more similar, and *structural assimilation*, in which the non-dominant groups participate in the social and economic systems of the larger society.

The integration option implies the maintenance of the cultural integrity of the group, as well as the movement by the group to become an integral part of a larger societal framework. In this case there are a large number of distinguishable ethnic groups, all co-operating within a larger social system. Such an arrangement may occur where there is some degree of structural assimilation but little cultural and behavioural assimilation, to use Gordon's terms.

When there are no positive relations with the larger society, and this is accompanied by a maintenance of ethnic identity and traditions, another option is defined. Depending upon which group (the dominant or nondominant) controls the situation, this option may take the form either of segregation or of separation. When the pattern is imposed by the dominant group, classic segregation to keep people in "their place" appears. On the other hand, the maintenance of a traditional way of life outside full participation in the larger society may derive from a group's

Figure 1
Model Showing Types of Ingroup and Outgroup Relationships (Integration, Assimilation, Separation, and Marginalization)

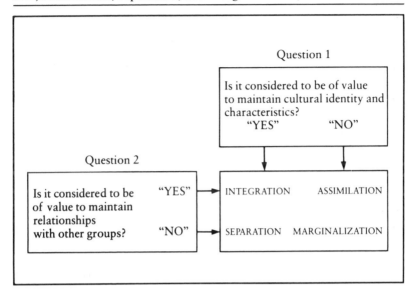

desire to lead an independent existence, as in the case of separatist movements. In our terms, segregation and separation differ only with respect to which group or groups have the power to determine the outcome.

Finally, there is an option that is difficult to define precisely, possibly because it is accompanied by a good deal of collective and individual confusion and anxiety. It is characterized by striking out against the larger society and by feelings of alienation, loss of identity, and what has been termed *acculturative stress* (Berry and Annis 1974, Berry et al. 1985). This option is *marginalization*, in which groups lose cultural and psychological contact with both their traditional culture and the larger society. When imposed by the larger society, it is tantamount to ethnocide. When stabilized in a nondominant group, it constitutes the classical situation of marginality (Stonequist 1935).

A number of points should be made with respect to the model in Figure 1. First, as we have noted, these options pertain to both individuals and groups in plural societies. One individual may follow a course toward assimilation, whereas another may not; and one ethnic group through its formal organizations may opt for separation, whereas another may seek integration. It should be obvious, however, that choices among the options are not entirely independent. At the group level, if all of one's group pursued assimilation, one is left without a membership group, rendering the other options meaningless; and if group assimilation is widespread, the culturally plural character of the larger society is eliminated, again voiding the other options.

Second, the various options may be pursued by politically dominant or nondominant groups. For example, if assimilation is sought by a particular ethnic group, it is an example of the melting pot, whereas if it is enforced as national policy, we may characterize it as a "pressure cooker." Similarly, as we have noted, separation occurs when a group wishes to set up shop on its own, whereas the classic forms of segregation exist when such apartness is forced on it by the dominant groups.

Third, there can be flux and inconsistency with respect to which options are pursued within a society. Flux occurs over time as an individual or a group experiments with differing options; for example, French Canadians, long in fear of assimilation, have been exploring the relative merits of the integration versus separation options. Inconsistency occurs when, at a single point in time, for example, an individual may accept linguistic and economic assimilation but wish to avoid it in all other areas of daily life.

Fourth, it is possible to create scales which may be used to assess an individual's attitudes toward these four modes of acculturation. We now turn to an examination of a series of empirical studies which attempt to operationalize the model, and to validate it.

Analysis of the Data
Studies with Native People

The first study (Sommerlad 1968, Sommerlad and Berry 1970), addressed the question: "How do Australian aborigines wish to be related to the larger Australian society?" At that time, Australian government policy was to assimilate aborigines, and we were interested in discovering aborigines' views on the matter. To do so, it was necessary to construct a scale (for use in a survey) which expressed the notion of assimilation. It was also thought to be useful to construct scales expressing some alternatives; hence the two additional scales of integration and separation were also drafted. At the time of this first study, the overall framework outlined previously was not yet developed, and no assessment of marginalization was attempted.

Scale construction began with a pool of items which were responded to by a number of aboriginal leaders attending a conference on aboriginal affairs. Items were selected which met the usual discrimination criteria. These scales were then used with a sample of sixty urban and fifty rural aborigines.

Validity (with ethnic identification as a criterion) was found to be high: 83 percent of those (N = 40) identifying as "Australian" favoured assimilation over integration, while only 14 percent of those (N = 34) identifying as "aborigine" did so; conversely 79 percent of those identifying as "aborigine" preferred integration, while only 13 percent of those identifying as "Australian" did so. Moreover, construct validation was supported by an interscale correlation of –.49 between assimilation and integration.

These scales were subsequently used by Berry (1970b) in a field study of an aboriginal community concerned with marginality and acculturative stress. In a sample of thirty-one individuals, the three scales exhibited similar relationships with ethnic identification; and a measure of Westernization correlated positively with assimilation attitudes and negatively with separation attitudes. The notion of marginality (Mann 1958) was introduced as a first attempt to assess the concept of marginalization; this correlated positively with high separation attitudes, and negatively with educational experience.

In Canada, versions of the scales have been used with a variety of native people, not only to discover how they wish to relate to the larger Canadian society, but also to assess the role of such attitudes in cognitive and stress-related phenomena. In a first round of studies (Berry and Annis 1974), six samples of about sixty persons each were drawn, two each from three native groups (James Bay Cree, British Columbia Plateau Carrier, and B.C. Coastal Tsimshian), one sample being relatively traditional and the other relatively acculturated. In addition, a Euro-Canadian village sample was asked to indicate their views about how native people should relate to the larger Canadian society (Berry 1975). A later study (Berry 1976) added three Ontario Ojibway samples, and most recently (Berry et al. 1982), a longitudinal follow-up of the original James Bay Cree samples was completed, after a major hydroelectric project was constructed in their midst.

Validation (against years of formal schooling as an index of exposure to Euro-Canadian life) revealed correlations which are consistently positive with assimilation (mean across samples of +.28) and with integration (mean of +.14) and negative with separation (mean –.27). In the Cree follow-up study (Berry et al. 1982) these were +.53, +.25 and –.61 respectively. Concurrent validation revealed correlations of

−.69 between assimilation and separation, −.25 between integration and separation, and + .22 between assimilation and integration.

In summary, work with various native people shows that these three scales tend to "behave" reliably, validly, and consistently. Some degree of usefulness (both scientifically and politically) seems to be present, and their continued use seems to be warranted in understanding the views of native communities.

Studies With Other Ethnic Groups

Most recently, a series of new scales has been developed for use with various ethnic groups in Canada in an attempt to judge whether the scales (and the model underlying it) have some generality in plural societies. Extended versions of these scales now exist for French Canadians living outside Quebec (Power 1983); for Portuguese first- and second-generation immigrants (Young 1984); for Korean immigrants (Kim 1984); and for Hungarian first- and second-generation immigrants (Bujaki 1985). The rationale for selecting these groups was to include in the research program one long-established ethnic group (French Canadians) which has (like native people) a special linguistic and political position within the larger society, and three relatively new groups, two of European background (the Portuguese and Hungarians) like French Canadians and one of non-European background (the Koreans) like native people. With such a diverse sample of peoples it is possible to search for the limits of generalizability of the model.

In the study of French Canadians (Power 1983) residing outside the province where they hold political and linguistic dominance, we wanted to produce scales with a sufficient number of items to provide for an analysis of internal consistency (reliability), as well as attempt some validity checks. An initial pool of 105 items was generated, and then given to seven bilingual judges who were familiar with the conceptual model in Figure 1. Their task was to sort the items into four categories, each representing one of the four acculturation attitudes. An item was considered to have face validity if six of the seven judges placed it in the intended attitude category. After item selection, 80 items were retained, 20 for each acculturation attitude, and within each, 10 were worded positively and 10 negatively. Items were then forward and back translated by a bilingual French and English Canadian respectively (Brislin 1980). Problems were sorted out by a third bilingual assistant in consultation with the first two.

The 80 items (in French) were randomly arranged in a survey instrument along with another set of questions concerning sociodemographic variables (including age, sex, language use, occupation, club membership, and ethnic identity). The whole instrument was given to a sample of 49 Franco-Ontarians, drawn from a list of the resident Francophones in Kingston.

With respect to validity, club membership and ethnic identity provided the criteria. The rationale was that those who belonged to French cultural clubs would score higher on integration and separation than those not belonging to such clubs; similarly, those not belonging should score higher on assimilation and marginalization than those belonging. The predictions were borne out for all but the assimilation scale, where the difference was in the predicted direction but with $p = .09$. The predictions for ethnic identity were that those with a "Canadien"/ "Canadian" identity would score higher on assimilation than those with other identities ($p = .17$), those with a "Français" or "Québécois" identity would score higher on separation ($p < .001$), and those with no identity would score higher on marginalization (however, no persons claimed to be without an identity). Thus of the seven possible validity checks, four were significant as predicted, and the other three were non-significant but in the predicted direction.

In the study of Portuguese Canadians (Young 1984), items were generated to reflect the four acculturation attitudes as they relate to the Portuguese in Canada, using Power's (1983) items as a guide. An initial pool of 97 items was categorized by four judges who were familiar with the model in Figure 1. An item was considered to have face validity if three of four judges categorized an item as reflecting the intended acculturation attitude; 80 items were retained, 20 for each of the four attitudes, with 10 positive and 10 negative phrasings. Forward and back translations were then performed.

The sample consisted of 31 families in Kingston of Portuguese (Azorean) ethnicity. There were 62 adults (31 father/mother pairs) and 55 children (27 boys/28 girls) aged 13 to 23 years. The language of interview was selected by each individual: 60 of 62 parents chose Portuguese, while all 55 children chose English. The 20-item scales were administered individually, along with a short sociodemographic questionnaire.

For validity, languages spoken at home and ethnic identity were used as criteria. With respect to language, it was predicted that English-speakers would score higher on assimilation, Portuguese-speakers higher on separation, and speakers of both higher on integration; only the difference for separation reached significance. For ethnic identity (with the same predictions as for French Canadians) predictions for integration and rejection reached significance, but assimilation did not. There was no test possible for the marginalization scale, since no person claimed no identity (or no language). Thus of the six possible validity checks, three were significant and three were not.

The third study, of Korean immigrants to Canada (Kim 1984), was intended to return to some of the acculturative stress-related issues addressed in the earlier studies with native people. Scales of acculturation attitudes were developed, in part, to understand relationships between these attitudes and the mental health status of immigrants (Berry and Kim 1984).

A new format for acculturation attitudes was used: twenty topics of concern to Koreans in Canada were selected on the basis of pilot work with thirty Korean respondents; four statements (all positively phrased) were then generated for each topic, one to express each acculturation attitude. To reduce acquiescent tendencies, the four items were presented in a block where their contrasting meanings would be readily apparent, since it would be obviously contradictory to agree to all four. A seven-point Likert-type response scale was provided for each statement, so that within blocks of four items, a person's response to each item would be independent. The sample (N = 150) of respondents in Toronto was individually administered, along with a sociodemographic questionnaire, and scales of marginality and stress.

Validity was checked against four criteria: club membership, newspaper readership, ethnic identity, and language preference, using similar predictions to those in the earlier studies. For club membership significant differences were found for the assimilation and integration scales (Canadian clubs only, and both Korean and Canadian clubs, respectively), but not for the other two scales. For newspaper readership and ethnic identity all but the marginalization scale received validation. For language preference, integration and separation received validation, but not assimilation and marginalization.

The fourth study (Bujaki 1985) was similar to the Portuguese-Canadian study (Young 1984) in design, with the intent being to develop scales to measure acculturation attitudes of both first- and second-generation Hungarian Canadians. Using previous studies as a guide, twenty topics were selected and ranked by eight Hungarian Canadians in terms of their importance to them as Hungarians living in Canada. The five least important topics (in terms of overall mean rank) were discarded, and forty-five statements were formulated, fifteen each for integration, assimilation, and separation; marginalization was not examined in this study. The forty-five items had an inter-rater face validity of 100 percent among five raters familiar with the acculturation attitudes theory and format.

A questionnaire was developed to measure objective acculturation, including a set of questions to obtain background information and demographic information, and others measuring language fluency and use, socioeconomic status, and organizational and group participation; a shortened version of the Rokeach Personal Values Task (as used in a national survey by Berry, Kalin, and Taylor 1977) was also used. The acculturation attitudes questions were presented in a random (but uniform) order.

The sample consisted of thirty first-generation and twenty second-generation Hungarian Canadians living in Ottawa; most were postrevolutionary refugees (who had come to Canada between 1956 and 1958) and their children. The same criteria were used to check validity as in the Korean-Canadian study (Kim 1984): organizational participation, newspaper readership, ethnic identification, and language preference, with similar predictions. For organizational participation, significant differences were found for assimilation and separation (Canadian clubs only, and Hungarian clubs only, respectively), but not for integration (since only three people belonged to both Hungarian and Canadian clubs). For newspaper readership, ethnic identity, and language preference, all three acculturation attitude scales received validation, although the evidence for the separation scale was primarily indirect due to the few people identifying themselves as "Hungarian" (N = 2), reading Hungarian newspapers only (N = 0), and reporting a preference for using the Hungarian language only (N = 2). In summary, assimilation and separation were found to be valid in all four checks, with integration being found valid in three of the four. Thus eleven out of twelve possible validity checks were significant.

Across these various studies, then, there seems to be fairly strong support for the validity of these scales, as developed and used in the various native and ethnic groups. To illustrate some of the correlations see Figure 2. Note that there is always a negative correlation between integration and assimilation for all groups; for most groups there is also a negative correlation between separation and assimilation; and there is a positive correlation between assimilation and marginalization for all groups. However, the degree of correlation varies considerably by the various groups, and correlations between several attitudes like separation and marginalization, or integration and marginalization may also vary. We turn next to the question: what accounts for individual differences in acculturation attitudes?

Figure 2
Interscale Correlations

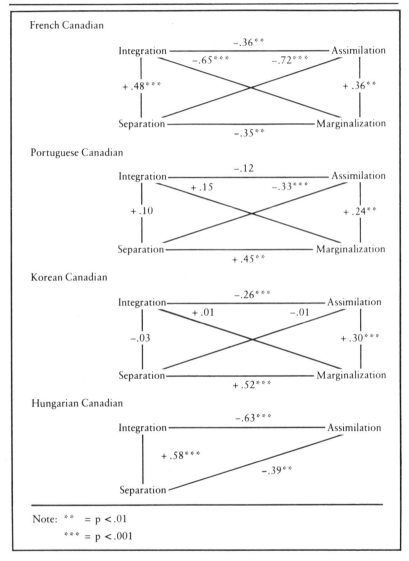

French Canadian

Portuguese Canadian

Korean Canadian

Hungarian Canadian

Note: ** = p < .01

*** = p < .001

Predictors of Acculturation Attitudes

In addition to the validation studies, where such variables as club membership, newspaper reading, and ethnic identity were shown to be related to acculturation attitudes, we can examine other factors which may be systematically related to them. In all studies correlational analyses were performed, and in two of the studies, multiple regression analyses were carried out, with each acculturation attitude as a predicted or outcome variable.

In studies of native people in Australia and Canada, various measures of actual degree of participation in the acculturation process were found to be predictive of more favourable attitudes toward assimilation and less favourable attitudes toward separation; there is a variable pattern with integration attitudes (although generally positive), while there is a consistently negative correlation with marginality. These measures of actual degree of acculturation include an index of Westernization (in the two aboriginal studies), of formal education (in one aboriginal and all Canadian native studies), and of wage employment experience, and ownership of Euro-Canadian manufactured goods (in the Canadian native studies). Thus there is an indication of consistency between a variety of behavioural measures of the actual degree of acculturation and attitudes toward the process. Of course, these correlations cannot indicate which variable preceded the other, attitudes or behaviour; this remains an urgent research question in dealing with acculturation.

In the French-Canadian study, beyond ethnic identity and club membership as validation criteria, education, socioeconomic status and travel experience formed a cluster of related variables: correlations were negative with assimilation and marginalization, positive with integration and separation. Thus, those higher in education and status tended to favour cultural retention (the common element in integration and separation attitudes) more than those lower on these variables. Age and sex did not appear to have any consistent relationship with acculturation attitudes.

In the Portuguese-Canadian study, formal schooling and status were uniformly low, and hence no correlations were likely to be found. For the parents, age and length of residence in Canada were positively correlated with assimilation attitudes, and for the children, length of residence was negatively correlated with integration and marginalization attitudes. Beyond these there is no strong pattern of predictors of acculturation attitudes in this sample.

In the Korean-Canadian study, in addition to simple correlational analyses, multiple stepwise regression analyses were carried out with each acculturation attitude as a predicted outcome, with behavioural measures and psychological variables included in the pool of predictors. For assimilation, the multiple R was .50, with the following variables contributing: viewing less Korean TV, independent (not sponsored) immigration, reading Korean newspapers less, having fewer Korean and more Canadian friends, lower desire for children to maintain their Korean language, and higher marginality. Thus, there is a fairly consistent pattern among the predictors which indicates nonmaintenance of Korean culture. For integration, the multiple R was .49, with four variables predicting: choosing English as the language of interview, reading Canadian newspapers more, direct entry to Canada, and greater participation in Canadian clubs and organizations. Thus, high-integration scorers tend to have a greater penetration into Canadian society. For separation, the multiple R was .60, with the following as predictors: less English usage, lower socioeconomic status, less education, more Korean friends, higher marginality, and having a "Korean" ethnic identity. Thus there is a clear lack of penetration into Canadian society among these high separation scorers. Finally, for marginalization, a multiple R of .60 was obtained, with three predictors: low education, high marginality (simple r of + .54), and having a "Korean" identity.

From these regression analyses, it is clear that assimilation and separation differ in the degree of "behavioural and cultural assimilation" (in Gordon's terms): relinquishing a Korean behaviour pattern is associated with assimilation attitudes, while maintaining it is predictive of separation. In contrast to separation, integration is predicted by the degree of penetration into Canadian society (which is lacking in separation). That is, the degree of "structural assimilation" distinguishes integration and separation. Marginalization and separation are similar in the maintenance of a "Korean" identity and high marginality, and in lacking the necessary skills (education) needed to penetrate into the larger society.

Multiple stepwise regression analyses were also carried out in the Hungarian-Canadian study, again with each acculturation attitude as a predicted outcome. Assimilation was predicted by three variables: a low importance of ethnicity, a low degree of participation in Hungarian group activities, and (for the first generation only) an increase in social status following migration (multiple R = .78). These factors are characterized not by an acceptance of Canadian society, but rather by a distancing from the Hungarian community. For integration, the predicting factors were a high importance of ethnicity, fluency in Hungarian, a strong desire to maintain the Hungarian language, and having married another Hungarian (multiple R = .77). In this case, the factors have in common an affinity for, and an appreciation of, things Hungarian, but again none of them reflects any degree of participation in Canadian society. For separation, the predicting factors were using the Hungarian language frequently, having a limited knowledge of English, and identifying oneself as either "Hungarian" or "Hungarian-Canadian" instead of "Canadian" (multiple R = .65). These factors have in common an acceptance of Hungarian language and culture, combined with an isolation from Canadian society.

Simple correlational analyses support these findings, with two main themes emerging: language and ethnic identity. Both integration and separation were characterized by such variables as fluency in the Hungarian language, high frequency of its use, and a strong desire to maintain it; they are distinguished from each other by fluency in English, with poorer knowledge of English predicting separation. Assimilation, on the other hand, was correlated with low fluency in Hungarian, low frequency of usage, and a preference for speaking English. Integration and separation are also characterized by such factors as a high importance of ethnicity, and maintenance of the Hungarian language and culture, as opposed to assimilation, which was associated with a marked decrease in "Hungarian-ness," as measured by ethnic identity, use of the Hungarian language, involvement in Hungarian organizations, and the maintenance of Hungarian traditions.

This pattern is very similar to the one found in the Korean-Canadian study. We find the same relationship between assimilation and separation, which differ in the degree of Hungarian cultural retention ("behavioural and cultural assimilation"), with cultural maintenance being associated with separation attitudes, and culture loss being predictive of assimilation. However, unlike the Korean-Canadian sample, integration was not predicted by or associated with the degree of penetration into Canadian society; the only difference between integration and separation was the latter's poorer knowledge of English. This fact may, however, have important ramifications for interactions with the larger Canadian society, even if quantitatively there appears to be little difference between the objective acculturation of people with integration and separation attitudes. This is an area where further research is necessary.

Conclusion

In this paper we have attempted to define conceptually and illustrate empirically the notion of acculturation attitudes. There is clear evidence for both the psychometric quality and the "behaviour" of acculturation attitude scales in a number of studies across a variety of acculturating groups. We hold that acculturation attitudes have been shown to have a reasonable scientific status, and that they have a value not possessed by the more traditional (and independent) research paradigms of modernity and traditional ethnic identity.

The conceptual framework takes us well beyond the thinking in both the modernization and ethnic enclave fields. With respect to the former, the model allows for other courses of events than the unidimensional drift toward assimilation which is assumed in modernization work: reaction to, novel combinations with, and disengagement from the dominant group are all possible alternatives to absorption. With respect to the latter, the model allows for shifts between the various orientations over time, and in different domains of life: youth may prefer assimilation, their parents integration, while others in political movements may seek separation; moreover, there may be assimilation in food preferences, integration in identity, separation in social relations, and marginalization in religious beliefs.

Beyond these advantages of the model, it is clear to see how at one level national policies can be classified within the framework, while public opinion can be assessed at another level: an articulated national goal may be to achieve integration, while public opinion may be in favour of assimilation. In addition, leaders of specific ethnic groups may articulate their collective goal (e.g., separation), while individuals may prefer another alternative (such as integration or assimilation). While in this chapter we have focused on research at only one of these four levels of analysis (acculturation attitudes of individuals), there remains much work to be done at these other levels.

Some usefulness of knowing about acculturation attitudes may be claimed. First, they permit an assessment of individuals' attitudes toward policy options in plural societies, thus permitting a better match between citizens' wishes and government policies and programs (Berry 1984b). Second, they permit an examination of the process of acculturation over time (longitudinally) or across generations (cross-sectionally), which should reveal important information to ethnic groups and their members about what is happening to them in their particular acculturation arena. And third, in schools (and other institutions), an awareness of such attitudes may help in the teaching, counselling, and placement process by fostering a better understanding of the individual caught up in the process of acculturation. Thus, in addition to their scientific merit, there is a potential for considerable practical utility.

Notes

1. Over the course of research on acculturation attitudes the names of these four orientations have changed somewhat, while the conceptualization in Figure 1 has remained constant. The terms assimilation and integration have been used consistently; however, separation has sometimes been referred to as "rejection"; and marginalization has been termed "deculturation," and has been approximated on occasion by a scale of marginality (Mann 1958).

part **IV**

Ethnic stratification and conflict

Ethnicity and Class: Bases of Sociality[†]

PIERRE VAN DEN BERGHE

The fundamental argument of this work is that ethnicity is a special basis of sociality, irreducible to any other, though often empirically overlapping with other principles of sociality. I have argued that ethnicity is an extension of kinship and that the sentiments associated with it are of the same nature as those encountered between kin, albeit typically weaker and more diluted. I have gone one step further to link ethnicity with the sociobiology of kin selection, a step that is bound to elicit passionate rejection and disagreement.

Ethnicity as Kin Selection

To restate the argument briefly, there is abundant evidence that natural selection favored nepotistic organisms, because, by favoring kin, organisms are contributing to their own inclusive fitness. Genes predisposing for nepotism will spread in an animal population, because their carriers thereby enhance not only their own direct reproduction but also that of related organisms which share certain proportions of their genes with the nepotist. Indeed, nepotism seems to be an important—perhaps the most important—basis of animal sociality. The most social and tightly integrated animal societies, the eusocial insects, are made up entirely of a reproductive couple and specialized, nonreproductive siblings.

It is admittedly a big leap to go from ants, bees and termites to humans, but the hypothesis of kin selection in the furtherance of inclusive fitness has received much corroboration from vertebrates, including mammals, and, as anthropologists have long known, *all* human societies are organized on the basis of kinship. Elsewhere, I have

†*The Ethnic Phenomenon* (New York: Elsevier Science Publishing Co., Inc., 1981), pp. 239–50.

shown that even the most specific and diverse forms of human kinship organization conform remarkably well to expectations derived from sociobiological theory (van den Berghe 1979a). The leap is thus not nearly as great or as implausible as most social scientists assume.

The next step in my analysis was an extension of the principles of nepotism from the nuclear and extended family to that group of inter-marrying (and thus interrelated) families that for most of human evolu-tion (and still for many people today) makes up the basic solidary social group, variously called sib, deme, tribe or whatever. This constituted the elemental ethny—until a few thousand years ago, a group of a few score to a few hundred people. This was the fundamental peace-keeping group of people who saw each other as related.

Over time, ethnies grew to thousands and even millions of people, and, as they grew, their underlying kinship basis became, of course, correspondingly diluted. Nevertheless, underlying ethnicity, wherever it is found, is some notion of shared ancestry, real or at least *credibly putative*. In the absence of such a belief—however vague and generalized—the basis of sociality is *not* ethnicity but something else.

From the basis of ethnicity as an extension of kinship (most likely with genetically selected nepotism), we turned to the *markers* of ethnicity, i.e., to the outward signs used by people to determine whether others share the same ethny or not. The more reliably, quickly and easily a marker is likely to establish or discount common ethnicity, the more likely that marker is to be used. Ethnic markers are usually cultural (especially linguistic), as we have seen, because under most historical situations until recently, cultural markers best differentiated even close neighbors who typically looked very much alike.

Race as a Special Marker of Ethnicity

"Race" as a primary marker of common descent is relatively uncommon and recent, because it does the job of discriminating accurately only after much rapid long-distance migration has taken place and then typically only for a few generations before interbreeding blurs again phenotypical distinctions. I must, once more, reassert that I attribute no *intrinsic* significance to phenotypes in determining group boundaries and, hence, no validity to any classification of our species into rigid subspecies. Nor am I arguing that we have an instinctive propensity to stick to people who look like us. Rather, to the extent that we do so, we are "race conscious" only as a test of common ancestry. The genetic propensity is to favor kin, not to favor those who look alike. This is clearly shown by the ease with which parental feelings take precedence over racial feeling in cases of racial intermixture.

We have not been genetically selected to use phenotype as an ethnic marker, because, until quite recently, such a test would have been an extremely inaccurate one. Racism is thus a cultural invention, a simple one to be sure, that is readily invented when the circumstances of long-distance migration across a wide phenotypic gradient make "race" a good test of kinship; there is no evidence that racism is in-born, but there is considerable evidence that ethnocentrism is.

Racism is thus a special case of ethnic sentiment, using a phenotype as an ethnic marker. Because, however, the markers themselves are largely immutable, ascribed at birth and genetically inherited, societies that use primarily phenotypes as ethnic markers are characterized by more rigid and invidious intergroup relations than societies using cultural markers. In practice, many societies, particularly the complex large-scale societies that developed out of European colonial expansion since the late 15th century have adopted a mixture of cultural and phenotypic markers of ethnicity. Nevertheless the analytic distinction between ethnicity and race is useful for the reasons just mentioned.

Class and Class Conflict

Ethnicity (and race, as a special case thereof) are thus extensions of the principle of kinship. The basis of ethnic solidarity is nepotism. The two other principal ways in which human societies are organized are reciprocity and coercion. Two unrelated individuals can enhance each other's fitness by cooperating in a mutually beneficial manner. Commonality of interest is therefore another fundamental basis of sociality in human collectivities. Broadly, we call human groups, organized for the pursuit of common interests, *classes*. Or, to utilize the useful Marxian distinction, a group of people who simply share common interests constitute a "class *in* itself," while a group consciously organized for the pursuit of these common interests is a "class *for* itself."

The third basis of human sociality, coercion, is, in fact, intraspecific parasitism. It arises when one group of people uses force or the threat of force to enhance the fitness of its members at the expense of another group. Different classes, as I have just defined them, can (and often are) linked to each other in such an unequal relationship of parasite and "host," thus making for class conflict in the classical Marxian sense.

It can readily be seen that my analysis is generally compatible with Marxian class analysis. One fundamental limitation of Marxian class analysis, however, is its reification of class as an entity superseding individual actors. It is this reification of class that leads many socialist utopians to expect that, once class distinctions have been abolished in a society, then class conflicts will disappear and general altruism will prevail. The first part of the prediction is true enough, but the second is a non sequitur. Eliminate exploitative relations between classes in a society, and you eliminate that particular basis of group conflict. But if the entire society becomes classless, then the basis of class solidarity, namely individual interest, disappears. Selfish interests are even more likely to emerge than in a situation of class conflict where overlap in individual interests can lead to solidary class action. Classes organize, not in the abstract, but against other classes with antagonistic interests; eliminate class differences, and you destroy the very basis of class solidarity.

Class solidarity, then, is nothing more than the overlap in the selfish individual interests of the members of a class. Workers, for instance, can only be expected to join a trade union if, by so doing, they individually benefit (or hope to benefit). That is, the benefit/cost ratio of unionization must be realistically predicted to be greater than one for successful unionization to take place. A reductionist model of class conflict and solidarity in terms of individuals maximizing self interests is thus perfectly adequate to understand "collective" behavior. Conversely, the reification of class adds nothing to the model and the gratuitous assumption of altruistic behavior in classless societies is empirically falsified. That is why Marxism has been so relatively successful in accounting for class conflicts (where it implicitly adopted the individual reductionist model of classical economics) and such an abysmal failure in predicting, much less changing, behavior in the utopian societies it attempted to create. Socialism has always foundered on the rock of individual selfishness. We are an organism biologically selected to maximize our individual inclusive fitness.

Ethnicity Versus Class

The two principal modes of collective organization in complex societies are ethnicity and class. The former is based on some notion of common kinship; the latter on common interest. The analytical distinction between these two types of social formation is crucial; both are, in principle, equally important, and neither is reducible to the other. They are fundamentally different in nature, and trying to redefine one as a special manifestation of the other impoverishes our understanding of plural societies (Leo Kuper 1974, Leo Kuper and M.G. Smith 1969).

Ethnicity tends to be the more permanent and the more basic of the two. Since it is based on common descent, changes in ethnic consciousness and boundaries, while they can and do occur, are contained within the limits of people's perceptions of biological relatedness. Thus, for example, ethnic boundaries can extend in scope by lumping together related groups that hitherto saw each other as different; conversely ethnic solidarity can break down into smaller components. Also, the salience of ethnic sentiments and the extent to which they can be mobilized for political purposes can fluctuate greatly in short periods of time.

All these changes, however, take place within a preexisting framework of ties of descent and marriage establishing a network of kin selection and sense of "we-ness" between people. Since descent, in the nature of the case, also creates the possibility of cleavage between collateral branches at each generation, the principle of fission and fusion (as called by British structural anthropologists in analyzing segmentary lineage systems) also operates in the definition of ethnic boundaries. This is why the latter often appear to fluctuate widely and capriciously. A closer examination shows, however, that these changes, while indeed responsive to environmental conditions and politically manipulable within limits, are not random, taking place within a preexisting structure with predictable lines of cleavage.

It will be objected that the sense of common descent in ethnicity is often a fiction, which is true enough. But for such a fiction to be effective, it has to be credible, and this cannot be achieved instantaneously, arbitrarily and at random. It takes time before an alien group becomes assimilated into an ethny, and, as the assimilation process is accompanied by intermarriage, generations of interbreeding indeed to transform the fiction into reality again. Two previously unrelated groups can fuse into one breeding population after a couple of generations of intermarriage.

It will also be objected that, for modern ethnies of millions of people, whatever biological relationship they may have is extremely tenuous at best, and this is quite true. Indeed, feelings of ethnic solidarity are more easily maintained in small, closely related groups than in large ethnies running into tens or even hundreds of millions of people. Nevertheless, even in very large ethnies, the basis of the solidarity remains the same, however diluted it may be. Ethnocentrism appeals to sentiments that have evolved in much smaller groups, and hence the appeal is often of reduced effectiveness, but the appeal strikes a responsive chord to the extent that the larger group is, in fact, a credible descent group. This typically can happen only after several generations of common history.

A commonly noted feature of ethnicity is its "irrationality." Appeals to ethnic sentiments need no justification other than common "blood." They are couched in terms of "our people" versus "them." The ethnic demagogue does not have to argue from logic or to mobilize interests. He merely has to activate preexisting sentiments of common descent. The most effective way to elicit this elemental ethnic solidarity is to create the illusion (or exploit the reality) of a threat by an outside group. Race riots, for instance, flare up by the mere spread of a rumor that one of "them" killed, hurt or simply offended one of "us."

The 1979–1980 seizure of hostages by Iranian militants at the American Embassy in Teheran is a classical example of the mobilization of ethnic sentiments. It elicited a groundswell of ethnic patriotism in the United States, as well as a wave of irrational retaliatory actions against totally innocent Iranians in the United States. Only a court injunction stopped, for example, the Immigration Service from discriminately deporting Iranians from the United States. It is also interesting how ineffective the Iranian militants' actions have been in trying to capitalize on the main line of cleavage in the United States. They released black American hostages in an attempt to exacerbate racial divisions, but they were unsuccessful. The detention of the American hostages was seen by Americans not as the actions of a small group of militants and not as an ideological struggle of Third World peoples against capitalism, but as an affront of Iranians against Americans.

Clearly then, ethnicity is more primordial than class. Blood runs thicker than money. This, however, is not to say that ethnicity is always more important or more salient than class. Nor is it necessarily the case that ethnicity can always be mobilized more easily than class for political action. Class solidarity, unlike ethnic solidarity, is dependent on a commonality of interests, which must be convincingly demonstrated before class solidarity can become effectively mobilized. Even then, it is vulnerable to the countervailing selfish interests of individual members of the class. A successful class organizer must persuade his target audience that they have a selfish interest in organizing for this common interest.

Class is therefore an alliance of convenience, based on selfish opportunism. It is vulnerable to changes in circumstances and can quickly disintegrate, because a class is not a preexisting solidary community, but class formation is not constrained by preexisting groups. Class groups can be formed out of coalitions of disparate groups sharing only a common interest in taking collective action. A classical example is the spectacular success of Jarvis' Initiative 13 in California in 1978. It was not difficult to convince California property owners that it was in their interest to vote themselves a substantial reduction in real estate taxes. The appeal was strictly rational, and it did not require any mobilization of ethnic or any other affiliation. Some minority ethnic groups attempted to organize against the initiative, because they tended to belong to the class that did not own property and whose social services would be negatively affected by the initiative, but they failed to organize an effective countermovement on a class basis, and they resoundingly lost the fight.

The Relationship Between Class and Ethnicity

Repeatedly in the case studies we examined, we saw that class and ethnicity, although they are clearly distinct principles of social organization, interpenetrate in complex and varying ways. Indeed, the interplay of class and ethnicity is probably the most difficult problem facing the analysis of complex societies. Empirically, a complete range of situations is found, from a Swiss-type situation where the correlation between class and ethnicity is close to zero, to a Peruvian-type case where the correlation is close to one. In between are situations like those of Québec or Northern Ireland where there is some relationship between ethnic and class status—but far from a perfect one. The intermediate situations are in fact the most common, and the ones where class and ethnic conflicts are most intricately intertwined. A priori, it is impossible and unwise to declare that one factor is more important than the other. The relative salience of class and ethnicity varies from case to case, and from time to time.

A few generalizations, however, seem to emerge from this bewildering diversity of situations:

1. Class and ethnicity seem to be *antithetical* principles of social organization. As one waxes, the other wanes in relative salience. Basically, if the cleavages are primarily ethnic, then the class divisions within the ethnies are correspondingly muted. Typically then, each ethny in the common polity is led by its elite. Each ethnic elite represents and acts on behalf of its respective ethny. The country may be ruled by a coalition of such ethnic elites, with each elite competing with the other for an ethnic distribution of resources under their supervision. Alternatively, if there is a clear ethnic hierarchy, the subordinate elite acts as a representative of its group and an intermediary between the subordinate group and the dominant elite. Sometimes the subordinate elite turns nationalist and revolutionary, challenging the dominant elite, but even then it is acting

on behalf of and, presumably, in the interest of its ethnic constituency, on whose support it relies. In all the variants of situations of great ethnic salience, the class distinctions within ethnies are secondary to the ethnic cleavages, and class organization is difficult.

In the opposite case, where class conflicts take precedence over ethnic cleavages, the definition of problems in terms of class interest militates against ethnic solidarity. Such situations are less common than ethnic-salient situations, which seems to indicate that, if ethnic cleavages are marked, they tend to take precedence over class cleavages.

The Andes of Peru are a case in point (van den Berghe and Primov 1977). There is a clear ethnic distinction between the Spanish-speaking dominant *mestizos* and the Quechua- or Aymara-speaking Indians who are almost all peasants. As there is a near identity of class and ethnic status (i.e., nearly all Indians are peasants), it is a moot question whether Indian peasants are oppressed *qua* peasants or *qua* Indians. The answer is that both factors are at work, although, at the national level, class relations tend to take precedence over ethnic relations. Indians can, however, redefine their class position by leaving the land and ceasing to be peasants. In time, they learn Spanish, become acculturated to local mestizo culture and assimilate into the mestizo group in one or two generations. This class mobility open to Indians automatically deprives Indians of potential leaders, since class mobility is almost inevitably accompanied by a change of ethnic identity. Thus, the class dynamics of the situation strongly militate against an ethnic definition of conflicts.

2. Where ethnic cleavages are complicated by class differences between ethnies, ethnic conflicts tend to be much more virulent. This is so because the issues then often shift from the right of each ethny to autonomy, self-determination and cultural identity, to more radical demands for ethnic equalization of resources and, hence, for an alteration of the class system. Interestingly, the outcome is often not radical, for generally it simply leads to the *embourgeoisement* of the formerly subordinate ethnic elite and a duplication of the dominant group's class structure in the subordinate group. Indeed, we are witnessing this process among American blacks. But the demands for ethnic (or racial) equalization often take very strident forms and elicit much conflict. Here again, we see that the ethnic definition of the problem of inequality deflects from a class solution, even though the subordinate ethnic leadership often adopts radical-sounding rhetoric. Nevertheless, class differences are not irrelevant, for they aggravate ethnic conflicts.

3. Both classes and ethnies vary greatly in their degree of openness and rigidity, with complex mutual repercussions on each other. Broadly,

where class groups are rigid and where class mobility is difficult, classes tend to acquire properties of ethnies. Conversely, where ethnic boundaries are fluid and permeable, ethnies tend to acquire the properties of classes.

Examples of rigid classes are "estates" (*Stände* in German), semihereditary occupational strata characteristic of pre-19th century Europe, in which social classes became much more than simply interest groups. Privileges of rank, status, wealth and occupational skills were passed on hereditarily at all levels of society: the nobleman passed on his title and lands to his sons; the merchant willed his wealth likewise; the craftsman apprenticed his sons and nephews, and so on. Therefore, each social class came, over time, to acquire many of the attributes of an ethny, with its own distinct subculture, style of dress, dialect, institutions and so on.

An even more extreme case of status rigidity is caste. Both castes and estates are thus "mixed" types of groups, sharing some of the properties of classes (notably functional interdependence in the system of production and complementarity in the division of labor) and some of ethnies (including, most importantly, a strong tendency to be endogamous). The existence of such mixed types does not invalidate, of course, the analytical distinction between class and ethny. It merely shows that the tendency for the two to be in an antithetical relationship is not absolute. Rigid classes tend to become like ethnies.

The reverse is also true. If ethnies are stratified but if the dominant group does not resist acculturation and assimilation of members of subordinate ethnic groups, then it can be expected that members of the subordinate ethnies will seek assimilation into the dominant one as a means of upward class mobility. We have seen examples of it in the assimilation of European immigrants in the United States, the Gallicization of the Flemings in Belgium, the Anglicization of Franco-Canadians outside of Québec, and the Mestizoization of Andean Indians in Peru. To the extent that this process of ethnic assimilation of the upwardly mobile has taken place over several generations, those members of the subordinate ethnic groups who have not assimilated find themselves in an *increasingly* subordinate and marginal position in both the class and the ethnic structure.

The Andean Indian case is an extreme one: nearly all Indians are peasants, and nearly all peasants are Indians. The conquered ethny had become first decapitated of much of its ruling class by the Spanish conquest and then systematically deprived by interbreeding, acculturation and assimilation over 20-odd generations of its more enterprising, successful and upwardly mobile elements. It is little wonder then, that those who today still remain Indian constitute, in fact, the bottom class of a highly stratified society by almost any objective correlate of class status one chooses to adopt: illiteracy, infant mortality, morbidity, life expectancy, per capita income or whatever.

Some scholars have termed such groups "eth-classes" (Gordon 1964) or "ethnic classes" [e.g., Rex and Tomlinson (1979) in their study of colored immigrants in Britain]. Others, stressing the tendency for ethnically or racially differentiated groups in industrial societies to occupy specialized niches in the division of labor, have spoken of a cultural division of labor (Hechter 1971, 1975, 1976, 1978). Others yet have explored the important consequences of the existence of a "split labor market" by ethnicity or race on intergroup relations (Bonacich 1972). All these studies point to the complicated relationship between class and ethnicity and the analytical irreducibility of one to the other, much as some would like to try to be class reductionists (e.g., Rex and Tomlinson 1979). Indeed, Max Weber's classical distinction between a class and a status group *(Stand)* was based on the same distinctions we have drawn here, except that he did not clearly distinguish the ethny from the status group (Weber 1968). Instead, he tended to identify the two.

Class and Ethnic Mobility

If we dichotomize the degree to which people move in and out of class and/or ethnic groups into "high" and "low," we can schematize the relationship between the two types of mobility as in Figure 1. The schema yields four logical combinations, which we have labeled A, B, C and D, but only three of which are found in practice. Cell B is empty for reasons that, by now, are fairly obvious. Given the inertia to remain in one's ethny unless there are powerful incentives to change, it follows that, in a system which offers little opportunity to improve one's *class* position, such incentives to change one's ethnicity are lacking. Even attempts at forced acculturation and assimilation are relatively unsuccessful if ethnic change is not supported by a system of positive rewards (such as access to better jobs, positions of power, high-status spouses and so on).

Type A societies—those characterized by low mobility in terms of both class and ethnic status—tend to be rigidly and highly stratified by both class and ethnicity. That is, they tend to be societies with a high degree of cultural division of labor in which ethnies occupy specialized niches in the economic system. Since class position and ethnicity tend to be closely associated, there is a trend toward occupational roles being hereditary or semihereditary. If, say, Jews in the Ottoman Empire tended

Figure 1
A Classification of Societies by Their Class and Ethnic Mobility

Class Mobility	Ethnic Mobility	
	Low	High
Low	**Type A** India Ottoman Empire Medieval Spain Tuzi Kingdom of Rwanda	**Type B** No clear cases
High	**Type C** Nigeria Belgium Switzerland	**Type D** Peru Guatemala Mexico

to be jewelers and money-lenders because Muslims were religiously excluded from these occupations, and if Jews had few other occupational outlets, then, obviously, these specialized occupations would become semihereditary in Jewish families.

By contrast, Type D societies, which have relatively high rates of both class and ethnic mobility, show much more dynamism. Yet, as in Type A societies, the ethnic groups are sharply stratified and specialized, and class status correlates highly with ethnic membership. Type D societies are thus dynamic cases of the ethnic division of labor, in which upward class mobility and change of occupation is possible, but only at the cost of leaving the subordinate ethnies and becoming absorbed into the dominant group. The clearest examples of such societies are in those Latin American countries where the peasantry is heavily Indian and where Indians are nearly all peasants. Indians thus constitute the bottom of a class system dominated by the group (variously called *mestizos*, *ladinos* or "whites") that, over the centuries, adopted the Spanish language and culture and, at the time of political independence from Spain in the 1810s, assumed power and became the "mainstream" of the new "national" societies.

In Type D societies, the possibility to leave the land and enter non-peasant occupations is relatively attractive, since the rewards for doing so are often substantial; but this can only be done by migration, generally to urban areas that are mestizo-dominated, and by leaving the cultural and social matrix of the local Indian peasant communities. Eventually this double process of social and geographical mobility leads to a change of ethnicity as well. Even in countries like Guatemala where ethnic boundaries are supposedly rigid and castelike (Tumin 1952), an analysis of changes in ethnic composition between population censuses clearly shows a continuous process of ladinoization of the Indian population (van den Berghe 1968).

The classic form of Type D societies is that of a multiplicity of fragmented, atomized, localized but internally unstratified peasant groups that are ethnically distinct from the culturally dominant group. The latter, often a majority of the total population, is much more *culturally* homogeneous but is itself highly internally stratified by social class. Indian peasants are thus a fragmented "ethnic class" at the bottom of a double hierarchy of class and ethnicity. They are dominated, both culturally and in politicoeconomic terms, by a class-stratified "national" mestizo society, the upper class of which rules the society (and traditionally owned much of the land cultivated by the Indian peasants).

Another interesting feature of Type D societies is their brand of paternalism in which extensive networks of patron-client relationships cut across both ethnic and class lines. In Latin America, this takes the form of *compadrazgo*, a ritual tie uniting the biological and godparents of a child and the child himself *(ahijado)* in a life-long set of mutual obligations. One generally seeks a class equal or a superior (but almost never a social inferior) to become a godparent of one's child. Thus, most Indians seek out powerful mestizos to become godparents *(padrino, madrina)* of their children, thereby consolidating a close but unequal relationship across both an ethnic and a class line.

Such ties almost invariably existed, for example, between *hacendados* and their Indian serfs. This paternalism obviously had the effect of perpetuating a quasifeudal relationship and undermining both class and ethnic solidarity among the Indian peasantry. The only tangible way of improving one's lot was to seek the protection and favor of one member of the oppressor class by maintaining a special, personal, privileged relationship with him. Class and ethnic domination reinforced one another as both class and ethnic solidarity was undercut by these particularistic ties of *compadrazgo* across class and ethnic lines.

Type C societies—those characterized by a high degree of class mobility but considerable ethnic stability—are markedly different from both Types A and D. This combination of ethnic stability and class mobility implies that one can change class status without altering one's ethnicity, and, therefore, that each ethny is internally stratified into social classes. To the extent that each ethny has its own class system, the ethnies themselves are less clearly stratified in relation to each other. Indeed, in some cases, the ethnic groups are in substantially the same class position, and one finds a nearly total absence of a cultural division of labor. Switzerland and contemporary Belgium are cases in point.

Sometimes, there are ethnic inequalities as well as class inequalities in Type C societies, but the overlap between the two is only partial. Nigeria is an example. Southern Nigerians, who are largely Christians, are, for a number of reasons traceable to the colonial period, greatly overrepresented in the upper echelons of the "modern" sector, have a much higher literacy rate, have far greater percentages of people with Western-style education and a knowledge of English and so on—compared to Northern Nigerians, who are mostly Muslims. Yet, despite these regional differences in levels of development and "modernization," one cannot rank-order Nigerian ethnic groups in a consensual hierarchy of status. Each ethny feels superior to the others, and each has its internal class distinctions and its elite that represents it in "national" politics.

Since, in Type C societies, social class mobility is possible without changing one's ethny, and since the ethnies themselves are often not clearly stratified, the incentives to assimilate are minimal. There is no point in severing one's ethnic ties, unless this is the main (or, indeed, the only) way of improving one's position. These conditions do not prevail in Type C societies, and this absence of incentives to assimilate largely accounts for the persistence of ethnic differences in these countries. It also accounts for the relative absence in Type C societies of patron-client ties *across* ethnic lines. Indeed, there is a striking contrast between Type C and Type D societies in the operation of networks of patronage and clientelism. In Type C societies, patron-client ties are typically *intra*ethnic. The elite distribute favors and resources to ethnic clients, thereby reinforcing ethnic and familistic ties and heightening the salience of ethnicity, at the expense of class, in the political game.

An overwhelming difference between African countries (most of which tend to be of the C Type) and Latin American countries (mostly D Type) is in the relative salience of class and ethnicity. In Africa, class conflicts tend to be muted, while ethnic conflicts are seldom far below the surface. Conversely, in Latin America, ethnic conflicts are almost completely defused through the mechanisms I have just discussed, and class conflicts, especially within the culturally dominant mestizo group, are paramount. This again points to the antithetical nature of class and ethnicity as modes of social organization. Generally, but not necessarily, a stress in one factor is accompanied by a deemphasis in the other. At least, this seems to be the case in terms of consciousness and solidarity.

As principles of *domination*, class and ethnicity often reinforce each other, as we have seen in the latin American societies of Type D.

Conclusions

Naturally, these societal types are but crude constructs to put some order into an extremely complex reality and attempt some generalizations on the interplay of class and ethnicity. At this level of analysis, we have used general and abstract concepts describing processes at the collective level. This is convenient as a short-hand device to describe a multiplicity of individual actions and decisions. In the last analysis, however, it is people who modify their behavior in accordance with their individual interests. Therefore, processes of ethnic change and persistence must be understood in terms of a model of individual benefit-maximizing behavior.

The Social Standing of Ethnic and Racial Groupings[†]

PETER C. PINEO

The coexistence of a status hierarchy based on socioeconomic factors and a second hierarchy based on ethnicity has remained a puzzle for Canadian sociologists. Since the "collapse of the vertical mosaic," to use Porter's own phrase (Pineo and Porter 1985: 390), the earlier resolution of the problem, that ethnic status was largely derivative of socioeconomic status, is no longer satisfactory. At a minimum, such an explanation would require us to assume that the public is highly responsive to the very modest socioeconomic differences between ethnic groups shown in recent research (Pineo 1976, Darroch 1979, Ornstein 1981), although somewhat stronger differences can be found in earlier decades (Pineo and Porter 1985).

The research reported in this article endeavours to measure the strength of the distinctions between ethnic and racial groupings made by the Canadian public, using several comparisons. A comparison with "occupational prestige" is possible since the methods used to collect the evaluations of ethnic and racial groupings are identical to those used in prestige studies. A further comparison can be made with the United States, since the study is a replication of U.S. work. Finally, the responses of different categories within Canada can be compared, and the responses coming from French Canada can be compared with those from English Canada.

The best known research in this area is that of Bogardus, who conceptualized the distinctions he found as measures of *social distance* (1959a). Canadian work including these measures has been done by

†*Canadian Review of Sociology and Anthropology* 14, 2 (1977): 147–57. This is a revised version of the original article.

Driedger and associates (for example, Driedger and Peters 1977, Driedger and Mezoff 1981). In the Bogardus approach, respondents are asked a series of questions about the admissibility of individuals to social interaction of varying degrees of intimacy. Phrased in this way, the questions imply a pre-judgement that the effects of any invidious distinction between ethnic or racial groupings will be principally in the area of primary relations. What is demonstrated in this article is that using a more general evaluative criterion, "social standing" rather than social intimacy, also elicits a ranking of ethnic and racial groups, similar to the Bogardus results but differing from them in some details.

The evaluative criterion of "social standing" is the same as is used in studies of the evaluation of occupations, the "occupational prestige" studies. Its appropriateness has been thoroughly reviewed (Goldthorpe and Hope 1972, Ridge 1974). While highly critical of the tradition of using the word "prestige" for these studies, these authors nonetheless appear to conclude that the criterion of "social standing" does capture a broad and general evaluation of social status. As Ridge notes: "A measure of 'occupational prestige' is relevant *only* if it can be taken as a statement of where occupations stand in a social value hierarchy.... There is good reason to believe that public-opinion surveys of the social standing of occupations provide just such a measure" (1974: 3). By extension, then, the location of ethnic and racial groups in a value hierarchy can also be measured by using the stimulus of "social standing."

To test if the stimulus of "social standing" would elicit a ranked ordering of racial and ethnic groups, 393 adult Canadians, forming a national sample, were asked to sort cards printed with the names of 36 ethnic, racial, and related groups. To provide a baseline for comparison, the same 393 were asked, at a different point in the interview, to sort in an identical manner 204 cards bearing occupational titles. With the social standing of the occupations and of the racial and ethnic groups measured in an identical way it is possible to ask a series of questions about how similar the ranking of ethnicities and racial groups is to the ranking of occupations. Are people as willing to rank ethnic and racial groups as they are occupations? Is there as much consensus? Is the range of rankings as great? Do subgroups within Canada agree about the ranking of ethnicities and racial groupings as fully as they do about the rankings of occupations?

Procedures

The details of the fieldwork for this study are available elsewhere (Pineo and Porter 1967). To elicit the evaluations of racial and ethnic groups the following question was asked:

> Canada is a country made up of many different kinds of people. Some of these groups of people have higher social standing than others do. Here is a card with the name of one such group on it. Please put that card in the box at the top of the ladder if you think that group has the highest possible social standing. Put it in the box at the bottom of the ladder if you think that group has the lowest possible social standing. If it belongs in between, just put it in the box that comes the closest to representing the social standing of that particular group of people.

After the first card was placed, the interviewer was to go on to say:

> Here are a few more groups. As you did before, just put them in the boxes on the ladder which match the social standing you think these groups have. Place them the way you think people actually treat these groups, not the way you think they *ought* to treat them.

Except for the final sentence, this instruction is identical to the one eliciting the sorting of occupational titles.

The sorting of both the ethnicities and the occupational titles was made upon a cardboard "ladder" with spaces numbered from 1 to 9. The scores were then transformed (using the formula $X = 12.5\,X - 12.5$) so that they ran from zero to 100, the common form of presenting prestige scores.

English-Canadian Rankings of Ethnicities and Racial Groupings

The English Canadians in the sample appeared able to rank the ethnic titles given to them, and the resulting rank order of the groups contains few surprises.[1] It closely resembles the ranking generally felt to exist in the U.S. (see, for example, Knoke and Felson 1974). Western and North European origins, which in the U.S. would be called the "old immigrants," are at the top; Eastern and Mediterranean, the "new immigrants," further down; coloured and Asiatics at the bottom. The actual scores, with standard deviations, are given in Table 1, organized in these broader origin categories. For 19 of the groups in Table 1, Bogardus social distance scores from U.S. college students are also available; the rank order by social distance and by social standing for these groups is high ($R = .95$). Only the Jews and Scots are to any degree out of rank (Bogardus 1967: 152).

The range from the lowest to the highest score in Table 1 is considerable. English Canadians got the highest score, at 83.1; Negroes were given the lowest, at 25.4. But this is not quite so great a range as that used in the sorting of the occupational titles. In that sorting task, English Canadians gave 88.7 to provincial premier and 14.3 to newspaper peddler.[2] This is the first of several clues indicating that the ethnic rankings have a weaker statistical form than do the occupational rankings.

The "don't know" rates provide a second clue. They are consistently somewhat higher for the ethnicity titles than for the occupational titles. The typical no-answer rate for an ethnic ranking was over 10 percent while for occupations it was only 6.3 percent. While people have, or think they have, sufficient information to rank quite exotic occupations, they appear less able or willing to rank certain of the smaller ethnic groups. Thus 16 percent did not rank "Lithuanians," 15.7 percent did not rank "Icelanders," and 12.7 did not rank "Finns." The title "People of Foreign Ancestry" was left unranked by 13.7 percent; it was possibly considered too broad a category. The smallest no-answer rates were for titles "English," "Scots," and "English Canadians," 7.3 percent, 7.7 percent, and 7.6 percent respectively. Some 9 percent declined to rank themselves; that is, the title "People of My Own Ethnic Background." By implication, then, 91 percent must have felt they had some identifiable, rankable ethnicity themselves, despite the fact that "Canadian," as opposed to English Canadian or French Canadian, was not included as a title and therefore not suggested as an ethnicity. In general, however, these no-answer rates are not so high, by the ordinary standards of survey research, as to lead to any serious concern about the meaningfulness of the ethnicity rankings.

A third clue that the ranking of ethnicities has not quite the same structural firmness as the occupational rankings is that the standard deviations in the rankings of ethnicities are higher. The average standard deviation for the ethnicity rankings was 24.1; only around 20 of the whole 204 occupational titles, even with the French rankings included, had standard deviations this high (Pineo and Porter 1967). This means there is less consensus within English Canada about the rankings of ethnic groups than there is about the occupations. No ethnic groups had low standard deviations; the lowest was for the title "English" at 20.1, followed by "English Canadians" at 20.5. Many occupations had standard deviations below 20 points. This suggests that one source of the lack of consensus is a tendency for people to base the scale around differing midpoints; such a tendency would contribute to uniformly high standard deviations. That is to say, there may be a tendency to shift the whole

Table 1
Ranking of Ethnicities by English-speaking Canadians

Ethnic Groups in Origin Categories	Mean Rank	SD
Charter Group Members and Related Groups		
British	81.2	21.4
English	82.4	20.1
English Canadians	83.1	20.5
French	60.1	24.8
French Canadians	56.1	27.8
Irish	69.5	22.8
Scots	75.2	22.1
Western and North European		
Belgians	49.1	22.9
Danes	52.4	23.7
Dutch	58.4	22.6
Germans	48.7	25.2
Icelanders	45.6	24.7
Norwegians	55.3	22.8
Swedes	56.6	23.3
Swiss	55.7	21.9
Mediterranean and Central European		
Austrians	49.6	22.2
Czechoslovaks	41.2	22.9
Finns	47.6	22.7
Greeks	39.9	23.7
Hungarians	42.6	22.6
Italians	43.1	25.0
Jews	46.1	28.0
Lithuanians	41.4	21.9
Poles	42.0	22.4
Roumanians	42.1	23.5
Russians	35.8	26.2
Ukrainians	44.3	22.6
Non-Caucasian Groups		
Canadian Indians	28.3	28.3
Chinese	33.1	25.4
Coloureds	26.3	26.2
Japanese	34.7	25.3
Negroes	25.4	26.1
Not Ethnicities		
Catholics	70.1	25.6
Protestants	75.3	23.4
People of Foreign Ancestry	50.1	24.6
People of My Own Ethnic Background	74.4	24.9

(N = 300 cases less the number not ranking each title)

ethnicity ranking up or down the scale more than there is to shift the whole occupational ranking. But this cannot explain away the whole effect because there are also some exceptionally high standard deviations: 28.3 for Canadian Indians, 27.8 for French Canadians, 28.0 for Jews, and 26.1 for Negroes. Lack of familiarity with the group does not seem to be the issue; the standard deviations for Finns and Lithuanians are quite low. Rather it would seem to be that groups felt to suffer some degree of overt discrimination, especially the more visible racial groupings, are the ones on which the lack of consensus is greatest.

There is, then, evidence that Canadians can rank ethnicities but that the consensus and knowledge about them are not quite so great as about occupations. The theorem that consensus implies social importance suggests that the ethnic ranking has not the same structural importance as the occupational ranking.

The ranking itself, as noted, has few surprises in it. The English and English Canadians did extremely well. With ethnicity ranks of 82.4 and 83.1 respectively, their ethnicity earns them, if one plays the game that the scales are transposable, about the same rank as being a member of the Canadian cabinet. They are followed, not unexpectedly, by Scots and Irish, although the fall off in rank is fairly swift, down to 75.2 for the Scots and 69.5 for the Irish. Following the Irish there is another dead spot in the scale, this time of almost 10 points. Thus English Canadians give a special status to those of British origin. The concept of charter group status, as used by Hughes (1952: 137) seems appropriate.

Pineo and Porter suggested, in their analysis of occupational rating (1967: 31), that a tendency to give inordinately high ratings to the very top jobs might be a statistical representation of the "elitist" pattern which Lipset suggested was important in Canadian society (1963: chap. 7). They note that only a small tendency of this kind is found in the occupational rankings. Here, in the ethnicity rankings, the effect is found, and it is of considerable magnitude. It is tempting to speculate that the expected elitist pattern may in fact exist in the realm of ethnic rather than socioeconomic status. There is no indication in the literature that the same exceptional status is given to any U.S. ethnic group; in fact there is no colloquial term quite like "English Canadian" in the U.S. Bogardus provides a social distance score for "Americans (U.S. White)" and it is not markedly ahead of the balance (1959a: 152).

The rating of the French Canadians, at 56.1, puts them near on the scale to the Dutch and Scandinavians. This is the traditional "old immigrant" group described in U.S. literature, and the ranking of them is about as expected. They are all ranked higher than the general title

"People of Foreign Ancestry," suggesting they might be considered among the "most desirable" immigrants. That the French Canadians should be seen by the English only as "desirable immigrants" is ironic, but it also should be noted that as the major minority group in Canada their status undoubtedly vastly exceeds that of the blacks in the U.S.

Belgians and Germans ranks slightly below the title "People of Foreign Ancestry" and also slightly below the logical midpoint of the scale, 50.0. These too would be among those called "old immigrants" in the U.S. and their rank in Canada may be somewhat lower than one would expect. The lower ranking of the Germans may be a clue that international politics and warfare, operating perhaps through the media, can affect the status of an ethnic group within Canada. The Russians, an important international enemy at the time of the study, were given an extraordinarily low rank of 35.8.

The "new immigrants" from Eastern Europe and the Mediterranean are closely bunched with those from the Baltic between 47.6 and 39.9. Again this would resemble the U.S. pattern.

The Jews are not found "at the bottom" as suggested for the U.S. by Knoke and Felson (1974: 631). Actual data which are presented below show them to be more in the middle of the hierarchy in the U.S., the same place as in Canada. They are not at the bottom in the Bogardus results either, but are, as might be expected, lower in social distance rank than in social standing (1967: 152).

The Japanese and Chinese rank low, at 34.7 and 33.1 respectively. Finally, Canadian Indians, at 28.3, the coloured at 26.3, and the Negroes at 25.4 enjoy a social standing about equivalent to the occupational rank of a construction labourer or railroad section hand. Clearly the non-whites are felt to be very much at the bottom, visibility apparently accentuating the phenomenon.

Ratings of ethnic groups in the United States were collected in an identical manner and at approximately the same time as the Canadian ones. Scores for some 19 ethnic groups are now available for comparison with the Canadian ones. The high degree of similarity is shown by a rank order correlation between the two sets of .95. The two rankings are shown in Table 2.

Table 2 reveals one matter which the rank order coefficient would hide—that is the tendency to give a sort of elite ethnic status to those of British origin is, as we suggested, a distinctively English-Canadian pattern. The title "British" was rated 81.2 in Canada and only 65.5 in the United States. In general, the U.S. scores cluster much more closely together, suggesting less differentiation in the rankings of ethnic groups

Table 2
Hierarchy of Ethnic Groups in the U.S. and English Canada

United States (N = 445)			English Canada (N = 300)
		81	British
	80		
		79	
		78	
		77	
		76	
		75	Scots
		74	
		73	
		72	
		71	
	70		Irish
		69	
		68	
		67	
British		66	
		65	
		64	
		63	
Irish		62	
		61	
	60		French
Scots, French		59	Dutch
Germans, Dutch		58	
		57	Swedes
Norwegians		56	French Canadians
Swedes		55	Norwegians
		54	
		53	
Danes		52	Danes
Finns, French Canadians		51	
Italians	50		
		49	Germans
		48	Finns
		47	
Jews		46	Jews
Hungarians		45	
Poles		44	
Lithuanians		43	Italians, Hungarians
Czechs		42	Poles
Greeks		41	Lithuanians, Czechoslovaks
	40		Greeks
		39	
		38	
		37	
Russians		36	Russians

Source: U.S. Data: Laumann (1973: 46).

in the U.S. than in Canada, perhaps since the period of heavy immigration is futher back in U.S. than Canadian history.

The only other major differences between the two sets of scores involved specific groups, although there may be a tendency in Canada to give systematically lower ratings to Eastern European and Mediterranean ethnicities. Among the specific titles, both Germans and Italians are much lower in Canada. This may be a legacy of the Second World War, in which Canada was more greatly committed than the U.S. On the other hand, the status of French Canadians is appreciably higher among English Canadians than Americans (56.1 as compared to 50.9).

Variation Within English Canada

In three tests so far, involving the incidence of no answers, the range and the size of the standard deviations, the amount of knowledge and degree of consensus surrounding the ranking of ethnicities is found to be lower than that of occupations. A fourth test can be made. One can compute correlation coefficients representing how similar the rankings were in different social categories within English Canada. Did women rank them in the same way as men? Did low and high income groups rank them similarly? This is a test traditionally applied to occupational prestige rankings, and the result, in that case, is uniformly high correlations which are offered as evidence of consensus.

By this test the amount of consensus in the rankings comes very close to the amount found in examining occupational rankings. The correlations were .99 for five variables comparing respondents from differing community sizes, comparing men and women, comparing those under and over 40 years of age, comparing those with any rural experience with those with none and comparing blue with white collar workers. The correlation was somewhat smaller for three other variables: between education levels it was .97; between income groups it was .98; and in comparing Catholics and Protestants it was .96.

The results seem inconsistent. The standard deviations were appreciably higher than those for the occupational ranking but the correlation coefficients are only slightly lower. The standard deviations imply some substantial dissensus within English Canada; the correlation coefficients suggest only moderate dissensus. In fact what has happened is that the dissensus which exists is not between the several social categories chosen for examination, and this reveals the limitation of this fourth test of consensus. As has been noted in the work dealing with occupational prestige, establishing that there is no important disagreement between major social categories is a very special test of dissensus (Burshtyn 1968:

176). It does not rule out the possibility of considerable individual variation within the categories or disagreement between less significant social categories. Those who have designed this test in the past must have adopted the position that dissensus across major, established social categories is theoretically and practically the more significant variety.

Inspection of the ratings given those of low and high education and those of low and high income, two variables producing correlations less than .99, reveals no obvious pattern. One might have expected simple effects of "liberalism" among the better educated and also that the income differences were derivative of this. But while the better educated English Canadians gave some 10 extra points to Japanese, and 9 extra to Jews, no extra points were given to Negroes or Canadian Indians. If liberalism does operate at all it operates to increase the standing of most. On the average, ethnic titles were ranked some five points higher by the better educated, and this did not include the top charter group ethnicities which were ranked at about the same level by both the less and better educated. So the pattern for the better educated is that most ethnicities are lifted some 5 or 6 points closer to the charter groups. Exceptions were the Negroes and Indians, and also the Italians, who dropped one point. The French Canadians also were not raised. Certain Scandinavian ethnicities were given much higher ratings by the better educated; Danes were ranked 58.4 by the better educated and 45.9 by the less well educated. The better educated, then, see a society with the charter group ethnicities well up at the top, most continental European ethnicities somewhat higher than they are seen by the less educated, but the most deprived groups still very much at the bottom. Possibly, the better educated are simply showing a greater capacity to describe the society accurately. Or, if this is projection, Canadian education serves to liberalize attitudes to most continental European and Asian ethnicities but not Negroes, Indians, Italians, or French Canadians.

Examination of the difference between the income groups suggests that the basic pattern is the same. The ratings given by high income people are virtually identical to those given by the highly educated ($r = .995$).

The comparison of Catholic and Protestant respondents yielded the third correlation which was less than .99. Catholics rate Catholics higher and Protestants lower, of course. Catholics give themselves 75.2 points and the Protestants 69.1; Protestants give themselves 79.2 and the Catholics 68.8. Similarly, certain highly Catholic ethnicities are given higher points: Italians are rated 48.3 by the Catholics and 40.5 by the Protestants. The effect is less great in the ratings of French Canadians: Catholics give them 58.3 while the Protestants give them 54.2.

The clearest difference in the rankings given by English Catholics is that they give lower rankings to the charter groups. English get 78.0 from the Catholics while the Protestants rank them 84.0. English Canadians get 79.3 rather than 84.2. Scots get 67.7 rather than 77.9.

Finally, the English Catholics are the first group identified which shows a sense of being second class citizens. The title "People of My Own Ethnic Background" was given a ranking of only 63.7 by the English Catholics. The Protestants rated themselves 80.0. Evidence shows that this low rating of themselves by the Catholics has even further complexities in that they also have a high standard deviation: 26.9. Among the English Catholics there remains a diversity in self-image. In contrast there is much less variation among the Protestants: the standard deviation is only 21.5. The standard deviations were high for the majority of the rankings given by English Catholics, averaging 26.2. The English Catholic population appears to be a quite heterogeneous component of Canadian society.

Even when the correlation is nearly perfect there can be a difference in the ratings, as virtually all tend to be higher in one group than another. There were such differences. Respondents under 40 tended to give ratings averaging 4.5 points higher than the older ones. White collar respondents gave ratings averaging 4.0 points higher than blue collar workers, which is consistent with the tendency for higher income and highly educated respondents to give higher ratings. Other differences were minute. Women gave slightly higher ratings than men; Protestants slightly higher than Catholics. Those with rural backgrounds and those now living in communities under 30,000 gave slightly lower ratings.

Rankings by French Canadians

French Canada provides the only minority group sufficiently large in this sample for a direct investigation of how the members of a specific group modify the ethnic ranking system in response to their own status. The rank order given the groups by French Canadian respondents is quite different from that given by English Canadians; the correlation coefficient is only .84 (or .83 for 32 pure ethnicity titles). By the standards of occupational prestige studies this is a very low correlation and it shows clearly that the statistical treatment of the data does not guarantee high correlations.[3]

The ratings by English and French are presented in Table 3. The general shape of the ranking by French Canadians puts virtually all non-English, non-French ethnicities further down the rank. Western and Northern Europeans were ranked around an average of 52.8 by the

Table 3
Hierarchy of Ethnic and Racial Groups in English and French Canada

English Canada (N = 300)		French Canada (N = 93)
English Canadians (83.1)	83	
English (82.4)	82	
British (81.2)	81	
	80	
	79	
	78	
	77	French Canadians, English Canadians
	76	Catholics (77.6)
Protestants (75.3) Scots (75.2)	75	
My Own Ethnic Background (74.4)	74	My Own Ethnic Background (73.7)
	73	
	72	French (72.4)
	71	English (71.0)
Catholics (70.1)	70	
Irish (69.5)	69	
	68	
	67	
	66	British (66.0)
	65	
	64	
	63	
	62	
	61	
French (60.1)	60	
	59	
Dutch (58.4)	58	
Swedes (56.6)	57	Scots (56.5)
French Canadians (56.1) Swiss (55.7)	56	
Norwegians (55.3)	55	Irish (55.2) Protestants (54.8)
	54	
	53	
Danes (52.4)	52	
	51	Italians (51.3)
People of Foreign Ancestry (50.1)	50	Dutch (49.7)
Austrians (49.6) Belgians (49.1)	49	
Germans (48.7) Finns (47.6)	48	
	47	
Jews (46.1) Icelanders (45.6)	46	
	45	Belgians (45.3) Swedes (44.8)
Ukrainians (44.3)	44	Swiss (44.4)
Italians (43.1) Hungarians (42.6)	43	Jews (43.10)
Poles (42.0) Roumanians (42.1)	42	
Lithuanians (41.4) Czechoslovaks	41	
(41.2) Greeks (39.9)	40	Germans (40.5) Ukrainians (40.0)
	39	People of Foreign Ancestry (38.9)
	38	Hungarians (38.4) Poles (38.0)
	37	Norwegians (38.0) Austrians (37.5)
Russians (35.8)	36	
Japanese (34.7)	35	
	34	Roumanians (33.9) Greeks (33.5)
Chinese (33.1)	33	Russians (33.2) Icelanders (32.9)
	32	Canadian Indians (32.5) Czecho-
	31	slovaks (32.4) Finns (32.3)
	30	Danes (32.2)
	29	Lithuanians (29.1)
Canadian Indians (28.3)	28	Japanese (27.8)
	27	Coloureds (26.5)
Coloureds (26.3)	26	
Negroes (25.4)	25	Chinese (24.9) Negroes (23.5)

English and 41.1 by the French. Mediterranean and Central Europeans were ranked around 43.0 by the English and 37.1 by the French. Non-Caucasians were ranked around 29.5 by the English and 27.0 by the French. The specific title "People of Foreign Ancestry" was ranked 50.1 by the English and 38.9 by the French. French Canada is not a nation of new immigrants and foreign ethnicities tend to be down-graded.

A second observation may be quickly made. The French do not agree with the English about where they themselves belong in the order. The French rank themselves at the top, giving themselves exactly the same score as they do the English: both ethnicities were ranked at 77.6. The tie, of course, suggests a model of a Canada formed of two equal founding peoples. This is the kind of image of Canada which underlay the Report of the Royal Commission on Bilingualism and Biculturalism. The commission apparently caught the main currents of thought in this respect within French Canada, at the time at least. Canada's problem, perhaps, is that this image is not shared by English Canada.

It must be noted that the extraordinary high ranking given to charter group ethnicities—those of British origin—by English Canadians is not found to be the pattern in the French Canadian responses. Rather they give the highest group only around 77.

While these broad patterns to the French responses are clear and perhaps expected, closer inspection of the French ratings reveals details which to an English Canadian seem peculiar. The Scots, for example, are much lower than the English. Finns and Danes are ranked with Canadian Indians. Norwegians are tied with Poles. The very categories in which English Canadians and Americans apparently think about ethnicity, such as Scandinavian, Eastern European, etc., seem to disappear as their component ethnicities are scattered through the list.

It is quite possible that the problem is one of sample size. Only 93 French Canadians did the ranking. This may be a sufficient number to reveal the general pattern of the ranking within French Canada but not sufficient to look at the specific ranking given to the smaller ethnic groups.

As well, there is some evidence that French Canadians are, quite understandably, less familiar with some of the smaller ethnicities and hence less able to rank them. Don't-know rates for certain ethnicities are quite high: 20.4 percent failed to rank Icelanders; 20.4 failed to rank Finns; 17.2 failed to rank Roumanians; and 16.1 failed to rank Danes. Thus, some of the titles which seem most peculiarly ranked are also ones for which the don't-know rates suggest there is less information within French Canada. When it came to some better known ethnicities, the don't-know rates were much lower: Chinese, 6.5; French Canadians, 6.5; English Canadians, 6.5.

While the don't-know rates are fairly high, they can be put in perspective. In ranking some of the religion groups in a separate rating task also in the same study, the don't-know rates among the French became enormous. For the title Christian Scientists, 43.0 percent failed to rank; for Mormon, 46.2 percent; for Seventh Day Adventists, 49.5 percent; and for Lutherans, 38.7 percent. From this perspective, then, it would seem that French Canadians feel they do have some knowledge about the smaller ethnic groups, at least in comparison with their knowledge about many religious groups.

Another test that was applied to the rankings by English Canadians can also be applied to the French. That is, are the standard deviations particularly high? The average standard deviation for the French was 23.8, and for the English, 24.1. The rankings from French Canada cannot be dismissed as mere statistical noise; where they do rank, they appear to rank with as much consensus as the English. (In ranking religions the standard deviations differed more: 24.3 for the English; 25.8 for the French.)

High standard deviations and high don't-know rates do not appear to indicate the same thing. For ethnicities such as "Finns" and "Danes," where the don't-know rate is high, the standard deviations are not particularly high. Rather the standard deviations within French Canada tend to be high for titles with low don't-know rates, suggesting they represent true differences of opinion rather than lack of information. There are high standard deviations for such groups as "English," "Protestants," "Germans," and "Jews."

Consensus Within French Canada

The final test of consensus, that of comparing the responses of major subgroupings within the society, can also be applied to the French-Canadian responses, although here sample sizes became quite small and interpretations risky.

Despite the small size of categories, the resulting correlation coefficients are quite substantial. They are listed in Table 4, with the size of the smaller category in the comparison also included. No correlation is less than .95 despite category sizes as low as 16 cases. On balance, there is evidence here that the consensus within French Canada closely approaches but does not equal that within English Canada. Again, as in English Canada, the dissensus across socioeconomic categories of income and education appears the greatest, although the category sizes are dangerously low. There is considerable agreement between those with and those without rural background and between those in bigger cities and the others. The strength of the rural-urban distinction in French Canada seems to have diminished considerably since the 1930s when Hughes (1944) did his field work. Finally, there is a hint of greater male-female differences in French than in English Canada.

The differences in the overall average rank given are not great—of about the same magnitude as in English Canada and varying in direction.

Table 4
A Test of Consensus Within French Canada: Correlation Coefficients Representing the Amount of Consensus Between Major Social Categories Within French Canada

Variable	Size of Smaller Category	Correlation
Education	16	0.951
Income	29	0.961
Occupation	18	0.958
Size of community	32	0.962
Ruralness	43	0.970
Gender	37	0.958
Age	39	0.972

Detailed inspection of the ratings given specific titles is unwise with such small categories. A few quick points may be made. Generally, the title "English Canadian" was rated about the same by all components of French Canada. It was highest (82.8) among those with higher incomes and lowest (74.4) among those with rural backgrounds. In contrast, the rating given "French Canadian" varied more extensively. It was highest (85.2) among the highly educated, and lowest (72.9) among those living in smaller communities.

In fact, the 85.2 rating indicated by the better educated is sufficiently greater than the 75.5 given by the less educated to achieve statistical significance. Also the 84.3 given by those in communities of 30,000 or more is significantly greater than the 72.9 given by those living in smaller communities. Thus a favourable self-image is more common among the more sophisticated, educated, and urban French Canadians than the rest.

Again, for the French as well as the English, we are left with the paradox that while higher standard deviations imply some dissensus, a check for its source using a list of standard sociological categories does not prove successful. Alternative axes of dissensus must exist. For the French we have one clue. The standard deviations are low among those with higher socioeconomic status and the more urban, but remain high among the rest. The dissensus largely exists among the less sophisticated component of the society. Some titles, such as English, English Canadian, and Jews do not follow this rule, however.

Conclusion

Canadians were able to rank ethnic and racial groupings according to their "social standing." By most tests, however, the degree of knowledge and consensus shown is less than that found when occupations are ranked. In so far as the assumption that consensus (and knowledge) imply social importance is valid, the ranking of ethnic and racial groupings appears to be a less crucial element in Canadian social structure than the ranking of occupations.

Proceeding beyond this observation is a matter of some difficulty. No one has successfully explained why occupations are ranked as they are, and it would seem unlikely that any easy explanation of the ethnic hierarchy will be found. One matter is largely settled, however. As noted earlier, the position that socioeconomic status is the major cause is no longer tenable. At the time the rankings were collected, the association between them and occupation level as shown in the Census of 1961 was extremely modest ($r = .11$, Pineo 1976: 119). Data in the Canadian mobility study dealing with the occupations of older cohorts suggest that earlier periods may have shown higher associations. Thus to some degree the rankings may represent an earlier time period, capturing the *entrance status* of immigrating groups and retaining that image as a form of *lag*.

Beyond this possibility it is likely that this phenomenon, like so many in sociology, is *multi-caused* and the accumulation of a large number of small associations will eventually produce some adequate level of explanation. While more consensus surrounds the occupational evaluations than the ethnic hierarchy, even for them recent research shows it is not total (Guppy 1984, Guppy and Goyder 1984). The departures from consensus may be used to provide some explanation of the ranks, as, for example, the education or religion of the respondent produce at least small differences in the rankings given. There are also hints in the data that the size of the group or its length of residence in Canada may be factors. It will be noted that these suggested factors fall into two categories—properties of the respondents, or the properties of the ethnic and racial groups themselves. Splicing these two kinds of data—one the usual explanatory variables of survey analysis, the other in aggregated form—into a single analysis is difficult, and some methodological innovations may be required to make it possible to do so gracefully.

The fieldwork and design of this study were done with sufficient care that a replication to measure social change is possible. One may speculate what changes are likely. Occupational ratings are known to change very little (Hodge, Siegel, and Rossi 1964). With less consensus behind them, however, the ethnic rankings could show more rapid change, but a variety of factors suggest considerable stability should be expected. Little has changed since 1932, for example. Anderson and Frideres have uncovered an embarrassingly forthright quotation from the 1932 *Canada Year Book*, an official government publication, which describes the "relative assimilability" of various groups, and it is much like the 1965 results (Anderson and Frideres 1981: 276). Further, if the U.S. is considered a likely model of Canada's future, it is not greatly dissimilar, although, as noted, the hierarchy is truncated. Within the Canadian data the rankings given by the young and the better educated might be considered bellwether; they show a tendency to rank most groups somewhat higher, but otherwise no major differences from the balance. It is probably more reasonable to expect a substantial number of very moderate shifts in ranking. This is perhaps an inevitable consequence of assuming that the hierarchy is multi-caused: that is, no single social event, or intervention, should be expected to cause major changes, but many small changes are likely. A replication of the research might serve as a sort of score card, showing which events and interventions appear to have had consequences.

Notes

1. For brevity, the term ethnicity (and ethnic group) is used frequently to encompass both ethnic and racial groupings.
2. The source for these and other occupational rankings is Pineo and Porter (1967).
3. Could the small size of the francophone sample have produced this "low correlation"? For comparison, 30 pairs of randomly selected subsamples were drawn from the occupational ranking section of the study. The subsamples had 30 cases in each. Treated in the usual statistical manner, with means calculated for each occupation and the ranks intercorrelated between each pair, the resulting Pearsonian correlations averaged about .955 and none were less than .94. Sample size has some effect but not enough to produce the correlation of .84.

Ethnicity and the Formation of the Ontario Establishment[†]

FREDERICK H. ARMSTRONG

Such writers as John Porter in the *Vertical Mosaic* (1965) and Peter C. Newman in *The Canadian Establishment* (1975) have correctly depicted the Canadian Establishment as a basically Anglo-Saxon group, although one with a certain French admixture.[1] Yet neither these authors, nor others, have looked at it historically to see how and why it so evolved. This present emphasis means that many questions remain unexamined in the light of eighteenth and nineteenth century conditions, even if they have been studied in the more or less current situation.

For instance, while emphasis has been placed on the Anglo-Saxon nature of the Canadian oligarchy, further study is needed on why it is Anglo-Saxon. Is this because initially only Anglo-Saxons were available, or was it through the deliberate exclusion of other groups; or when the elite was originally formed were factors other than ethnicity decisive? Those problems related to origin, of course, stand separately from the very different question of how far the established elite accepted non-Anglo-Saxons as they arose to influence. A third question is whether the original "Anglo-Saxons" saw any real ethnic differences among themselves in the period when they had a monopoly on power in the colonies.

Underlying the answers to these questions is the need for an analysis of the genesis of the Establishment. We must find how the original elites obtained their positions and power in the formative years of the various colonies. A variety of additional questions present themselves. What were the pioneer roads to political and economic power? How were they seized upon by the initial settlers? Also, what minorities were present, was there any inclusion of these groups in the elite, and if not why not?

[†]"Ethnicity in the Formation of the Family Compact: A Case Study in the Growth of the Canadian Establishment," in *Ethnicity, Power and Politics in Canada*, edited by Jorgen Dahlie and Tessa Fernando (Toronto: Methuen, 1981).

To determine the answers to these types of questions it will be necessary to examine carefully the process of settlement in several contrasting colonies and the relationship between the Imperial and colonial governments. This paper, as a preliminary contribution to such an examination, will concentrate on Upper Canada, the Southern Ontario of today, the events at its capital of York (or Toronto, as it became in 1834[2]) and the activities of its elite, which became known as the Family Compact. The time frame for investigation of the consolidation of the elite will begin with the arrival of the first Loyalist settlers in 1784, continue through the 1788 creation of local government administrative districts and the separation of Upper Canada from Quebec to create an independent colony in 1791, and end with the 1841 reunification of the colony and Quebec (or Lower Canada) to form the United Province of Canada.

The Ethnic Picture

But first, before we discuss the roads to power, it is necessary to present a picture of the ethnic structure of the province. This can be done most clearly by first showing the ethnic structure as it existed at the end of the Upper Canadian period in 1841 and then working backwards to examine its evolution, for the numerical representation of ethnic groups presents several difficulties in an analysis of the power structure of Ontario. First there is the impossibility of obtaining accurate figures for the early period. The Census of 1790 did not include the western districts beyond Montreal and there is no further census until that of 1824, which only enumerates the male and female population per county, both under and over 16.[3] The same is true of the virtually annual censuses of the decade following; it is only with the Census of 1842 that we get a breakdown of ethnicity, or rather by place of birth. This is worth citing here, both because it represents the situation at the end of the period with which we are dealing and because it is the first certain take-off point for population distribution. It also demonstrates the problems of attempting an analysis using statistics. The figures for place of birth are:

England and Wales	40,684
Scotland	39,781
Ireland	78,255
Canada: French Canadian	13,969
Canada: English Canadian	247,665

United States	32,809
Europe	6,581
Not given	27,309
Total	487,053[4]

What comes through immediately are the innumerable problems created by using place of birth interchangeably with ethnicity. Extrapolating from the numbers born in Great Britain, it might seem that the nearly 50 percent of the population of the province who were native born were Irish by origin, yet we know from emigration patterns that the Irish had only begun to come in large numbers in the years after the War of 1812.[5] Of course, the Irish must be subdivided into Protestant and Catholic groups to understand their actions. Earlier information would point to the "native-born English Canadian" population being largely English and Scots, with the former predominating. The Pennsylvania Germans would also be included in that figure.

Similarly, we do not know the ethnic origin of those who emigrated from the United States. To say that these were Americans is dangerous, for many recent immigrants would have felt strongly that they were Scots, or English, or Irish. On the other hand, some would have come from families which had been in North America for generations and would have regarded themselves as Americans. Still others would have had a mixed background and might have had divided loyalties, or might have changed their minds from time to time.

"Ethnicity" in such cases was probably largely a factor of how long the individual, or his family, had been on this continent, and it would fluctuate with individual circumstances. To try to understand how people thought, acted, or were appointed to office, including Americans as a separate ethnic group is highly dangerous, even if beautifully simple when used to create a neat line-up of statistics. Further problems are created by the fact that 5.6 percent of the population were of unknown ethnic origin. Where the census is of value is in showing that, by 1842, the population of the province was half native born, that the percentage of Upper Canadians of European birth was still very small, indicating a limited emigration from the continent, and that the population of French-Canadian origin had shrunk to less than 3 percent.

Thus, in any ethnic analysis of the power structure of Upper Canada, we are little helped by the available statistics, especially when they start late and the power structure was formed early. Even if the statistics were comprehensive enough to make an analysis of the power structure we would need the percentage of the people of influence who belonged to each ethnic group, rather than the percentages for population as a whole. It is those of influence whom we must examine. One way to approach this problem is to look at those groups which were present during the period under examination and see what leadership roles their members played.

Naturally, the Indians should be examined first. Some of the Loyalists were Indians, and the intermarriage of some of the successful early fur traders with the families of Indian leaders, or sometimes with unknown Indian women, meant that some of the most influential families were part Indian: the interconnected Askins and Babys of Detroit and Sandwich (Windsor) and the Hamiltons of Niagara and London form one example. Several members of these families became magistrates; some went on to the Legislative Council. These men could be said to provide an Indian element in the power structure, but it was indirect, through intermarriage, not through Indians who retained their own customs. Basically, the Indian peoples lived their own life in their territories outside the regular provincial power structure.

The French form the second ethnic group in order of appearance. Their major settlement at the time of the establishment of the province was in the far west at Detroit, not yet ceded to the Americans. This was the home of several influential fur trade families, particularly the Babys, who were a cadet branch of the important Quebec clan of that name, and were intermarried with such local families as the Barthes and the Réaumes. All of these families provided Justices of the Peace for the local government. The Babys not only succeeded in playing a lead role at Detroit/Sandwich, but—with Lieutenant-Governor Simcoe's approbation—also managed to establish a beachhead at Toronto through Jacques-Duperon Baby, who became Receiver General of the province and a member of the Councils. Other members of the family became MLAs.[6] In most parts of the province however, the French element was virtually nonexistent. Naturally, French participation in the distribution of potential wealth was not welcomed by British immigrants. At Toronto, where some of the leading French-Canadian families resident in Quebec had succeeded in establishing land claims prior to 1791, Governor Simcoe quickly bypassed their interests and made sure the land was transferred into English hands, for he wanted both to reward his own men at the new capital and to limit any Quebec influence in Upper Canada. Also, he was pursuing an anglicization policy which quickly wiped out virtually all French and Indian connections and names.

Nevertheless, aside from Quebec French influence in the elite, note should be made of the attempted settlement of Royalist refugees from the

French Revolution in 1798. The man who envisaged the unlikely idea of having nobles from the court of Versailles develop frontier Canadian farms was Joseph-Geneviève, Comte de Puisaye, an officer of the army of the Vendée,[7] who brought out several unhappy lords and their servants. These individuals attempted to settle land at Windham on Yonge Street north of Toronto, while the Comte himself located in the much more amenable region of Niagara for a brief period, before going back to his English comforts. His settlement was hardly a success, although some of the nobles lingered until the liberation of France in 1814 before returning home.

As aliens, the French Royalists did not play any part in the local power structure, though they did receive large land grants. The only member of the group to achieve real success in the province was Laurent Quetton de St. George, who before returning to France became an important merchant of Toronto and accumulated vast estates. (Later in the century his son Henri returned to Toronto and became something of a figure of note in the area.) Again, although he established various important commercial connections and acted as an army paymaster, St. George hardly engaged in politics. Because of his nationality, he could not be appointed a magistrate. What his career showed was how a man of ability, but of non-British background, could play a major role in the commerce of the colony if he was ready to adopt what were basically British methods of business and was willing to operate within the power structure established by the Imperial government—a type of career parallelled by many of his French contemporaries in Quebec.

One other non-British group should be particularly noted: the largely Mennonite Pennsylvania Germans who, at the opening of the nineteenth century, settled in the Waterloo County area and the townships north of Toronto. Later, they were joined by others, including immigrants who came directly from the German states. Unlike the French nobles, they made excellent farmers, developed some of the finest land in the province and frequently attained considerable wealth and holdings. In the Upper Canadian period at least, however, their religious convictions kept them largely separate from the power structure; the Mennonites, then as now, preferred to keep to themselves, with their own ways of life, the preservation of which was, after all, the reason for their migration north from Pennsylvania. Thus, for all practical purposes, they eliminated themselves from office. Despite their prosperity, few Germans turn up as office holders or on the commissions of the magistrates.

With these groups thus eliminated, it was inevitable that the elite which grew up would be composed of those whose ancestors had come from the British Isles, or who had themselves been born there. Dividing this group into Americans and emigrants from Great Britain is difficult; the names get us nowhere; the Loyalists were Americans, and some later wealthier British emigrants tended to come via the United States, where they might stop for some years. Many Americans did have a tendency to drift into the ranks of the Reformers and thus oppose the oligarchy; conversely, many others were happy to join it, or in the case of Loyalists to help found it. But, especially after the War of 1812, those Americans who were strongly opposed to Britain and the pro-British oligarchy in the colony were less likely to emigrate to Upper Canada.

In studying the ethnic rivalry in Upper Canada, then, it is the ruling groups from the British Isles that we must examine to see how they rivalled each other and forwarded their compatriots' interests. The actual details will be discussed below. First, however, some general comments should be made. Also, an analysis should be provided of the factors, other than ethnicity, that played a role in the evolution of the provincial elite.

The Origins of the Elite

In examining the growth of the elite, it is necessary to understand how power was held in Upper Canada: the crucial element in this picture was the Imperial connection. Today, we naturally think of ourselves as a nation, albeit one in some danger of fragmentation, and look inside our borders—at least inside the continental borders—for the foci of power. To understand the situation in the late eighteenth and early nineteenth century, when some of the most important branches of the present Canadian Establishment first obtained affluence and power, we have to see ourselves as only one of many farflung outposts of a world Empire and to remember that power in such empires was frequently acquired not because of an individual's local importance, but rather because of connections in the distant colonizing country. Thus, many of the future elite families received their initial impetus because of associations that had nothing to do with Canada, or because of wealth they brought with them from another place. Whether or not they retained these positions or passed their wealth on to another generation usually hinged on their own merits, not their imported connections; but, initially, the origins of the elite were not linked directly to Canada itself. The ruling coterie, in essence, was to a large extent superimposed from outside.

Of course, as each colonial elite became established, it resented and resisted such appointments and influences from outside, however loyal it was to the Motherland, and making such appointments became progressively more difficult as a local elite matured. This process can be seen clearly in the examination of the origins of the Upper Canadian Establishment, the Family Compact which for so long dominated York/Toronto and its province of Upper Canada. First, how did the appointees obtain their places?

The initial component in The Family Compact were the Loyalists. Their leaders, sometimes individuals who had played some important role in the old American colonies, came to hold key posts in the local or district governments of the colony, although Loyalists were unable to obtain a parallel importance on the provincial scale, except in a few special cases. The second component were the Imperial appointees—sometimes Loyalists—who, through some connection in Great Britain, were granted posts in such new colonies as New Brunswick or Upper Canada, created after the American Revolution, or who were injected into the already extant elites of colonies like Quebec or Nova Scotia.[8] Some of these early officeholders successfully founded dynasties, either through their own progeny or through the various relatives whom they brought out and helped establish. These emigré families might, initially at least, join together to form small ethnic-oriented groupings within the power structure of the province.[9]

Thirdly came another group of people, who were in some ways rather a specialized combination of the first two, that is, people appointed not because of random Old World connections, but rather because of one very specific connection: the governor. These people were to be found in every colony. In Upper Canada, the founding governor, Colonel John Graves Simcoe, a man of exceptional energy, not saddled with an already existing oligarchy, took a very eighteenth-century pleasure in the distribution of patronage to his cohorts. Consequently, the recipients of this beneficence were in an ideal position to found dynasties. Naturally, such individuals would attempt to retain the favour of the next governor; but in Upper Canada loss of favour was not to prove too great a hazard. Although governors came and went, appointments tended to be for life and one could carry on reasonably well even when out of favour.

Ethnicity could play a considerable role in such appointments if the governor strongly favoured any one group. In the case of Simcoe (1791–98), who achieved an amazing amount during the four brief years during which he actually resided in his wilderness, the factor that was particularly considered was not ethnic, but rather military service with his old Revolutionary War regiment, the Queen's Rangers, or with its revived successor and namesake which he brought with him to his colony.

Naturally, many of these soldiers were Loyalists, often from the New York State area—the only group of Loyalists whose interest Simcoe took major steps to advance. Thus they were reasonably well suited to life in

North America, although they may have been used to and would have much preferred a more civilized region. Some came after an initial exile in New Brunswick, some had influence beyond their acquaintance with Simcoe: for instance, Christopher Robinson, scion of one of the first families of Virginia; his descendants were to retain their connections with other members of the Robinson family who had fled to England and attained high position there.

Fourthly, an important and immediate cause of advancement was the acquisition of wealth which, in a colony such as Upper Canada, usually meant engaging in commerce and speculating in land. From the 1780s, some individuals were transacting business; when Upper Canada was established, several already had sufficient wealth to command respect. These "smart" individuals—the term originally connoting an individual capable of some dubious practices—could often move quickly to the highest offices. Some of the first great merchants, Richard Cartwright at Kingston, Robert Hamilton of Niagara and William Robertson of Detroit, were immediately appointed to the first Legislative Council, a body that in many ways became the voice of the great landed magnates. Since many of these merchants were of Scottish extraction, a sort of Scottish connection came to play a major part in trade, a point that will be further examined below.

Primary Factors in Advancement

Such were the initial routes to obtaining influence: Loyalism, British connection, governor's favour and commercial success. Once established, by what means did the new elite augment wealth and power? The first road was through office holding. Appointment to office, or the hope of appointment to office, may well have been the factor that originally brought such emigrants to the colony. And, at least initially, there were a large number of posts available. Upper Canada, of course, formed part of the old province of Quebec before 1791; but as the Loyalist population began to flourish in these western regions of that colony, some form of local government run by local residents was necessary. As a result, in 1788 the future territory of Upper Canada was divided into four administrative districts, each with its own officials. The overall administration of these districts was carried on by a Court of Quarter Sessions comprising all the justices of the peace, or magistrates, of each district. These men met four times a year to handle both local administrative problems and minor judicial matters.

Above the level of district, Upper Canada was given a complete colonial power structure in 1791, as had happened in New Brunswick only seven years earlier, and Prince Edward Island (Isle St. Jean) fifteen years before that. This consisted of a bicameral legislature, a cabinet (or Executive Council), ministers, clerks, and all the other officialdom necessary in a colony. Here was the arena in which Simcoe and the colonial office officials were able to make their appointments, and it was an arena in which considerable flexibility was possible, for there were few limiting rules. Plurality of office holding was taken for granted and in many cases residency was not required, although the incumbent would have to hire a clerk to carry out the duties. Nor was there any separation of local government offices from provincial ones, for an individual could hold both types simultaneously and even add certain appointments made in Quebec and London.[10] Finally, there was no term, as noted: once appointed to almost any office, the holder could stay on for life.[11] Naturally, an hereditary tendency also developed; some Upper Canadian families held on to local government offices until well into this century. In fact, Family Compact names may still be found today.

The districts were unaffected by the creation of Upper Canada, and became the local government structure of the new province. After 1793 there were town meetings and township officials; however, these were to exercise little influence before 1841. Acting for the magistrates were certain local officials in each district, such as the clerk of the Quarter Sessions, the sheriff, the treasurer and a separate judge for the district, all of whom drew comfortable emoluments, which were frequently composed of both salaries and fees. Furthermore, as the population of the province grew, the districts were gradually subdivided, so that by midcentury there were twenty in the province. Naturally, each time a new district was created, there were more offices to be filled, so that the up and coming generation of the Family Compact would have offices to assume and others, newly rising to power, could also be satisfied, at least to an extent.

One office that did not pay any direct salary, although fees were frequently involved, was that of justice of the peace.[12] As noted, these were the men who were basically responsible for handling the local administration of the province, as well as the minor judicial cases. The office was regarded as an honourable one; the members of the Executive and Legislative Councils, as well as the justices of the highest court, the King's Bench, were automatically justices of the peace for all districts of the province. In each district the members of the leading families were usually appointed under what was called a general commission of the peace, that is, a list of new magistrates, and thus sat on the Quarter Sessions. The first justices were appointed in the 1780s for the District of Montreal, which included what was to be Upper Canada before the separate districts were created in 1788; regular commissions of peace for each district were issued right through the Upper Canadian period and long afterwards. Further, the justiceship was a sort of life appointment, with a man retaining his post through each new commission. It also assumed an hereditary tendency as new justices, often their sons, were added. A new name appearing was evidence that a man had succeeded.

The magistracy thus can provide us with something of a convenient yardstick in establishing who belonged to the elite of the province. Naturally, the percentages of the various ethnic groups among the names listed in the commissions of the peace provide a further indication of the relative position of each ethnic group in the Canadian community. This is worth analysis, although some caveats will be presented.

Beyond holding offices and gathering the perquisites of office, how did an individual become wealthy in the new country? A related method was through the accumulation of land, which was amply available in the colony and provided a way to pay bonuses to the officials, or Loyalists. Further, with the landed gentry outlook of the late eighteenth century, possession of land symbolized a gentleman. The fact that the property, however good, might be inaccessible, was irrelevant; the potentiality and the status were there, the development could come later, either as a farm, or for the more clever or fortunate, as urban subdivisions. The progenitor had it in prestige, although being land poor could be vexatious; the grandchild could reap the fortune in cash.

In keeping with the aristocratic, or landed gentry outlook of the government, special provision was made for receiving extra land grants for those who had previously held high rank in the military, or currently held high office in the government. The ordinary private in a Loyalist regiment might receive 100 acres, with 50 for wife and each child; initially, the member of the Executive Council received 6000, with 1200 for wife and each child. In addition, there were various ways of rewarding people with land; for instance, surveyors were partly paid in land grants. The amassing of great estates was underway.

There were also indirect ways in which to gather extensive landed estates. Many Loyalists did not want to claim their land grants, or would not settle them. Therefore their rights, represented by what are called "location tickets," could be sold, often cheaply, and the purchaser would thus add to his estates. In addition, the more affluent could become mortgagors and as payments frequently could not be met in the fluctuations of the pioneer economy, more land would be picked up this way. Before many years had passed some remarkably large holdings were accumulated, particularly by the merchants. Colonizers, too, could do well: the greatest of them, Colonel Thomas Talbot, the founding genie of the southwestern peninsula, who developed some 28 townships including what is now the city of London, held no less than 48,520 acres in 1838.[13] He was not the exception.

There was yet another way to acquire wealth beyond office and land: through the continued advance of commerce and later finance and manufacturing. It was there that the really huge fortunes were made, though caution should be taken, for frequently no separation is possible between those who made money in commerce and those who held office. In fact, the converse was the norm. William Allan, the financial genius of the Family Compact, was a member of both the Executive and Legislative Councils, collector of customs, postmaster, a leading figure in local government, a colonel of the militia, and possibly above all, a merchant, a leading landholder, the president of the Bank of Upper Canada, the first governor (president) of the British America Assurance Company and a commissioner of the Canada Land Company.

In the districts, in the structure of both commerce and government, the story was the same: the merchant was usually the key figure. He imported and exported everything, ran mills, loaned money, acted as postmaster and collector of customs, provided mortgages, sat as a member of the Legislative Assembly (eventually, possibly, even of the Legislative Council), and generally filled many of the functions of the modern lawyer—a post for which his son was often formally trained. What had begun as a commercial dynasty frequently became a legal one.

Secondary Roads to Power

Beyond these factors—office, land, wealth—there were what might be called secondary routes to advancement. One that was increasingly important as the province became established was family connection. As time went on and the elite intermarried, most of the upper crust of society gradually became interrelated. Families were large, marriage outside the circle presented some difficulties, and there was the inevitable hereditary tendency in office holding. The governor, even if he wished to change things, would have had to be a man of unbelievable energy if he was to take on an entrenched oligarchy.

The leading families naturally spread their tentacles everywhere; the Hamiltons of Niagara, Queenston, Hamilton, Kingston and London provide one good example. Robert Hamilton of Queenston, who began as a business partner of the equally wealthy Richard Cartwright of Kingston, married Catharine Askin (in whose honour St. Catharines was latter to be named), a daughter of the great fur trading family of Detroit/ Sandwich (Windsor), who was also the widow of John Robertson, of another prominent Detroit merchant family. Robert was so affluent that he was one of the first appointees to the Legislative Council in 1792 and remained a member until his death in 1809. One of their sons, John Hamilton of Queenston, attained the same dignity in 1831, as did another in 1836, the George Hamilton after whom the city of Hamilton is named. George was to die in 1838; but John was reappointed through all the various midcentury changes and died a Senator of Canada in 1882, after fifty years' service in the upper house. Of the other sons, James Hamilton became sheriff of the London District, Alexander Hamilton sheriff of the Niagara District and Peter Hunter Hamilton a magistrate at Hamilton.[14] The Hamiltons are only one of many examples.

Education also tied the elite together, or divided them, to look at it in a different way. In a pioneer community the opportunities for advanced education were naturally limited to the more wealthy classes. Much of the education was in private schools, and one of the first and certainly the most influential school in the Upper Canadian period was that located at Cornwall and run by John Strachan, a Scottish emigrant who became a Church of England clergyman and finally bishop of Toronto. In his years as schoolmaster, before he moved to Toronto on the eve of the War of 1812, Strachan's excellent reputation as a teacher meant that a large percentage of the leading families sent their sons to him to be educated. In later years, as he rose to power and as they grew up and joined him in office, they formed a network, a sort of pseudo-family, that extended across the colony, sometimes in rivalry to the graduates of the grammar schools established in 1807.[15] It was only towards the end of the period, in 1829, that Upper Canada College was founded as the first really good school in the colony. Even then, that institution was under the domination of the same Church of England leadership.

Religion was another important factor in advancement, one that could tie in with ethnicity to create even stronger interconnections; but the religious structure of the colony was complex. The Church of England was the state church in England and had pretensions to being the state church in the colonies. In Upper Canada such official recognition was never enacted; nevertheless, the Church of England did receive special consideration in many ways. To complicate the picture in the colonies, the Church of Scotland was always ready to exert its influence as the state church of another part of the Motherland, and that Church also demanded and received special privileges. As if this quarrelsome pair were not enough, in Upper Canada the Catholic Church, although not recognized in England until 1829, retained the special privileges granted under the Quebec Act of 1774, when the colony had formed the western part of the old province of Quebec. Like the Anglicans and Presbyterians, the Catholics received lands, subventions and privileges.

Later these denominations were joined by others. The Methodists were originally regarded as being too American and possibly disloyal, even if they were probably the largest denomination. But, with the union of the various Methodist churches of the colony in 1829, a new picture emerged, subsidies flowed in their direction and the appointment of Methodists to the magistracy became frequent. Thus the modern Canadian phenomenon of a sort of composite state church in which several denominations hold privilege and prestige was already making its appearance. This did not, of course, mean that these denominations particularly liked each other or, indeed, that they did not have internal divisions. What it did mean was that religion was progressively no bar to admission to the ruling class. Nor were there many qualms displayed about changing religion as one achieved success; Strachan himself was a convert from Presbyterianism to the Church of England. Some groups, such as Mennonites and Quakers, may have deliberately excluded themselves, yet for most the religious path was open.

Possibly outlook, more than religion, provided the "theological" entrée to the Establishment. Members were expected to accept the idea of a state church, even if they did not agree on which one. Also, they were expected to support the idea of an ordered society, loyalty to Great Britain, and distrust for the United States and its institutions—principles that would not be too difficult for the man of ambition to adopt, in public anyway. And all cut across ethnic lines.

Finally, in studying the growth of the "Canadian Establishment" at this early stage, one important factor must be stressed, that is, while society was relatively fluid in the first years, given that advancement could still be greatly aided by connections; after each new district or colony was settled the structure of power underwent a change that can well be likened to a jelly setting. Those who were in at the top remained there, those who were down the scale, or who came late, had to work that much harder to join the power elite. For members of a new ethnic group this would be particularly difficult, even more so because they had to take on the business methods and social characteristics of the ruling group in order to advance. A first-generation merchant might rise to the Legislative Council as one of the great magnates of the province, a successful second-generation merchant would probably merely be appointed one of the magistrates. Yet, as land was available and new districts were periodically opened up, particularly in the west, there was an escape valve for the ambitious, or the well connected, throughout the period.

There was always a shortage of trained men in any pioneer community—having ability and education and the willingness to conform might be enough for one to advance. Sir Francis Bond Head's secretary, John Joseph, who was Jewish, had no difficulty in marrying into the Family Compact.[16] Later, a noble Polish refugee, Casimir Stanislas Gzowski, became a leading engineer who was to rise eventually to the dignity of Administrator of Ontario, just as his compatriot Alexander Edouard Kierzkowski was to do well in Lower Canada.

The British Emigrant and the Structure of Power

To return to the role of the British ethnic groups in the formation of the elite of the province, first, it should be pointed out that no one group ever succeeded in achieving a really dominant place. Although at times much was said about one faction or another advancing their own interests, generally the need for new men in administration, plus the ethnically random Imperial appointments, prevented any real takeover by one ethnic group.

Each individual was, of course, going to forward the interests of his one family and kinsmen, and probably cooperate with those who come from the same general region. For the first-generation immigrant this would, of necessity, mean that those in power would be helping their own nationals. Nevertheless, as time passed such clannishness was bound to change. Provided that there was not some bar, such as religion, or violent political differences, the marriage patterns of the next generation might well begin to establish a new picture, except in areas that were ethnically homogeneous. For the elite, with its ties across the province, intermarriage by wealth between various ethnic groups became the norm and the mixed ethnic pattern of the future which began to develop quickly ran counter to any attempt to form an oligarchy dominated by one ethnic group. The commissions of the magistrates never show a picture of one British race moving towards a monopoly. In addition, the early social organizations that were formed tended to be on other than ethnic lines; for instance, the various Masonic lodges welcomed all Protestant comers. The national societies, when they were finally established in the mid-1830s, represented ethnic cross sections of society— not elite groupings.[17]

Of the direct emigrants from Britain, the Welsh were few in number and frequently joined with the English in such activities as social clubs, for instance the St. George's Society. One or two Welsh families did rise to a position of importance, such as that of Chief Justice William Dummer Powell, perhaps because he was one of the first lawyers to settle in the province—though his lack of connections in England may have been a factor in it taking so many years for him to reach the chief justiceship.[18]

The English presented a very different picture. They were initially the largest ethnic group and the one most directly connected with the colonizing power; with the exceptions of Scottish Hunter and part-Jewish Head, all the governors were English, as were many of the other officials who were sent out. Further, a very large number of the second rank members of the ruling class came from this group. Finally, it should be noted that many other immigrants, with family origins in different parts of the British Isles, had either migrated to England, or had been born there. Therefore, it is difficult to say that being English, as opposed to belonging to one of the other ethnic groups of the British Isles, served as any advantage in advancement; there were no claims of English takeovers, or cabals. In fact, being English may have, at times, been a detriment, for the largest group does not need to develop a protective network of connections in the same way as the minorities.

It is the Irish and the Scots who present the most interesting examples of power blocks—or would-be power blocks—although neither actually formed a single unity. The Irish must be divided into the Anglo-Irish and the poor Catholic Irish.

The Anglo-Irish were usually Protestants, generally reasonably well off, often well connected, sometimes with reform tendencies, and often early arrivals on the scene. They were to represent a very influential group in the colony. After Simcoe's departure in 1796, Peter Russell, who took over as administrator (acting governor) for three years, was one of their numbers. Whether or not Russell strongly favoured his own compatriots and relatives in land grants is arguable; but certainly, with his Baldwin connections, he did belong to a power grouping in the colony. And that group was rather excluded from the seats of the mighty in the period after his term ended in 1799. Possibly it is not surprising that it was Anglo-Irish emigrants, such as Robert Thorpe and Joseph Willcocks, who were to play a leading role in the early reform demands.[19]

The impoverished Catholic Irish, who had begun to arrive in large numbers by the late 1820s, provide an entirely different story. They arrived when the power structure had already been formed, they generally were poorly educated and, as they rose to influence, the Protestant-Catholic split, which earlier was at least partly hidden by the Tory-Reform split, was developing rapidly. Naturally, the Catholic Irish played no part in the Establishment until well on in the century when they had had an opportunity to become settled and to gain wealth.

The Scots were another matter. Again, it should be noted that they did not form one monolithic block. The Gaelic-speaking Catholic Highlanders, such as those who settled in 1804 at the east end of Upper Canada in Glengarry county, were a very different people from the Protestant Lowlanders, who played a major role in the commerce and government of the province as a whole. The Highlanders were less educated, tended to stick to their own area, and followed their bishop, Alexander Macdonell. He was, however, a leading Tory figure in the politics of the colony and a fair number of the Highlanders became magistrates and held various local offices.

It is the Protestant Lowlanders who probably played the greatest role, disproportionate to numbers, in the governance and commerce of the colony. They probably had the best system of advancing each other's interests, although it should be stressed that there was never a conscious Scots combination to monopolize offices. Again, they had the advantage of being there from the first, were well aided by their excellent commercial connections in the Old Country, and they were diligent. The Scottish commercial network deserves much more attention than it has received to date, although some very interesting research has been done.[20]

Much of the commerce of the Empire centred on Glasgow and adjacent Greenock—aside from the number of Scots merchants who had operations in England—and these Scots entrepreneurs were quick to establish commercial connections in the New World, either through branches, which might later become independent, or through agreements with rising local businesses. Similarly, the older commercial houses of Montreal, and later Kingston and Toronto, were always ready to open branches on the expanding frontier, which might become independent shops as society developed. The immigrant Scots youth, with commercial training in the old country, a good letter of introduction, or better, an arranged clerkship, who was willing to work long hours for many years, had the road cleared for his progress and was better assured of an affluent future than almost any other type of emigrant.

To cite two examples from the beginning and end of the Upper

Canadian period, William Allan came to Canada in 1787 and worked for the great commercial house of Forsyth, Richardson & Company in Montreal before going on to Niagara and then to Toronto. He became the richest man in the colony, the financial genius of the Family Compact and a leader in railway ventures at the end of his long life. Much later, about 1835, John Birrell came to Montreal, then went on to Hamilton, where he worked for Isaac Buchanan & Company, and then to London. There he opened his own wholesale dry goods company and died as president of the local trust company (now the Canada Trust) and the railway that was being built to the hinterland.[21] In all, the number of Scots merchants in the colonies, as compared to the population as a whole, was quite out of proportion. Yet, it must be noted that, while they may have preferred to work with their own kind, if business interest dictated it the Scots had no hesitation in taking English partners—such as in the long-term Clark-Street partnership at Niagara—or French partners. Also, they were quite ready to intermarry into the local elite regardless of nationality. Their flexibility may well have been a major factor in their success.

In the government, they played a major role, and many were appointed to the Legislative Council and the judiciary; but again the claims of Scottish exclusiveness cannot be substantiated. Many of these accusations came as a result of the governorship of the autocratic Perthshireman, Peter Hunter (1799–1805), and were voiced by the Anglo-Irish radicals who attacked his rule in the first outburst of reform demands, which arose immediately after he was safely dead and could not answer. The Anglo-Irish may not have done very well under his regime and Russell may have lost influence; but an examination of Hunter's activities provides little evidence that he was forwarding Scots unduly. Many of the Scots who came to power, such as Attorney-General Thomas Scott, were sent out from England; Hunter's chief advisors were Englishmen, John Elmsley Senior and Henry Allcock.

Later there were renewed claims of Scottish collusion when the Legislative Council was dominated by the two Aberdeenshiremen, Strachan and Allan, as the Family Compact reached its apogee under the governorship of the English Sir Peregrine Maitland (1818–28). Yet it should again be noted that Strachan did little to forward the cause of Scots who were not Anglicans, and that he did advance those of his non-Scottish pupils who were. His chief protégé was John Beverley Robinson of English-Virginian descent, who rose to the chief justiceship under his regime.

Conclusion

Thus, ethnically there was a composite Establishment that arose in Upper Canada centering on its capital of Toronto, one that encompassed all the founding groups who fitted in with the political outlook of the period, yet one that was open to new men as they arose to wealth and power. The fact that it took time for the latercomers to attain such a position is not surprising in a developed colony; the fact that they did obtain status indicates an open elite in the province. After 1841, when Upper Canada and Lower Canada were reunited as the Province of Canada, the old Toronto Establishment may have lost considerable political power; but it remained the focus of the wealth, society and aristocracy of the colony. Canada has never had a successful revolution and retirement from the political fray has not meant retirement from wealth, power and influence. In local government the old families retained office even longer than in the provincial sphere, because of the more gradual process of change rather than because of any exclusiveness.

In conclusion, then, the origins of the present Canadian Establishment, at least as far as Upper Canada/Ontario is concerned, go back to the earliest times, when the elite was formed from among the first settlers and officials. In the rise of various individuals to power, the possession of wealth, education and the right attitude and connections were the major determinants. Ethnicity played a rather secondary role, yet still one that was always present. Further, in considering ethnicity and the Family Compact—or really ethnicity and any elite group—we should not lose sight of the fact that the elite are after all part of an ethnic group. They are not somehow "de-ethnicized" by being in power. Rather, it is a case of have and have-not ethnic groups, or established and unestablished, as new generations grow up in the New World, gain wealth and intermix in the new society.

Notes

1. The words ethnic and race, elite and establishment have been defined in many ways. Brewton Berry and Henry L. Tischler demonstrate the difficulties in dealing with the first two in their *Race and Ethnic Relations* (Boston: Houghton Mifflin, 1978), pp. 30–42. For the purposes of this paper we shall use ethnic to differentiate cultural distinctions. Peter C. Newman really does not define the Establishment in his *The Canadian Establishment* (Toronto: McClelland and Stewart, 1975), but I would agree with his thesis that the Establishment is made up of a variety of elites (p. 14).

2. The town of York was incorporated in 1834 and the name then changed to Toronto, probably to get away from the appellation "Muddy York." For simplicity, Toronto will be used throughout this paper.

3. See *Canada, Census of, 1871*, 5 vols. (Ottawa: Minister of Agriculture, 1876). Volume 4 contains the historical statistics from 1665.

4. *Census, 1871*, vol. 4, p. 136.

5. Helen I. Cowan, *British Emigration to British North America* (Toronto: University of Toronto Press, 1961). Pages 38–39 show the first peak of Irish emigration in 1818.

6. F. H. Armstrong, "The Oligarchy of the Western District of Upper Canada," *Canadian Historical Association: Historical Papers*, 1977, p. 97.

7. The story is told in Lucy A. Textor, *A Colony of Emigrés in Canada* (Toronto: The University Library, 1905).

8. The Sewell family provides a good example here. From their original base in Massachusetts, members went on to hold office in Quebec, where Jonathan Sewell (1766–1839) was chief justice for thirty years, and in Nova Scotia and New Brunswick.

9. The Baldwin family of Toronto, who played such an important role in Responsible Government, are a good example of this, with their various branches and their connections with other Anglo-Irish immigrants.

10. For instance, the headquarters of the post office for British North America was at Quebec and customs were regulated from London, England.

11. Probably the last Upper Canadian officials to die in office were the County Registrars of Norfolk and Oxford: Francis Leigh Walsh, who held his post from 1810 to 1884, and James Ingersoll, who was in office from 1834 until 1886.

12. For a discussion of how the justices of the peace operated and their influence in a district, see my article on the "Western District" cited above and J. H. Aitchison, "The Municipal Corporations Act of 1849," *Canadian Historical Review* 30 (1949): 107–22.

13. Public Archives of Canada, MG 24A7, Durham Papers, Sec. 2, vol. 49, p. 141.

14. See E. Marion Chadwick, *Ontarian Families*, vol. 1 (Toronto: 1894), pp. 143–48 for a complete genealogy of the family.

15. For instance, some of the leading reform families, such as the Baldwins and the Smalls, sent their sons to the York Grammar School. For an analysis of Strachan's school, see F. H. Armstrong, "John Strachan, Schoolmaster, and the Evolution of the Elite in Upper Canada / Ontario," in *An Imperfect Past: Education and Society in Canadian History*, edited by J. Donald Wilson (Vancouver: University of British Columbia, 1984), pp. 154–69.

16. Joseph married a daughter of Attorney General Christopher A. Hagerman.

17. The St. George's Society (which included Welsh as well as English) was instituted in 1835, the St. Andrew's Society and the St. Patrick's Society in 1836. Basically, they were social. However, the St. Andrew's Society had the aid of needy immigrants as its avowed purpose.

18. Powell became a puisne, or associate justice of the Court of King's Bench as early as 1791. However, three men were appointed to the chief justiceship before he received the office in 1816.

19. For Thorpe's opinion, see W. Stewart Wallace, *The Family Compact* (Toronto: Glasgow, Brook & Company, 1915), pp. 4–5.

20. See David S. Macmillan, "The 'New Men' in Action: Scottish Mercantile and Shipping Operations in The North American Colonies, 1760–1825," in his edited *Canadian Business History, Selected Studies, 1497–1971* (Toronto: McClelland and Stewart, 1972), pp. 44–103; and also "The Scot as Businessman," in *The Scottish Tradition in Canada*, edited by W. Stanford Reid (Toronto: McClelland and Stewart, 1976), pp. 179–202. Bruce G. Wilson's biography, *The Enterprises of Robert Hamilton* (Ottawa: Carleton University Press, 1983), provides an interesting study of one of the greatest Scottish merchants.
21. For Allan see M. L. Magill, "William Allan: A Pioneer Business Executive," in *Aspects of Nineteenth Century Ontario*, edited by F. H. Armstrong, H. A. Stevenson, and J. D. Wilson (Toronto: University of Toronto Press, 1974), pp. 101–13; and for Birrell see F. H. Armstrong, "John Birrell, 1815–75," in *Dictionary of Canadian Biography*, vol. 8 (Toronto: University of Toronto Press, 1972), p. 68.

Minority Conflict: Ethnic Networks versus Industrial Power[†]

LEO DRIEDGER

Recently, Eldorado came into conflict with the residents of Warman, Saskatchewan, when they sought to build a hexafluoride refinery in a largely pacifist rural Mennonite community. There was a great deal of opposition to the invasion of an unwanted refinery, much conflict resulted, and eventually after federal hearings, Eldorado Nuclear decided not to build. The extended struggle which ensued provides us with an excellent opportunity to study community conflict (Galaskiewicz 1979).

Two useful conceptual frameworks for the study of community conflict, one macro and the other micro, have been developed by Laumann and associates (Laumann 1973, Laumann and Pappi 1973, 1976, Laumann, Verbrugge, and Pappi 1974, Laumann, Marsden, and Galaskiewicz 1977) and by Wellman and associates (Wellman 1979, Wellman and Leighton 1979, Wellman, Carrington, and Hall 1983) respectively. The studies of Laumann and associates of communities such as Altneustadt (Laumann and Pappi 1973, Laumann, Verbrugge, and Pappi 1974, Laumann and Pappi 1976), Towertown (Laumann and Marsden 1979) and River City (Laumann et al. 1977) have produced useful models of bargaining and opposition, which help explain how active proponent and opponent networks are formed around dynamic controversial issues (Laumann, Marsden, and Galaskiewicz 1977: 594–631). Although Laumann and associates found support for their bargaining model, they found less evidence of opposition than we expect in this Warman study.

†"Community Conflict: The Eldorado Invasion of Warman," *Canadian Review of Sociology and Anthropology* 23, 2 (1986): 247–69.

While the macro models of Laumann provide insights into the dynamics of the larger organizational structures, the studies by Wellman and associates (Wellman 1979, Wellman and Leighton 1979, Wellman, Carrington, and Hall 1983) provide much needed micro insights into "lost," "saved," and "liberated" network qualities, leadership patterns such as brokers, and the multiple strands of relationships, of solidarity, intensity, density, and boundedness.

This paper will use both the macro and the micro network approaches for one study of the Warman conflict, first outlining the two models more extensively, after which the two will be combined to study the Warman conflict.

Laumann's Bargaining and Oppositional Models

As illustrated in Figure 1, Laumann, Marsden, and Galaskiewicz (1977: 607) outlined two bargaining and oppositional models for issue organization "derived from differing conceptions of the manner in which preference and activation serve to organize discussion contacts." Both models assume some level of homophily; the difference between the two lies in their expectations of the process and the outcome.

Bargaining Controversial Issues

The bargaining model assumes that the communication distance between active proponents and opponents is small, and that these highly involved persons on each side of the controversy negotiate the outcome by compromise and trading of concessions to come to a mutual agreement. Laumann, Marsden, and Galaskiewicz (1977: 608) "imply that active persons, on both sides, will be central nodes in the discussion network."

We wish to enlarge and enrich the bargaining network model by asking three questions. First, are the active proponents and opponents equally powerful, represented by the size of two active groups on each side of the fault line (Figure 1a)? Second, do the active proponents seek to gain an advantage over their opponents, by building up support secretly or otherwise recruiting sub-networks (A,B,C,D,E) to support their cause and surprise their active opponents (Figure 1b)? Indeed, the active could recruit strength so quickly and successfully, that active community opponents might be almost nonexistent. There is evidence that some industrial or governmental bureaucracies do seek such advantages when they set up new factories and programs in new territories. Bargaining for land rights between governments and Indians in northern

Figure 1
Bargaining and Oppositional Models for Issue Organization

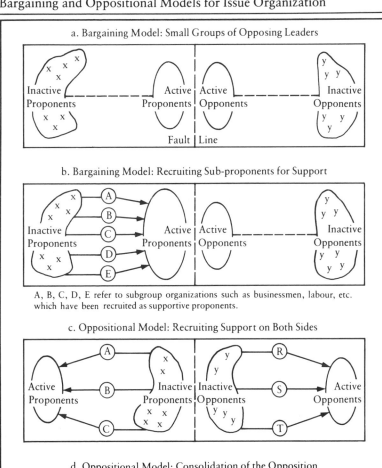

a. Bargaining Model: Small Groups of Opposing Leaders

b. Bargaining Model: Recruiting Sub-proponents for Support

A, B, C, D, E refer to subgroup organizations such as businessmen, labour, etc. which have been recruited as supportive proponents.

c. Oppositional Model: Recruiting Support on Both Sides

d. Oppositional Model: Consolidation of the Opposition

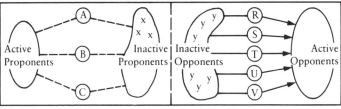

A, B, C, R, S, T, U, V refer to subgroup organizations such as business, farmers, churches, ethnic groups, etc. which have been recruited as opponents or proponents.

Source: Basic schema taken from Laumann et al. (1977) and modified.

Canada and bargaining between urban corporations and rural communities can become quite one-sided where power is concerned.

Crucial to winning support for an active proponent are such issues as more jobs for workers when an industry enters a community, or land rights for native Indians up north, or greater profits for businessmen, who become supporting sub-networks. Instrumental issues usually appeal to economic self-interests for sub-networks in a community and "they involve a limited level of controversy in which many aspects of an issue are negotiable" (Laumann, Marsden, and Galaskiewicz 1977: 608).

Oppositional Model for Issue Organization

In contrast to the bargaining model, Laumann, Marsden, and Galaskiewicz (1977: 608) also pose the oppositional model presented in Figures 1c and d which we have expanded:

> The oppositional model, in contrast, is the one implicit in discussions emphasizing divergent issue preferences as an indicator of a factional influence structure. It assumes a polarized community (Coleman 1957) in which sharp differences of opinion, often associated with mutual feelings of antagonism, cause direct discussion among active persons with opposed preferences to be avoided . . . . This model implies intensified discussion contacts within groups of persons sharing the same strongly held views.

Consummatory issues are usually part of controversies involving the oppositional model. Laumann and Pappi (1973: 226) clearly show how "consummatory or expressive issues, are concerned with controversies regarding the maintenance or change in organization of basic values, commitments, and orientations that shall guide or control community affairs." Such issues are usually highly charged with emotion, and tend to polarize people, making negotiation and settlements difficult. School and pop festival issues in a religious community such as Altneustadt were highly consummatory issues (Laumann and Pappi 1973: 226), resulting in considerable opposition, as did issues in Towertown (Galaskiewicz 1979: 101–20).

In Figure 1c we present the oppositional model with the active proponents and opponents at opposite ends, with considerably more distance between them than in the bargaining model. Again, we have expanded the oppositional model, as we did the bargaining model, to include sub-networks. We expect that when a community issue is sufficiently consummatory (such as the nuclear industry), in a community which may be opposed to war (Mennonite pacifists), and if they have the will and time to organize themselves, then the active opponents may be able to gain an advantage by recruiting a greater number of opposition sub-networks to support them (Figure 1d). We wish also to examine the dynamics between the sub-networks which are in opposition, and the extent and form in which they support the active opponents.

Bargaining and Oppositional Interaction

Must we assume that issue organization will take either the bargaining or oppositional form? Which assumptions or ways of contact will gain the upper hand? Two opposing parties may be assumed to begin with different assumptions, but either the bargaining or oppositional model could begin to dominate in a controversy. We also predict that when proponents enter a community with a proposed plan or issue they must proceed with bargaining, and they must dominate the bargaining, or lose the controversy. Finally, we predict, that when one of the parties views the issues as consummatory, the opposition model will increasingly dominate, forcing adversarial relations to the advantage of the opponents, especially if the issue is fought in their home territory and if they can gather community support. Figure 2 illustrates the expected respective advantages of proponents (bargaining and focusing on instrumental issues) and opponents (focusing on consummatory issues) in opposition.

Figure 2
Model Showing Expected Advantages of Proponents (Bargaining with Instrumental Issues) and Opponents (in Opposition because of Consummatory Issues) for Issue Organization

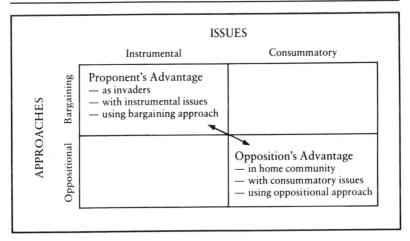

Wellman's Lost, Saved, and Liberated Communities

Wellman's (1979: 1204–27), and Wellman and Leighton's (1979: 363–90) discussion of "lost," "saved," and "liberated" communities appears to have some predictive power as to when opponents will be able to bargain successfully, or when they will succeed in opposition.[1] They propose that as society becomes increasingly industrial, basic human needs such as effective ties and primary experiences will need to be nurtured not only within traditional rural, isolated, segregated, closed community boundaries, but within social networks developed by more accessible space, increased communication velocity, and through transactional density and links to multiple social circles. They begin with a network analytic perspective of the community as their starting point in a search for social linkages and flows of resources. This approach frees the community study from spatial and normative bases. While the rural "traditional" community is more spatially bound, the "liberated" community is freed from spatial boundaries. The "saved" community lies between the two, with some spatial boundedness and primary concerns, but branching out into new urban multiple social networks, both rural and urban. "The saved argument contends that urbanites continue to organize safe communal havens, with neighbourhood, kinship, and work solidarities mediating and coping with bureaucratic institutions" (Wellman and Leighton 1979: 373). We expect that it will be easier to find leaders in religious and ethnic communities who commit themselves to fight threatening consummatory issues, and that it will be possible, through informal networks to rally a cohesive opposition to their community's invasion, especially if it threatens their ideology. As Granovetter suggests, "whether a person trusts a given leader depends heavily on whether there exist intermediary personal contacts.... Trust in leaders is integrally related to the capacity to predict and affect their behaviour" (1973: 1374).

The problem with closed traditional rural communities is that their boundaries tend to stifle new ways and means of creating networks outside the segregated community (Tilly 1967, 1970). Thus, Native Indian reserves, Hutterite colonies, or many rural communities are easy prey for industrial bureaucracies whose invasion involves a network of corporate political, economic, and educational powers. It is here where Wellman's (1979: 1206–7) "liberated" community has additional advantages: cheap, effective transportation independent of local-area proximity and widespread facilities for interaction that create possible access to loosely bounded multiple social circles. Many traditional rural communities are changing in this direction.

The community "saved" argument does not accept the urban social disorganization assertion of the "lost" community advocates, but documents the persistence of changed community in the city. Some of the most interesting saved arguments have been made by Janowitz (1952), Greer (1962), Suttles (1972) and Hunter (1975) who have been concerned with external linkage from a bounded communal base—often a small-scale territory or neighbourhood. They have clearly demonstrated that city community solidarity exists in bounded population aggregates, often with ethnic or religious cores.

We expect that when "saved" opponents of a proposed invasion of a community have the combined advantages of the "traditional" and "liberated" communities, they will have both the will and commitment to fight, as well as the social networks and skills to do so successfully. Like Granovetter (1973: 1373) we wish to discover "why some communities organize for common goals easily and effectively whereas others seem unable to mobilize resources, even against dire threats." Gans (1962: 229–304) suggested that working-class residents could not effectively defend themselves, while middle-class residents could. We expect that this may be a factor, but success depends on more.

Granovetter (1973: 1374) suggests that "studies of diffusion and mass communication have shown that people rarely act on mass-media information unless it is also transmitted through personal ties" (Katz and Lazarsfeld 1955, Rogers 1962). This opens the door for important (sometimes charismatic), brokers or middlemen, who deeply understand their community and its aspirations, are respected and accepted as its legitimate leaders, and at the same time are also involved in important social networks and contacts outside of their community. Usually these brokers are more educated and upwardly mobile occupationally. Thus, brokers can take advantage of both the trust placed in them by members of their community, as well as reach other communities which can be rallied for added strength. Many rural communities do not have such a resource of sophisticated ingroup brokers, but those that do have an added advantage over invader bureaucracies. Industrial bureaucracies may have specialized expertise and secondary political contacts, but they will find it harder to compete with educated, charismatic, upwardly mobile "saved" leadership based in a solid local primary community, which also has "liberated" access and influence in both the regional and the national arenas.

This study will examine the Warman refinery controversy, to see whether the following propositions gleaned from the Laumann and Wellman literature are supported by the data.

1 Crucial to community support for an active proponent of community invasion will be the effective use of instrumental issues coupled with a bargaining position.

2 Crucial for success in opposing a community invasion will be consummatory issues to arouse opposition, so that an adversarial strategy can be developed.

3 We expect that members of a "saved" community are the most likely to have the will, commitment, and ability to fight invasion, and will be most successful in resisting intrusion.

4 We expect that members of a "traditional" community will have neither the ability nor the will to fight an invasion; and that members of a "liberated" community will have neither the conviction nor the commitment to fight community invasion.

Methodology

To help understand the community solidarity, the potential social networks, and the social dynamics involved in community opposition to a proposed uranium refinery, we will use six data sets. The first three will aid in understanding the ethno-religious solidarity ties and community networks which were involved, and the fourth, fifth, and sixth directly relate to the appearances of the levels of open opposition.

Driedger (1955) did a community study of the traditional Mennonites in the Warman area thirty years ago to document their history, the extent of their institutional completeness, the village structures, their maintenance of a distinctive culture, and the quality of their social institutions. The 1955 study shows the area contained a wide range of Mennonites from very conservative to more liberal. Many of the most traditional Old Colony Mennonites who came to the area first in 1895 settled in fairly isolated traditional villages, many of which still exist (Friesen 1975). More liberal General Conference Mennonites, and Mennonite Brethren arrived later in the 1920s, and they were better able to enter the educational and economic institutions in the community. This research was replicated by Driedger (1977a) twenty years later, research that indicated considerable change with the continued maintenance of a distinctive Mennonite identity. These two studies will be used to examine Warman Mennonite community solidarity and their social networks.

Alan Anderson's (1972) study in the same larger Saskatchewan area included samples of Mennonites as well as Polish Catholics, Hutterites,

Doukhobors, Ukrainian Catholics, Ukrainian Orthodox, Scandinavian Lutherans, French Catholics, and German Catholics. His total sample of 1,000 provides comparative information on language maintenance, cultural identity, and the extent of institutional completeness of these nine groups. These rural ethnic communities vary considerably with respect to maintenance of identity, but their social networks have been maintained and they are important to most members of these groups.

When it became apparent that the proposed refinery in his constituency was creating serious controversy, Ralph Katzman, a member of the legislative assembly for the province of Saskatchewan representing the Rosthern constituency (including Warman) sent out 5,625 questionnaires to all households in his constituency. Of these questionnaires, 1,117 were completed and returned to him. He asked nine questions related to a nuclear plant, a refinery, nuclear wastes, a uranium mine, use of uranium products, and more specific questions related to location of such facilities. This survey will be used to assess community attitudes toward a proposed refinery.

It is difficult to document conflict situations, but we were able to observe the public hearings held by a Canadian Federal Environmental Assessment Panel, January 1980, on a proposed uranium hexafluoride refinery planned by Eldorado Nuclear for Warman, Saskatchewan. Verbatim recordings of the twenty-two sessions held over twelve days were made, and the 3,091 pages of the proceedings in twenty-two volumes were published (Federal Environmental Assessment Report No. 13, 1980). We studied copies of these volumes to objectively confirm the proceedings.

In addition to the report on the hearings, we interviewed members of the federal panel, Eldorado representatives, leaders of the Concerned Citizens Groups, pastors in the rural Warman area as well as in Saskatoon, the mayor of Warman, town officials, and numerous Hutterite and Mennonite leaders and lay people after the hearings. While the first four data sets provide community context which help explain the outcome, the hearings and interview data provide qualitative data for assessment of Laumann's and Wellman's models for understanding the Warman Eldorado Nuclear conflict with Warman Mennonites.

Findings

First we present data on the federal hearings held in the Warman-Saskatoon area, the battleground for building a hexafluoride refinery near Warman. This will be followed by addressing the four propositions which emerged out of a review of Laumann's community conflict and Wellman's community network models.

Federal Hearings: The Battleground

Twenty-two sessions of hearings were held by a Federal Environmental Assessment panel and Table 1 lists the times of the hearings, where they were held, who presented the briefs, and the position they took. A total of 347 speakers appeared before the panel. Some briefs were extensive scholarly, documented papers, which took half an hour to present. Others were as short as a minute or two, where individuals simply recorded their position on the proposed refinery. Three fourths (74.1 per cent) of the briefs, presented by 257 individuals were against the location of the refinery near Warman, and one quarter were in favour (25.9 per cent). The qualitative data provided good opportunities for content analysis (Public Hearings, Volumes 1–22, 1980).

Physical Structure of the Hearings

When the hearings began, Eldorado succeeded in creating a formal intimidating environment for opponents, by placing four permanent representatives at a table immediately to the left of the head table, where the seven federal panel representatives were located. Opponents were given no permanent place, and were asked to speak at the very end on the right, farthest removed from the panel (about twenty-five feet), placed after the secretaries, and recorders (symbolically the most inferior position). The spatial setting implied that Eldorado was in a strong position, while opponents were in the last place. The space was structured to intimidate opponents. The bright lights of the local and national TV cameras hovering near the scene, the press from the East and elsewhere interviewing the speakers, and the two hooded verbatim recording specialists speaking into their receivers did not encourage the timid.

At the first hearing, many of the opposition did not accept their assigned lowly spatial disadvantage, and spoke in front of the panel. Hildebrand, the chairman of the Concerned Citizens Group, the major organized opposition, began by commenting on the intimidating structure, asking for changes which were made in the hearings that followed. Eldorado was also given the right to question opponents after each presentation, which at times became intimidating to grandmothers, youth, and lay people who testified in opposition.

Table 1
Public Meetings of the Federal Environmental Assessment Panel on the Proposed Hexafluoride Refinery at Warman (Volumes, Dates, Places, and Briefs Presented)

Published Reports: Volumes	Time of Hearings	Place of Meetings	Briefs Presented by		Briefs Presented		
			Mennonites	Others	For a Refinery	Against a Refinery	Total
1, 2	8 Jan, 1980	Martensville	18	8	6	20	26
3, 4	9 Jan, 1980	Martensville	23	13	3	33	36
5, 6	10 Jan, 1980	Martensville	4	14	9	9	18
7, 8	15 Jan, 1980	Saskatoon	1	24	5	20	25
9, 10	16 Jan, 1980	Saskatoon		25	4	21	25
11, 12	17 Jan, 1980	Saskatoon		19	10	9	19
13	18 Jan, 1980	Saskatoon		34	11	23	34
14, 15	19 Jan, 1980	Saskatoon	4	65	8	61	69
16	21 Jan, 1980	Martensville		3	3		3
17, 18	22 Jan, 1980	Martensville	17	13	5	25	30
19, 20	23 Jan, 1980	Martensville	5	21	12	14	26
21, 22	24 Jan, 1980	Martensville	13	23	14	22	36
Total			85 (24.5)	262 (75.5)	90 (25.9)	257 (74.1)	347

SOURCE: *Public Hearings of the Environment Assessment Panel on the Proposed Uranium Hexafluoride Refinery at Corman Park Saskatchewan*, Volumes 1–22, 1980.
Note: percentage is in parentheses.

Grassroots Opposition and Politics

It soon became evident that the larger community contained many more inactive opponents than proponents, as illustrated in Table 2. Ralph Katzman's survey of his constituency suggests this conclusion (Table 2). He found that attitudes were similar in all parts of his constituency— Rosthern, Warman and Allen. Of the respondents 73 to 82 per cent favoured a referendum as to whether a uranium plant, refinery, wastes or mine should be introduced into the community.

Two thirds or more (60–78 per cent) did not favour development of uranium activity in Cluff Lake and Warman, and they did not favour uranium exports. More than three quarters (78 per cent) did not favour a uranium refinery in the Warman area. Katzman reported in his brief that as a result of the survey he was shifting from support to active opposition to the proposed refinery.

The constituency's general latent opposition to nuclear-related issues provided the opponents with a large pool of potential recruits illustrated by models 1c and 1d in Figure 1. The issue consistency was sufficiently salient (anti-nuclear related activity) to create a high level of open controversy involving mobilization of non-elite members of the community (*Why People Say No* 1980).

Technical Resources: Bringing in the Big Guns

When the hearings took place in January 1980, Eldorado provided stacks of studies and technical reports, chiefly on the safety of the proposed operation and the advantage this would provide to the community (Environmental Impact Statement 1979). At first Eldorado succeeded in getting opponents to respond to the technical parts of its proposal when it brought forward the best experts from across North America. However, the opponents shifted ground to Eldorado's weaknesses, scoring points for the opponents as they mounted their opposition.

Specialists were brought in by both sides as heavy artillery, to legitimize the opposing positions. In the beginning, Eldorado had hoped that their specialists and reports on the safety of the refinery and the benefits this would create for the community would overwhelm the panel, with little technical opposition on the other side. However, when the brokers and the concerned citizens brought in specialists who could speak to the issue on the same grounds (physical safety, economic benefits), and in addition brought in experts on ethics, theology, and sociology where Eldorado was ill prepared, the experts of the opposition began to set

Table 2
Attitudes of Residents in the Provincial Constituency of Rosthern to Issues Concerning the Production and Use of Uranium and Related Nuclear Products (%)

| | Responses to Questions | | | |
	Yes		No	
1. Are you in favour of a vote by residents of an area which has been designated as a site for a nuclear power plant?	82	(840)	18	(183)
2. Are you in favour of a vote by residents of an area which has been designated as a site for a uranium refinery?	82	(840)	18	(183)
3. Are you in favour of a vote by residents of an area which has been designated as a site for a dump of nuclear wastes?	80	(834)	20	(203)
4. Are you in favour of a vote by residents of an area which has been designated as a site for a uranium mine?	73	(818)	27	(299)
5. Are you in favour of the use of uranium products in medical research and treatment?	68	(599)	32	(282)
6. Do you feel you have been given enough information by the media or other sources to properly answer questions asked here?	63	(638)	37	(367)
7. Are you in favour of the development of the Cluff Lake uranium mine in Northern Saskatchewan?	40	(351)	60	(537)
8. Are you in favour of Canada exporting uranium products?	38	(334)	62	(550)
9. Are you in favour of a uranium refinery in the Warman area?	22	(224)	78	(803)

Source: Ralph Katzman, brief, *Public Hearings,* Volume 4, pp. 546–55, 1980.
Note: N is in parentheses.

Eldorado forces back. These battles were fought in twenty-two skirmishes at as many meetings of the hearings in Martensville and Saskatoon. The high level of open opposition on the floor of the hearings, also reported in the media nation-wide, mobilized non-elite members of the community and elsewhere against the refinery.

As previously indicated, when the twenty-two volumes of recorded presentations to the panel were published, they revealed that of the 347 briefs, one quarter (25.9 per cent) supported the proposed refinery, and three quarters (74.1 per cent) were against (see Table 3). The proponents and opponents lined up as predicted in Figure 1. The 90 briefs supporting the proposed refinery came mainly from five Eldorado representatives (19 briefs), governmental representatives (27), and representatives of business and labour (16). Most proponents came from outside the immediate community (Saskatoon and farther away). Almost all the Mennonites (83 briefs) and other church groups (15) lined up solidly in opposition. The 159 individuals who were opposed represented farmers, dairymen, professionals, some businessmen, labourers, politicians, housewives, young people, and the representatives of peace groups. It was a grassroots community effort which surprised the federal panel and Eldorado Nuclear. They had not seen such an organized grassroots opposition before.

Table 3
Supporters and Opponents of the Proposed Eldorado Refinery at the Hearings in Saskatoon and Martensville, January, 1980

Briefs Presented By	Support for a Refinery	Against a Refinery	Total
Eldorado Panel Members (5)	19		19
Government Agencies	27		27
Business and Labour	16		16
Individuals	26	159	185
Mennonites	2	83	85
Other Church Groups		15	15
Total	90 (25.9)	257 (74.1)	347 (100)

Source: Public Hearings of the Environment Assessment Panel, Volumes 1–22, 1980.
Note: percentage is in parentheses.

Conflict: The Emergence of Opposing Networks

Refinery Proponents and Bargaining

Eldorado Nuclear, the company which proposed the refinery, clearly planned for a bargaining situation, and it hoped as much as possible to stay away from oppositional confrontation. First, they chose "jobs for the community" as the "instrumental issue...which would involve a limited level of controversy in which many aspects of the issue could be negotiable" (Laumann, Marsden, and Galaskiewicz 1977: 608). They hoped that such an issue would give rise to recurrent discussion channels, which would facilitate forming a bargaining structure around economic issues to benefit 1) the Saskatoon businessmen and organized labour fifteen miles away, 2) merchants in the small town of Warman, two miles away, 3) residents of the community who would find jobs, 4) the municipality in terms of $300,000 in new tax income, and 5) a general boost to the province's image and welfare (Environmental Impact Statement 1979, Public Hearings 1980). As Laumann and Pappi point out,

> instrumental issues are concerned with controversies over differing allocation of scarce resources, such as land, jobs, and money, and find their particular locus in the adaptive and integrative sectors of community concern....For such issues there is usually a fairly obvious calculus of costs and benefits to various interested parties. Conflict over such issues tends to be moderate, often characterized by bargaining and compromise...(1973: 224).

Second, Eldorado Nuclear sought to gain an advantage over potential community opponents by secrecy, providing limited information. Land accumulated for the refinery was purchased by another company, giving vague information about needs for future development, from Mennonites who later were opposed. Next, Eldorado created a network of business, labour, and political leaders who were persuaded to back the refinery because it was in their own interests, and these recruits also talked very little. Thus, Eldorado spent several years creating a supporting network (when there were still no active opponents), seeking to gain a power advantage for any bargaining which might be necessary later.

Third, as the bargaining model implies, they sought to enlarge the network of proponents by gaining active support from the Saskatoon merchants, organized labour, political proponents at all levels, the Warman town council, and community supporters (the Hutterites). The strategy was to transfer more proponents from the inactive to the active circle, to join Eldorado Nuclear in support of a refinery (Figure 1).

Eldorado offered most of the leaders of churches, business, mayors, prominent teachers, and Hutterites an expense-free trip to their Port Hope, Ontario refinery for a tour. Some accepted the offer, and they came back with varying reports.

Eldorado Nuclear clearly began by seeking to gain community support for their proposed refinery by presenting instrumental issues coupled with a bargaining position as Proposition 1 suggests. At first it seemed that this approach might work, but later their strategy waned because of community opposition. How did this opposition develop?

Refinery Opponents: Defining Consummatory Issues

While opponents for the refinery were forced to begin under circumstances set up for bargaining, where Eldorado had an enormous advantage, they defined the proposed refinery as a consummatory issue, and they forced the panel and Eldorado to increasingly work under an oppositional model (Laumann, Marsden, and Galaskiewicz 1977: 608). Opponents refused to bargain, because they saw the nuclear industry as a non-negotiable issue, where they could not compromise. They saw the proposed refinery and their own community aims at opposite poles, and they succeeded in polarizing the controversy. Eldorado proponents soon were forced to focus on new issues, and found themselves reacting to ethnic, social, and community values which they had not researched, and for which they were ill prepared.

Eldorado proposed to build its refinery in a solidly Mennonite community. As illustrated in Table 4, it is a cohesive ethno-religious community where endogamy (98 per cent), regular church attendance (86 per cent), ability to speak the mother tongue (97 per cent), and use of it (69 per cent) is high. A uranium refinery clashed with the Mennonite peace position, a tenet which they have upheld since the Protestant Reformation (Epp 1974, 1980). Non-resistance and opposition to war was definitely a consummatory issue, for which Mennonites have emigrated, suffered, and died over the centuries. Numerous speakers at the hearings were puzzled as to why Eldorado chose such a community. They seem to have thought that Mennonites were too "traditional" or uninvolved to promote a challenge, or they were unaware of the salience of Mennonite beliefs.

Driedger's 1955 study of the Warman area illustrates a "traditional," rural, segregated ethno-religious community of Mennonites; the 1977 study documents considerable change in educational patterns, occupational status, family roles, emerging contacts and networks including other groupings beyond the immediate community. While Eldorado

Table 4
Endogamy, Attendance at Church Services, Ability to Speak, and Use of Mother Tongue by Nine Ethno-Religious Groups in Northern Saskatchewan

Group	Indicators of Ethnic Solidarity				
	Extent of Endogamy	Regular Church Attendance	Ability To Speak Mother Tongue	Frequent Use of Mother Tongue	
Hutterite	100	100	100	100	(6)
Mennonite	*98*	*86*	*97*	*69*	*(244)*
Scandinavian Lutheran	96	87	90	37	(86)
French Catholic	91	91	99	78	(15)
German Catholic	90	94	93	29	(190)
Ukrainian Orthodox	89	70	100	63	(83)
Ukrainian Catholic	88	82	99	69	(154)
Polish Catholic	69	53	100	87	(15)
Doukhobor	60	55	95	70	(20)
Total Sample	91	86	97	60	(1000)

Source: Alan Anderson, "Assimilation in the Bloc Settlements of North-Central Saskatchewan: A Comparative Study of Identity Among Seven Ethno-Religious Groups in a Canadian Prairie Region." Saskatoon, Ph.D. dissertation, 1972.

Note: N is in parentheses.

Nuclear thought they were dealing with a 1955 type of "traditional" ethnic community, which they observed among the Amish in Ontario, they were actually dealing with a large segment who represented a "saved" community which had advanced well into creating broader "liberated" social networks. Thus, maintaining a "saved" community was very important as well.

The community study data show that the consummatory issue (the peace issue) played an important part (Proposition 2). The Mennonites felt very deeply that the introduction of a refinery was inconsistent with their historical peace position, and they also felt it would undermine their "traditional" and emerging "saved" communities.

Brokers: "Saved" Leadership Gathering Community Opposition

As indicated, Eldorado spent several years laying the groundwork for entering the community by grooming a network of business, labour, and governmental proponents who would present the merits of a refinery. While there were many different Mennonite denominations in the Warman community, as well as many ethno-religious groups who were against introduction of a refinery, they required organization, co-operation, and leadership for the coherent oppositional force most rural communities find difficult to provide. Leaders used both "strong ties" of intimacy within the traditional community, and "weak ties" with the many non-Mennonite groups to mold consensus (Granovetter 1973: 1361, 1376).

The community very quickly organized a Concerned Citizens Group with a membership of 860, many of whom presented briefs at the hearings. The chairman was a Mennonite pastor, the vice-chairman a former warden of several correctional institutions in Canada, and the secretary an elementary school principal in the area ("saved" leaders). These leaders and others on the executive served as brokers and brought with them religious, educational, and social service networks which were quickly molded into a cohesive unit of contacts. From many sub-networks they created an effective action group, often a difficult proce-dure with Mennonites especially (Craven and Wellman 1973: 65). Belatedly, Eldorado attempted to organize an Informed Citizens Group, to combat the work of the Concerned Citizens Group with the former Warman mayor as the head, but it never gained more than a dozen members. Guenther, the chairman, was no longer an active Mennonite and was considered suspect by Mennonites, so Eldorado's first counter attack failed.

These "saved" Mennonite brokers, long-time residents of the commu-nity, had the trust of the Warman community, and they also provided bridges to much-needed contacts with outside resources. All three execu-tive members had studied in Mennonite theological schools as well as state universities, so that they were aware of ideological, technical, and social resources. To counter Eldorado's professional reports on the natural environment and the safety of a refinery presented by experts in their respective fields, leaders of the Concerned Citizens Group brought in their own professionals who were experts in the nuclear and social sciences, as well as experts in ethics and theology, where Eldorado's research was almost non-existent. Most effective were the professionals (several sociologists, medical doctors, ethics professor, biologists) which the Concerned Citizens Group brought in from universities in Saska-toon, Winnipeg, and Toronto to present lengthy scholarly papers on Mennonite beliefs, the Mennonite sociological community, and the ethics of Mennonites (Public Hearings 1980). These scholarly presenta-tions turned the focus of the hearings from instrumental economic issues as Eldorado desired, to consummatory ethical and social issues related to the refinery's impact on the community. Eldorado had done almost no work in this area, and later complained that the frame of reference for the hearings had been redirected. Various peace groups (some radical) also testified, but they had relatively less influence, since their briefs were fairly predictable, and to some extent, radical.

These brokers also rallied allies to their cause. Anderson's (1972) samples in the Hague-Osler-Warman community, of Mennonite, Polish Catholic, Hutterite, Doukhobor, Ukrainian Catholic, Ukrainian Orthodox, Scandinavian Lutheran, French Catholic, and German Catholic ethnic bloc settlements surrounding the Warman area (see Table 4), demonstrated a combination of "traditional" ethnic community solidarity with "saved" types who maintained their identity. While each of these nine groups were segregated solitudes in the earlier years of existence, they still had many identity maintenance interests similar to those of the Mennonites. The potential for social networks and alliances to fight common enemies who threatened their communities, their cultures, and their religious beliefs and values was considerable.

These many religious and ethnic communities rallied their resources behind Mennonites (Public Hearings 1980). Although the peace issue was not necessarily a part of the history of all groups, many were able to oppose a refinery on such grounds, and most could support the exclusion of the refinery on grounds that it was an invasion of a rural, religious and ethnic community which had a right to direct future developments, a right which each of them also wished to reserve for their own communities.

As predicted in Proposition 3, we found "saved" Mennonite leaders who had the will and commitment to organize diverse community groups into a Concerned Citizens Group; able opponents were willing to rally around the consummatory issue of "peace," and help fight their cause.

Uncommitted "Traditional" and "Liberated" Bystanders

While the "saved" leaders were able to rally many Mennonites as well as others to their cause, there also were two distinct groups which did not participate—the "traditional" and the "liberated" Mennonites.

The Mennonites first came to the Osler-Hague-Warman area in 1895 (Driedger 1955). These conservative Old Colony Mennonites settled on a reserve north of Warman designated especially for them, and located in old European house-barn combinations in about twenty villages (Epp 1974). Hundreds of these conservative Mennonites left for Mexico in the early 1920s because of loss of control of their own German schools. Many stayed and some continued in their "traditional" ways (the Old Colony and Bergthaler Mennonites).

The "saved" leaders sought to involve these inactive "traditional" opponents (Figure 1d), but were unable to involve the Old Colony Mennonites because they were reluctant to enter political controversy. The leaders did rally the support of one leader of the Bergthaler Mennonites, but even he could not persuade his ministerial council to officially join the opposition. Since then he and some of his followers have separated from the Bergthaler and formed a separate group.

The opponents of the refinery also tried to rally a network of urban "liberated" Mennonites to support their rural cause, but without success. The author later interviewed a dozen Mennonite pastors in Saskatoon to learn why they did not support their rural coreligionists. Some claimed that their members were older and did not approve of active methods of opposition; others claimed that the primary purpose of the gospel was to redeem mankind, not get involved in social action. Still others looked upon their coreligionists as rural traditionalists intolerant of change and modernity, and many thought Eldorado would win in any case so why fight a bureaucracy unsuccessfully. The Concerned Citizens Group was deeply disappointed that they could not add the urban Mennonite network to oppose the refinery. Instead, they had to rely on other churches in Saskatoon to support them, who were not historic peace churches.

In Proposition 4 we predicted that members of a "liberated" community would have neither the conviction nor the commitment to fight community invasion. We found this true amongst the Mennonites in Saskatoon. The issue of peace did not seem sufficiently salient for urban Mennonites, so that they would join rural Mennonites in opposing the refinery. Interviews with the urban Mennonite pastors indicated that for some the peace issue was not salient, and for many ethnicity was not a binding force either. As for maintaining a solid rural Mennonite community, they had abandoned this quest earlier when they moved to the city. It is hard to tell whether they were "liberated" or assimilated ("lost").

The bargaining and oppositional models proposed by Laumann et al. (1973, 1977) provide considerable explanatory power for this study. We have demonstrated how Eldorado chose the bargaining model, a popular model with most industrial and political proponents, because they usually have the staging and power advantage. The study also shows that opponents can shift to an oppositional model and fight effectively, if they see the invasion as a consummatory issue, if they have cohesive community backing, if they can find leaders and brokers who will commit themselves to battle, and if they can rally other networks to support them (Figure 3).

Figure 3
Bargaining (Eldorado) and Oppositional (Mennonite) Strategies in the Warman Refinery Conflict

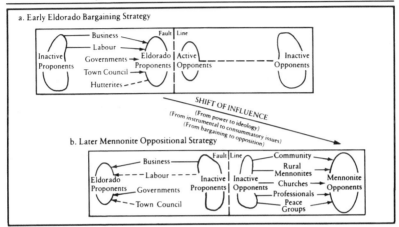

In their Altneustadt study, Laumann and Pappi (1973: 226) found that two of the five issues (school and pop festival), seemed to provide some consummatory and ideological potential for opposition. In their Tower-town and River City studies (Laumann, Marsden, and Galaskiewicz 1977), the issues for each of the two cities seemed largely instrumental, so that opposition did not develop. We think this Warman study illustrates that if the issue is sufficiently consummatory, and if there is a group (such as the Mennonites), whose beliefs are sufficiently salient in opposing an issue, the oppositional model will develop. We found that our Warman study supports the oppositional model of Laumann and others (1973, 1977) very well.

While Laumann, Marsden, and Galaskiewicz (1977: 607) diagrammed the broad features of the bargaining and oppositional models, we were able to enlarge and enrich the models by examining and documenting some of the groupings that supported both the proponents (business, labour, government, town elite) and the opponents (community, churches, professionals, peace groups) in the Warman study. It is difficult to demonstrate the dynamics and shifts during conflict and controversy, but the published hearings provided unique objective qualitative and quantitative data to analyze community solidarity and conflict.

We were also able to link two of Wellman's (1979) three communities to the Laumann model. While most traditional and "liberated" communities could not be recruited as opponents, the strong "saved" leadership was able to rally a cohesive opposition to the invasion of Eldorado, by drawing inactive opponents from all communities.

Conclusions

Eldorado Nuclear clearly selected "jobs for the community" as the instrumental issue, where they calculated the costs and benefits to the various interested parties (Laumann and Pappi 1973: 224). They also expected that a bargaining model would permit negotiation, compromise, trading, and concessions between Eldorado and the community in which they wished to build a refinery. They mobilized representatives of business, labour, governments, and the town elite to strengthen their bargaining power, hoping to surprise any potential opponents. They sought to persuade the panel and the community that the refinery would be safe, and that it would be an economic boost to all. Eldorado's proposal persuaded the panel that indeed the plant would be safe. However, they were not able to confine the controversy to instrumental issues, and bargaining soon turned to opposition.

The immediate Mennonite community quickly saw the proposed uranium refinery as a consummatory issue symbolizing a threat to their basic peace position and their way of community life. They took a strong oppositional stance, mobilized the community, other churches, professionals and peace groups to oppose the refinery on social, ethical, and ideological grounds. Thus they shifted the issue from instrumental to consummatory issues, removing any potential for bargaining and compromise (Laumann, Marsden, and Galaskiewicz 1977: 608). A few new jobs and dollars for the community seemed paltry in the light of the negative symbols the refinery would bring to the community. Eldorado was unprepared for the shift, and was forced into an oppositional stance where they reacted to Mennonite issues, ethics, and social factors, for which they were ill-prepared. The panel asked Eldorado for more intensive and extensive community impact studies, and Eldorado complained that the focus had been changed, deciding that it could not provide the social studies requested, and withdrew.

Like Granovetter (1973) we wanted to discover why some communities organize for common goals effectively. We conclude it was because "saved" leaders of the Warman Mennonite community combined strong "traditional" community ties, and extensive "liberated" networks to fight the invasion. Thus, they were able to shift the controversy from instrumental economic to consummatory peace issues, and from a bargaining to an oppositional strategy, where they gained an advantage and resisted the intrusion of Eldorado successfully.

As expected, the "saved" leaders were able to rally the middle range of the community to support their opposition, but they were not able to gain the support of the most "traditional" and "liberated" Mennonites at opposite ends. The conservative "traditional" Old Colony Mennonites have always been reluctant to enter the political fray; here too they remained on the sidelines. Urban Mennonites in Saskatoon who could be viewed as more "liberated" also did not join the "saved" movement in fighting the invasion. While they had the ability to fight, they had neither the conviction nor the commitment to do so.

Notes

1. While we wish to use part of Wellman's model of three types of urban communities, there have been changes in nomenclature. In 1979 Wellman (1979) and Wellman and Leighton (1979) wrote about "lost," "saved," and "liberated" communities in the city. Later Wellman, Carrington and Hall (1983) relabelled them as "lost," "retained," and "unbound" urban communities. Since we are examining both rural and urban communities, we find that the rural "traditional" community with its bonds of kinship, neighbourliness, and common folk traditions is still alive and well in the Warman area (they are not lost). Therefore, we shall use the terminology "traditional," "saved," and "liberated" communities with only the last two of Wellman's three. For our purposes "saved" and "liberated" express the Warman–Saskatoon scene better than "retained" and "unbound," which Wellman and associates used later.

part V

Human rights and social inequalities

Ethnicity and Collective Rights in Canada†

EVELYN KALLEN

On April 17, 1985, three years after the patriation of Canada's Constitution, the equality rights section of the Charter of Rights and Freedoms (CRF: S.15 (1) and (2)) became law. Presumably, under the nondiscriminatory provisions of S.15 (1) members of Canada's many ethnic communities, as individual citizens, will be protected against overt forms of racial and ethnic discrimination. Presumably, also, under the provisions of S.15 (2) members of disadvantaged minorities will be able to seek collective redress against past, systemic discrimination, through programs of affirmative action and other means.

What S.15 does not directly address is the need of ethnocultural communities, as collectivities, for recognition and protection of their collective cultural rights. The concept of equality, under the equality rights section of the CRF is essentially individualistic in thrust: it does not speak directly to the Canadian multicultural ideal of equality of status for all ethnic groups; nor does it recognize or protect equality of ethnocultures.

The equality rights provisions of our Charter accordingly afford no protections, at the group level, for the collective cultural status and collective cultural rights of Canada's ethnic communities.

The only section of the CRF which even indirectly speaks to the collective notions of ethnicity and multiculturalism is S.27, in its vague commitment to the preservation and enhancement of the "multicultural heritage" of Canadians.

In light of these observations, we will argue that if the Charter of Rights and Freedoms [CRF] (Canada Act 1982) is to pave the way for a

---

†This article has not been previously published. This is a revised version of a paper originally presented at the Canadian Ethnic Studies Association conference, 1981.

national transformation predicted on the multicultural principle of *unity in diversity* it must be amended so as to recognize and protect not only the individual human rights of all citizens, but also, and equally importantly, the collective cultural rights of all Canada's ethnic groups.

For the most part, human rights issues as they pertain to ethnic collectivities have been approached by legal scholars and by social scientists from a negative stance, i.e., in the context of the effort to combat and eradicate ethnic prejudice and discrimination. The importance of combatting racism notwithstanding, we will adopt a positive approach, focussing on the recognition and protection of collective ethnic (ethnocultural) rights. Drawing upon existing international human rights instruments, we will posit a conceptual framework for the analysis of the state of collective cultural rights in Canada. In light of this framework we will assess the provisions of the Charter and its potential for a national transformation to a truly multicultural Canada.

As individuals, all Canadian citizens can justifiably claim the same kinds of fundamental human rights and freedoms. But, at the group level, all of Canada's different ethnic collectivities cannot claim the same kinds of collective rights. Central to the argument of this paper is the thesis that status differences between charter (or founding) peoples, (later) immigrants, and (earlier/original) aboriginal peoples provide the basis for a tripartite division in the kinds of collective ethnic rights which can, justifiably, be claimed.[1] As each set of group claims is based on a different version of the Canadian ethnic mosaic, each envisages a different kind of national transformation. To some degree, then, the three sets of claims are in conflict.

To what extent are the claims of each of the three categories of Canadian ethnic groups recognized and protected in the CRF?[2] Our analysis should shed light not only on the ethnic *priorities* governing the Charter, but also on the concomitant version of Canadian "unity in diversity" underlying its provisions for a national transformation.

The International Level: Unity, Diversity, and Human Rights

While the majority of international human rights codes and covenants express the dominant principle of the *unity* of humankind and, accordingly, are directed toward the individual *qua* human being, the twin principle of group diversity also is given global recognition under the International Bill of Human Rights (1978).

Minority Rights of Ethnocultural Groups

Article 27 of the International Covenant on Civil and Political Rights (ICCPR) addresses the *cultural diversity* of humankind and recognizes the collective rights of ethnocultural minorities[3] within the states where they exist:

> In those States in which ethnic, religious or linguistic minorities exist, persons belonging to such minorities shall not be denied the right, in community with other members of their group, to enjoy their own culture, to profess and practice their own religion, or to use their own language.

Whether or not this article can be interpreted in its present form as providing a basis for minority claims based on collective ethnocultural rights remains a matter of some debate among legal scholars. Some suggest that the wording refers to individual members of minorities rather than to minorities as collectivities. Increasing numbers of scholars, however, seem to be of the opinion that the article should be interpreted collectively.[4]

Under Article 27 (above) it is clearly the *ethnocultural* underpinnings of minority status which provide the international basis for *minority* rights. This observation is a critical one for our examination of collective rights claims for it sets apart *ethnocultural* minorities from all other socially disadvantaged and disprivileged minorities in Canadian society. Like ethnocultural minorities, other minorities (women, children, aged, homosexuals, mentally and physically impaired populations, etc.) have long been subject to negative, collective discrimination and have come to occupy an inferior and disadvantaged social status in Canadian society, and elsewhere. What distinguishes ethnocultural minorities from the others is the attribute of *culture* (or ethnoculture) in the transgenerational, anthropological sense of the term.

Anthropologists generally agree that for a distinctive culture/way of life of a particular human group to be categorized as a culture/ethnoculture, it must have both a spatial/empirical and a temporal/historical dimension. When the available evidence shows that a given constellation of collective beliefs and lifeways has been transmitted by members of an ethnic group over at least three generations, it can be regarded as a "genuine" ethnoculture rather than a subculture (alternate lifestyle within a given culture). This conceptual distinction between ethnoculture and alternate culture or subculture has important implications for the question of minority cultural rights: under Article 27

(ICCPR), minority linguistic, religious, and (broader) cultural rights would seem to accrue only to members of ethnic communities maintaining transgenerational ethnocultures.

With regard to the kinds of protections for minority ethnic groups afforded under Article 27, legal opinion strongly suggests that states (like Canada) which have ratified the covenant have assumed only negative obligations: they have agreed not to interfere with the legitimate cultural activities of minorities. However, a guarantee of noninterference by the state does not mean that the state is under any obligation to take positive measures to protect minority ethnocultures nor does it imply the recognition of the right to self-determination of minorities. The legitimacy of the latter kind of collective minority right (which, in theory, includes the right to secession) remains a question beset by continuing controversy at the international level.

Peoples' Rights and the Right of Self-Determination

Article 1 of the International Covenant on Economic, Social, and Cultural Rights (ICESCR) provides the international norm for the right of self-determination of peoples. It reads as follows:

> All peoples have the right of self-determination; by virtue of that right they freely determine their political status and freely pursue their economic, social, and cultural development (International Bill of Human Rights 1978: 10).

The concept of *peoples*, as employed in international human rights instruments, has been narrowly interpreted by legal scholars. A recent sociological overview and analysis (Wiberg 1981) indicates that the concept applies only to a nation: a people whose ethnocultural/territorial boundaries (potentially or actually) coincide with the political boundaries of a state unit. Moreover, in its application until the present time, international law has interpreted the concept of people(s) even more narrowly, so as to support the right to national self-determination *only* in cases of non-self-governing territories, formerly under colonial rule by overseas states ("saltwater colonialism").

In its customary application, then, international law offers little support to ethnic collectivities living *inside* the territories of recognized sovereign states, when they strive for independence or autonomy. Accordingly, proponents of current, internal movements for national self-determination, for example, the Franco-Québécois and the Inuit of Nunavut—cannot expect formal support from international human rights bodies, since the collective rights to *nationhood* upon which their claims are based have not as yet achieved recognition at an international level.

Accountability to International Human Rights Principles

The various international instruments which provide the global directives for human rights have not, as yet, achieved the customary status of international law through legal invocation.[5] Their power is that of moral persuasion.

In ratifying the International Bill of Human Rights (1978), states have undertaken a moral obligation to abide by these principles and to enact human rights legislation in accord with them. In the Canadian context, federal, provincial, and constitutional human rights legislation are modelled, to varying degrees, on these international guidelines. Yet, it should be noted here, *none* of this legislation, including the CRF, actually *incorporates* the international covenants ratified. What this means is, their moral obligation notwithstanding, Canadians are not legally bound to act in accordance with all of these international directives, at the present time.

Collective Rights in Canada: The Differential Claims of Charter, Immigrant, and Aboriginal Peoples

The distinction between Canadian ethnocultural collectivities, *with* and *without* territorial bases for nationhood within the state, has important implications for the nature of collective claims which can justifiably be made. All Canadian ethnocultural collectivities, in accord with the international principle of minority rights (Article 27, ICCPR), can justifiably seek recognition of their collective linguistic, religious, and (broader) *cultural group rights*. But only those ethnic groups with territorial bases for their ethnocultural claims within the Canadian state can justifiably seek recognition of their collective *national group (nationhood) rights*. We will argue (for the Canadian context) that nationhood claims, based on the international principle of peoples' rights (Article 2, ICESCR), can justifiably be put forward only by *some* ethnic collectivities within the two categories of charter and aboriginal peoples. Immigrant ethnic groups, as a whole, cannot justifiably put forward such claims.

The legal and quasi-legal premise for this argument rests on several grounds.

Mede (quoted in Leavy 1979: 3–4) draws a distinction between two kinds of ethnic minorities:

> 1. *voluntary* minorities, composed of those who, individually or in families, left their country of origin and moved to another country where they live as a community. They preserve certain parts of their own culture and transmit them to their descendants, while integrating to a certain degree with the majority culture of the new country.
> 2. *involuntary* minorities, those groups which for reasons of war, territorial request or frontier adjustments find themselves in a state where their culture is in a minority situation.

Involuntary minorities (e.g., Canada's Franco-Québécois and aboriginal peoples), Mede argues, are justified in making more collective human rights claims than voluntary minorities (e.g., Canada's immigrant ethnic collectivities). Voluntary minorities would be justified in claiming the right to "institutional" autonomy, e.g., ethnic schools or social services. But only involuntary minorities would be justified in claiming the right to a measure of "jurisdictional" cultural autonomy, e.g., the right to establish standards applicable to their ethnically distinctive school system. The rationale for this distinction, Mede argues, is that there can be no cultural autonomy without territorial autonomy.

Within the category of "involuntary" minorities, a further conceptual distinction with implications for the kinds of collective claims put forward by ethnic minorities is the distinction between charter group status and aboriginal status. Nationhood claims based on charter group status, such as those proposed by the Franco-Québécois, essentially represent constitutionally-based claims to nationhood within Canada made on the basis of the ethnic group's historically, and constitutionally, recognized status as a "founding people." Nationhood claims based on aboriginal right, such as that proposed by the Inuit of Nunavut, represent aboriginal claims to nationhood (national self-determination) based on "original peoples" ("First Nations") occupancy and use of their aboriginal territories "from time immemorial"—aboriginal right.[6]

Frideres (1983: 85) points out that the concept of aboriginal right to land stems from an incontrovertible fact of Canadian history: that Indian and Inuit peoples were the original, sovereign inhabitants of this country prior to the arrival of the European colonial powers. He goes on to say that, while its content has never been clarified in Canadian law, aboriginal title has been referred to by the judiciary as "a personal and usufructuary right," or right of use and occupancy, "dependent upon the good will of the Sovereign."

The *aboriginal peoples'* conception of this right, however, is much broader: it goes far beyond the legal notion of aboriginal title. It is a comprehensive concept which connotes the integral link between an aboriginal nation, their aboriginal territory and self-government, and their aboriginal, land-based ethnoculture. It is this comprehensive concept of aboriginal *sovereignty*, from time immemorial, which underlies current aboriginal nationhood claims.

For the Inuit, according to John Amagoalik, co-chairperson of the Inuit Committee on National Issues:

> Our position is that aboriginal rights, aboriginal title to land, water and sea ice flows from aboriginal rights and all rights to practise our customs and traditions, to retain and develop our languages and cultures, and the rights to self-government, all these things flow from the fact that we have aboriginal rights.
> ...In our view, aboriginal rights can also be seen as human rights, because these are the things that we need to continue to survive as a distinct people in Canada (Canada 1983a: 130, quoted in Asch 1984: 27).

The generally held legal view towards recognition of aboriginal title to land in Canada is that as long as the title of the band or tribe from which an aboriginal people is descended has not been recognized and extinguished, the collective aboriginal rights of the group have not been abrogated. Following from this, for purposes of collective rights claims, aboriginal peoples can be arbitrarily divided into two categories: Status Indians (with legal Indian status under the Indian Act) and all the others (non-Status Indians, Métis, and Inuit).

Within the legal category of Status (or Registered) Indians, the difference between the subcategories of Treaty and non-Treaty Indians has important implications for the question of collective claims based on aboriginal rights. In the case of Treaty Indians, their aboriginal title has been *recognized* and *extinguished* through the process of signing land cession treaties.[7] In the case of non-Treaty Indians, whose ancestors did not sign *land cession treaties* (while they may have been party to other treaty arrangements, e.g., peace and friendship treaties), their aboriginal title has *not* been recognized or extinguished.

The non-Status Indians, Inuit, and Métis, whose ancestors did *not* sign land cession treaties or engage in other transactions with the Crown that would abrogate their aboriginal rights (e.g., taking scrip) can, like non-Treaty (Status) Indians, make collective claims based on aboriginal right.

Summary: Differential Claims of Charter, Immigrant, and Aboriginal Peoples of Canada

In the foregoing discussion we have attempted to elaborate the basis of the difference in the kinds of collective rights claims which may justifiably be put forward by representatives of Canadian ethnic groups. We have argued that *all* ethnic communities may collectively claim religious, linguistic, and (broader) cultural rights, but that only those ethnocultural collectivities with historical/ancestral links to a specific territory within the Canadian state may make legitimate claims to nationhood. Because immigrant ethnic collectivities cannot provide evidence for such ethnic-territorial links, they cannot, justifiably, put forward collective claims to nationhood within Canada. Alternatively, the collective, nationhood claims put forward by charter and aboriginal peoples derive from a demonstrable historical association between ethnicity and territory, a link between an ethnocultural group and their ancestral homeland. The constitutionally recognized, historical association of French Quebeckers with a distinctive language, religion, and ethnoculture maintained within their ancestral homeland, the province of Quebec, underlies Franco-Québécois demands for nationhood (see, especially, Lévesque 1968). Aboriginal peoples' nationhood claims rest on the demonstrable link, "from time immemorial," between aboriginal peoples, their aboriginal territories, and their living, land-based ethnocultures (see, especially, the 1979 *Nunavut* proposal put forward by the Inuit Tapirisat of Canada). Such claims are rooted in the concept of aboriginal rights.

On the basis of the foregoing discussion, we will now attempt to schematize the categories of collective, ethnic rights claims which can justifiably be put forward by group representatives from aboriginal, immigrant, and charter populations within Canada.

Typology of Collective Ethnic Rights Claims

Cultural group rights: Claimants seek recognition and protection of their collective right to freely express and enjoy their distinctive ethnic language, religion, and culture, in community with their ethnic fellows.
National group rights: Claimants seek recognition and protection of their right to politico-economic and cultural sovereignty, i.e., nationhood, within the geocultural boundaries of their ancestral territory within the society.

Aboriginal rights: Claimants seek recognition and protection of their collective right to occupy and use their ancestral lands and resources and/or to claim adequate compensation in exchange for the extinguishment of their aboriginal rights.

The foregoing scheme will provide a framework for our analysis of the provisions of the CRF (Constitution Act 1982). In the following pages, we will assess the degree to which the CRF recognizes and protects collective ethnic rights, the kinds of collective rights entrenched, and the ethnic priorities underlying the Charter's provisions. In this process we will seek to determine whether or not the CRF, in its present form, can be held to pave the way for a national transformation to a truly multicultural Canada.

CRF and the Canadian Mosaic Ideal

Before proceeding to assess the various provisions for collective ethnic rights contained in the Charter we should ask: To what extent does the CRF endorse and protect the Canadian multicultural ideal? In its original (1980) version, reference to the notion of multiculturalism was notably absent. Later, in response to submissions from a wide variety of ethnic groups the Charter (1982), under Section 27, states that: "This Charter shall be interpreted in a manner consistent with the preservation and enhancement of the multicultural heritage of Canadians." However, the somewhat amorphous notion of "multicultural heritage" is nowhere defined or elaborated. Nor are any positive guarantees for collective cultural rights mentioned or specified.

As compared with *egalitarian* multicultural models projected by some scholars and concerned citizens, the present Charter, under the Constitution Act, 1982, represents a highly conservative document. Overall, it perpetuates the status quo by focussing on individual rights for ethnic minorities on grounds essentially the same as those in the 1960 Bill of Rights, and by spelling out protections for the collective linguistic, religious, and cultural rights only for the established English and French charter groups.

The Issue of Linguistic Rights

The issue of linguistic rights is clearly related to the view of Canada and Canadian culture held by various scholars, politicians, and the people they purportedly represent. The conception of Canada as a *multicultural* society clearly implies some equitable form of recognition of the collective rights of all of Canada's ethnocultural collectivities. To constitutionally entrench such rights, however, would require a radical departure from the concepts of human rights and of Canadian society which underlie our original constitution (the BNA Act), the 1960 Bill of Rights, and the current CRF, under our new (1982) Constitution.

The BNA Act contains only two references to collective rights: S.93, dealing with separate (Protestant and Catholic) denominational schools, and S.133, concerning the use of English and French in certain federal and Quebec institutions. These provisions have been incorporated under the present (1982) Constitution and further extended under the CRF, S.16–22 (Official Languages of Canada) and S.23 (Minority Language Educational Rights). Through these provisions, the collective religious and linguistic rights of Canada's two charter groups have been legally secured. Alternatively, as in the original Constitution, under the current Constitution and its CRF, the collective rights of non-Protestant and non-Catholic, non-English and non-French ethnic collectivities are neither recognized nor protected.

The present Charter, which represents the unwavering position of former prime minister Trudeau, strongly endorses the position of proponents of bilingualism and biculturalism. Scholars who support this view (notably Rocher 1976) refer to Canada as a nation with "a unique bicultural heritage" and suggest that constitutional guarantees are necessary for the preservation of English and French cultures through the protection of their language rights.

While considerable support was voiced during the constitutional debate for the retainment of the privileged situation of the two official languages at the federal level and in some provinces (notably Ontario, Manitoba, and New Brunswick), there was far less support for constitutional entrenchment of linguistic rights under a new bill or charter (McKinnon 1979). Moreover, among those who have favoured this idea there has been some support for the extension of the principle of linguistic rights to include guarantees for the protection of non-official minority languages, where numbers warrant.

From a legal perspective, some scholars have argued that it is only appropriate to speak of language rights where an ethnic collectivity has the requisite population numbers to ensure the maintenance of the effective use of the language. Douglas (1979) contends that, where numbers warrant, the effective protection of linguistic rights requires positive measures by the state to ensure: 1) the right to understand and be understood by the state; 2) the right to use one's language before the courts; and 3) the right to be educated in one's mother tongue.

While these measures for the recognition and protection of non-official minority languages would clearly meet some of the demands put forward by the proponents of multilingualism and multiculturalism in

Canada,[8] they were rejected outright by former prime minister Trudeau, first, under the federal policy of multiculturalism within a *bilingual* framework (1971), and second, in the CRF under the Constitution Act, 1982.

The sections dealing with language rights under the CRF are designed to enshrine constitutionally the provisions of the Official Languages Act and to pave the way for Canada-wide recognition of institutional bilingualism. Accordingly, constitutional guarantees are provided to ensure the equality of status of English and French in federal institutions and before federal courts. Further, constitutional guarantees are provided for minority language instruction in English or French, where numbers warrant, in both primary and secondary schools throughout Canada.

The established, constitutional, "cultural duality" of the English-Protestant, French-Catholic *majorities* in Canada is clearly reinforced and perpetuated by recognizing and protecting their collective linguistic and religious rights in locales where their numbers constitute *numerical* minorities. This highly political interpretation of *minority rights* neither applies to nor protects the collective rights of the other ethnic groups, the true ethnic minorities.

Religious Rights

In the foregoing discussion of linguistic rights, it was pointed out that the religious rights of English Protestants and French Catholics, from the very beginning of Canadian life, have been recognized through S.93 and S.133 of the BNA Act. But the protection for Protestant and Catholic minority education provided in S.93 proved, over time, to be highly controversial; education was a provincial matter, and provincial governments were not always supportive of minority religious education, especially when instruction was given in the minority language.

Religious Rights and the Issue of Denominational Schools in Canada

The issue of public funding for "minority" denominational schools has been further complicated over the years by two factors: first, the migration to Canada of increasing numbers of non-Protestant and non-Catholic religious minorities dedicated to the preservation of their religious distinctiveness, and second, the guarantees for religious freedom included under the 1960 Bill of Rights, under the non-discriminatory clauses of federal and provincial human rights legislation, and under S.2a of the CRF.

Like the question of minority linguistic rights, the question of minority religious rights has become inextricably interwoven with the education issue. Increasingly, spokespersons for non-Catholic and non-Protestant religious minorities have taken the view that the constitutional recognition of the right of parents to determine the education of their children should apply equally to parents of all religious persuasions. Further, it has been argued that in a truly multicultural society a freedom of religion provision (S.2a, under the CRF) should be interpreted as an extension of the provisions of S.93 of the BNA Act to include *all* minority religious denominational schools. In economic terms, proponents of this view have argued that government funds for denominational schools should be extended to include non-Protestant and non-Catholic religious minorities *or* that the parents of religious communities who voluntarily choose to support separate non-Catholic, non-Protestant, denominational schools should be exempt from taxation for public education.

For some religious minorities (Jews, for example) the idea of government funding for denominational education poses a serious ideological conflict: on the one hand, there are those who support the argument that multiculturalism is meaningless unless it implies equal government support for all ethno-religious communities; on the other hand there are those who oppose government funding because it implies the right of government intervention and control in private, religious matters (Glickman 1976: 239–42).

For members of various sectarian religious communities like the Hutterites (Macdonald 1976), the Sons of Freedom Doukhobors (Lyons 1976), the Lubavitcher Chassidim (Shaffir 1976) and the Holdeman Mennonites (Levy 1979), the notion of government interference and control is anathema. These religious minority groups do not seek government funding, for what they prize above all is the freedom to pursue their distinctive religious lifeways unhampered by outside interference. However, they are not exempt from compulsory education legislation. Thus various compromises have been made. Hutterites, for example, have managed to persuade governments to allow them to locate schools on their isolated colonies (Macdonald 1976), where they are able to screen carefully both potential teachers and curricular content (Flint 1975).

The current, heated controversy surrounding the issue of provincial government funding for Catholic denominational secondary schools in Ontario points up the glaring inequities (not to mention the ethnic hostilities) deriving from constitutional provisions favouring the collective religious rights of charter groups at the expense of ethnic minorities.

Current lobbying for "equal treatment," in the form of hundreds of briefs to government bodies from a wide variety of ethno-religious minority representatives and non-Catholic church groups demonstrates beyond doubt that members of these minorities take the *egalitarian* multicultural ideal seriously. Their interpretation of multiculturalism is evident in their demands that, where numbers warrant (100 + students), *all* religious denominational schools should be funded, on an equitable basis, by the Ontario government (personal communication with minority spokespersons).

To return to the CRF's "omission", it seems clear that there are no guarantees for the collective religious/denominational education rights of ethno-religious minorities. While CRF (S.2a) protects the individual right of all citizens to freely choose their religion, there is no comparable provision which protects the collective right of non-Protestant/non-Catholic ethnic communities to transmit their religious heritage to future generations.

"God and the Constitution"... An Ongoing Debate

The 1980 version of the constitutional package made no reference to God in the preamble, nor did the revised versions developed during the process of debate in 1981. Finally, reportedly in response to more than 8,000 letters supporting some mention of God received by then justice minister Jean Chretien (*Globe and Mail*, 24 August 1981), a phrase recognizing the supremacy of God was inserted into the preamble to the CRF before a list of guaranteed freedoms, including the fundamental freedoms of conscience and religion (S.2a).

The insertion of the "God phrase" sparked immediate controversy, and some expressions of hostility, from theologians, legal scholars, ethnic community spokespersons, and others. Some scholars called it "ambiguous," others said it was "sanctimonious" or "discriminatory." One Buddhist scholar was quoted as saying: "Such a reference to God clearly discriminates against non-Christians" (*Globe and Mail*, 24 August 1981). A professor of Hindu religions suggested that the wording of the phrase in question would surely come before the courts in order to clarify precisely to which religion the word God refers (*Globe and Mail*, 24 August 1981). The head of the religious studies department at a Canadian university in Western Canada saw problems for minorities in the proposed preamble: would minorities be expected to recognize the same God as recognized by a court? Whether or not the reference to God is discriminatory to non-Christians, he felt, would depend on the interpretation placed on the word "God," by the courts.

The Rights of Aboriginal Peoples

The original (1980) version of the CRF made no mention of aboriginal or treaty rights. Indeed, the only direct reference to aboriginal peoples was the vague and negatively-phrased guarantee, under S.24, that the existing rights and freedoms that pertained to "the native peoples of Canada" would not be denied.

Under later versions of the Charter, protections for the rights of aboriginal peoples were more clearly specified. In response to representations by more than forty bodies speaking in favour of stronger guarantees for aboriginal peoples' rights, the drafters included the guarantee, under S.25, that nothing in the Charter was to detract from any aboriginal, treaty, or other rights or freedoms that may pertain to the aboriginal peoples of Canada. Mention of relevant historical documents was also added. After further debate, an additional clause (S.34) was inserted, which gave unequivocal recognition to the aboriginal and treaty rights of Canada's aboriginal peoples. Section 34 read:

1. The aboriginal and treaty rights of the aboriginal peoples of Canada are hereby recognized and affirmed.
2. In this Act, "aboriginal peoples of Canada" includes the Indian, Inuit, and Métis peoples of Canada.

In the tense period of federal-provincial negotiations culminating in final agreement on the constitutional package by all provincial premiers except Quebec's, then prime minister Trudeau agreed to the deletion of two key clauses in the proposed Charter in order to win the majority provincial support prior to patriation. The two clauses temporarily deleted were section 28, guaranteeing equality of men and women, and section 34, recognizing and affirming aboriginal and treaty rights. But fierce lobbying efforts on the part of supporters of women's rights and of aboriginal peoples' rights led to the reinstatement of both clauses. Section 34 was reinstated as S.35, under Schedule B, Part II: Rights of the Aboriginal Peoples of Canada. In the final version of this section, the word "existing" was added before "aboriginal and treaty rights." Some legal scholars interpret this addition as a move designed to ensure that the legal rights of aboriginal peoples are not *extended* beyond those already recognized. It should be noted here also that the concept of aboriginal right was *not* defined under the (1982) Constitution and that the guarantees pertaining to aboriginal and treaty rights did *not* include provisions for positive measures by the state.

Asch (1984: 1) points out, nevertheless, that Section 35 of the Constitution Act, 1982, acknowledges for the first time in Canada's legal history that there are "aboriginal people" and "aboriginal rights." What (he asks) are the implications for Canada of the inclusion of Section 35 in the Constitution? Although all parties agreed to put "aboriginal rights" into the Act, there was no consensus regarding its meaning. Rather, as the Constitution makes clear, this meaning would emerge through further dialogue and discourse. In March of 1983, a conference was held with the prime minister, the ten provincial premiers and representatives of aboriginal groups in attendance, to discuss the identification and definition of the rights of aboriginal peoples to be included in the Constitution of Canada (Section 37 (2)). This conference produced an initial agreement to continue the discussions at further conferences to be held over the next five years.

A central area of concern about the meaning of aboriginal rights emerged at this early meeting and continued to plague participants at conferences over the ensuring years, namely whether or not the definition of aboriginal rights would include political as well as economic rights, and particularly, whether the definition would specify the right to self-determination for aboriginal peoples.

Asch (1984: 37) argues that the position of aboriginal peoples' organizations is that aboriginal peoples have the right to maintain ways of life that are distinct from those of the various ethnic groups among immigrants to Canada. These aboriginal ways of life are autonomous systems which integrate language, economy, social organization, political organization, religion, and other institutions and values into a total culture. Central to the ongoing viability of an aboriginal culture is a land base and self-government. Asch argues further, that the right to preserve and develop such autonomous systems in Canada is perceived by aboriginal groups to derive, in part, from the utter failure of programs designed to establish viable non-traditional lifeways for the majority of the aboriginal population. More importantly, however, it derives from a view of Canada as a colonial manifestation and from the perception of aboriginal peoples as internally colonized nations like those indigenous populations on other continents, who (Canadian aboriginal peoples believe) have an inherent collective right to assert their self-determination and control over their own cultural destinies. This goal is perceived to be attainable within the context of Confederation; it does not necessitate secession from Canada.

Claims put forward by aboriginal peoples, whether for local, regional, or national autonomy, increasingly have come to represent demands for constitutional recognition and protection of their national group rights. These nationhood claims require constitutional recognition of the aboriginal and treaty rights of aboriginal peoples as well as recognition of their collective, national, and cultural rights. But, as suggested earlier, the Canadian federal government has not, as yet, formally *defined* aboriginal rights even though it has undertaken to negotiate with respect to aboriginal peoples' claims.[9]

Clear manifestations of aboriginal commitment to the goal of self-determination were evident as early as 1976, in the original Dene Nation proposal, and again, in 1979, in the Nunavut proposal (Inuit Tapirisat of Canada). But this aboriginal view was not widely shared by other Canadians, particularly by government representatives. The hiatus between aboriginal and government positions on definitions of aboriginal rights and aboriginal self-determination has presented a formidable obstacle to progress in the three constitutional conferences (1983, 1984, and 1985) which have been convened to date. Equally serious stumbling blocks, however, have been posed by the internal differences between representatives of various governments and of different aboriginal groups. Where there is general agreement among aboriginal representatives is in their commitment to the position that aboriginal peoples have an inherent right to self-government and that this right should be constitutionally acknowledged and guaranteed (*Globe and Mail*, 4 April 1985). The latest federal proposal put forward by Prime Minister Mulroney at the conference in March of 1985, was for a constitutional amendment to entrench the *principle* of a right to aboriginal self-government, subject to further aboriginal–government negotiations and agreements. But, like earlier attempts by former prime minister Trudeau, no agreement was reached, and the conference ended in failure. The fourth, and final, conference is to take place in 1987.

The Rights of the Franco-Québécois

For the Franco-Québécois, the constitutional accord of 5 November 1981 to which Quebec was the single dissenter, has been interpreted as an act of outright denial of their charter group status as an equal founding people/nation with the English within Canada. Following the constitutional conference, then premier René Lévesque put forward a resolution to the National Assembly of Quebec outlining several conditions for accepting patriation of the Constitution. First and foremost, he insisted upon recognition of the fundamental equality of the French and English as the two founding peoples of Canada. In the same declaration, he demanded recognition of Quebec as a society, within the Canadian federation, distinct by its language, culture, and institutions and possessing all the attributes of a distinct *national community* (*Globe and Mail*, 25 November 1981).

A vital part of former premier Lévesque's position has been that Quebec, as a founding nation, has the right to veto the constitutional accord; denial of this right is a denial of the special status of the Franco-Québécois, which, in turn, represents a violation of the original terms of the BNA Act.

Section 33: Override Clause

In the final stages of the constitutional debate, the federal government granted a dramatic concession to the provinces by agreeing to the insertion of an override clause (S.33) in the 1982 Charter. This clause allows provinces to pass legislation that overrides the Charter in the areas of legal rights, equality rights, and fundamental freedoms. The overriding legislation must be renewed every five years.

The controversial override clause sparked heated public response, because it gives provincial governments the power to overrule unilaterally the fundamental freedoms, legal rights, and equality rights of Canadians within their jurisdictions. And there is no appeal from an act of a provincial legislature or the federal Parliament under an unlimited override (*Globe and Mail*, 12 December 1981).

Prospects for a National Transformation to a Multicultural Canada

In light of the foregoing discussion, the question is: What are the priorities built into the CRF which will shape Canadian public policy and practice regarding the collective rights of different ethnic collectivities?

First and foremost, on the basis of our assessment of the provisions of the CRF, it seems clear that unless future amendments are made, there will be no positive guarantees for collective ethnic rights, except in the case of securing the linguistic, religious, and (broader) cultural rights of the English and French charter groups. Further, it appears likely that the kind of protections afforded *individual* members of ethnic minorities will continue to be largely of a negative nature, i.e., anti-discrimination legislation as well as the guarantees of non-interference by the state provided by the fundamental freedoms. The only basis for *positive* measures for the protection of minority rights outlined in the 1982 Charter is the provision allowing affirmative action measures, contained in S.15(2).

In light of the premises and *requirements* of an egalitarian ideal of multiculturalism, the provisions of the CRF are weak, indeed. Our charter's most serious *omission* lies in its lack of specified protections for the collective rights of *all* Canadian ethnic communities. Overall, it perpetuates the established ethnic hierarchy—the *vertical* mosaic of ethnic group inequality—by limiting protections for ethnic minorities to the area of individual rights, while clearly spelling out protections for the collective (linguistic, religious, and educational) rights of Canada's entrenched ethnic majorities, the English/Protestant and French/Catholic "charter groups" or founding peoples.

In closing, then, we must conclude that insofar as the CRF under the *Constitution Act*, 1982 fails to *equally* recognize and protect the collective rights of *all* Canadian ethnocultural collectivities, the prospects for a national transformation based on the multicultural ideal remain no more than illusory.

Notes

1. The social scientific concept of "rights" employed in this paper refers to just or justifiable claims for specified kinds of treatment made by or on behalf of individuals or social collectivities against other individuals, groups, or the state. This concept should not be confused with the concept of legal rights, i.e., rights recognized as such in law.
2. For a further discussion of the collective claims and issues raised in connection with the constitutional debate, see E. Kallen (1982: chap. 9).
3. The fact that the cultural rights of *minorities*, rather than the cultural rights of members of *all* ethnocultural collectivities are singled out in this covenant reflects the global reality of dominant status, i.e., that the cultural rights of dominant ethnic groups tend to be entrenched in all human societies at the state level.
4. The July, 1981, decision by the United Nations Human Rights Commission, in support of Canadian Indian women's rights (in the Sandra Lovelace case) invoked Article 27 in a collective, cultural sense and thus lent strong support to the interpretation favouring *collective* minority rights.
5. The one exception is the *Universal Declaration of Human Rights* which sets out the fundamental rights and freedoms for humankind.
6. For a cogent elaboration of the legal and quasi-legal underpinnings of aboriginal rights, see P. A. Cumming and N. H. Mickenberg (1972).
7. The *Treaty rights* of Treaty Indians derive from the provisions set forth in the treaties negotiated between representatives of various Indian peoples and the British Crown. In many cases, Indians argue today, treaty negotiations were not

carried out in good faith, and/or these provisions have not been carried out. Much of the continuing wrangling between Treaty Indians and the federal government stems from conflicting interpretations of the process of treaty negotiation and the terms of the treaties themselves.

8. For an elaboration of this position, see E. Kallen (1982: chap. 8).

9. At the time of writing, negotiations are well advanced in the Northwest Territories and Ottawa is committed to self-government there within two years. However, the boundary between Nunavut (Eastern Arctic/Inuit) and Denedeh (Western Arctic/Dene/Métis coalition) has not been finalized, as yet, and aboriginal groups remain seriously divided on this issue (*Globe and Mail*, 5 April 1985). Moreover, the exact nature of "self-government" in the Northwest Territories remains a contentious issue: Will political authority be "delegated" or "legislative"?

Finding and Defining Discrimination[†]

JOHN HAGAN

This is an account of an attempt to find "discrimination." In one sense, the effort is unsuccessful. It was found that "discrimination" is a concept with multiple meanings, each of them vague and lacking in empirical criteria that allow a clear boundary to be drawn around the referent. The research experiences generating this conclusion are described. New strategies of conceptualization are then suggested for use in future research.

The Search

On January 1, 1973, the Alberta Criminal Justice Project received a generously funded mandate to discover when, where, and how Indian and Métis persons in the Province of Alberta (Canada) were experiencing "discrimination" at the hands of the provincial judicial system. Few doubted the occurrence of "discrimination." There were charges that the province imprisoned its citizens at a rate higher than any other jurisdiction in the Western World, and it was known that native persons were incarcerated far beyond their representation in the general population (Matthews 1972). Yet, interviews with native leaders, court personnel, and concerned citizens failed to identify consensually the location and content of the "discriminatory" practices. Instead, the conclusion that emerged was diffuse: Discrimination was perceived to occur, by one group or another, at nearly every stage of the judicial process.

The scope of the allegations, then, matched the generosity of the financial mandate. As Director of the Project, it became the author's responsibility to develop a research design equal to the task. The

†"Finding Discrimination: A Question of Meaning," *Ethnicity* 4 (1977): 167–76. This is a revised version of the original article.

resulting design first involved a comprehensive reanalysis of data abstracted from 20 American studies of race and sentencing. Second, three new samples were drawn: i) 1018 persons charged and handled by the prosecutor's office in the City of Edmonton; ii) 776 questionnaires based on pre-sentence reports completed by probation officers in all offices of the Province; and iii) 1000 offenders sentenced and admitted to the five largest prisons in the Province. Analyses of the data are presented elsewhere (Hagan 1974a,b,c, 1975a,b, 1976). It will be argued here, however, that the findings of the research further confuse, rather than resolve, the issue of what discrimination is. This argument is built around four common denotations of the term.[1] It is suggested that each of these denotations of discrimination is encumbered by problems of *inclusion* and *exclusion* of events. The resultant difficulties form a basis for the suggestion of new orientations to the issue at hand.

Discrimination as Differential Treatment

The crudest denotation of discrimination is found in lay practice rather than in formal definition. It consists of equating discrimination with differences in the treatment of one group by another. This denotation postulates the world as a projection of the experimentalist's laboratory, with all variables other than the apparent group-related stimulus and its hypothesized treatment response assumed equal. The problem with this denotation is, of course, that "other things" seldom are equal. Fortunately, most sociological definitions, though not all research applications, acknowledge this problem. Thus, sociological definitions of discrimination generally include a provision holding institutionalized standards theoretically constant. Probably the most frequently cited of these definitions is provided by Robin Williams: "Discrimination may be said to exist to the degree that individuals of a given group who are otherwise formally qualified are not treated in conformity with these nominally universal institutionalized codes" (Williams 1947: 39).

The adequacy of this type of definition is limited by several methodological and theoretical problems. The source of these problems is the residual character of the definition. The definition equates discrimination, once the impact of institutionalized standards is removed, with residual group-connected differences in treatment. However, problems of inference result from identifying discrimination with the differences in outcome remaining when institutionalized standards are controlled. These difficulties involve knowing when all relevant factors have been considered and being certain as *to what* the residual differences can be attributed. In short, the problems are those of insuring the consideration of all known contaminating variables and identifying the origin(s) of remaining differences in outcome. Methodologically, this situation is aggravated by the use of tabular analytic techniques. An example, abstracted from the literature on race and sentencing, will illustrate some of the problems involved.

In studies of criminal sentencing, it is common to find four intercorrelated independent variables associated with final disposition. These variables are race, number of charges, prior convictions, and gravity of offense. It has been the custom in the sentencing literature to examine the effects of these variables with the use of tabular techniques. However, because tabular analysis requires a prohibitively large sample to consider the *simultaneous* effects of four independent variables, the pattern has been to drop at least one of these variables from consideration.[2] Given our disciplinary interests, it would be the rare social scientist who would eliminate the racial variable from his analysis; thus, one of the legal variables is customarily the first to go. Since the legal variable dropped from the analysis is intercorrelated with the remaining independent variables and, thus, likely to be responsible for some part of the latter variables' effect on final disposition, the causal meaning of any one of the residual relationships is subject to doubt. In particular, it is not possible to make any causal inferences regarding the residual relationship between race and sentence without engaging in a suspect assumption about the association between race and the missing legal variable.

Methodologically, the efficiency of a structural equation model improves this situation. With a reasonably large sample, it becomes possible to consider a large number of independent variables simultaneously. However, the residual character of our definition remains problematic. As long as our definition is operationalized in residual terms, the source(s) of the relationships observed remains unknown. An example of the uncertainties involved in this situation is available in the Alberta prison data described earlier.

Analysis of the 1000 cases resulting in incarceration revealed that Indian and Métis alcohol offenders, less frequently than whites, receive referrals to open institutions with special programs for alcoholics. Although this differential treatment qualifies as discrimination under Williams' residual definition, we are left uninformed of the recipient's role in the selection of treatment. The notion of discrimination implies the existence of a "perpetrator" and a "victim." It follows that differential treatments "freely chosen" by the "recipients" are not clear cases of discrimination. Determining the freedom with which choices are made is, of course, a problematic task. Nonetheless, there were indications in the course of the research that Indian and Métis offenders defined and rejected the open institutions as providing less desirable locations and atmospheres for "doing time" than the local jails of the province. While this finding may suggest policy changes (i.e., decentralization and the reorientation of programs), it also vitiates the basis for calling the differential treatment discriminatory.

We have indicated, thus far, that equating discrimination with residual differences in treatment may result in an unintended inclusion of events within the boundaries of the concept. There may also be problems of exclusion. Considering again the Alberta prison data, it was found that Indian and Métis offenders, more frequently than whites, were incarcerated in default of fine payments. Further analysis revealed, however, that these differences did *not* result from disparities in fines assigned to offenders of varying background. That is, when the number of charges, prior record, and gravity of offense were held constant in a regression analysis, the amount of fine imposed was found unrelated to racial background. In this instance, then, *equal treatment was associated with differential outcomes*. The differences in outcome were apparently linked to the offender's ability or willingness to pay fines, rather than to the unequal application of institutional standards. Assuming that willingness and ability to pay fines could be empirically distinguished and that differences in outcome could be attributed reliably to the latter, then, it could be argued that the *absence* of residual differences in treatment indicates discrimination. In short, there are instances where *equality* of treatment might be called discriminatory. One way out of this situation, of course, is to redefine "equal treatment" in terms of a sliding scale of assets and abilities. Arguments against this revisionist approach deserve consideration.

First, if notions of mitigating conditions requiring differential treatment are included in our calculations, it is difficult to conceive how the boundaries on such conditions could be defined. For example, in the case of fines, we would have to consider not only income, but also source and stability of income (i.e., welfare and seasonal work), dependents, personal property, medical expenses, outstanding debts, fluidity of assets, budgeting skills, and a variety of other extenuating circumstances. Second, it is not clear that all such mitigating conditions (e.g., budgeting skills) can be reliably measured. Third, the weighting to be assigned to each of these factors is not apparent. Without answers to these questions, it is impossible to determine *how much* differential treatment is needed to produce "equality." Conversely, it is therefore also impossible to determine *when* such differential treatment becomes discriminatory. All of this does not deny the importance of these considerations, but rather indicates the problems of clarity they pose for a definition of discrimination.

Discrimination as Prejudical Treatment

A second denotation of discrimination defines it as the behavioral expression of prejudice. This definition requires, in addition to residual differences in treatment, malice of motive on the part of the perpetrator. Thus, for Allport, discrimination is the expression of prejudgment: "The net effect of prejudice, thus defined, is to place the object of prejudice at some disadvantage not merited by his own misconduct" (Allport 1954: 10). The distinctive feature of this definition is, of course, that it requires an attitude as well as an action. According to this denotation, discrimination begins with a thought and ends with its expression. Wolfgang phrases this type of definition in the following terms: "Discrimination refers to behavior that resides in the mind of the actor which is expressed overtly for observation by others" (Wolfgang 1974: 243).

A difficulty with this approach, however, involves the circular tendency to infer malevolent motivation on the basis of the behavior to be explained. Such inferences seem convincing when used to explain the differential imposition of the death penalty for interracial rape cases in the South. However, the relative frequency of interracial cases is small, and the practice of inferring motives from behaviors becomes more clearly problematic as its use is expanded. For example, one frequently cited study reports that black offenders in a southern state receive *shorter* sentences than do whites for *intra*racial offenses. This finding is then used as evidence of discrimination based on "prejudice" (Bullock 1961).[3] Yet, a similar response to the predominantly intraracial offenses of Indian and Métis offenders in the Northwest Territories of Canada is attributed to *benevolent* motives, including the attempt to adapt Anglo-Canadian law to native culture (Cooney 1974). The question that emerges is whether it is possible to designate the former situation as "discriminatory" and the latter as "nondiscriminatory" when their immediate consequences are identical.

Even more problematic may be the cases of the white offenders in both of the situations described. In each instance, *white* offenders receive longer sentences, suggesting the charge of "reverse discrimination." However, prejudicial motivation is inferred in neither situation.

There are additional problems. For example, many researchers have noted that prejudice can be a consequence, as well as a cause, of discrimination (Merton 1949). Additionally, historical processes can presumably create self-fulfilling prophecies that may eventually conceal the conditions that create them. For example, patterns of differential treatment can create attitudes of resignation and acceptance on the part of recipients that eventually make moot the possibility of their prejudicial origins. A case in point may be the situation described earlier involving the willingness of Indian and Métis persons to forfeit fine payments and spend time in jail. The problem is in knowing at what historical stages such processes can be called discriminatory. This problem is only artificially resolved by the denotation of "discrimination as prejudicial treatment."

Discrimination as Disadvantaging Treatment

A third denotation of discrimination involves disadvantaging treatment. Antonovsky offers a succinct example of this type of definition: "Discrimination may be defined as the effective injurious treatment of persons on grounds rationally irrelevant to the situation" (Antonovsky 1960: 81). The immediate difficulty with this definition involves the designation of a standard of judgment. Social scientists must rely upon empirical indicators in their analysis, not their own sympathies and resentments (Mackie 1985: 232). Simpson and Yinger appropriately note that, "It is apparent from such a definition that a given act can be labelled discriminatory only when particular values or a particular labelling group is specified" (Simpson and Yinger 1972: 27). But as Yinger indicates, "Discrimination is an analytic concept, not a moral term" (Yinger 1968: 449).

It is sometimes suggested that moral entanglements can be avoided by using "fundamental values" as yardsticks against which the consequences of differential treatments are measured. Unfortunately, most institutions that we will want to study offer only vague and contradictory statements of their goals. "Fundamental values" are seldom indicated, and empirical referents of such values are infrequently specified. Beyond this, the standard suggested demands attention to both the short- and long-range consequences of alternative types of treatment. The situation of Indian and Métis alcohol offenders again provides a useful example. It has been suggested that the incarceration of native alcohol offenders for forfeiture of fine payments may be discriminatory. It can be agreed that in the short range, such treatment clearly seems disadvantaging. However, law enforcement personnel argue that, if alcohol offenders were *not* incarcerated at regular short-term intervals, the lives of such offenders would be shortened. It is argued that periods of incarceration offer these offenders their only opportunity to escape the physical decline that attends an uninterrupted alcoholic life-style. It is further suggested that denying law enforcement officers powers of institutionalization places them in the unenviable position of having to return native alcohol offenders to the conditions of their imminent death. In the long range, then, the basis for calling such incarceration discriminatory using the criterion of disadvantage, is unclear.

It also follows that, if the attribution of disadvantage depends upon the time span employed, then treatment initially considered advantageous can become detrimental. For example, in the future, we may find that the lenient treatment accorded native offenders in the Northwest Territories of Canada is damaging to their economic assimilation or to maintenance of their cultural integrity. Thus, differential treatment, initially judged non-discriminatory may later prove the opposite if the criterion used is some measure of disadvantage.

In short, the referent of discrimination as disadvantage changes. It varies with the period of time and set of values used to assess disadvantage. This type of shifting referent does not lend itself to rigorous use.

Discrimination as the Denial of Desire

A fourth denotation of discrimination involves the denial of preference. This variation of the term's meaning takes two forms. In its restrictive form, a United Nations publication argues that "Discrimination comes about only when we deny to individuals or groups of people equality of treatment that they may wish."[4] The essence of this definition is that things unwanted cannot be the subject of discrimination; only things desired can be unjustly denied.

There is also a more permissive form of this type of definition. The groundwork for this more expansive use of the term discrimination is provided by Peterson and Matza. They argue that "A minority that accepts the general norms of society and wants to live by them is fundamentally different from one that is defined precisely by its insistence on different norms" (Peterson and Matza 1963: 157). Simpson and Yinger summarize the implications of this distinction: "... to discriminate against a group because of what it is and wants to be is different from discriminating against a group because of what others believe it to be or because of what it is despite its own plans or desires. The first is cultural or subcultural conflict..., the latter is discrimination...."[5] According to this definition, then, if there are group-connected differences in current circumstances that are contrary to the group's plans or desires, then differential treatment based on these differences is regarded as discriminatory.

Problems in the restrictive version of this type of definition can be considered first. The emphasis in this definition on the expression and denial of desire artificially confines the focus of study. In particular, no attention is given to the influence of historical and structural processes in determining awareness of circumstances and the expression of desires. In short, there are independent historical and structural dimensions of differential treatment that are ignored in this definition.

The more permissive version of this type of definition also has its difficulties. It suggests that, if there are group differences in abilities and behaviors that are in contradiction to the group's plans or desires, then differential treatment on the basis of these abilities and behaviors is discriminatory. Unfortunately, this type of definition opens a door to *ad hoc* justification that is probably impossible to close. It is for this reason that our laws disallow ignorance as a mitigating circumstance and insist on penalties for negligence. It is difficult to imagine living in a society without such provisions, and it is utopian to label the sanctions involved as "discriminatory."

The criteria to be used in resolving the problems of inclusion and exclusion considered under this definition are not apparent. There are no empirical referents available that allow a clear boundary to be drawn around the events regarded as discriminatory using this definition of the term. In review, this was the case with each of the definitions we have discussed. From our analysis of the four common definitions of discrimination, it seems difficult, if not impossible, to determine an empirical content of acts that can be reliably designated as discriminatory.

The Social Construction of Discrimination

Before exploring the final implications of our "findings," it should be noted that there is a simple escape route from the definitional problems we have discussed. This strategy demands only an acknowledgment of these definitional problems by reclassifying the search for discrimination as the study of the antecedents and consequences of "differential or alternative treatment." This strategy would, of course, include attention to variables considered in the various denotations of discrimination, but would avoid the need for the characterizing judgments implied in the term's usage. Such an approach would be particularly useful in examining the long-range consequences of programs (e.g., those involving "affirmative action" policies) designed to redress past discrimination.

It must be acknowledged, however, that most social scientists will probably feel uncomfortable with this strategy. Most of us feel that we know some events as "clear cases of discrimination," and that these events deserve serious study. Our suggestion is that the *manner* in which these events come to be *known* as discriminatory is an appropriate point at which to begin our research. Some examples will help to clarify what is being suggested.

Few disagree with the conclusion that the differential imposition of the death penalty for interracial rape in the South is a clear historical example of discrimination. That black men should be disproportionately electrocuted for raping white women is an affront to our collective sense of social justice. Yet, if the differential were reversed, that is, if white men were disproportionately electrocuted for raping black women, it can be hypothesized that the consensual level of agreement regarding the judgment of discrimination would be reduced, particularly among northerners who feel that black women are unprotected victims of a caste system. In short, then, some part of "finding discrimination" involves the social context in which events occur and are perceived. It can be further hypothesized that the influence of social context will become more prominent as the stimulus situation becomes logically more complex. An example will again be useful in clarifying this point.

A recent study of the police in several large American cities revealed that black juveniles, more frequently than whites, were charged for offenses known to the police (Black and Reiss 1970). Further analysis revealed that the major source of the differential treatment was the tendency of black complainants to demand such action of the police in response to black defendants. Is this discrimination? And, if so, by whom? It can be hypothesized that the attribution of discrimination will vary according to vantage point in and on the situation. Thus, the complainant and suspect will likely view the same situation quite differently, whereas observers will probably also disagree according to the party with whom they identify. The resulting double bind of the policeman is that he will likely be charged with discrimination by one group or another, no matter what decision he typically makes.

Our argument is simply that "finding discrimination" is in part a process of moral judgment socially constructed within a social context and, therefore, suitable for study as such. Our conclusion is that the social attribution of discrimination deserves study. Such research, when combined with analyses of the antecedents and consequences of differential treatment, could ultimately produce a type of information that a social scientific approach to the study of discrimination can very usefully provide.

Finally, an interesting approach to expanding the study of differential treatment beyond what we have described is provided in Driedger and Mezoff's (1981) study of "Ethnic Prejudice and Discrimination in Winnipeg High Schools." This research reveals evidence of discrimination under all four of the definitions we have discussed. That is, evidence was found of behaviors that involved differential treatment, that was prejudicial in origin, contrary to the desires of its targets, and disadvantaging as well. The effect of this study is to make the alternative criteria used in defining discrimination the basis of a typology to be used in researching discrimination. An attractive feature of this research strategy is that it allows important empirical research to continue in the face of definitional uncertainty.

Notes

1. The four definitions discussed were located by consulting ten current and popular text books in the area of racial and cultural minorities. It is possible that additional definitions exist; however, if they do, they are not in common use by practicing sociologists. Our interest is in determining if common usage of the term "discrimination" in social science is underwritten by a valid and reliable set of empirical criteria (see also Westen 1982, Mackie 1985, and Feagin and Eckberg 1985). Finally, it should be noted that we are not concerned here with the definition of "discrimination" used in the sociopsychological study of perception.
2. For documentation of this pattern, see Hagan (1974c), "Extra-legal Attributes and Criminal Sentencing: An Assessment of a Sociological Viewpoint."
3. For an example of how this problem may complicate court testimony, see Wolfgang (1974).
4. Cited in Allport (1954: 51).
5. Simpson and Yinger (1972: 27–8).

Ethnic Stereotypes: A Psychological Analysis[†]

DONALD M. TAYLOR AND
RICHARD N. LALONDE

What is an ethnic stereotype? Do stereotypes play an important role in intergroup relations? Why do members of another ethnic group all look the same? How are stereotypes related to prejudice? Is there any truth to stereotypes? Do only bigots use stereotypes? Do stereotypes threaten unity in multicultural societies?

In this chapter we will explore tentative answers to these questions from a social psychological perspective. Certain strengths and weaknesses of this perspective will become evident as our attention shifts from a solid research base to a more speculative analysis. The strength of the social psychological approach lies in the lengthy tradition of viewing stereotypes as cognitive structures that organize our experience and guide our behaviour in the context of interactions across ethnic group boundaries. Indeed, recent advances in the field of stereotyping have been precisely in the area of gaining insights into how stereotypes operate as a mental process.

Less well developed is an appreciation for the implications of stereotypes for intergroup relations, in short their broader societal implications. There are fundamental reasons for why interest in the social implications have not kept pace with research on the purely psychological component of stereotypes. Theory and research in social psychology generally have been biased toward the individual with less attention

[†]"Stereotypes and Intergroup Relations," in *A Canadian Social Psychology of Ethnic Relations*, edited by Robert G. Gardner and Rudolf Kalin (Toronto: Methuen, 1981). This is an expanded and updated version of the original chapter by D.M. Taylor. The research was sponsored, in part, by grants from the Social Sciences and Humanities Research Council of Canada to Donald Taylor for a sabbatical and to Richard Lalonde for postdoctoral work.

given to the social context. A number of North American (e.g., Sampson 1977, Steiner 1974, Taylor and Moghaddam 1986) and European (e.g., Billig 1976, Tajfel 1972a) writers have criticized social psychology for this bias. The overriding theme is that the prevalent ideology in the United States, the genesis of most social research, is individualistic, and thus the individual takes precedence. As Canadian researchers who have been socialized to believe in the reality of cultural diversity, we hope in this chapter to redress the balance somewhat.

The chapter is divided into two main sections. In the first section the current cognitive approach to the study of stereotypes is examined. Here a definition of an ethnic stereotype is proposed and its function is examined in detail. The second section focuses on the role of stereotyping in a multiethnic society. Specifically, a framework developed by Taylor and Simard (1979) for thinking about stereotypes and intergroup relations will be outlined.

Stereotypes: Definition and Function

Walter Lippman (1922) is credited for applying nomenclature from the printing trade to describe stereotypes as the "picture in the head" we have of others (for major reviews of the stereotype literature see Ashmore and Del Boca 1981, Brigham 1971, Campbell 1967, Cauthen, Robinson and Krauss 1971, Fishman 1956, Gardner 1973, Mackie 1985, Stephan and Rosenfield 1982, Tajfel 1969).

A sampling of the many definitions of stereotypes will illustrate the recurring themes that warrant more detailed comment. Brigham (1971), for example, defines stereotypes as "a generalization made about an ethnic group, concerning a trait attribution, which is considered to be unjustified by an observer." An early definition by Katz and Braly (1935) proposed that a stereotype is a rigid impression, conforming very little to the facts and arises from our defining first and observing second. That stereotypes are an inferior cognitive process is reflected in definitions such as the one proposed by Allport (1954) who described the stereotype as an exaggerated belief about a category, or Middlebrook (1974) who notes that they are often defined as an inaccurate, irrational overgeneralization. Lippman (1922), claimed that the stereotype "precedes the use of reason, is a form of perception, imposes a certain character on the data of our senses before the data reach the intelligence" (p. 98). Finally, in a recently published social psychology text, Myers (1983) defines a stereotype as follows: "A generalization about a group of people that distinguishes those people from others. Stereotypes can be overgeneralized, inaccurate, and resistant to new information" (p. 421).

Before discussing the adequacy of these definitions it may be instructive to describe the basic procedure for measuring stereotypes since the method represents, in concrete form, the operationalization of the stereotype concept. The basic procedure was developed in 1933 by Katz and Braly, and while there have been several innovations (Brigham 1971, Gardner, Wonnacott and Taylor 1968, McCauley and Stitt 1978, Triandis and Vassiliou 1967), the basic underlying rationale remains unchanged. Respondents are presented with the name of a particular ethnic group and are asked to check off which of a large number of traits best describes the group in question, or to indicate to what extent these traits are characteristic of the group. Although the conceptualizations underlying certain measurement techniques appear to be different, Gardner, Lalonde, Nero, and Young (1986) have demonstrated that the content of the stereotypes identified by these methods have considerable overlap. They suggest that inherent in each of the different measures is the idea that the stereotype involves a shared perception about the characteristics of a particular group.

In order to place these definitions and assessment procedures in context, Table 1 presents the attributes most associated with French Canadians and English Canadians, which are two ethnic groups that have received considerable attention by Canadian researchers. The stereotypes of other ethnic groups also have been assessed in the Canadian context and examples are offered in Table 2. The longitudinal perspective provided in Table 1 shows that despite wide differences in the respondents sampled and the particular year the study was conducted, there is a remarkable consistency in the stereotypes about these groups. While Anderson and Frideres (1981) believe that the traditional stereotype of the French Canadian is changing, the present data indicate that this process of change may be relatively slow.

From the various definitions, and the procedures used for assessment, certain common themes emerge. First, stereotypes refer to the personality characteristics of another group, or one's own group (auto-stereotype). Second, a stereotype refers to people's perceptions or beliefs about others rather than factual statements. Third, the focus is on shared beliefs: that is a set of characteristics believed by many members of one group to be true of another. Fourth, stereotypes are described as poor judgments of others since in applying characteristics to an entire group they involve overcategorization and overgeneralization.

In this chapter a stereotype will be defined as: *consensus among members of one group regarding the attributes of another.* The key elements of this definition are now examined in order to specify precisely how it relates to the four themes common to most definitions.

Table 1
Examples of Research Assessing Stereotypes of French and English Canadians

Investigators	Respondents	Target Group	Stereotype Attributes
Aboud, F.E. 1973	English Canadians (Quebec)	French-Canadian male sociology students	Sensitive, separatist, socialistic, talkative
	English Canadians (Quebec)	French-Canadian male	Excitable, colourful, emotional, artistic
		English-Canadian male	Materialistic, competitive, conservative, reserved
Aboud, F.E., and Taylor, D.M. 1971	English Canadians (Ontario)	English Canadians	Likable, competent, proud, ambitious
		French Canadians	Proud, emotional, dissenting, demanding
	French Canadians (Quebec)	English Canadians	Educated, dominant, ambitious, authoritarian
		French Canadians	Proud, humane, materialistic, studious
Gardner, R.C., Taylor, D.M., and Feenstra, H.J. 1970	English Canadians (Ontario)	French-speaking people	Artistic, religious, proud, colourful
		English-speaking people	Proud, pleasant, loyal, intelligent
Gardner, R.C., Wonnacott, E.J., and Taylor, D.M. 1968	English Canadians (Ontario)	French Canadians	Talkative, excitable, proud, religious
Kirby, D.M., and Gardner, R.C. 1973	English-Canadian adults (Ontario)	French Canadians	Religious, emotional, talkative, sensitive
		English Canadians	Clean, intelligent, modern, good
Lay, C.H., and Jackson, D.M. 1972	English Canadians (Manitoba)	French Canadians	Excitable, emotional, impulsive, tenacious
Lalonde, R.N. 1985	English Canadians (Ontario)	English Canadians	Educated, materialistic, loyal, proud
		French Canadians	Proud, artistic, talkative, romantic

Table 2

Examples of Stereotypes of Canadian Groups Other than French and English Canadians

Investigators	Respondents	Target Group	Stereotype Attributes
Grant, P.R., and Holmes, J.G. 1981	University students (Ontario)	Chinese	Scientific, ambitious, industrious, courteous, neat, reserved
		Irish	Happy-go-lucky, talkative, religious, pleasure-loving, stubborn, quick-tempered, argumentative
Kirby, D.M., and Gardner, R.C. 1973	Adults (Ontario)	Canadian Indians	Poor, quiet, followers, sensitive, primitive
Lalonde, R.N. 1985	University students (Ontario)	Chinese	Responsible, loyal, short, dependable, scientific, ambitious, honest
Mackie, M. 1974	Adults (Alberta)	North American Indians	Not materialistic, poor, large families, lazy, uneducated
		Hutterites	Religious, self-sufficient, old-fashioned, cliquish, hard-working
		Ukrainians	Religious, not neglectful of child, hard-working, retention of culture

First we note that most definitions, or more accurately the methods derived from them, focus on personality characteristics. However, there is no need to restrict stereotypes to personality characteristics; surely any set of shared beliefs can be important. If English Canadians believe French Canadians to be separatists, and in return English Canadians are stereotyped as politically conservative, such stereotypes can affect relations between the groups as much as stereotypes about personality characteristics. Social class also can be an important element in an ethnic stereotype. For example, La Gaipa (1971) found that his American respondents associated Negro with unskilled worker, while proprietor and clothing merchants were related to Jewish people. Included in the stereotype, then, should be any set of shared beliefs about a group. Some Canadian researchers such as Aboud (1973, 1975, 1977), Gardner and Taylor (1969), Mackie (1974), and Mann (1976) have already studied attributes other than the usual personality characteristics.

Stereotypes clearly refer to peoples' perceptions and beliefs, but do these stereotypes have any basis in reality? Many argue that they do not. This position is of course consistent with the prevalent view of stereotypes; they are manufactured judgments that rationalize prejudice. And there is some indication that stereotypes may have little basis in reality. Often, for example, conflicting traits are contained in the same stereotype. How can Jewish people be both clannish and trying to intrude into Gentile society at the same time (Adorno, Frenkel-Brunswik, Levinson and Sanford 1950)?

These possibilities notwithstanding, the view adopted here is that many stereotypes do contain a "kernel of truth"—a position that is consistent with that of Mackie (1973) whose excellent review addresses this issue in detail. This is not to suggest that stereotypes are accurate and sophisticated cognitive descriptions of a group of individuals. Far from it, but they are often useful characterizations of a group's attributes.

The definition adopted here emphasizes that stereotypes are shared beliefs. This is a central feature of stereotypes but one that is not often acknowledged by researchers in the field. One person's beliefs about a group does not constitute a stereotype. The procedures used for measuring stereotypes make this clear. Only if a number of respondents check the same trait is it included in the stereotype.

This aspect of stereotyping is crucial since it emphasizes the *social* importance of the process. Taking into account the social or shared feature of stereotypes has important implications. A number of group processes must be involved if members of one group attribute precisely the same characteristics to another group. There are likely social pressures to conform, and a shared meaning to permit communication within the group, which in turn will enhance ingroup solidarity and create more clearly defined ingroup and outgroup boundaries.

Although this shared feature of stereotypes has been a neglected area of research, the clear exception to this tradition is the work by Gardner and his associates (Gardner 1973). Gardner, Kirby, and Finley (1973), for example, have demonstrated empirically that the shared feature of stereotypes facilitates communication among ingroup members about an outgroup. Only if there is consensus that members of group X are backward do statements such as "Isn't that just like an X?" or "Well, he is an X after all" have any meaning. Indeed, it is precisely such stereotypes that make it possible for members of a group to share ethnic jokes at the expense of an outgroup.

Finally, the present definition contains no evaluative pronouncements about the process of stereotyping. This represents somewhat of a departure from traditional conceptualizations of social scientists who openly condemned the process. Past definitions alluded to undesirable features in ethnic stereotypes. They were referred to as morally wrong, inaccurate, unjustified, overgeneralizations, overcategorizations, erroneous causal attributions, or arrived at through some inferior cognitive process. In short, stereotypes were viewed as undesirable because they relied on faulty judgmental processes, and because they were the outgrowth of prejudicial motivations. There have always been researchers, however, who did not espouse the traditional interpretations of stereotyping (e.g., Berry 1970a, Gardner 1973, Mackie 1973, Tajfel 1969, Triandis 1971, Vinacke 1957) and the past decade has been characterized by research that treats stereotyping as a normal and inevitable cognitive process (Hamilton 1979, 1981, Tajfel 1981).

Why were stereotypes viewed so negatively in the traditional approach? One answer perhaps is that researchers react in human ways to psychological processes they view as destructive. Many people no doubt believe that characterizing an ethnic group in the form of a stereotype is socially destructive, prejudicial, and detrimental to good relations between groups.

But this is only true if one adopts the ideology that ethnic differences lead to intergroup conflict. Such a rationale would be based on the assumption that similarity relates strongly to attraction, a view that has received considerable empirical support (Byrne 1969). Cultural differences, especially those that become reified in the form of a stereotype, are not conducive to mutual attraction among members of different ethnic groups. Such a view of course is consistent with the often referred to "melting pot" philosophy of cultural integration associated with the United States. According to this philosophy, producing homogeneity by eradicating cultural differences enhances the potential for peaceful intergroup relations. Clearly then, in terms of the ideology of cultural homogeneity, which has until recently been characteristic of the United States (Glazer and Moynihan 1970), ethnic stereotypes would be viewed as undesirable.

The Canadian experience, however, is somewhat different from that of its neighbour to the south. Throughout our history, French Canadians have maintained their language and culture while participating in Confederation. Furthermore, multiculturalism was adopted as an official policy by the Government of Canada in 1971. This policy advocates that every ethnic group should be encouraged to retain its cultural distinctiveness. The multicultural ideology implies that the ethnic stereotypes that reflect a group's cultural distinctiveness may be desirable and even perhaps necessary for effective relations between groups. As Kalin and Gardner (1981) point out, culture influences science, and the position that has been adopted by Canadian researchers of ethnic stereotypes may reflect their cultural and political tradition.

This is not to imply that all forms of stereotyping are desirable but only to suggest that the value judgments that become expressed in the very definitions of stereotypes may be linked to a prevalent ideology. Stereotyping is a cognitive process that operates in us all because of the functions it serves and hence the basic definition of stereotypes should not, we believe, contain evaluative judgments.

Having discussed at some length a definition of the ethnic stereotype, there are four fundamental issues about the operation of stereotypes to be addressed in detail. First, do stereotypes play an important role in intergroup relations? Second, does ingroup stereotyping differ from outgroup stereotyping? Third, how are stereotypes related to prejudice? And finally, what functions do stereotypes serve?

Stereotypes and Intergroup Relations

In raising the issue that stereotypes play an important role in intergroup relations we must confront directly the possibility that stereotypes only exist in the minds and theories of social scientists, and in fact have no role to play for normal people in the course of everyday encounters. Volunteer participants in a study will, if asked by an experimenter, check off personality traits judged to be characteristic of a particular group. But does this mean that people actually use stereotypes when they interact with members of another ethnic group? The point is that in traditional studies of stereotypes the respondent is given no information whatsoever except for the name of an ethnic group. In such circumstances the respondent is forced to rely upon the information contained within the social category associated with the group in question. Are we to believe that the same respondent would apply these stereotypes in situations where there is an abundance of detailed information about the other person?

The results of a series of experiments (Aboud and Taylor 1971, Gardner and Taylor 1968, Mann 1976, Taylor and Gardner 1969) on perceptions of ethnic group members suggest that stereotyping is not an artifactual phenomenon but is rather fundamental to the process of intergroup relations. In these experiments individual members of an ethnic group (French Canadian) were presented to Anglophones by means of tape or videotape recordings, and it was the observer's task to form an impression of the specific individual group member. In different conditions in the experiments the stimulus person, whose ethnicity was clear from his accented English, described himself in a way that either a) was consistent with the stereotype of French Canadians, b) was totally inconsistent with the stereotype, or c) revealed little or no information about himself.

From the results it was evident that while anglophone respondents did take into account what the speaker said about himself, their judgments were always modified by the group stereotype. Thus even when the French-Canadian speaker negated the stereotype by indicating that he was neither religious, sensitive, proud or emotional, the anglophone respondents' stereotype seemed to prevent them from taking this information at face value. In short, the stereotype operated as a cognitive filter, systematically modifying information about an individual from another ethnic group.

The application of stereotypes to *individual* group members was also found by Grant and Holmes (1981) who explored anglophone stereotypes of the Irish, among others. They found that the Irish are stereotyped as happy-go-lucky, talkative, and pleasure-loving. In an interesting design, Grant and Holmes (1981) presented respondents with an Irishman who was described as scientific and ambitious, two traits that are not normally associated with the Irish stereotype. The participants were willing to believe that this particular Irishman was scientific and ambitious, but they were also insistent that he was happy-go-lucky, talkative, and pleasure-loving. It would seem that people not only stereotype entire ethnic groups, but also apply their stereotypes to individual members of ethnic groups even in the face of contradictory evidence.

There is another feature of stereotyping that points to its potential importance for intergroup relations. The original Katz and Braly study of stereotyping described earlier was conducted in 1933 at Princeton University. Some eighteen years later the study was repeated by Gilbert (1951) again at Princeton. The results showed that the stereotypes of the ten ethnic groups were remarkably unchanged, although the stereotypes appeared slightly less crystallized than they did in 1933. The study was again repeated at Princeton in 1969 (Karlins, Coffman and Walters

1969) and despite some replacement in stereotype traits for certain groups, similar stereotypes emerged. It would seem that once a stereotype is formulated it is extremely resistant to change. This observation is supported further by the stereotypes presented in Table 1 as well as a study conducted by Gardner, Wonnacott, and Taylor (1968). Stereotypes, then, are shared cognitions that are stable over time and, as we have seen, across situations. This feature along with the fact that people apparently apply their stereotypes to individual group members, even in the face of contradictory evidence, suggests that stereotyping is an important phenomenon with profound implications for intergroup relations.

Ingroup-Outgroup Differences in Stereotyping

Everyone has heard, and maybe even used, such popular expressions as "They all look the same to me" or "Those Xs, they're all alike." Such expressions are always in reference to "them" and never to "us," suggesting that our perception of others (outgroups) is different from the perceptions we have of our own group (ingroup). This observation raises some fundamental questions with respect to stereotypes. Is ingroup stereotyping different from outgroup stereotyping? Why should stereotyping change with the group membership of the perceiver? What conditions affect the way groups are stereotyped?

All of the preceding questions have been addressed from a cognitive perspective. When one person encounters another, some form of group membership of the other may become salient and a social category associated with that membership will be activated. This category may be more or less complex in its representation, and the more ingroup members have shared representations concerning a group, the more stereotyping is occurring. It has been suggested that the representation of an ingroup is more complex than that of an outgroup (Linville 1982, Linville and Jones 1980). More specifically, Quattrone and Jones (1980) have proposed that we perceive more variability in the characteristics of members of our ingroup than in the characteristics of outgroup members, hence the expression "they're all alike." This phenomenon, known as the *outgroup homogeneity hypothesis*, has recently been discussed in detail in an excellent review by Quattrone (1986). Considerable support for the hypothesis has been obtained using a variety of strategies for measuring perceived variability and using groupings based on race (Linville and Jones 1980), sex (Park and Rothbart 1982), age (Brewer and Lui 1984, Linville 1982), student or club affiliations (Jones, Wood and Quattrone 1981, Park and Rothbart 1982, Quattrone and Jones 1980), and ethnicity (Lalonde 1985).

Given that we perceive little variability in the characteristics of outgroup members, there should be considerable agreement among ingroup members concerning these characteristics. The implication is that there will be more stereotyping of outgroups than of an ingroup. This was found to be the case for two studies of ethnic stereotyping in a Canadian context conducted by Lalonde (1985). In a first study, with English Canadian participants, stereotyping on a given set of attributes was found to be more pronounced for French Canadians and Americans (outgroups) than for English Canadians (ingroup). This finding was replicated in a second study that focused on Canadians and Chinese as ingroups and Americans as a salient outgroup. There were two conditions to be met for this effect to occur. First, stereotyping of outgroups will be more polarized than that of ingroups only for attributes that are largely descriptive (e.g., athletic, educated, artistic). When attributes are highly evaluative (e.g., courteous, just, responsible) an ingroup favouritism bias is evoked and ingroup members show stronger polarized agreement in ratings of their own group than in those of outgroups.

The second condition for differential stereotyping pertains to outgroup salience. In the multicultural setting of Canada a variety of ethnic groups are present, but not all of these groups will be of relevance to a particular ingroup. Lalonde found no evidence of stereotyping of an unknown group (Pireneans) and very little stereotyping of groups that were not salient in the research setting (Mexicans and Filipinos). To summarize, stereotyping will be more pronounced than ingroup stereotyping when the outgroup is a meaningful comparison group in the intergroup context, and when the characteristics on which stereotyping is compared are not highly evaluative in nature.

Why is it that the process of stereotyping changes as a function of group membership? The most common explanation revolves around *differential contact*. Given that frequency of contact is greater with ingroup members than with outgroup members, a more complex social representation of the ingroup is likely to result. Even in the strong bicultural milieu of Montreal, Taylor and Simard (1975) found that the actual amount of daily interactions occurring between English and French Canadians was extremely limited when compared to the frequency of interactions taking place within groups. However, although differential contact is an appealing explanation of differential stereotyping it cannot explain the effect of outgroup homogeneity obtained for groupings based on sex (Park and Rothbart 1982) when the frequency and intimacy of interactions between females and males are considered.

A number of other reasons have been offered by Quattrone (1986) to explain differential perceptions as a function of group membership. For one, intergroup interactions are often restricted to a number of set situations and the interpretation of behaviours exhibited by group members may be attributed to invariance in their characteristics when in fact the observed behaviours may be dictated by situational constraints. For example, Ted's stereotype of Japanese women is that they are clean, polite, submissive and traditional. However, the extent of his interactions with Japanese women has been confined to waitresses in Japanese restaurants. In these instances, the Japanese women are behaving within role constraints determined by the situation. If Ted were to observe these women in informal settings such as their home, the observed behaviours may run counter to their traditional stereotype.

Another factor that influences the maintenance of outgroup stereotypes is *selective attention*. Laboratory studies (Hamilton 1979) have indicated that people tend to overestimate the frequency of confirming evidence of stereotypes while underestimating the frequency of disconfirming evidence. Furthermore, Quattrone (1986) suggests that when we are infrequently exposed to a group, we tend to focus on the similarities in behaviour that are exhibited in order to maximize our impression of the group. The perfect example could be provided by any friend who has recently had the experience of being a tourist in an unfamiliar country. Just ask him or her what he or she thought of the natives. The answer is sure to be a simple caricature, based on the few characteristics shared by most members of that society.

One would expect that certain counter-stereotypic behaviours are noticed at times, thus providing evidence of variability in the characteristics of outgroups. However, since all individuals are members of a number of ingroups, it is possible to shift the categorization of social information from one group to another. Certain stereotypes become salient in the presence of a confirming behaviour and eliminate the possibility of that behaviour being encoded as disconfirming evidence of another stereotype. Furthermore, when disconfirming evidence cannot be overlooked a perceiver can always interpret the instance as being the "exception to the rule."

We have seen that ingroup members tend to perceive outgroups in a relatively homogeneous fashion while perceiving a good deal of variability in the characteristics of their own group. As a result, salient outgroups will be more stereotypically represented than the ingroup. The reasons offered for this perceptual bias of outgroup homogeneity included differential contact, constrained interaction episodes, selective attention and selective encoding.

One additional point remains to be made with respect to group differences in stereotyping. Although people perceive more variability in the characteristics of their ingroup, thus permitting a greater sense of individuality, there are social forces operating that can push towards ingroup similarity (Brown 1984). According to social identity theory (Tajfel and Turner 1979) individuals strive to maintain a positive social identity through identification with the ingroup. They will attempt, therefore, to enhance the prestige of their group by making it appear to be positively distinct from other groups on certain dimensions. We have reported the results of one study (Lalonde 1985) where ingroup members stereotyped their own group to a greater extent than outgroups on evaluative dimensions. Ingroup favouritism is one mechanism that will push towards ingroup homogeneity. Dion (1973) has also demonstrated that conditions associated with ingroup cohesiveness engender greater differentiation between ingroup and outgroup. We suggest that in conditions of competition and conflict, the need for ingroup cohesiveness and between group distinctiveness will intensify, such that homogeneous perceptions and stereotyping of both the ingroup and outgroup will result.

Stereotyping and Prejudice

Prejudice, as the label implies, involves prejudgment, the forming of an opinion prior to being exposed to all the evidence. In this sense the stereotype can be equated with prejudice since stereotypes refer to beliefs about the attributes of members of a group that become applied before account is taken of the actual attributes of the particular individual. If I stereotype Gianetto as emotional even before I meet him, I am being prejudiced.

In another sense, however, stereotyping and prejudice should not be equated. Prejudice usually implies an emotional, attitudinal, or evaluative attribution, and in the case of ethnic groups the attribution is usually negative. As we have seen, negative evaluative overtones are traditionally associated with the stereotype. But the present view is that stereotypes are not synonymous with attitudes and so in a very fundamental sense stereotypes and prejudice are not the same. That is, a stereotype is not by definition a negative attitude. Stereotypes are shared beliefs, attitudes are evaluative orientations.

For example, a community may have a stereotype of a particular group, but some members of the community may have a positive attitude and others a negative attitude toward the group. Many might agree that the Germans are scientific, but they may disagree in their attitudes towards them. This point is supported by studies where outgroup stereotypes and attitudes were found to be independent of one another in a Canadian context (see Gardner, Wonnacott, and Taylor 1968, Gardner, Taylor, and Feenstra 1970, Kirby and Gardner 1973, Lalonde 1985, Lay and Jackson 1972). For example, Gardner, Wonnacott, and Taylor (1968) asked English-speaking university students in Ontario to rate French Canadians on a number of characteristics, some of which were expected to reflect the stereotype, others to be highly evaluative. In addition respondents' evaluative reactions toward French Canadians were assessed by means of traditional well validated measures of attitude. A factor analysis of the entire battery of scales demonstrated that stereotypes and attitudes are orthogonal. Thus, French Canadians were stereotyped as "religious, sensitive, proud, and emotional," by the majority of anglophone respondents. An examination of the attitude scales indicated that this same stereotype was held equally by respondents with a positive and those with a negative attitude toward French Canadians.

This does not mean that stereotypes and attitudes toward outgroups are totally unrelated, but only that they are not equivalent concepts, so that one term cannot be interchanged with the other.

What is the relationship between these two concepts? The view taken here is that the ethnic stereotype is a perception of the *descriptive* characteristics of an ethnic group, but the nature of the descriptive elements in the stereotype can reveal much about the perceiver's attitude toward the ethnic group in question. Specifically, there are three ways by which a person might reveal his or her attitudes through the stereotype. First, descriptive attributes of the stereotype may be chosen for the express purpose of reflecting attitudes. So, to express a negative attitude, negative attributes such as dirty, stupid, and backward, might be chosen because of their evaluative connotation. But since stereotypes endure over time and across situations, choosing attributes *only* because of their evaluative connotation is unlikely. Choosing attributes on this basis probably only occurs where the intergroup situation has deteriorated to open conflict. The American stereotype of the Japanese before and after Pearl Harbour (Seago 1947), the stereotype of Germans before and during the Second World War (Dudycha 1942) and the stereotype changes that resulted from the Sino-Indian border dispute (Sinha and Upadhyay 1960) are examples of this process. However, in most instances, attitudes are not expressed by only choosing attributes for their evaluative meaning with no consideration for their descriptive component.

A second mechanism for expressing attitudes in the context of the stereotype involves a more subtle selection of descriptive stereotype attributes. The traits which form the basis of most group stereotypes have both descriptive and evaluative components (Kirby and Gardner 1972, Peabody 1967). Hence, it is possible to maintain the descriptive aspect of a stereotype and at the same time express one's attitudes via the choice of specific evaluative labels. A group might be stereotyped as either bold or rash, generous or extravagant, eccentric or neurotic, and so forth, depending upon attitudes toward the group. The earlier example of the stereotype of Scots illustrates the point: those with positive attitudes might stereotype them as "thrifty," whereas they might be "stingy" to those who hold negative attitudes.

The first two mechanisms for expressing attitudes involve selecting the descriptive content of the stereotype to reflect attitudes directly. However, most stereotype labels cannot be easily interchanged in order to reflect individual attitudes. Thus, the third and most important mechanism, involves maintaining the descriptive attribute of the stereotype independent of the attitude being expressed.

How is this possible? There is no reason to believe that attributes have evaluative connotations independent of the social object being judged. Hence the term "religious" when applied to a priest may mean one thing, and when applied to a French Canadian mean something totally different.

People with different attitudes toward French Canadians will then attribute different evaluative connotations to traits such as religious, sensitive, proud and emotional when they are applied to French Canadians. While certain traits are potentially more variable in their meaning than others (see Lamarche 1975), even traits that seem evaluatively straightforward can have different connotations; loyalty to one's own group is a good thing but loyalty among members of another group is negatively valued.

The latter line of reasoning agrees with a model of category-based affect, developed by Fiske and her colleagues, that purports to link affect with cognition (Fiske 1982, Fiske and Pavelchak 1986). The model's premise is that once a social category is cued by the act of categorization, an "affective tag" associated with the category label is immediately evoked. In our illustrative example of the French Canadian, some type of affective reaction would be set off as soon as an individual is classified as being a French Canadian. This affective response would then serve to colour the stereotypic attributes of the category (religious, sensitive, proud, emotional).

Stereotypes, then, are not to be equated with attitudes or prejudice, although attitudes are expressed through the stereotype. Two of the mechanisms for expressing attitudes involve selecting the actual descriptive attributes of the stereotype to reflect attitudes directly; such mechanisms are likely to be applied only where there is open intergroup conflict. A more usual and subtle mechanism for expressing attitudes involves an individual interpretation of the evaluativeness of the specific stereotype attributes.

The Function of Stereotypes

There are two important functions to stereotyping. First, stereotypes serve an organizational function and second they satisfy emotional needs by protecting our self-image.

In his review of the stereotype literature Hamilton (1979) has neatly summarized the cognitive or organizational function of stereotypes.

> Stereotypes, as cognitive schemas, can influence the encoding, interpretation, retention, and retrieval of subsequently obtained information about members of stereotyped groups, as well as the perceiver's causal attributions regarding the target person's behaviour (p. 80).

Our position is that a stereotype involves a shared organizational structure in the sense that the same attributes are applied to all members of a group. Shared categorization can be functional in two complementary ways. In the case where there is little or no information about an ethnic group, stereotypes "fill in," thus providing an organized perception of the group. More often, however, there is far too much information about a group. In this case the person can categorize in order to reduce the extremely complex environment into manageable units. Thus the categorization involved in stereotyping is a useful guide for behaviour both in situations having a lack of information as well as where there is information "overload."

Stereotypes, therefore, guide behaviour both with outgroup members as well as with members of the ingroup. To the extent that an outgroup stereotype has some basis in reality it allows a person to judge how to behave most effectively with members of the outgroup as well as how to interpret the behaviour of the outgroup member. With regard to ingroup members, the shared stereotype facilitates communication and mutual understanding among members of the ingroup regarding all issues to which the outgroup is relevant.

There are certain important implications that can be drawn from the organizational function served by stereotypes. First, to the extent that stereotypes contain a "kernel of truth" they are reasonable guides to behaviour. Second, stereotyping helps in indirect ways in terms of self-definition. By categorizing others, important contrastive social categories are created which, by comparison, serve to help us know who we are and where we fit into the complex social environment. Third, if stereotypes are to be truly functional the form of the categorization should correspond to the context for which it was designed.

A simple stereotype with only a few unqualified attributes would be expected for little known and referred to outgroups. On the other hand, people would be expected to have well-defined stereotypes about groups to which they are frequently exposed. This exposure does not have to be the result of direct contact but may be brought about by the mass media. The complexity and sophistication of information regarding one's own group, however, will not necessarily lead to one well-defined overriding stereotype. Rather, this complexity would be handled by several sub-stereotypes within the ingroup. For example, while English Canadians may see French Canadians as a broad undifferentiated category, French Canadians may organize information about themselves into subordinate differentiated categories (e.g., urban vs. rural French Canadian, or Québécois vs. Acadien).

The second important function served by stereotypes is that of satisfying individual emotional needs, particularly the need people have to view themselves positively. This function is related to other psychological concepts such as ego-protection, self-image and self-esteem. The underlying theme is that perceptions and cognitions of the environment are designed, in part, to reinforce people's own positive view of themselves. For example, most people are inclined to take greater credit for successes than they probably deserve, and are quick to blame anyone but themselves for personal failures.

It is worth noting as well that stereotypes are not the only cognitive structure to serve this emotional function. If a person's attitudes toward his or her own group are extremely favourable and their attitudes toward an outgroup are not so favourable, this ethnocentric pattern of attitudes indirectly reinforces the view that they are a good person. Similarly, in attribution terms, if the person attributes desirable behaviours to their own group as motivated by internal causes (e.g., we are honest) but those of the other group to external causes (e.g., they want to take advantage of us) the person's self-image is enhanced (see Taylor and Jaggi 1974). The expression "one man's terrorist is another man's freedom fighter" captures this process succinctly.

Stereotypes operate in the same way. First, the fact that all ingroup members have the same outgroup stereotype reinforces ingroup members' views that they are correct in their judgments of others. Similarly, if all members share a stereotype of their own group, they can mutually reinforce each other for having these stereotyped attributes which are generally very positive. More subtly, stereotypes provide group members with a sense that they "understand" the social world. That is, stereotypes provide ready-made explanations for the behaviour of other groups. Finally, and most directly, because attitudes can be expressed through the evaluations associated with the attributes in the stereotype, an ethnocentric view of the outgroup can be maintained which enhances the esteem of all ingroup members.

Unfortunately, stereotypes are not so neatly arranged that it is possible to say, "This person is stereotyping for organizational purposes whereas this one is only concerned with enhancing his or her self image." Rather, the two functions operate simultaneously within a single act of stereotyping. The view adopted here is that people have a normal operating balance between the two functions in their use of stereotypes. For most people this probably involves holding stereotypes that maximize the organizational function while still not presenting any threat to the self. So one might, in normal circumstances, stereotype Japanese Canadians as traditional, polite, and politically conservative. This stereotype poses no threat to the self-image or the image of the ingroup, and thus serves as a useful orientation in dealing with members of that group.

This normal balance operates only when the person is in a psychologically healthy and unthreatened frame of mind. When members of a group are threatened, the balance of functions for the stereotype may change—the emotional function becoming more important at the expense of the organizational function. What changes might be expected in a threatening situation? Certainly the stereotype might be reduced to only a few negatively valued attributes, the complexity of the relationship among the attributes to the entire ethnic group would become more rigid and extreme. Under threatening conditions, then, the loss of information arising from the process of categorization in stereotyping would reach a point where the stereotype interferes with effective interaction rather than serving as a useful guide. At this stage certain aspects of our functional analysis of stereotypes are very speculative, and programmatic research will be required for their confirmation or modification.

Stereotyping in a Multiethnic Society

The role that ethnic stereotypes play in a multicultural society will depend upon the ideology associated with ethnicity in that society. In societies where ethnic categorization is viewed as undesirable, where the operating principle is that ethnic differences are the basis of conflict, and where the aim is to produce an ethnically homogeneous society, ethnic stereotypes will be viewed as socially undesirable. However, not all societies value cultural homogeneity. Canada's "multicultural" policy encourages members of different ethnic groups to retain their cultural distinctiveness. Ethnic categories are viewed as desirable, indeed as essential for members of all groups to feel a sense of security within the fabric of Canadian society. Furthermore, preserving ethnic identity not only has political importance, but psychological significance as well. That is, there has been some research to indicate that under certain conditions when group members feel secure about their ethnic identity, they tend to be more open toward other groups (see Berry, Kalin, and Taylor 1977, Lambert, Mermigis, and Taylor 1986).

Stereotypes can be an important mechanism for recognizing and expressing pride in ethnic distinctiveness. Stereotypes refer to a group's major distinctive attributes, and to the extent that they are accurate reflections of the group, and refer to attributes the stereotyped group is proud of, stereotypes can play a constructive role in intergroup relations. So, the claim that stereotypes can have socially desirable consequences refers to situations where the particular intergroup stereotypes satisfy the desires of all groups in a community involved, and where intergroup interaction is not characterized by destructive forms of conflict. More specifically, it refers to situations where intergroup stereotypes reflect mutual attraction, even though the members of each group maintain through stereotypes their own ethnic group distinctiveness.

The pattern of intergroup stereotyping which gives rise to these idealistic, socially desirable consequences, is represented schematically in Figure 1. The column classifications represent the group (I or II) doing the stereotyping while the rows refer to the group being stereotyped. The capital letters in each cell represent specific stereotype attributes, which may include traits, beliefs, values, political ideologies and so forth, and the (+) sign is used to indicate a positive attitude associated with the stereotype attributes.

What is depicted in Figure 1, therefore, is an idealized situation where each group stereotypes the other in a manner that is consistent with each group's stereotype of itself (autostereotype). Further, members of each group have pride in their own attributes, while at the same time respecting the attributes of the other group. Thus we have a socially desirable intergroup situation where each group retains its own cultural distinctiveness but is favourably disposed to the other group.

Figure 1
Schematic Representation of Situation Where Stereotyping May Have
Desirable Consequences

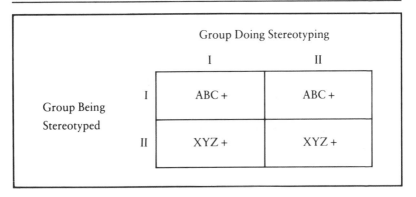

The obvious question at this stage is whether the socially desirable stereotyping depicted here actually operates in society. Examples might not seem easy to find. However, they do exist and, if not ideally, at least at a level where mutual tolerance is characteristic of the intergroup situation. It is less difficult to imagine socially desirable stereotyping in other than interethnic group situations. While the discussion has focused on *ethnic* stereotyping it is clear that stereotyping is a process that is characteristic of social perception in general (see Taylor and Aboud 1973). Doctors stereotype lawyers and vice versa, as do teachers and students, children and parents, students from different universities, and men and women. In these examples of role stereotyping it is relatively easy to imagine the potential for role distinctiveness co-occurring with mutual tolerance and respect.

In the domain of ethnic stereotyping the relations between the French and English Canadians in Quebec may be illustrative. Although there can be no question that tensions do exist, there is evidence to suggest that in certain contexts and among certain sub-groups of English and French Canadians, mutually positive attitudes prevail (see Berry, Kalin, and Taylor 1977). Furthermore, the mutual stereotypes and autostereotypes are well defined. English Canadians stereotype themselves and are stereotyped by French Canadians as conservative, formal and reserved, while French Canadians are stereotyped as sensitive, proud and emotional (Mann 1976). Thus both groups maintain their cultural uniqueness and respect each other in the process.

Studies by Mann (1976) and Aboud (1973) provide some empirical support for the notion that individuals can be attracted to members of an ethnic group who conform to the stereotype of that group. In Mann's (1976) experiment French- and English-Canadian actors were video-taped while playing the role of a lawyer presenting arguments for the defence before a jury in a murder trial. The same arguments were presented in two guises; an "emotional" guise which involved a portrayal of the French Canadian stereotype and a "formal" guise which repre-sented the English Canadian stereotype. The guises were differentiated by means of postures, gestures and voice inflection. English-Canadian respondents did not prefer English- to French-Canadian actors, nor did they favour one guise to the other. Rather, respondents reacted equally favourably to the French-Canadian stereotype and English-Canadian actors in the "formal" guise. Both French- and English-Canadian actors who behaved inconsistently with the stereotype of their respective group were rated less favourably.

Aboud (1973) examined the attraction English Canadians felt for members of familiar and unfamiliar ethnic groups. The groups in order of familiarity were English Canadians, French Canadians from Mon-treal, French Canadians from Northern Quebec, Indians, Eskimos and Hutterites. She found that for unfamiliar ethnic groups, respondents were attracted to individual members who conformed to the stereotypes of that group. However, for familiar ethnic groups, respondents fa-voured individuals who did not conform to the stereotype of that group but were rather similar to themselves. The results were replicated in a second study using Jewish respondents from Montreal. Taken together these studies indicate that, at least for unfamiliar ethnic groups, individ-uals are attracted to members of other ethnic groups who conform to the stereotype. That this is not the case for familiar groups serves as a reminder perhaps of the difficulty involved in achieving an intergroup situation where stereotyping has socially desirable consequences.

These examples emphasize personality traits contained in the stereo-types, although Aboud's (1973) studies did focus on aspects of culture and occupation. If further studies were to be conducted that included other components such as the language differences between the two groups, cultural differences which are reflected in every day life (e.g., cuisine, theatre and music), differences in emphasis in education (e.g., European vs. American), and social philosophy differences (e.g., collec-tivity vs. individualistic), we may well find that there would emerge an admiration for some of the stereotyped attributes of the other group.

Although members of one group may respect certain stereotypic attributes of another group, it will be recalled that stereotypes and prejudice are conceived here as being relatively independent. One group may perceive certain positive and distinctive features in another group, but still want to maintain their distance from that group. Work by Mackie (1974) with adults, and by Driedger and Mezoff (1981) and Driedger and Clifton (1984) with high school students, demonstrates that majority Canadians (i.e., Caucasians of European descent) have a rather well defined hierarchy in the degree of social distance they want to maintain between themselves and others. Recognition of an outgroup's positive characteristics, therefore, may not necessarily engender a general openness towards that group.

Distinctive and Shared Aspects of Culture

One of the difficulties in finding examples of the ideal situation for stereotyping is that rarely are two groups totally distinctive, as is implied in Figure 1. In multiethnic societies the focus is on relations between groups who, despite a tendency to live in separate neighbourhoods, nevertheless share the same geographical space. By sharing the same environment such groups come to share important attributes derived from common political, social, educational and religious institutions. While from the point of view of stereotyping our focus is usually on the distinctive cultural features of each group, the attributes that these groups have in common, because of the mutual influence involved in sharing the environment, are also crucial. Indeed, they may enhance the possibilities for positive attitudes between groups to develop.

Figure 2
Schematic Representation of Socially Desirable Stereotyping Involving Both Shared and Distinct Attributes

		Group Doing Stereotyping	
		I	II
Group Being Stereotyped	I	ABC + xyz +	ABC + xyz +
	II	ABC + pqr +	ABC + pqr +

An analysis of intergroup stereotypes which takes account of shared attributes is described in Figure 2 where the capital letters (ABC) represent common or shared attributes and the lower case letters (xyz, pqr) are used to denote distinctive attributes. The consequences of sharing important attributes and remaining distinct on other ones may be particularly desirable in contexts where both groups are familiar with each other, where there is a high level of contact and where both groups are interdependent with regard to important shared goals. On the one hand, the shared attributes might facilitate two major social needs of members of the community; the emotional satisfaction derived from mutual attraction and the achievement of important goals. On the other hand, the unique attributes would permit the development and maintenance of a distinctive group identity, and allow for some novelty and interest in intergroup interaction.

The idea that different ethnic groups in Canada may share certain basic attributes has been considered by Isajiw (1977). His theoretical position deals with the relationship of technology to ethnicity. His focus is not just on modern industry but rather on an entire set of related values such that the term technological *culture* is adopted. In answer to the question, "Why focus on technological culture?" Isajiw (1977) answers, "Because it is something that, in our society, ethnic groups seem to share more than anything else" (p. 79). We have, then, one example of what might constitute the shared values depicted as ABC in Figure 2.

Evidence for elements of a common culture has been reported by Lalonde (1985) who found that English Canadians stereotyped both themselves and French Canadians as being loyal, proud, sociable and educated while maintaining distinctive attributes in the stereotypes of both groups. The notion of common culture can also surface in a broader context. Given that we share a technological culture (Isajiw 1977) it would be expected that Canadians and Americans would evidence some degree of common culture. In fact, Lalonde (1985) found that Canadians stereotyped both themselves and Americans as materialistic, sociable, athletic, scientific and ambitious, all characteristics that typify modern society.

The idea that two groups may share certain attributes raises an important question—where do the shared attributes or where does this "common culture" (ABC in Figure 2) come from? For example, English and Italian Canadians living in Toronto may share certain fundamental attributes—beliefs in technological culture, in specific forms of democracy, justice and freedom—while at the same time retaining distinctive attributes regarding beliefs about the role of family and interpersonal relationships. But where do the shared beliefs in technological culture, democracy, justice and freedom come from? The likely answer is that the "common culture" comes more from one group than the other. The point is that in most intergroup situations the distribution of power is not equal.

English Canadians are by all accounts the dominant group in Canada. Hence it is this group which over time has defined the "common culture." If the Italian community shares these values it is largely because they have assimilated to them rather than having had an active role in their creation. Generally, then, it is dominant groups whose attributes define the common culture.

It must be stressed that it is not realistic nor even desirable to contemplate a) that a minority group will contribute as much to the common culture as a majority group, or b) that all of a group's values, majority or minority, will be contained in the common culture. Rather, the common culture forms the basis for a shared identity and one that insures participation by all groups in society. Over and above the common culture, group distinctiveness is maintained by attributes a particular group is proud of and hopefully that others respect.

A qualification to be added to Figure 2 then is that the common culture (ABC) must involve an agreed upon set of attributes based on contributions from both groups, not those which by default become the common attributes through the natural outcome of social power.

Unequal power relations between groups poses another difficulty which must be noted before one can talk realistically about achieving socially desirable intergroup stereotyping. Two or more groups may have, through mutual contribution, articulated a "common culture." Beyond this the two groups may agree upon their mutual "auto" and "other" stereotypes, and both groups may value their own attributes as well as those of the other groups; however, for one of the groups the attributes in question may be superficial or trivial. Such a situation might take the form of tokenism where a dominant group values selected trivial attributes of the other group as a means of placating the other group while protecting its own self interests.

An example might be the plight of native peoples of North America. Aspects of Amerindian and Inuit culture and art have undergone re-evaluation such that they now comprise a crystallized stereotype that is positively valued by both white society and native peoples. Although this stereotype provides for a positively valued cultural distinctiveness it may well be that the attributes it consists of are those that white society is willing to entertain, because they are of little importance and in no way threatening in terms of the fundamental rewards society can offer. So

white society respects these aspects of the stereot\
but these attributes may not really permit native p\
more fully in the rewards society can offer.

The appropriate conditions for socially desirable\
typing can now be summarized. First both groups wil\
culture that will become stereotyped as the shared attrib   ⌐ers
of both groups. Beyond this each group will retain and be   ⌐cotyped by
distinctive attributes that are valued by the person's own group and
respected by members of the other group, with the one provision that the
distinctive stereotype attributes do not serve as a barrier to full participation in society.

Ethnic stereotypes can in these specific circumstances be socially
desirable, indeed perhaps necessary for effective intergroup relations.
What must be emphasized is that only when the specific conditions
described in Figures 1 and 2 are present can intergroup stereotyping be
viewed in this light. A change in the attitudes associated with the
stereotype, represented schematically by the replacement of plus with
minus signs in Figures 1 and 2 would produce a less than desirable
pattern of intergroup stereotyping. Similarly, changes in the attributes
themselves, denoted by the letters in any of the four cells in Figure 1
producing a lack of shared perception about stereotyped attributes,
would naturally lead to misunderstandings and misattributions in the
course of relations between members of different ethnic groups.

Conclusion

At the outset of the chapter a series of questions was posed. The present
view of stereotypes implies a set of tentative answers which can be
summarized briefly.

What Is a Stereotype?

A stereotype is a consensus among members of one group regarding the
attributes of another. It is a socially important process because of its
consensual nature; it can refer to any beliefs about a group, not just
personality characteristics, and there is no reason to assume that it is
necessarily an inferior cognitive process.

Do Stereotypes Play an Important Role in Intergroup Relations?

Yes. They are fundamental cognitions which serve organizational and
emotional functions. More directly they influence perceptions and judg-

dividual ethnic group members even in the face of contradic-
ܢ:ormation.

Why Do Members of Another Ethnic Group All Look the Same?

Given the complexity of our social world certain biases have developed that make us focus on the common characteristics of outgroup members, not on their differences. The fact that we perceive outgroups as homogeneous may be a function of the frequency of interactions with outgroups, the set situations in which these interactions occur and the process of selective attention and encoding.

How Are Stereotypes Related to Prejudice?

In one way stereotypes are the same as prejudice in the sense that they both represent prejudgments. In another way they should be equated. Prejudice implies a negative attitude and this is not necessarily the case for stereotypes.

Is There Any Truth in Stereotypes?

While this is a controversial issue the present view is that in many instances there is some truth to stereotypes. The stereotype can be a useful guide to behaviour in intergroup relations, however, in times of conflict where the emotional function of stereotypes becomes predominant, they can seriously detract from intergroup interaction.

Do Only Bigots Use Stereotypes?

It is clear that the present perspective views stereotypes as being used by everyone, and that they are a normal cognitive process for organizing the social environment. The prejudicial person may express negative attitudes about a group through a variety of processes including his or her values, attributions, opinions, intentions and behaviour itself.

Do Stereotypes Threaten Unity in Multicultural Societies?

This is the most difficult question of all. The framework presented in this chapter is based on the premise that a secure ethnic identity is a necessary prerequisite for effective intergroup relations. Preserving ethnic identity and the stereotypes that symbolize this cultural distinctiveness need not be a divisive force. The "common culture" comprised of the fundamental attributes shared by all of society forms the basis for a shared identity. Beyond this, cultural distinctiveness represented cognitively in the form of a stereotype can be maintained. Where a group is proud of this distinctiveness, and is at the same time respectful of the stereotypes of others, it should be possible to attain unity not through diversity but with diversity.

The Banished Japanese Canadians[†]

THOMAS BERGER

During the hearings of the Special Joint Committee on the Constitution, which sat during the winter of 1980–81 to consider amendments to the Charter of Rights, it was generally conceded that the evacuation and internment of the Japanese Canadians during the Second World War represented an evil instance of mass racial hysteria, made worse by the pusillanimity of the federal government. All agreed that it was an event which must never be repeated. It should be remembered, however, that the expulsion of the Japanese Canadians from Canada's west coast in 1942 was not a sudden manifestation of anti-Japanese feeling which occurred as a result of the Japanese attack on Pearl Harbor on December 7, 1941, and was gone as soon as the war with Japan ended. The crisis of 1942 had its origins in racial prejudice against Orientals in British Columbia which began in the nineteenth century, with the founding of British Columbia itself, and persisted into the middle of the twentieth century and reached its shameful climax into the Second World War.

The story of the Japanese Canadians is not simply the story of a painful episode which may now safely be forgotten. As Gordon Kadota, speaking for the National Association of Japanese Canadians, told the Special Joint Committee on November 26, 1980, "Our history in Canada is a legacy of racism made legitimate by our political institutions." Although our institutions and our laws no longer foster racial prejudice, it still exists in Canada, disfiguring the face of society. A knowledge and understanding of the Japanese Canadians' experience may enable us to isolate the virus of racial prejudice—endemic in history—when it threatens to escape again.

---

†*Fragile Freedoms: Human Rights and Dissent in Canada* (Toronto: Clarke, Irwin, 1981).

British Columbia had, before the Second World War, a long history of animosity towards and of discriminatory legislation against Orientals. This anti-Oriental feeling lapped near the homes of Japanese Canadians on the west coast many times before the Japanese assault on Pearl Harbor generated a wave of anti-Japanese hysteria which swept their homes away, destroyed their communities, and dispersed them as a people.

In 1941, there were some 22,000 Japanese Canadians in British Columbia. They had many enemies and, with the outbreak of war with Japan, there were few to defend them. Thousands of Japanese had chosen to become Canadian citizens, and thousands more had been born in the province. But, when they found themselves under attack, vulnerable and helpless, and looked for protection to those who held the highest political offices, they found none. They were removed from the west coast, interned, their property confiscated, and many of them were sent into exile, all because they were of Japanese descent. Nothing in our history demonstrates so well the necessity to constantly be aware of our own attitudes towards racial minorities, and the wisdom of entrenching in the Constitution our belief that racist measures are wrong and of providing legal safeguards that will protect racial minorities against such measures.

The Japanese were preceded in British Columbia by the Chinese. It may be said that anti-Oriental feeling in British Columbia began in 1858, the year the Crown Colony of British Columbia was established. That was the year of the Cariboo gold rush, when prospectors, a few of them Chinese, came from California seeking gold. More Chinese came to the colony in the 1860s and 1870s, but virtually all of them came from China, not as prospectors, but as cheap labour.

No Japanese came to British Columbia before 1877. Japan had kept herself isolated from the rest of the world until 1852, when Admiral Perry of the United States Navy forced his way into Tokyo Bay. In 1867, the Japanese began to look outwards, and undertook a program of rapid industrialization. Population grew and men unable to find employment in the new industrial centres started to go abroad. Thus began the migration of Japanese across the Pacific Ocean to Hawaii, California, and British Columbia.

When the Japanese began to arrive on Canada's west coast in the 1880s, they were hired as cheap labour, as the Chinese had been before them. They found work in railway construction, mining, logging camps and sawmills. Most of the Japanese who came to Canada were young men. They did not intend to stay; they wanted only to make some money, then return to their villages in Japan. But many of them did not return, and by 1900 concentrations of Japanese had emerged in a number of British Columbia communities along the coast, as far north as the Skeena River. The most important of these were "Little Tokyo" in Vancouver, whose residents had a Japanese-language newspaper; and Steveston, a fishing port at the mouth of the Fraser River. By 1901, out of a provincial population of 178,657 there were 4,738 Japanese. The Chinese by this time numbered 14,885. Thus, Orientals constituted ten per cent of the province's population.

These numbers of Orientals caused apprehension, resentment and fear among the White majority of British Columbia. While the railway builders and other industrial magnates insisted upon the advantages of cheap Oriental labour, the White working class feared this influx of workers of a different race and colour who were prepared to accept lower wages than they were. The competition for jobs was felt mainly by the working class, but all classes in British Columbia felt that the burgeoning Oriental population represented a long-term threat to the White character of the province. They regarded the Orientals, few of whom spoke English, as unassimilable. Thus, they endangered the ideal of White homogeneity in British Columbia.

From the late 1870s onwards, there were many attempts to curb Oriental immigration into British Columbia. Under the BNA Act, however, the provinces had no jurisdiction over immigration: only the federal government could stem this flow. In 1880, at British Columbia's insistence, the federal government imposed a head tax of $50 on Chinese immigrants. Not satisfied with this, the British Columbia legislature passed a series of anti-Chinese statutes in the early 1880s, but the federal government disallowed them. John A. Macdonald, the prime minister, favoured the immigration of Chinese to work on the railway he wanted to build to the Pacific. Macdonald did say, however, as he told the House of Commons in 1882, that he had no desire to see the Chinese remain in Canada when the railway was finished. After that, he said, he would "be quite ready to a reasonable extent to prevent a permanent settlement in the country of Mongolian or Chinese emigrants." In the meantime, he had no objection to excluding the Chinese from enjoying elementary rights of citizenship. In 1885, when his government passed the first federal franchise act, it denied Orientals the right to vote. "Person" was defined in the act so that it excluded Chinese and Mongolians.

At the turn of the century the British Columbia legislature attempted to pass what were in effect provincial immigration laws. In 1900 the province tried to impose English-language qualifications as a condition of admittance for persons entering the province. The federal government disallowed the legislation, just as it did when the province passed similar legislation in 1903 and in 1905.

Laurier and the Liberals had succeeded the Conservatives in 1896. Laurier, like Macdonald, would not let the province pass its own immigration laws. Laurier was prepared to acknowledge, however, that once Orientals had become naturalized, they should have the right to vote: in 1898, his government granted to naturalized Orientals the right to vote in federal elections. But though legally they now had the right to vote in federal elections, they couldn't exercise their right because the provincial list of voters was used to prepare the federal list. And in 1895, the British Columbia legislature had passed an amendment to the Provincial Elections Act to deny the vote to Orientals, including those who had become naturalized, and those born in Canada.

In 1900, Tomey Homma, a naturalized Japanese Canadian, applied to enroll his name on the provincial voters' list. When the registrar of voters rejected his application, he asked the Supreme Court of British Columbia to order the registrar to allow him to vote. This court, in a remarkable judgement for the time, upheld Tomey Homma's right to vote. Chief Justice Angus McColl wrote:

> ... the residence within the province of large numbers of persons, [citizens] in name, but doomed to perpetual exclusion from any part in the passage of legislation affecting their property and civil rights would surely not be to the advantage of Canada, and might even become a source of national danger.

The court affirmed the right of the Japanese Canadians and the Chinese Canadians to vote in provincial elections, holding that the legislation in question went beyond the powers of the province. In 1902, the case went to the Privy Council, which continued its virtually unbroken record of denying minority rights in Canada. It reversed the decision of the Supreme Court of British Columbia, holding that the legislation was within provincial powers. The editor of the *Victoria Colonist* rejoiced.

> We are relieved from the possibility of having polling booths swamped by a horde of Orientals who are totally unfitted either by custom or education to exercise the ballot, and whose voting would completely demoralize politics.... They have not the remotest idea of what a democratic and representative government is, and are quite incapable of taking part in it.

The Japanese Canadians could still theoretically claim the right to vote in federal elections. But even that shadowy claim passed away in 1920, when Parliament passed an act providing that persons disenfranchised by any province because of their racial origin would be disqualified for federal elections unless they were war veterans.

But it was not only the right to vote that was denied to Orientals, citizens or not. Though every citizen was eligible for employment in the public service of British Columbia, Canadians of Oriental descent were excluded *de facto*. Professor H. F. Angus, of the University of British Columbia, writing in 1931, said that while such employment would not be illegal, it "would occasion general amazement." They were, in the same way, excluded from municipal employment. Provincial legislation prohibited the employment of Orientals in the construction of public works. If a contractor violated this provision, he was liable to forfeit any money that was due under his contract with the government. It was a condition of sales of Crown timber that Orientals could not be employed. Nor could they enter certain professions. For example, no person who had not been on the voters' list at the age of 21 could be enrolled as an articled clerk with the Law Society of British Columbia. And when the law did not overtly bar Orientals from professional employment and other callings, discriminatory practices were effective enough to do so. Thus a network of law, regulation, and custom kept Orientals out of a whole range of occupations. As Angus wrote in 1941, "You will look in vain in British Columbia for Japanese lawyers, pharmacists, accountants, teachers, policemen or civil servants."

These measures were sanctioned by public opinion. By the turn of the century anti-Orientalism had become entrenched in the political culture of British Columbia. This antipathy was especially keen in the case of the Japanese. When, during the late nineteenth century, Japan began to emerge as an industrial power, the rest of the world began to look upon the Japanese as very different from the Chinese. In the Sino-Japanese War, 1894–95, Japan easily defeated China and established herself as a military power. Then came the Russo-Japanese War. It was all very well for Japan to modernize its economy and to crush the Chinese, but Japan's triumph in 1905 over Russia was greeted with unease, even alarm, by the Western nations. It was the first victory in modern times of an Asiatic nation over a European nation. These events affected the way in which the Japanese in Canada were perceived. They came to be regarded as more enterprising, competitive, and ambitious than the Chinese and, like Japan herself, as a greater threat to British Columbia than the Chinese.

Japan was able, through treaties with Great Britain which were binding at that time on Canada, to assure entry into Canada for Japanese immigrants. China, truly a helpless giant, could not assure such access for Chinese immigrants; in fact, the head tax on Chinese immigrants had risen to $500 by 1900. This head tax was to last until 1923. But while Japan could ensure Japanese access to Canada, her reach was limited. Japan could do nothing for the Japanese once they arrived in British Columbia, and mounting hostility toward the Japanese there exploded in 1907. In that year, the legislature had passed yet another statute to limit Japanese entry into British Columbia. The lieutenant-governor, James Dunsmuir, refused to assent to the act. A summer of protest against Oriental immigration culminated in a gathering of 5,000 persons before City Hall in Vancouver. The crowd became a mob, and it stormed through Chinatown, breaking windows and destroying storefronts. The Chinese Canadians did little to resist. But, when the mob reached "Little Tokyo," the Japanese Canadians defended their homes and their property and pelted their attackers from the rooftops with bottles and clubs, until the mob turned back.

Mackenzie King, then deputy minister of labour, was sent to British Columbia to investigate Japanese Canadians' claims for damages and the question of Japanese immigration. King was then only 29 years old. He had come to Ottawa to edit *The Labour Gazette*, the department of labour's monthly publication. Soon he became the department's deputy minister and, before long, he had persuaded Laurier to find him a seat in the House of Commons and a place in cabinet. This visit to British Columbia was the first occasion on which the path of this strange man crossed that of the Japanese Canadians.

King urged that restrictions be placed on Japanese immigration, and Ottawa took up the matter with the Japanese government. Japan agreed to limit emigration by those leaving Japan to enter the Canadian labour force, but there were to be no restrictions on emigration of wives and families. The nature of Japanese immigration to Canada changed at once: young women replaced young men. Japanese workers already in Canada, through an exchange of photographs, arranged for brides to be sent to them from Japan. During the next 20 years, the so-called "picture brides" made up the majority of Japanese immigrants to Canada. Families were formed, new communities were established, and the Japanese-Canadian population rapidly increased; by 1920 there were more than 4,000 children born in Canada of Japanese descent, and the Japanese population in British Columbia had risen to 15,000. By the late 1930s the population of Japanese Canadians exceeded that of the Chinese Canadians in British Columbia. Many of the men still worked in logging camps and sawmills. But now in Vancouver Japanese-Canadian families ran rooming houses, grocery stores, dry-cleaning and dressmaking shops. A growing number of Japanese-Canadian fishermen lived in Steveston, at the mouth of the Fraser River. Forbidden by law to acquire Crown lands directly, the Japanese Canadians could buy property privately. In this way they acquired farms in the Fraser and Okanagan valleys.

Attempts to restrict the expansion of the Japanese Canadians over the economic fabric of British Columbia were concentrated on the fishing industry, for it was there that the Japanese Canadians were to be found in gretest numbers. As early as 1893, Japanese Canadians held 20 per cent of the salmon gill-net licences issued in the province. By 1901, they had nearly doubled this percentage. By 1919, Japanese Canadians held half of the salmon gill-net licences issued in the province. That year, at the insistence of White fishermen, the federal department of marine and fisheries promised to "gradually eliminate Orientals from the fishery" and, by 1925, half of the licences held by Japanese Canadians had been cancelled. A variety of other measures were taken, some of them bizarre forms of discrimination. For instance, between 1921 and 1930 Japanese-Canadian fishermen were barred from using gas-powered boats on the Skeena River. The Japanese-Canadian fishermen had to row their boats along the Skeena to the fishing grounds, while White and Indian fishermen sped by under power. These measures achieved their purpose. By 1941, Japanese Canadians held only 12 per cent of the fishing licences in British Columbia. The confiscation of Japanese-Canadian property did not begin after Pearl Harbor; it had been going on for some 20 years.

All of these measures, whether taken by the provincial government or by the federal government, were explicitly racial. There was no constitutional limitation on the power of either government to enact discriminatory legislation against particular racial groups. To be sure, there was a division of legislative power between the federal and provincial governments, but if a particular measure was within the legislative competence of the government which passed it, nothing could be done to challenge it. The Charter of Rights provides that every individual is equal before the law and under the law and has the right to the equal protection and equal benefit of the law without discrimination based on race. This is a guarantee of racial equality which should take from Parliament and the provinces the power to pass legislation which discriminates against any group on account of race, and prevent the federal government and the provinces from erecting a network of laws and regulations designed to restrict the opportunities available to any racial group in Canada. The Charter does not, however, provide a complete guarantee. The changes to the Charter agreed to by the prime minister and the premiers on November 5, 1981, reserve to Parliament and the provinces the power to declare that a statute shall operate notwithstanding the Charter provisions relating to racial equality. This is the *non obstante* clause (it allows parliament and the legislatures to override the Charter provisions relating to fundamental freedoms and legal rights, as well).

In British Columbia in the 1920s, there was such a network. But these restrictions, designed to deal with the Japanese population the province already had, were not enough to satisfy the militants. They believed no more Japanese should be allowed to come to Canada. In 1922, Premier John Oliver of British Columbia urged Mackenzie King, now prime minister of Canada, to ban further Oriental immigration. The province's attorney-general, A. M. Manson, said, "The Oriental is not possible as a permanent citizen in British Columbia because ethnologically they cannot assimilate with our Anglo-Saxon race." It was true that British Columbians claimed that the Japanese would not or could not assimilate, but at a deeper level there was a fear that, if they were assimilated, the White character of the province would be drowned in a sea of brown-skinned fecundity.

In 1923, Mackenzie King brought in legislation to restrict Chinese immigration; as a result, few Chinese entered Canada until after the end of the Second World War. British Columbia politicians continued to press for legislation against Japanese immigration and for yet stronger measures, including repatriation to Japan. In 1927, Premier Oliver told King that:

> The stopping of Oriental immigration entirely is urgently necessary, but that in itself will not suffice, since it leaves us with our present large Oriental population and their prolific birth rate. Our Government feels that the Dominion Government should go further, and by deportation or other legitimate means, seek to bring about the reduction and final elimination of this menace to the well being of the white population of this province.

King undertook to negotiate a new arrangement with Japan. In May, 1928, Japan agreed to limit the number of emigrants to Canada to 150 persons a year. The Japanese-Canadian population would now depend on natural growth for its increase. King was not prepared to act on Oliver's call for deportation—that would have to wait until 1946.

Of course, the politicians were reflecting popular prejudice. Few argued that this prejudice had no rational foundation. Few spoke in defence of the Japanese Canadians. There may be a liberal establishment that speaks for the rights of minorities today, but it did not exist in the days before the Second World War. Newspaper editors inveighed against the Chinese and the Japanese. Nor did the churches preach tolerance. Far from it. The Anglican Bishop of New Westminster told his synod, "We should have a province that will be white; that will be British and that will be Christian." No political party was prepared to urge the enfranchisement of the Japanese Canadians and Chinese Canadians until the advent of the Co-operative Commonwealth Federation (CCF) in 1933. Indeed, during this long period, no more damaging allegation could be made against a political opponent in British Columbia than to suggest that he favoured giving Orientals the vote.

The Regina Manifesto, the party platform adopted by the CCF in 1933, announced that the new party would seek "equal treatment before the law of all residents of Canada, irrespective of race, nationality or religious or political beliefs." J. S. Woodsworth, leader of the CCF, carried this policy to the House of Commons, and the Liberals used it against the CCF in British Columbia in the federal election of 1935. The Liberals opposed giving Orientals the vote, and they ran newspaper advertisements to say, "A vote for any CCF candidate is a vote to give the Chinamen and the Japanese the same voting right as you have." In 1938, the Conservative party in national convention passed a resolution in favour of the complete exclusion of all Orientals from Canada.

Entreaties to reason did no good. In May, 1936, a delegation led by S. I. Hayakawa, a Vancouver-born Nisei who had become a university professor in the United States (and was elected to the United States Senate from California in 1976), appeared before a parliamentary committee in Ottawa with a brief in support of the Japanese Canadians' right to vote. Two British Columbia Members of Parliament, Thomas Reid and A. W. Neill, urged that the franchise should not be extended to them. They advanced the same old reasons: the Japanese were a race that lived apart and would not be assimilated. Nor could assimilation be any kind of answer, for it would lead to the full horrors of miscegenation.

Nevertheless, the social landscape of British Columbia had begun to change. During the 1920s, the growth of the Japanese-Canadian population had slowed, and during the 1930s, with immigration from the old country reduced to a trickle, the population stabilized. The Japanese Canadians were themselves changing, too. Few of the immigrant generation of Japanese, the Issei, spoke English. But the Canadian-born generation, the Nisei, spoke English as well as Japanese. They attended public schools, although many students also attended Japanese-language schools after public school. Many families were converted from Buddhism to Christianity. Between the rising generation and the older generation, there was often distance and tension. In his book *The Enemy That Never Was*, Ken Adachi has written:

The life of the school and of the street widened the separation between generations. If it did nothing else, the school introduced a rival source of authority, the image of the teacher competing with that of the father. In the process, the child came to believe in a universe divided into two realms, one for school and one for home, each with rules and modes of behaviour of its own. As the children grew up, they felt an increased compulsion to choose between the one way and the other. The immigrants themselves were torn by a conflicting desire to have their sons and daughters be like themselves and yet lead better lives. Still, they rarely saw their children as mediators between the culture of the home and the culture of the wider society. Even if they did, they resented it, for it reversed the "proper" order of things. In their eyes, the second generation was undisciplined and ungrateful.

In the 1930s the stereotype held by White Canadians of their Japanese-Canadian neighbours began to crack. In 1931, the Trades and Labour Congress of British Columbia passed a motion calling for the enfranchisement of all native-born Canadians. The CCF urged that all citizens, including those of Oriental descent, be granted the vote, and some academics such as H. F. Angus spoke out in their favour. But any changes that might have come from these stirrings were thwarted by the warlike course of the Japanese Empire on the other side of the Pacific Ocean.

In 1931, Japan invaded Manchuria and, in 1937, she invaded China. Japan's invasion of China crystallized and legitimated anti-Japanese feeling in British Columbia. Even the Chinese Canadians joined in boycotting Japanese-Canadian merchants. The Japanese Canadians were virutally isolated. In case of conflict with Japan, wouldn't the Japanese Canadians constitute a subversive element behind the Canadian lines? The reasons that had led Colonel Lawrence in 1755 to conclude that he could not defend Nova Scotia against the French so long as the Acadians were at his back loomed large in British Columbia. There were demands that Japanese Canadians should carry identification cards; that they should be denied trade licences; that Japanese-language schools should be closed; and that the Japanese Canadians should be removed from the west coast.

On September 10, 1939, Canada declared war on Germany. Many Nisei immediately tried to enlist, and some who signed up east of the Rockies were accepted but, in British Columbia, there was *de facto* exclusion. (During the First World War, 202 Japanese Canadians enlisted and 59 of them died overseas.) On January 8, 1941, Mackenzie

King announced that Canadian citizens of Japanese ancestry were to be exempted from military service.

Exemption from military service was prompted by King's desire to forestall any claim the Japanese Canadians might make to a right to vote based on military service. It would be difficult to argue that the Japanese Canadians might die for their country, but that they should not have the right to participate in choosing who should govern it. In 1931, the British Columbia legislature had granted (by one vote) the franchise to Japanese veterans of the First World War, and it was a precedent that the province's politicians did not wish to expand. Duff Pattullo, the premier of British Columbia from 1933 until 1941, wrote to King urging him to prevent the recruiting of Nisei. "If they are called up for service, there will be a demand they be given the franchise, which we in the province will never tolerate...."

Japanese Canadians were anxious and apprehensive as war with Japan drew ever closer. Throughout 1941, Members of Parliament from British Columbia urged the federal government to take drastic measures against the Japanese Canadians. Only one MP from the province, Angus MacInnis of the CCF, defended the Japanese Canadians. Here is MacInnis speaking in House on February 25, 1941:

> If we are to have harmonious and friendly relations between the orien-tal population and the rest of our British Columbia citizens, we must stop discriminating against and abusing the orientals. We must find some common ground on which we can work, and I think it can be found. Is there any reason, if we should get into difficulties with Japan on the Pacific coast, why the Japanese in British Columbia should be interested in helping Canada, after the way in which we are treating them? I am satisfied that if we treat the Japanese and our other oriental citizens aright, we shall get their loyalty, because they are no longer orientals in the accepted sense of that term. They would feel as much out of place in Japan as we would. I know them, speak to them; I visit them and have them in my home, and I have not the slightest doubt that what I say is correct. If we are to avoid the troubles that other countries have had with racial minorities, then we must take a realistic view of the situation in British Columbia and attempt to make these people feel at home among us. We will secure their loyalty by fairness and kindness and by the practice of other attributes which we exercise in our relations with other people.

But MacInnis was the only parliamentarian to come to the Japanese Canadians' defence. They had no one in high office they could rely upon; and they had no constitutional guarantees. They would have to rely on the "regime of tolerance" to which Laurier had appealed. The Japanese Canadians themselves understood this very well. With war against Japan imminent, an editorial in *The New Canadian*, the weekly newspaper of the Japanese Canadians, on November 14, 1941, said, "We need now to place our assurance in the inherent tolerance, good sense and decency of our Canadian neighbours and the democratic way of life."

Three weeks later, on December 7, 1941, the Japanese attacked Pearl Harbor. Immediately, 38 Japanese Canadians were interned, and 1,200 Japanese-Canadian fishing boats were impounded. Within a month, all persons of Japanese origin, whether they were citizens or not, were banned from the fishing industry, and their fishing boats were sold. At a stroke, the Japanese Canadians had finally been removed from the fishing industry.

Not surprisingly, immigrants who had retained their Japanese citizenship were required to register with the Registrar of Enemy Aliens, in the same way that Germans and Italians in Canada had been obliged to do. That was on December 7. On December 16, however, an order-in-council was passed requiring all persons of Japanese descent, citizens or not, to register. No similar measure had been taken with respect to Canadians of German and Italian origin, although Canada had been at war with Germany and Italy since September, 1939.

After the Japanese attack on Pearl Harbor, the virus of racial antagonism infected the whole province, and virtually all of its politicians, federal and provincial, jostled one another in proposing draconian measures to be taken against the Japanese Canadians. In his book *White Canada Forever*, Professor W. Peter Ward has described the wave of hostility which fell upon the Japanese Canadians. It was one

> ...in force and amplitude surpassing all previous racial outbursts....
> This sudden, dramatic attack roused the racial fears and hostilities of white British Columbians to heights never before attained. In turn, they loosed a torrent of racialism which surged across the province for the next eleven weeks. This outbreak of popular feeling demanded an immediate response from the King government. In attempting to placate white opinion it offered a succession of policies, each one aimed at further restricting the civil liberties of the west coast Japanese. As it proved, nothing short of total evacuation could quiet the public outcry.

Mackenzie King told the nation by radio that the authorities "were confident of the loyal behaviour of Canadian residents of Japanese origin." This was a toothpick in a typhoon. The public clamour for the Japanese Canadians, citizens or not, to be evacuated and interned mounted steadily with each day's news of Japan's stunning victories in the Far East and the South Pacific.

On January 14, 1942, King announced that Japanese nationals between the ages of 18 and 45 would be removed from the west coast. Twenty-two hundred men were placed in road camps in the interior of the province. But this was only a partial evacuation. It did not satisfy the militants. "Take them back to Japan," demanded MP Thomas Reid on January 15, "they do not belong here...." Parliament reconvened on January 22, and its British Columbia members made another round of demands in even more strident language for complete evacuation to locations "east of the Rockies." They asserted, without the least evidence, that the Japanese Canadians constitued a fifth column. Early in 1942, Conservative MP Howard Green told the House:

> We should be protected from treachery, from a stab in the back....
> There has been treachery elsewhere from Japanese in this war, and we
> have no reason to hope that there will be none in British Columbia....
> The only complete protection we can have from this danger is to
> remove the Japanese population from the province.

There were wild rumours of Japanese subversion, but no evidence at all for the rumours. Many persons were, of course, genuinely afraid of Japanese landings on the west coast of Canada. But, apart from taking some remote islands in the Aleutian chain, the Japanese had not menaced North America. On June 20, 1942, a Japanese submarine shelled the lighthouse at Estevan Point on Vancouver Island, but there were no casualties. In any event the shelling occurred well after King had decided to evacuate the Japanese Canadians. Even if King had feared a Japanese attack on the west coast, he had no reason to believe that the Japanese Canadians were likely to aid and abet such an attack.

Today the apologists for the evacuation say that it was necessary for the protection of the Japanese Canadians themselves, that Canadians might spontaneously have fallen upon their fellow citizens in rage and frustration. An argument can, indeed, be erected on this footing. On Christmas Day, 1941, Japan had taken some 1,600 Canadian troops prisoner in the capture of Hong Kong. Was King thinking of the Vancouver riot of 1907, more than 30 years before? Did he fear that anti-Japanese riots in British Columbia might lead to reprisals against the Canadian prisoners taken in Hong Kong? It seems unlikely: the argument had little currency at the time. Certainly, none of those who were most vociferous in their denunciation of the Japanese Canadians advanced it then.

There was, in fact, no justification for their evacuation. No compelling military advice urged the course that King took. Compare the evacuation of the Japanese Canadians with the expulsion of the Acadians. In 1755, except for the English garrison, the Acadians constituted the whole population of Nova Scotia. The Japanese Canadians were only a small minority of the population of British Columbia and their numbers were of no significance at all in Canada as a whole. The Acadians had refused to swear an oath of loyalty to the British king and they had refused to serve against the French king. The Japanese Canadians had professed and amply proved their loyalty. Far from refusing to serve in the Canadian forces, they tried to enlist—but they were refused.

On February 26, 1942, King gave in to the militants. There would be a complete evacuation. He announced that all persons of Japanese ancestry would be evacuated from the west coast. Orders-in-council established a British Columbia Security Commission, which had the power to remove any person of Japanese origin from his or her home, and gave the Custodian of Enemy Property jurisdiction over the evacuees' property. More than 2,000 men had already been sent to work in road camps in interior British Columbia. Any who resisted were sent to a concentration camp at Angler, Ontario. There they wore clothing with red circles painted on their backs to make them easy targets, should they try to escape. Four hundred and fifty-two were still in custody at Angler when the war ended. Another 4,000 Japanese Canadians were sent to work on sugar beet farms in Alberta, Manitoba and Ontario. The rest were to be sent to the interior of British Columbia.

As a first step, Japanese Canadians were collected in the Pacific National Exhibition grounds in Vancouver where they were housed in converted livestock pens. In late spring they were sent to mining towns and newly built shack towns in the interior of the province. There the men working in the road camps were allowed to rejoin their families. Evacuation to the interior continued all that summer and into the fall. Finally, all Japanese Canadians, well-to-do, middle-class and poor, had been evacuated from their homes on the west coast. (The only exception made was in the case of Japanese Canadians who had married Whites.) Their land, their homes, and their personal property were taken from them.

By the time the evacuation was completed, Japan's star was waning. The rapid Japanese advance in the South Pacific was at last checked at the Battle of Midway on June 6, 1942. It was now clear that Japan could not win the war. The possibility of a Japanese invasion of the west coast of North America, always remote, was no longer a strategic consideration. The grounds for the evacuation had ceased to exist. So now the question was—what to do with the Japanese Canadians? Should they be allowed to return to the west coast? Should they be dispersed all over Canada? Or should they be sent to Japan when the war ended?

Members of Parliament from British Columbia were in no doubt. The Japanese Canadians should not be allowed to return to the west coast.

At the very least they should be dispersed; better still, send them to Japan. Only the voice of Angus MacInnis was raised in defence of the principles for which Canada had ostensibly entered the war. In 1940 he was the only CCF MP elected from British Columbia. MacInnis displayed political courage throughout his political career, but never more so than during the years when he was the lone defender of the Japanese Canadians in the House of Commons.

But the government could not be dissuaded. Events were in train. The Japanese Canadians had been evacuated from their homes and their property had been confiscated. By July, 1944, some 4,000 of them had relocated east of the Rockies. But the great majority were still in the camps in the interior of British Columbia, forbidden to return to the west coast. King decided to force them to choose between relocating east of the Rockies and "repatriation" to Japan. They were not to be allowed to return to the west coast. A notice posted in the camps read:

> Japanese Canadians who want to remain in Canada should now re-establish themselves east of the Rockies as best evidence of their intentions to co-operate with the government policy of dispersal. Failure to accept employment east of the Rockies may be regarded at a later date as lack of co-operation with the Canadian Government in carrying out the policy of dispersal.

A wish to return to the west coast, their home for three generations, was to be held over their heads as "lack of cooperation" in carrying out government policy.

What choice did the Japanese Canadians have? The orders-in-council which forbade them to return to their homes on the west coast were still in force. At the same time, they knew they would not be well received in the other provinces. Angry and bitter, many of the Japanese Canadians agreed to be "repatriated" to Japan. These, together with their children, exceeded 10,000. This was not repatriation. Japan was not their homeland; it was a country the majority of them had never seen. Their consent was obtained by foreclosing any other possibility. Thousands of persons—two-thirds, in fact, of those who signed applications for "repatriation"—later applied to cancel them.

The Canadian policy of "repatriation" or dispersal of the Japanese Canadians, undertaken on grounds of national security, was morally wrong. Throughout the war, not a single Japanese Canadian was ever charged, let alone convicted, of espionage. King's policy of "repatriation" or dispersal was founded on racial prejudice and political convenience. Even those Japanese Canadians who had complied with the government demand to relocate east of the Rockies, as 4,000 of them had by 1944, were not to be given the rights of citizenship. The provinces east of the Rockies had little or no Oriental population and had not enacted measures to disqualify them as electors. So there was nothing to stop the Japanese Canadians claiming the right to vote in federal elections. What did King's government do? In 1944, it had the House of Commons pass a bill to prevent the Japanese Canadians who had relocated east of the Rockies from voting in federal elections. On August 14, 1945, the Japanese government surrendered unconditionally, and on September 2 the formal document of surrender was signed. What lay in store for the Japanese Canadians, now that the war was over? In an editorial on August 1, 1945, *The Vancouver Sun* had asked that question. "What British Columbians want to know is whether the Japs can be sent out of the country and kept out."

The war was over, so the federal government had Parliament enact, on October 5, 1945, the National Emergency Transitional Powers Act, which continued the powers assumed by the federal government under the War Measures Act. Acting under the new legislation, the cabinet, on December 15, passed orders-in-council providing for deportation of all Japanese Canadians who had requested "repatriation" in 1944 and for the loss of their Canadian citizenship.

King's policy would make these Japanese Canadians a people without a country. His insensitivity to the enormity of his government's action was complete. Announcing to Parliament the government's policy of deporting loyal citizens who had committed no crime, King's gift for the banal did not fail him. "May I say that we have sought to deal with this problem and in doing so we have followed that ancient precept of doing justly but also loving mercy, and the Orders-in-Council...will give expression to that approach."

The first of the orders-in-council recited that "Whereas during the course of the war with Japan certain Japanese nationals manifested their sympathy with or support of Japan by making requests for repatriation to Japan and otherwise...." King had decided to treat Japanese Canadian requests for "repatriation" made in 1944, requests that the federal government had solicted from them, as evidence of disloyalty.

The orders-in-council provided for the deportation to Japan of any person of 16 years or more who had requested repatriation, including Japanese nationals, naturalized citizens, and persons of Japanese descent born in Canada, together with their wives and any children under the age of 16. Naturalized or Canadian-born citizens who were deported would lose their Canadian citizenship. Altogether, 10,347 Japanese Canadians were to be "repatriated." Three-quarters were Canadian citizens; half of these were Canadian-born.

But the war had ended in August, and thousands of the Japanese Canadians applied to cancel their requests for "repatriation." Moreover, some Canadians were now beginning to feel a sense of shame over what was happening, and they began to come to the aid of the Japanese Canadians. The protests they made led to concessions by the government. An announcement was made that naturalized and Canadian-born Japanese (but not Japanese nationals) who had applied for cancellation of their requests for "repatriation" before September 2, 1945, the date of the official signing of Japan's surrender, would be considered. The government justified this limitation by asserting that persons who had applied only after Japan's surrender must have been hoping that Japan would win the war, else why didn't they apply earlier?

The campaign against deportation continued. Applications for *habeas corpus* were brought to test the legality of the orders-in-council. King agreed to refer the question of the legality of the orders-in-council to the Supreme Court of Canada. On February 20, 1946, the court handed down its decision. Chief Justice Thibaudeau Rinfret held that the cabinet "was the sole judge of the necessity or advisability of these measures," and a majority of the Supreme Court agreed with him.

An appeal was taken to the Privy Council, which handed down its opinion on December 2, 1946. It went even further than the majority in the Supreme Court of Canada and held that the orders-in-council were valid in all respects and that even the forcible deportation of wives and children was valid. These judgements of the Supreme Court of Canada and of the Privy Council reveal how much the judges were inclined to defer to the cabinet. The issue was regarded as one for political judgement, in no way subject to the jurisdiction of the courts. The War Measures Act gave the cabinet power to act and, so far as the Privy Council was concerned, that was the end of the matter. So the Japanese Canadians were banished by their own government. (The last Canadian before them to be banished had been Louis Riel in 1875).

But not all Canadians agreed with their government and the courts. New ideas of human rights and human freedom were gaining currency in the world. No longer were there just a few protesting against the federal government's policy; now there were many. On January 24, 1947, King gave in. The government, he announced, would not carry out its deportation program after all. But, by this date, almost 4,000 persons, half of whom had been born in Canada, had left for Japan. No doubt many of them would have remained in Canada, rather than share postwar Japan's weak prospects, had not the years of persecution embittered them to the point where they had no reason to stay in Canada and no faith in Canada. We must think of them as exiles.

There was no attempt made in the United States to send the Japanese Americans to Japan. There had been, after Pearl Harbor, an outbreak of anti-Japanese hysteria in California, followed by the evacuation and internment of 120,000 Japanese Americans from the west coast. These measures had been upheld by the Supreme Court of the United States on the ground of the paramountcy of national security. But on December 17, 1944, the United States government rescinded the orders excluding the Japanese Americans from the west coast and announced that all detention centres would be closed down within one year. Japanese Americans were permitted at once to return to California and the west coast. Certainly, no attempt was made to banish them to Japan.

In April, 1947, the Canadian cabinet formally revoked the orders-in-council which had sent the Japanese Canadians to Japan. But the orders-in-council passed in 1942 stood. Japanese Canadians still could not return to the west coast. In 1948, three years after the war had ended, they could not travel freely in British Columbia or fish commercially anywhere in Canada. In that year one of them was sentenced to a year's hard labour for returning to British Columbia without permission.

On June 15, 1948, Parliament granted to Japanese Canadians who were citizens the right to vote in federal elections. But though these citizens at last could vote in federal elections, they still could not return to the west coast. The orders-in-council that forbade them to do so were finally rescinded in 1949, four years after the end of the war. By that time, many of them had settled east of the Rockies, especially in Ontario; in fact the largest population of Japanese Canadians in Canada now is in Toronto. In that same year, 1949, they were given the right to vote in provincial elections in British Columbia as well. In 1949, the United Fishermen and Allied Workers Union agreed to let Japanese Canadians return to the fishing industry in the province.

Mackenzie King could write in his Diary that it was "fortunate the use of the [atomic] bomb should have been upon the Japanese rather than upon the white races of Europe." But public attitudes were changing. The world stood appalled by the holocaust to which racial hatred in Europe had led. Canada had become a member of the United Nations Organization, and a subscriber to the Universal Declaration of Human Rights. Racism was no longer in vogue.

In the postwar years the principal concern of the Japanese Canadians was to establish themselves and their children in Canadian society. They wished only to be inconspicuous, and in Toronto deliberately dispersed themselves about the city. Many of the Nisei moved into professional and white-collar occupations, and their acceptance and assimilation, which had once been thought to be impossible, occurred virtually unnoticed. Intermarriage became commonplace. The years of abasement were over.

The "it was all for the best" argument is founded on the notion that the state has the right to scatter the members of any minority whenever it is deemed to be for their own good. If the evacuation of the Japanese Canadians from their homes can be justified as social engineering, which of us will be the next group to be scattered, our communities destroyed, our property confiscated—all in our own best interest?

Such wrongs are beyond redress. The confiscation of property, however, is amenable to redress. Yet there has not been adequate redress for the loss of the Japanese Canadians' property. Their fishing boats, impounded at the very beginning of the war, were sold without any compensation to their former owners. As for the rest of their property, after evacuation it was vested in the Custodian of Enemy Property, who had wide discretionary powers to dispose of it. Without the owners' permission—indeed, over their protests—the Custodian sold their property, often at ridiculously low prices. For instance, Japanese Canadians owned some 700 farms covering about 13,000 acres in the Fraser valley. They were appraised, together, at $836,256 (approximately $64.00 an acre for the finest agricultural land in British Columbia)—that is what the owners received for them—and held by the government for soldiers then serving overseas. The irony is that some of these farms belonged to Japanese Canadians who had served in Canadian forces during the First World War.

Canada opened its doors to Asian immigrants in the 1960s. Perhaps the counterparts today of the Chinese and Japanese immigrants of the nineteenth century are the immigrants from India and Pakistan. Since the early years of this century, Canada had virtually excluded immigration from the Indian subcontinent. As late as 1941 there were no more than 1,500 East Indians in Canada. Since the 1960s, however, immigration from India, Pakistan and Sri Lanka has risen dramatically. This has had a visible impact on many communities in British Columbia and in other provinces, too, for these immigrants do not arrive only on the west coast, by sea, as in the old days. Today they arrive by air, and their destinations may include Winnipeg, Toronto or Montreal. Thus people from the Indian subcontinent may now be found in increasing numbers in many Canadian centres. East Indian immigrants appear to some Canadians as alien, clinging to their own language, dress and customs. There has been a recrudescence of racial feeling, directed against these most recent Asian immigrants. There have been beatings, vandalism, and fire bombings in communities with significant East Indian populations. But these have been isolated outbreaks, generally deplored by all.

The racial virus has been so far kept in check in British Columbia and the other provinces. There has been no attempt to erect a network of discriminatory laws and regulations. There is today a liberal establishment ready to speak out in support of the rights of Asians in Vancouver or West Indians in Toronto or Moroccans in Montreal. There are human rights commissions at the federal level and in every province. And there are the provisions of the Charter of Rights. These things give minorities the confidence to speak out, to protest the violation of their freedom, and to assert their claim to rights we have all been taught they should enjoy.

But might one of the provinces nevertheless have the power to pass racist legislation in the future? Might the federal government, in the exercise of its emergency power, invoke the War Measures Act against a racial minority again? How secure actually are racial minorities in Canada?

The Charter guarantees to every individual the right to equality under the law and the right to the equal protection of the law "without discrimination based on race, national or ethnic origin, (or) colour." But there is the *non obstante* clause. It is difficult to say how often legislators may exercise their power to override the Charter provisions.

The fact is that the Constitution, the Charter, and the law will not provide complete protection for racial minorities. It would be difficult to draft a statute that did. Equality for racial minorities depends, in the end, on the attitudes of the citizenry. But we have progressed. The trial and torment of the Japanese Canadians have taught us something about the obligations of citizenship in Canada. In British Columbia legislators used to strive to devise statutes that would limit the rights of racial minorities. In 1981, the legislature of the province passed the Civil Rights Protection Act to combat racism by prohibiting racist propaganda. Similar legislation was passed in Saskatchewan in 1979. This type of legislation presents a problem. Discrimination in employment, housing, and so forth on racial grounds can properly be made subject to the sanctions of the law. These are overt acts of discrimination. But legislation banning racist propaganda, such as the federal legislation of 1969 banning hate propaganda, entails the enactment of curbs on freedom of speech, something not to be undertaken except for the most compelling reasons and, in the case of racial intolerance, with an awareness that legislation may not be the answer to every evil in the state. While the wisdom—and efficacy—of such legislation is open to question, the change in public and legislative attitudes is important. Such legislation affirms society's commitment to racial equality.

The third generation of Japanese Canadians, the Sansei, have grown up without the linguistic and cultural connections that the Issei handed on to the Nisei. But this does not mean the Japanese Canadians are vanishing. Like the Acadians, the story of their expulsion has provided them with a legend, has given them a graphic tale of the hardships of their parents and their people, of those trying to strengthen their links with the past and to redress past wrongs. But the sense of vulnerability still persists. Should the Japanese Canadians, even today, be silent about the past, lest reminding others of it provoke another outbreak of racism? In *A Dream of Riches*, a book published by The Japanese Canadian Centennial Project in 1978, to commemorate the history of their one hundred years in this country, the Japanese Canadians have given their answer:

> Let us break this self-damaging silence and own our history. If we do not, estrangement from our past will be absorbed and driven deeper, surfacing as a fragmentation in ourselves and coming generations. But in retracing the journey of our people through time, in going back to our roots, we find ourselves made whole, replenished in spirit. We return from that journey deeply proud of our people, of their contribution to this country.

The racism once made legitimate by our political institutions is no longer legitimate. But as long as it finds a place in our collective psyche, it will constitute a threat, sometimes near, at other times far off. Nothing is to be gained by pretending it doesn't exist, or by temporizing with evil. Each of us has an obligation to uphold the regime of tolerance. In *A Dream of Riches* the Japanese Canadians have expressed what should be the aspiration of us all:

> Having gained our freedom . . . we must not lose sight of our own experience of hatred and fear. Too often we have heard "damn Jew," "lazy Indian," from those who were once called "dirty Japs." The struggle of the generations and the meaning of the war years is completely betrayed if we are to go over to the side of the racist. Let us honour our history . . . by supporting the new immigrants and other minorities who now travel the road our people once travelled.

The Predicament of Racial Affirmative Action[†]

KOGILA A. MOODLEY

The Politics of Combatting Racism

The March 1984 publication of the "Report of the Special Committee on Visible Minorities in Canada," entitled *Equality Now*,[1] is a landmark in the ongoing controversy about multiculturalism, immigration policy and race relations in Canada. The extensive cross-country hearings by an all-party committee of the House of Commons under the chairmanship of Liberal MP Bob Daudlin resulted in eighty recommendations on new policies from social integration to employment, from changes in the legal and justice system to media representation and educational issues. Regardless of how the government bureaucracy will respond to the proposals for affirmative action in many realms, the report has already received almost unanimous endorsement from ethnic organizations that would be difficult to ignore.

Despite the widespread support for this imaginative and well-intentioned blueprint, it is necessary to subject the document to a critical review. As may be expected, many reservations have been forthcoming from voices that dislike a multiracial immigration policy in the first place, not to speak of special considerations for disadvantaged visible minorites. However, fundamental questions need to be asked also by those who will benefit from this progressive state intervention. Instead of uncritically embracing short-term gains, they should clarify the long-term implications of affirmative racial action, explore the underlying assumptions and question the motives of state representatives, as noble

†"The Predicament of Racial Affirmative Action," *Queen's Quarterly* 91: 795–806.

as they may sound, in the quest for equality. This critical analysis, therefore, departs from the ideological debate about affirmative action to focus on interests and implications that only a decoding of the public consensus can reveal.

The formation of the Special Committee was prompted by the alarming reports of increasing racial incidents in many Canadian cities at the beginning of a major recession.[2] The ruling Liberal party, as the champion of a relatively open immigration policy, had to protect its image as the party of the bulk of the non-Anglo vote, particularly in Ontario. A progressive policy on racism also allowed the Minister for Multiculturalism to achieve a higher profile in interbureaucratic competition and public opinion. At the same time, the Conservatives could not afford to be seen as opposing racial justice if they were to make inroads into the ethnic vote in the forthcoming federal election. Although it can be safely assumed that the 31 percent of Canadians who in a 1981 Gallup poll supported an all-white Canada are overrepresented in the Conservative constituency, the party leadership had to downplay its bigoted segment and also uphold the image of an all-group party, abhorring discrimination while tacitly adhering to Anglo dominance where it matters. Such tactical considerations do not, however, excuse genuinely held commitment to improvements in race relations by members of all parties. The ethnic lobby, on the other hand, fits into this constellation well. As the recommendations show, ethnic spokespersons basically represent genuine middle-class concerns of those on the verge of becoming part of the managerial elite. The guiding thread of the report is easier access to funds and positions of status and power by qualified members of visible minorities. Buzzwords such as dialogue, interchange, creative encounters, sharing, outreach, and networking indicate the methods with which most witnesses proposed to tackle racial antagonism. Systematic educational efforts, together with a higher profile of visible ethnics in public institutions through affirmative action, it is held, will result in greater interracial tolerance.

This political context colors much of the Report's recommendations, which are progressive and, at the same time, reinforce the status quo. An example of this is: "The committee does not believe that racist groups should be outlawed," but instead suggests that Human Rights Commissions should be strengthened and various provisions of the Criminal Code be amended to allow for more severe punishment of racially motivated crimes. This civil rights approach, however, hardly addresses the problem. Legal sanctions against racist associations, while not changing attitudes, can at least prevent the open propagation of denigration. The legal flaunting of racial intentions in itself constitutes psychological violence.

Canadian "ethnics" wish not only to succeed in the wider society and have easier access to managerial and public positions. While this remains their first political priority there is a second, more specific political concern held by immigrants. In the new environment, many are still interested in the politics of their country of origin. For ethnicity maintenance, this interest, after all, provides the vital link, if heritage is to mean more than the cultivation of food and dance. In this sense, the policy of multiculturalism embraces the continued political involvement of the new citizens with their former homeland. It is a legitimate concern that is not shed with the acquisition of the new citizenship. In fact, the new Canadian status entitles the immigrant to participate in the formulation of Canadian foreign policy toward his or her country of origin like any other citizen.

However, there is no receptive institutional channel for such legitimate concern. The Committee report is silent on the issue while the public stereotype often considers "immigrants" as importing foreign troubles into tranquil Canada. The sporadic mobilization of ethnic constituencies has been disdained by External Affairs. Several commentators have pointed out how ill-prepared and disinclined External Affairs is to leaven foreign policy with emotional input from partisan advocates.[3] As Sheldon E. Gordon aptly remarks: "External has always been an elitist department; while it represents Canada abroad, it disdains real-life Canadians at home."[4] If businessmen are invited to affect foreign policy, so should other interest groups whether the issue is recognition of Palestinians, boycott of South Africa or civil rights in the Philippines. Diplomats keeping aloof from the emotional undergirding of foreign policy issues deprive themselves of the valuable experiences of ethnic constituencies that could, at the very least, sensitize an allegedly neutral policy to the psychology of foreign controversies.[5] More than the necessary inclusion of visible Canadians in the representation of the Canadian foreign service to change the image of the country at home and abroad, it is the actual influence of legitimate ethnic interests on Canadian policy that matters but remains unaddressed.

Ideally, the Committee envisages Canadian society as a happy family where everyone can "feel really and truly a part of the whole Canadian fabric." The report stipulates a duty for "all Canadians to promote a sense of belonging and community for all minorities and foster active participation in the social, cultural and political life of the country." Such a utopia obfuscates the reality of wealth, differential power and political conflict generally. The image deflects criticism away from the dominance of the few and the manipulation of the many to the false sentiment that everyone is equal if he or she is only made to feel welcome. Despite the professed concern for more active political involvement, the ideology of equal opportunities and harmonious partnership in fact depoliticizes the newcomers.

The adjustments necessary to make this happy family image more credible do not upset the existing economic and political hegemony. On the contrary, the state machinery benefits from greater legitimacy by demonstrating its openness. Incorporating the racial outsiders streamlines the tasks of the state. Bigoted police forces cause friction and unnecessary costs. When only fifteen out of a 5472 member police force in Toronto come from visible minorities, it is no longer a question of altruistic justice but of effective policing to recruit from different groups. When half of the children in Vancouver schools come from non-English-speaking homes, effective language training is a precondition for their adequate functioning in the workforce later, rather than a charity extended by well-intentioned policy-makers. Indeed, it unwittingly places minorities in the position of recipients, rather than initiators of their own struggle. Even ethnicity, the ultimate tool which can be mobilized to define a collective self-image and to voice demands and express dissatisfaction, has been stripped of motive power through co-optation.

However, it is the unquestionable merit of the report that it forcefully recognizes such necessities, in opposition to the many ideological zealots who would like to dictate their ethnocentric vision to the rest. The reiteration that cultural pluralism is "the very essence of Canadian identity," the insistence on equality regardless of length of residence and the institutional rather than individual approach to racism make the report a valuable and progressive document despite its many deficiencies.

Race as an Invidious Distinction

From a sociological perspective the most startling shortcoming of the report lies in its treatment of visible minorities as more or less monolithic. Aboriginal people, blacks in Nova Scotia, Chinese and Indo-Canadians in British Columbia are subsumed under the concept "visible minority communities," whose common bond lies in exclusion. However, the history of these four major visible groups in Canada is so different, their expectations and claims so varied, and their experience of and reaction to discrimination so distinct, that the common denominator of being "non-white" makes the formulation of a common policy problematic. In addition to these intergroup distinctions, there are significant intragroup differences that make the racial label meaningless, except to those who have invented it. The crucial distinction between ethnic and racial groups is not adequately dealt with by the report. Ethnic characteristics, based on cultural heritage or common territory, are usually considered worthy of preservation by group members as long as their individual identity is bound to this origin. In this sense, aboriginal people form an ethnic group or a "first nation" whose visibility merely overlaps with ethnicity. The same applies to religious or language groups.

Unlike ethnicity, however, racial characteristics have no intrinsic social significance of their own. Racial characteristics acquire salience because of discrimination. Exclusion serves as a bond only as long as discrimination lasts. In and of themselves, racial classifications are meaningless, having no more reality than eye or hair color. The conceptual confusion in advocating multiracialism as a component of multiculturalism is evident. Nonracialism, but not multiracialism, can be a worthy ideal. Color blindness remains the logical outcome of "eradicating racism." To aim at both—multiracialism and the eradication of racism—is surely an unrecognized contradiction. If one wishes to combat racism and achieve color blindness as much as possible one cannot simultaneously "activate positive racial attitudes." All racial attitudes, whether positive or negative, represent stereotypes. Positive multiracialism is a dangerous supplement to a praiseworthy multiculturalism because it heightens invidious racial perceptions where multiculturalism is rightly silent on the question of race.

The conceptual confusion is of course the result of a unique Canadian political tradition. In the 1960s and early 70s it had become intellectually fashionable to deny any racial problems in Canada. Race Relations denoted an unrecognized discipline. Few, if any, social science departments offered a course in a field that was at best considered applicable to foreign countries, such as South Africa or the US. In Canada, however, the view that "we do not have a black problem" has become part of the folk wisdom. With the changing immigration patterns in the late 1970s, the visible newcomers from the Third World outnumbered immigrants from Europe.[6] This brought the latent racism—despite a forgotten history of anti-Asian discrimination in the West and an even more blatant neglect of aboriginal people—finally into the open. No longer could obvious exclusion of visible Canadians be kept invisible. The continual series of racial incidents in major cities together with a more vocal human rights lobby demanded government recognition beyond the rhetorical celebration of cultural diversity. Multiculturalism, the policy designed to appease the European ethnics from outside the charter groups, did not address the problems of racial discrimination of people who could never hope to blend into the mainstream as long as they were considered aliens regardless of their culture or behavior. But in its eagerness to reconcile the liberal creed of equality of opportunity with a contradictory reality—the Canadian dilemma revisited—the blueprint confuses the solution with the problem. In our eagerness to recognize the salience of race as a mark of deprivation, in contrast to an apolitical multiculturalism, we have tended to go overboard by reifying "race." Hence, the goal of curing racism through the recognition of multiracialism has in fact become part of the problem, rather than part of the solution.

Immigrants and Caste-like Minorities

The report fails to distinguish between immigrants and conquered or colonized groups. Visible minorities in Canada belong to both categories. The far greater portion of the estimated 1.9 million "visibles" (7 percent of the population) can be found in the immigrant group while the aboriginal people or blacks in Nova Scotia (who migrated as slaves or escapees from US slavery) would be examples of colonized/conquered segments.

There are two important differences between the two categories: 1) Conquered people can lay legitimate claims to restitution for past injustices. The native people in particular can evoke ownership rights to land and other symbolic resources. Visible immigrants do not possess such entitlement. The state does not owe immigrants anything more than equal rights.[7] 2) Colonized people often form what the Nigerian sociologist John Ogbu called "caste-like minorities."[8] They have, until recently, internalized their stigmatization. A self-fulfilling prophecy reinforces low expectations which lock many members of these groups into a vicious circle of poverty, underachievement, low status, and general anomie. No such destiny normally befalls voluntary immigrants in search of economic improvement. With the backing of an extended family and a culturally transmitted work ethic of high motivation, many Asian immigrants to Canada soon outperform the average member of the dominant group. Their vision of self-worth is increasingly sustained by a booming video industry which keeps alive the language and culture of origin. It also keeps out the devalued Canadian image of themselves. The same educational success story applies to many South Asians in the UK and Chinese and Japanese in the US.

On both grounds (entitlement to restitution and need) a good argument can, therefore, be made that colonized minorities in Canada, above all native people, both deserve and need affirmative action programs, while this is not so for visible immigrants. It is simply not true that the statistics about "missed opportunities to education and job skills" characterizing aboriginal people are "applicable to other visible minorities as well." The report recommends, for example, that "postsecondary institutions need to identify recruitment procedures which encourage more visible minorities to take advantage of their programs." If this advice were to apply to Canadian students of South and East Asian origin, and the US situation where detailed racial statistics are kept is any guide, Canadian universities will most likely find that students from the two largest visible groups (Chinese and Indo-Canadians) are proportionally overrepresented, at least in certain disciplines. If an ill-advised racial quota system were to apply, it could in fact be used to restrict such upward mobility. The racist backlash would only claim its proper quota. In short, visible immigrants do not need affirmative action. But apart from such opportunistic considerations there are more fundamental reasons why the clamor for quotas needs to be questioned.

Entrenching Racial Stigmatization

Affirmative action for Asian-Canadians and other visible immigrants can hardly solve continuous racism. On the contrary, a good case can be made against affirmative racial action for perpetuating invidious distinctions by attaching advantage to them. Affirmative action institutionalizes race. Visible minority members will perceive a strategic value in classifying themselves as racially distinct as long as a quota favors them in the market over competitors. There have been cases in India, for example, where individuals applied for reclassification to the "untouchable" caste, after a generation of conversion to Christianity, clearly to gain entrance to a coveted university seat.[9] Such racialization will not be a temporary measure until racial equality is achieved. The proposed changes require a racial categorization of the population. This is stated in a matter of fact manner in the report, as some items to be included in the census. Nowhere is the morality of requesting information about racial descent questioned. Once census data are collected on invidious distinctions both the racists and their victims find more justifications for fortifying the barriers. How liberal philosophy, that traditionally espouses universalism and the unity of humankind, can lend itself to unofficial pigmentation of Canadian society, remains to be explained by the well-meaning authors of *Equality Now*. Where are the lines to be drawn for children of "mixed" marriages? Will the immigrants from the Middle East qualify for visibility or have to undergo a test for skin fairness? When the entire civilized world abhors the compulsory race classification laws of South Africa, Canada, regardless of its benign intentions, is about to institutionalize voluntary apartheid. Stigmatized, newly benefiting groups may well see it as in their interest to keep alive the racial separateness for the advantage it brings.

As in the cases of India and the United States, those who benefit most from affirmative action programs will be the least disadvantaged members of minority groups. For India, this involved higher income members of "scheduled castes,"[10] for the US, Asian-Americans and members of the black bourgeoisie,[11] and for Canada a similar pattern may well be anticipated. It is these privileged groups who will reap most from such actions and suffer least from the stigmatization of such labels.

The shortsightedness of such a policy is further evident in the counterproductive implications for those members of visible minorities who succeeded in the absence of affirmative action. They will have to cope with the suspicion that they owe their position more to the color of their skin than to their merit. Although affirmative action programs stress that they are no substitute for adequate qualifications, they are always perceived as overriding merit with ascriptive assets. The inevitable denigration of actual minority achievement could lead to a setback rather than an advancement of minority success. There is evidence that as issues of affirmative action were percolating in the US, some white patients who had sought the services of black doctors ceased to do so. At Harvard University, a day after discussion of the issue in the press, white patients refused to be examined by black medical students.[12] Those who have made it at least know that they have reached their position on their own, despite racial obstacles. Once this certainty is removed, all members of visible minorities will labor under the suspicion of incompetence and psychological insecurity. They will be restigmatized through the very efforts meant to destigmatize visibility.

Changing the Mainstream or the Victim?

The visibility of a brown skin *per se* is not different from the visibility of a white one. The former is noticeable only because the latter belongs to a majority, a convenient norm of what is perceived as normal and familiar. Therefore, the problem of racism lies mainly with the majority community that singles out physical traits for differential treatment and esteem. Yet: "The Committee agrees with the view that racial harmony is best served by helping minority communities." However, all historical evidence of racial conflicts indicates that it is not the victims who are in need of intervention but the perpetrators of the crime. For example, no amount of help could have saved the Jews of Nazi Germany from their persecutors. Neither their deepening "sense of ethnicity" and vocal self-confidence, which the report recommends as the appropriate answer for minorities, nor their complete assimilation made any difference. Applying such lessons to Canada would mean that, above all, it is the mainstream that has to be educated. Why should it be so "important for governments to provide organizational and leadership skills training for groups and organizations" save to co-opt and control the outsiders by such offers? Given appropriate channels of access, ethnics, if they indeed have significant grievances, will articulate them without the advice of the condescending adversary on how to speak up. What is far more important is the training and sensitization of the public service to adequately accommodate the ethnic outsiders and the assurance of an unbiased hearing.

Ultimately it is the superordinates, not the subordinates, who need to be made psychologically secure so that they do not need to project inevitable frustrations onto outgroups. Minorities are best protected, not when they are most vocal, but when the dominant group has learned to accept and live with difference and live by its purported standards of fair play. As much as state assistance in this task is appreciated, placing the burden of combatting racism primarily on the victims overestimates their power.

In this focus the Committee may have been led astray by their chief witnesses. Those advocates *for* ethnic groups are not necessarily representative *of* their claimed constituency. Robert Harney states: "National lobbies, self-proclaimed ethnic spokesmen in federal politics, and the national committees for most ethnic organizations are, more often than not, the most ethereal and ephemeral part of any ethnic group."[13] A flourishing ethnic relations industry, from special consultants to intercultural communicators in a state-sponsored bureaucracy, has now reached the stage of developing an interest in its self-perpetuation and further expansion, regardless of need. Needs can also be manufactured and one of the consistent requests to the Committee concerned more funds for assessing, meeting and stimulating additional needs. Had the Committee not solely relied on this self-interested advocacy of ethnic spokespersons and instead commissioned independent surveys of grassroots sentiment, quite a different picture may well have emerged.

The lack of reliable data seems particularly obvious in the section on media and advertising. The report rightly castigates the media for omitting non-whites from its coverage, for biased reporting of visible minorities and for the absence of journalists from the ethnic communities in the image-setting depiction of Canadian society. It is one thing, however, to be concerned about the commercial lie portrayed in advertising that Canada is a white-only society but an altogether different one to aim at the incorporation of minorities into the all-pervasive consumer culture. Minorities may be best served by not being the target of advertising, contrary to the Committee's recommendation that "consumer information on visible minorities should be made available." In any case, visibility has little to do with consumer behavior, which may be influenced by cultural traditions, but certainly not race. According to the available research in Canada, the race of the characters in advertising does not affect the purchases of viewers. This finding contrasts with the US context, where black images are associated with low purchasing power as well as low esteem. The Canadian advertising industry has simply not realized that since the introduction of the point system, many Canadian immigrants are better educated than American minorities. It is, on the other hand, precisely this background that makes Canadian visible minorities impervious to racial consumption and advertising. One wonders why a Ministry of Multiculturalism should help the advertising industry by doing its research. In the meantime, sophisticated market researchers have wisely decided that the present low levels of immigration together with the inevitable Canadianization of consumer expectation based on length of residence, particularly in the second generation, do not warrant an ethnicization of sales in the longer term.[14]

Conclusions

The Report of the Commons Committee advocates the extension of existing affirmative action programs for the handicapped, women and native people to visible minorities in general. However, it is doubtful whether the same justifications applied to these groups can be legitimately extended to visible immigrants. Handicapped people face an objective disadvantage in the market and, therefore, need special protection. The same applies to native people in remote areas where externally based exploration companies would not hire local labor without being compelled by the state. In addition, one can argue well for the desirability of preserving aboriginal ethnicity. This is not a racial categorization because the group members themselves consider it important to preserve their ethnicity. In the case of racial discrimination, in addition to unequal treatment, group membership is always imposed on outsiders, regardless of their self-identification. The fact that the victims in some cases may assume the outside categorization resulting in a self-fulfilling prophecy does not make racial distinctions less invidious. Furthermore, it has been argued that not all stigmatized groups need affirmative action. The decisive criterion is the effect of historical exclusion and degradation on present behavior. Fortunately, visible immigrants have, on the whole, hardly internalized their stigmatization. They are not caste-like minorities in Canada. The unintended consequences of home-language maintenance and comparisons with their country of origin have been to allow their own definitions of themselves to persist. Many women and native people, on the other hand, have not escaped from age-old role stereotyping. Hence special assistance *is* needed to alter their customary behavior. What is called for is dispassionate analysis to assess realistically the extent to which the problem is a lack of qualification and merit on the part of the groups in question, or "the established system of markers and controls" which must be monitored.[15] There is little value in lumping together the different needs of native people, the handicapped, women, and immigrants in the demand for quotas.

Van den Berghe has argued for the American scene that policy-makers have three courses of action from which they can choose: 1) to ignore the racial or ethnic cleavages and enforce universalism and individual merit; 2) to "restore the balance" by instituting quotas and affirmative action-type measures; 3) to steer a midway course between the above extremes, by adhering to universal standards, yet incorporating some measure of ethnic particularism. While the first liberal option may initially seem progressive, it has not resulted in significantly altering the status quo.

The second option, it has been argued in this analysis, merely entrenches differences and exacerbates existing cleavages. Furthermore, it permanently stigmatizes minority groups. The third option, as van den Berghe points out, encompasses all the conflicts of group inequalities and problems of ethnic and racial particularism.[16] Despite its likelihood of antagonizing everyone, it is, by far, the best approach for the unique Canadian situation. Instead of forced access through preferential hiring, greater emphasis ought to be placed on safeguards against racism through legalized sanctions. While it may still be defensible to support preferential hiring for women, native people and "the handicapped," the integration of visible immigrants can come only through emphasizing universalistic criteria. Though the immediate short-term gains may not be as spectacular, the long-term acceptance of minorities will be of a very different caliber.[17]

Notes

1. Canada, House of Commons, Report of the Special Committee on Visible Minorities in Canadian Society, *Equality Now* (Ottawa: March 1984). All citations are from this report. The Special Committee consisted of four Liberal MPs (B. Daudlin, M. Veillette, N. Kelly, G. McCauley), two Conservatives (G. Mitges, S. Paproski) and one New Democrat (L. Lewycky). John Kehoe of the Education Faculty of the University of British Columbia was the Study Director who supervised a research team of a dozen staff members and consultants, some of them members of visible minorities. The Committee itself, it was often noted, comprised only white males, as is representative of the Canadian power elite.

2. See the "Situation Reports on Race Relations" commissioned by the Minister of State—Multiculturalism for eleven cities across Canada (Vancouver, Winnipeg, Williams Lake, Calgary, Regina, Windsor, Toronto, Ottawa, Montreal, Halifax, and St. John's).

3. See, for example, the contribution by Howard Stanislawski in *The Middle East at the Crossroads: Regional Forces and External Powers*, edited by Janice Gross Stein and David Dewitt (Oakville: Mosaic Press, 1983). The Jewish lobby has been in the forefront of trying to influence Canadian foreign policy towards Israel, but so have other groups, particularly from Eastern Europe, in trying to have Ottawa adopt certain stances, especially on human rights issues.

4. *Globe and Mail*, 28 January 1984. The case for the legitimacy of concern with the political affairs of their country of origin by new Canadians should not be construed as making allowances for extremism, be it support for the IRA, Khalistan or Armenia. But inasmuch as a Jewish or Ukrainian lobby, for example, has an unquestioned right to pressure External Affairs, so have Arab Canadians, in support of their perspective, provided such concern does not violate Canadian law. The displeasure of a government with which Ottawa has diplomatic ties cannot be the criterion of what involvement Canadian citizens are allowed. The civil rights of people everywhere ought to be of universal concern, particularly when kinship and ethnic ties make it a burning issue. The demand that new Canadians abstain from involvement with the politics of their former home not only violates the spirit of multiculturalism (that always must include culture maintenance as a political issue at its source), but also ignores natural sentiments and rights. With a heterogeneous population, Canada has become a "United Nation" that inevitably reflects the conflicts of that forum. That some agitation on foreign issues, such as the Polish-Canadian support for Solidarity, finds more public support and official sympathy than other causes, however, cannot be the criterion for their legitimacy.

5. I know of long-time new Canadian academics, for example, who have been repeatedly consulted by the US State Department and other foreign governments but have never been sought to advise External Affairs. One doubts whether the Canadian policy-makers are even aware of the local expertise outside Ottawa, not to speak of utilizing it.

6. By 1982 immigration from Third World countries outstripped recruitment from Europe and the US by a margin of 54 to 46 out of a total of 120,000 immigrants. The relative increase of non-white immigrants was mainly due to the cutback in the economic category of immigrants from 18,000 to 7000 (due to the recession), so that persons in the social and humanitarian categories (family reunification and refugees) accounted for almost three-quarters of the total. In the latter group, people from Third World countries are over-represented while in the economic category the opposite is the case.

7. I leave out here the question of how the Canadian government will compensate the estimated 2500 surviving early Chinese immigrants who paid a discriminating head tax and the approximately 4000 cases of Japanese-Canadian internees in B.C. whose property was confiscated during World War II. Why Ottawa stalls on an even symbolic compensation after formally acknowledging the injustice is surprising.

8. John Ogbu, *Minority Education and Caste* (New York: Academic Press, 1978).

9. *All India Reporter* 1976. Guntur Medical College Case, as cited in Lewis Killian, "Affirmative Action and Protective Discrimination: A Comparison of the United States and India," Occasional Paper No 3, Centre for Multicultural Education, University of London, Institute of Education, 1981.

10. See Mysore N. Srinivas, *Social Change in Modern India* (Berkeley: Univ. of California Press, 1969); and L. Dushkin, "Scheduled Caste Politics," in *The Untouchables in Contemporary India*, edited by J. M. Mahar (Tucson: Univ. of Arizona Press, 1972).

11. See T. Sowell, *Economics and Politics of Race* (New York: William Morrow, 1983), p. 201.

12. W. Williams, "On Discrimination, Prejudice, Racial Income Differentials and Affirmative Action, in *Discrimination, Affirmative Action and Equal Opportunity*, edited by W. E. Block and M. A. Walker (Vancouver: Fraser Institute, 1982).

13. Robert Harney, *Ethnic Forum*, Fall 1982.

14. See, for example, the statement by N. Pleasants, Vice President of media for Grant Tandy Advertising that the need to use ethnic communities in Canada will decline during the rest of the decade. He cites multilingual television station CFMT of Toronto as an example that will "drop more and more ethnic programming in favour of English-language programs," *Globe and Mail*, 2 May 1984.

15. J. Rothschild, *Ethnopolitics* (New York: Columbia Univ. Press, 1981).

16. P. L. Van den Berghe, "The Benign Quota: Panacea or Pandora's Box," *The American Sociologist* 6 (Supplementary Issue, 1971), 40–3.

17. I am grateful to Heribert Adam for many discussions of these issues.

Bibliography

Abella, I., and H. Troper. *None Is Too Many: Canada and the Jews of Europe 1933-1948*. Toronto: Lester and Orpen Dennys, 1982.

Aboud, F.E. "Evaluation and Information Seeking Consequences of Social Discrepancy as Applied to Ethnic Behaviour." Ph.D. dissertation, McGill University, 1973.

_____. "Seeking Information About Different Ethnic Groups: The Role of Motivation and Confirmation." *Journal of Applied Social Psychology* 5 (1975): 331-41.

_____. "The Functions of Language in Canada: Discussion of Paper by J.D. Jackson." In *The Individual, Language and Society in Canada*, edited by W.H. Coons, D.M. Taylor, and M.A. Tremblay. Ottawa: Canada Council, pp. 77-89.

Aboud, F.E., and D.M. Taylor. "Ethnic and Role Stereotypes: Their Relative Importance in Person Perception." *Journal of Social Psychology* 85 (1971): 17-27.

Abu-Laban, B. *An Olive Branch on the Family Tree: The Arabs in Canada*. Toronto: McClelland and Stewart, 1980.

Adorno, T.W., E. Frenkel-Brunswick, D.J. Levinson, and R.N. Sanford. *The Authoritarian Personality*. New York: Harper & Row, 1950.

Aitchison, J.H. "The Municipal Corporations Act of 1849." *Canadian Historical Review* 30 (1949): 107-22.

Allport, Gordon. *The Nature of Prejudice*. Reading, Mass.: Addison-Wesley, 1954. Reprinted New York: Doubleday, Anchor, 1958.

Anderson, Alan. "Assimilation in the Bloc Settlements of North-Central Saskatchewan: A Comparative Study of Identity Change Among Seven Ethno-Religious Groups in a Canadian Prairie Region." Ph.D. dissertation, University of Saskatchewan, 1972.

Anderson, Alan, and Leo Driedger. "The Mennonite Family: Culture and Kin in Rural Saskatchewan." In *Canadian Families: Ethnic Variations*, edited by E. Ishwaren. Toronto: McGraw-Hill Ryerson, 1980.

Anderson, Alan B., and James S. Frideres. *Ethnicity in Canada: Theoretical Perspectives*. Toronto: Butterworths, 1981.

Anderson, G.M., and D. Higgs. *A Future to Inherit: The Portuguese Communities of Canada*. Toronto: McClelland and Stewart, 1976.

Anderson, Robert. *The Cultural Context: An Introduction to Cultural Anthropology*. Minneapolis: Burgess, 1976.

Andrew, J.V. *Bilingual Today, French Tomorrow*. Richmond Hill, Ont.: BMG Publishing, 1977.

Antonovsky, A. "The Social Meaning of Discrimination." *Phylon* 21 (1960): 81-95.

Armstrong, Frederick H. "John Birrell, 1815-75." In *Dictionary of Canadian Biography*, vol. 8, edited by Frances G. Halpenny. Toronto: University of Toronto Press, 1972, p. 68.

_____. "The Oligarchy of the Western District of Upper Canada." *TheCanadian Historical Association: Historical Papers*, 1977, pp. 86-103.

_____. "Ethnicity in the Formation of the Family Compact: A Case Study in the Growth of the Canadian Establishment." In *Ethnicity, Power and Politics in Canada*, edited by Jorgen Dahlie and Tissa Gernando. Toronto: Methuen, 1981.

Asch, M. *Home and Native Land: Aboriginal Rights and the Canadian Constitution.* Toronto: Methuen, 1984.

Ashmore, R.D., and F.K. Del Boca. "Conceptual Approaches to Stereotypes and Stereotyping." In *Cognitive Processes in Stereotyping and Intergroup Behavior*, edited by D.L. Hamilton. Hillsdale, N.J.: Lawrence Erlbaum, 1981, pp.1-35.

Aun, Karl. *The Political Refugees: A History of the Estonians in Canada.* Toronto: McClelland and Stewart, 1985.

Azkin, Benjamin. *State and Nation.* London: Hutchinson University Library, 1964.

Balakrishnan, T.R. "Ethnic Residential Segregation in the Metropolitan Areas of Canada." *Canadian Journal of Sociology* 1 (1976): 481-98.

_____. "Changing Patterns in Ethnic Residential Segregation in the Metropolitan Areas of Canada." *Canadian Review of Sociology and Anthropology* 19 (1982): 92-110.

Balakrishnan, T.R., and J. Kralt. "Residential Concentration of Ethnic/Visible Minority Groups in the Metropolitan Areas of Montreal, Toronto and Vancouver." Paper presented at the Canadian Ethnic Studies Association conference held in Montreal, 1985.

_____. "Segregation of Visible Minorities in Montreal, Toronto, and Vancouver." In *Ethnic Canada*, edited by Leo Driedger. Toronto: Copp Clark Pitman, 1987.

Banton, Michael. *Racial and Ethnic Competition.* Cambridge: Cambridge University Press, 1983.

Barry, Brian. "Political Accommodation and Consociational Democracy." *British Journal of Political Science* 5 (October 1975): 477-505.

Barth, Fredrik, ed. *Ethnic Groups and Boundaries.* Boston: Little, Brown and Company, 1969.

Bausenhart, Werner A. "The Ontario German Language Press and its Suppression by Order-in-Council in 1918." *Canadian Ethnic Studies* 4 (1972): 35-48.

Bell, D. "Ethnicity and Social Change." In *Ethnicity: Theory and Experience*, edited by N. Glazer and D. Moynihan, pp. 141-76. Cambridge: Harvard University Press, 1975.

Bell, David, and Lorne Tepperman. *The Roots of Disunity.* Toronto: McClelland and Stewart, 1979.

Berger, Peter L., and Thomas Luckmann. *The Social Construction of Reality: An Exercise in the Microsociology of Knowledge.* Garden City, NY: Doubleday and Company, 1967.

Berger, Thomas. *Fragile Freedoms: Human Rights and Dissent in Canada.* Toronto: Clarke Irwin, 1981.

Berry, Brewton, and Henry L. Tischler. *Race and Ethnic Relations.* Boston: Houghton Mifflin, 1978, pp.30-42.

Berry, Brian. *The Human Consequences of Urbanization.* New York: St. Martins Press, 1973.

Berry, J.W. "A Functional Approach to the Relationship Between Stereotypes and Familiarity." *Australian Journal of Psychology* 22 (1970a): 29-33.

_____. "Marginality, Stress and Ethnic Identification in an Acculturated Aboriginal Community." *Journal of Cross-Cultural Psychology* 1 (1970b): 239-52.

_____. "Amerindian Attitudes Toward Assimilation: Multicultural Policy and Reality in Canada." *Journal of Institute of Social Research and Applied Anthropology* 1 (1975): 47-58.

_____. *Human Ecology and Cognitive Style: Comparative Studies in Cultural and Psychological Adaptation.* New York: Sage/Halsted, 1976.

_____. "Acculturation as Varieties of Adaptation." In *Acculturation: Theory, Models and Some New Findings*, edited by A. Padilla. Boulder: Westview Press, 1980a.

———. "Social and Cultural Change." In *Handbook of Cross-Cultural Psychology, vol. 5, Social Psychology*, edited by H.C. Triandis and R. Brisin. Boston: Allyn & Bacon, 1980b.

———. "Cultural Relations in Plural Societies: Alternatives to Segregation and Their Sociopsychological Implications." In *Groups in Contact*, edited by N. Miller and M. Brewer. New York: Academic Press, 1984a.

———. "Multicultural Policy in Canada: A Social Psychological Analysis." *Canadian Journal of Behavioural Science* 16 (1984b): 353-70.

———." Finding Identity: Separation, Integration, Assimilation, or Marginality?" In *Ethnic Canada*, edited by Leo Driedger. Toronto: Copp Clark Pitman, 1987.

Berry, J.W., and R.C. Annis. "Acculturative Stress." *Journal of Cross-Cultural Psychology* 5 (1984): 382-406.

Berry, J.W., and U. Kim. "Acculturation and Mental Health: A Review." Paper presented to W.H.O. Workshop, Mexico City, August 1984.

Berry, J.W., R. Kalin, and D.M. Taylor. *Multiculturalism and Ethnic Attitudes in Canada*. Ottawa: Ministry of Supply and Services, Canada, 1977.

Berry, J.W., R. Wintrob, P.S. Sindell, and T.A. Mawhinney. "Psychological Adaptation to Culture Change Among the James Bay Cree." *Le Naturaliste Canadien* 109 (1982): 965-75.

Berry, J.W., U. Kim, T. Minde, and D. Mok. "Comparative Studies of Acculturative Stress." Paper presented to Canadian Psychological Association, Halifax, June 1985.

Bibby, Reginald. "Bilingualism and Multiculturalism: A National Reading." In *Ethnic Canada*, edited by Leo Driedger. Toronto: Copp Clark Pitman, 1987.

Billig, M. *Social Psychology and Intergroup Relations*. London: Academic Press, 1976.

Black, D., and A. Reiss, Jr. "Police Control of Juveniles." *American Sociological Review* 35 (1970): 63-77.

Blalock, Hubert M., Jr. "Economic Discrimination and Negro Increase." *American Sociological Review* 21 (1956): 584-88.

———. *Toward A Theory of Minority Group Relations*. New York: Wiley, 1967.

Blau, Peter. "A Formal Theory of Differentiation in Organizations." *American Sociological Review* 35 (1970): 201-18.

———. "A Macrosociological Theory of Social Structure." *American Journal of Sociology* 83 (1977): 26-52.

Blauner, Robert. "Internal Colonization and Ghetto Revolt." *Social Problems* 16, 4 (1969): 393-408.

Blishen, Bernard R. "A Socio-economic Text of Occupations in Canada." *Canadian Review of Sociology and Anthropology* 12 (1967): 53-64.

Blumer, Herbert. "Society as Symbolic Interaction." In *Human Behavior and Social Process*, edited by Arnold M. Rose. London: Routledge and Kegan Paul, 1962, pp. 179-92.

Bogardus, Emory S. *Social Distance*. Yellow Springs, Ohio: Antioch Press, 1959a.

———. "Comparing Racial Distance in Ethiopia, South Africa and the United States." *Sociology and Social Research* 52 (1959b): 149-56.

Bonacich, Edna. "A Theory of Ethnic Antagonism: The Split Labor Market." *American Sociological Review* 37 (October 1972): 547-59.

———. "Abolition, the Extension of Slavery and the Position of Free Blacks: A Study of Split Labor Markets in the United States, 1830-1863." *American Journal of Sociology* 81 (1975): 601-28.

_____. "The Past, Present, and Future of Split Labor Market Theory." In *Research in Race and Ethnic Relations*, edited by C.B. Marrett and C. Leggon, vol. 1. New York: JAI Press, 1979, pp. 17-64.

Bourdieu, Pierre. "Le Fétichisme de la Langue." *Actes de la Recherche en Sciences Sociales* 4 (1975): 2-32.

_____. "Les trois états du capital culturel." *Actes de la Recherche en Sciences Sociales* 30 (1979): 3-6.

Bourdieu, Pierre, et Jean-Claude Passeron. *La Reproduction: Eléments pour une theorie du système d'enseignement.* Paris: Les Editions de Minuit, 1970.

Boxhill, W.O. "A User's Guide to 1981 Census Data on Ethnic Origins." Statistics Canada, Catalogue 99-949 (Occasional). Ottawa: Minister of Supply and Services, 1985.

Brandmeyer, Gerard A., and R. Serge Denisoff. "Status Politics: An Appraisal of the Application of a Concept." *Pacific Sociological Review* 12 (1969): 5-12.

Breton, Raymond. "Institutional Completeness of Ethnic Communities and the Personal Relations of Immigrants." *American Journal of Sociology* 70 (1964): 193-205.

_____. "Ethnic Stratification Viewed from Three Theoretical Perspectives." In *Social Stratification: Canada*, edited by James E. Curtis and William G. Scott. Toronto: Prentice-Hall, 1979, pp. 271-93.

_____. "The Production and Allocation of Symbolic Resources: An Analysis of the Linguistic and Ethnocultural Fields in Canada." *Canadian Review of Sociology and Anthropology* 21 (1984): 123-44.

Brewer, M.B., and L. Lui. "Categorization of the Elderly By the Elderly: Effects of Perceiver's Category Membership." *Personality and Social Psychology Bulletin* 10 (1984): 585-95.

Brigham, J.C. "Ethnic Stereotypes." *Psychological Bulletin* 76 (1971): 15-38.

Brislin, R.W. "Translation and Content Analysis of Oral and Written Material." In *Handbook of Cross-Cultural Psychology, vol. 2, Methodology*, edited by H.C. Triandis and J.W. Berry. Boston: Allyn & Bacon, 1980.

Brody, M. Kenneth. "Yankee City and the Bicentennial: Warner's Study of Symbolic Activity in a Contemporary Setting." *Sociological Inquiry* 52 (1982): 259-73.

Brotz, Howard. "Multiculturalism in Canada: A Muddle." *Canadian Public Policy* 6 (1980): 41-6.

Brown, David L., and Glenn V. Fuguitt. "Percent Nonwhite and Racial Disparity in Nonmetropolitan Cities in the South." *Social Science Quarterly* 53 (1972): 573-82.

Brown, R.J. "The Role of Similarity in Intergroup Relations." In *The Social Dimension: European Developments in Social Psychology*, vol. 2, edited by H. Tajfel. Cambridge, Mass.: Cambridge University Press, 1984, pp. 603-23.

Brunet, Michel. "Trois dominantes de la pensée canadienne-française." *Ecrits du Canada français* 3 (1957): 98-100.

Buchignani, N., and D.M. Indra. *Continuous Journey: A Social History of South Asians in Canada.* Toronto: McClelland and Stewart, 1985.

Bujaki, M. "The Acculturation Experience of First and Second Generation Hungarians in Ottawa." B.A. thesis, Queen's University, 1985.

Bullock, H. "The Significance of the Racial Factor in the Length of Prison Sentences." *Journal of Criminal Law, Criminology, and Police Science* 52 (1961): 411-17.

Bullough, Bonnie. "Alienation in the Ghetto." *American Journal of Sociology* 72 (1967): 469-78.

Burgess, E.W. "The Growth of the City: An Introduction to a Research Project." In *The*

City, edited by R.E. Park, E.W. Burgess, and R.R. McKenzie. Chicago: University of Chicago Press, 1934, pp. 47-62.

Burnet, J. *The Definition of Multiculturalism in a Bilingual Framework*. Paper presented at Conference on Multiculturalism and Third World Immigrants in Canada, University of Alberta, Edmonton, 1975a.

_____. "Multiculturalism, Immigration and Racism." *Canadian Ethnic Studies* 7, 1(1975b): 35-39.

_____. "The Policy of Multiculturalism within a Bilingual Framework: An Interpretation." In *Education of Immigrant Students*, edited by Aaron Wolfgang. Toronto: Ontario Institute for Studies in Education, 1975c, pp. 205-14.

_____. "The Policy of Multiculturalism within a Bilingual Framework: A Stock Taking." *Canadian Ethnic Studies* 10 (1978): 107-13.

_____. "Myths and Multiculturalism." *Canadian Journal of Education* 4 (1979): 43-58.

Burshtyn, Hyman. "A Factor-Analytic Study of Occupational Prestige Ratings." *Canadian Review of Sociology and Anthropology* 5, 3 (1968): 156-80.

Burshtyn, Hyman, and Derek G. Smith. "Occupational Prestige Ratings Among High School Students in the Canadian Arctic." In *The Canadian Ethnic Mosaic*, edited by Leo Driedger. Toronto: McClelland and Stewart, 1978.

Bushnell, J.H. "From American Indian to Indian American." *AmericanAnthropologist* 70 (1968): 1108-16.

Butler, R.V. "The Bureau of Indian Affairs: Activities since 1945." *The Annals* 436 (March 1978): 50-60.

Byrne, D. "Attitudes and Attraction." In *Advances in Experimental Social Psychology*, vol. 4, edited by L. Berkowitz. New York: Academic Press, 1969, pp. 35-90.

Campbell, D.T. "Stereotypes and the Perception of Group Differences." *American Psychologist* 22 (1967): 817-29.

Canada, House of Commons. Report of the Special Committee on Visible Minorities in Canadian Society. *Equality Now*. Ottawa: March 1984.

Canada, Public Archives. MGZ 4A7, Durham Papers, Sec. 2, 49 (1838): 141.

Canadian Consultative Council on Multiculturalism. *First Annual Report*. Ottawa: Minister of State for Multiculturalism, 1975.

_____. *A Report*. Ottawa: Minister of State for Multiculturalism, 1977.

Cappon, Paul. "Nationalism and Inter-ethnic and Linguistic Conflict in Quebec." In *The Canadian Ethnic Mosaic*, edited by Leo Driedger. Toronto: McClelland and Stewart, 1978, pp. 327-44.

Carneiro, Robert L. "Ascertaining, Testing, and Interpreting Sequences of Cultural Development." *Southwestern Journal of Anthropology* 24, 4 (1968).

Cauthen, N.R., I.E. Robinson, and H.H. Krauss. "Stereotypes: A Review of the Literature 1926-1968." *Journal of Social Psychology* 84 (1971): 103-26.

Census of Canada, 1870-71. Ottawa: Minister of Agriculture, 5 vols., 1873-79.

Chadwick, E. Marion. *Ontario Families*, 2 vols. Toronto: 1894-98.

Chapais, T. "Cours d'histoire du Canada." *The French Canadians, 1760-1945*, vol. 4. London: Macmillan, 1967, p. 27.

Charyk, J.C. *Those Bittersweet Schooldays*. Saskatoon: Western Producer Prairie Books, 1977.

Chimbos, P.D. *The Canadian Odyssey: The Greek Experience in Canada*. Toronto: McClelland and Stewart, 1980.

Cipywnyk, S. "Multiculturalism and the Child in Western Canada." In *Multiculturalism and Education*. Proceedings of the Western Regional Conference, Canadian Association for Curriculum Studies, 1976, pp. 27-50.

Clark, S.D. *The Canadian Society and the Issue of Multi-Culturalism*. Saskatoon: University of Saskatchewan, 1976.

Cohen, Abner. *Custom and Politics in Urban Africa*. Berkeley: University of California Press, 1969.

_____. *Urban Ethnicity*. London: Tavistock, 1974a.

_____. *Two-Dimensional Man*. London: Routledge and Kegan Paul, 1974b.

_____. "Symbolic Action and the Structure of the Self." In *Symbols and Sentiments*, edited by Ioan Lewis. New York: Academic Press, 1977, pp. 117-28.

Coleman, James S. *Community Conflicts*. Glencoe, Ill.: Free Press, 1957.

_____. "Race Relations and Social Change." In *Race and Social Sciences*, edited by Irwin Karz and Patricia Gurin. New York: Basic Books, 1969, pp. 274-341.

Connor, Walker. "Self-Determination. The New Phase." *World Politics* 20 (October 1967): 30-53.

_____. "Ethnonationalism in the First World: The Present in Historical Perspective." In *Ethnic Conflict in the Western World*, edited by M. Esman. Ithaca: Cornell University Press, 1975, pp. 19-45.

Constitution Act/Canada Act. Ottawa: 1982.

Cooney, J. "Dispensing Justice Is A Very Serious Matter to 'Judge of the North'." *Wall Street Journal*, January 14.

Cortese, C.F., R.F. Falk, and J.K. Cohen. "Further Considerations on the Methodological Analysis of Segregation Indices." *American Sociological Review* 41 (1976): 889-93.

Cowan, Helen I. *British Emigration to British North America: The First Hundred Years*. Toronto: University of Toronto Press, 1961.

Cox, Bruce. *Cultural Ecology: Readings on the Canadian Indians and Eskimos*. Toronto: McClelland and Stewart, 1973.

Cox, Oliver C. *Caste, Class and Race: A Study in Social Dynamics*. Garden City, N.Y.: Doubleday, 1948.

Craven, Paul, and Barry Wellman. "The Network City." *Sociological Inquiry* 43 (1973): 57-88.

Crowe, Keith J. *A History of the Original Peoples of Northern Canada*. Montreal: McGill-Queen's University, 1974.

Crowley, R.W., and J.P. Whitridge. *Human Rights in Canada Legislation*. Ottawa: Supply and Services, 1978.

Cumming, P.A., and N.H. Mickenberg. *Native Rights in Canada*, 2nd ed. Toronto: General Publishing, 1972.

Darroch, A. Gordon. "Another Look at Ethnicity, Stratification and Social Mobility in Canada." *Canadian Journal of Sociology* 4, 1 (1979): 1-25.

Darroch, A. Gordon, and Wilfred G. Marston. "Ethnic Differentiation: Ecological Aspects of a Multidimensional Approach." *International Migration Review* 4 (1969): 71-95.

_____. "The Social Class Basis of Ethnic Residential Segregation: The Canadian Case." *American Journal of Sociology* 77 (1971): 491-510.

_____. "Patterns of Urban Ethnicity: Toward a Revised Ecological Model." In *Urbanism and Urbanization: Views, Aspects and Dimensions*, edited by Noel Iverson. Leiden: E.J. Brill, 1984.

Dashefsky, Arnold. "And the Search Goes On: The Meaning of Religio-Ethnic Identity and Identification." *Sociological Analysis* 33 (1972): 239-45.

_____. "Theoretical Frameworks in the Study of Ethnic Groups: Toward a Social Psychology of Ethnicity." *Ethnicity* 2 (1975): 10-18.

Dashefsky, A., and H.M. Shapiro. *Ethnic Identification Among American Jews.* Lexington, MA: Lexington, 1974.

Department of Manpower and Immigration. *The Green Paper on Immigration*, vols.1-4. Ottawa: Information Canada.

Despres, Leo, ed. *Ethnicity and Resource Competition.* The Hague: Mouton, 1975.

Deutsch, Karl. "Social Mobilization and Political Development." *American Political Science Review* (September 1961): 493-506.

Deutsch, M., and R.M. Krauss. *Theories in Social Psychology.* New York: Basic Books, 1965.

Diefenbaker, J.G. "To Be a Canadian." In *Multiculturalism and Education*. Proceedings of the Western Regional Conference, Canadian Association for Curriculum Studies, 1978, pp. 89-99.

Dion, K.L. "Cohesiveness as a Determinant of Ingroup-Outgroup Bias." *Journal of Personality and Social Psychology* 28 (1973): 163-71.

Douglas, R.A.A., cited in J. Leavy, "Working Paper for a Conference on Minority Rights," held in cooperation with York University (Ontario), October 1979, pp. 11-14.

Dreisziger, N.F. *Struggle and Hope: The Hungarian Canadian Experience.* Toronto: McClelland and Stewart, 1982.

Driedger, Leo. "A Sect in a Modern Society: The Old Colony Mennonites of Saskatchewan." M.A. thesis, University of Chicago, 1955.

_____. "Mennonite Change: The Old Colony Revisited 1955-77." *Mennonite Life* 42 (1977a): 1-12.

_____. "Toward a Perspective on Canadian Pluralism: Ethnic Identity in Winnipeg." *Canadian Journal of Sociology* 2 (1977b): 77-96.

_____. "Ethnic Boundaries: A Comparison of Two Urban Neighborhoods." *Sociology and Social Research* 62 (1978): 193-211.

_____. "Maintenance of Urban Ethnic Boundaries: The French in St. Boniface." *The Sociological Quarterly* 20 (1979): 89-108.

_____. "Community of Conflict: The Eldorado Invasion of Warman." *Canadian Review of Sociology and Anthropology* 23 (1986): 247-69.

Driedger, Leo, and Glenn Church. "Residential Segregation and Institutional Completeness: A Comparison of Ethnic Minorities." *Canadian Review of Sociology and Anthropology* 11 (1974): 30-52.

Driedger, Leo, and Jacob Peters. "Identity and Social Distance: Towards Understanding Simmel's 'The Stranger'." *Canadian Review of Sociology and Anthropology* 14, 2 (1977): 158-73.

Driedger, Leo, and R.A. Clifton. "Ethnic Stereotypes: Images of Ethnocentrism, Reciprocity or Similarity?" *Canadian Review of Sociology and Anthropology* 21 (1984): 289-301.

Driedger, Leo, and Richard A. Mezoff. "Ethnic Prejudice and Discrimination in Winnipeg High Schools." *Canadian Journal of Sociology* 6 (1980): 1-17.

Driver, Harold E. *Indians of North America*, 2nd ed. Chicago: University of Chicago, 1969.

Dudycha, G.J. "The Attitudes of College Students Toward War and the Germans Before and During the Second World War." *Journal of Social Psychology* 15 (1942): 317-24.

Duncan, J.D. *Symbols and Social Theory.* New York: Oxford University Press, 1969.

Duncan, Otis Dudley, and Beverley Duncan. "A Methodological Analysis of Segregation Indices." *American Sociological Review* 20 (1955): 210-17.

riminal Justice: A Study of the Pre-
b): 620-37.
mmunities: A Study of the
(1976): 597-612.
Meaning." *Ethnicity* 4 (1977): 167-76.
n City, New York: Doubleday, 1966.
lysis of Stereotyping." In *Advances in*
ed by L. Berkowitz. New York: Academic

and Intergroup Behavior. Hillsdale, N.J.:

ndaries in Modern States." In *National*
. Meyer and M. Hannan. Chicago:
.

s. New York: Norton, 1964.
rk: Vintage, 1974.
ropos of a Solution of Race Problems."
Letters 30 (1944): 667-74.
ess, 1950.
rary Indians of Canada*, 2 vols. Ottawa:

the Assimilation of White Persons
row, 1973.
ort in Hudson's Bay to the North Ocean
1958, Toronto: Macmillan of Canada.
: Change." *Politics and Society* 2 (Fall

nge." *American Journal of Sociology* 79

ge and Kegan Paul, 1975a.
e in British National Development.
5b.
e Proliferation of the Cultural Division of

vision of Labor." *American Journal of*

a." In *The New Christian Right*, edited
. New York: Aldine Publishing Co., 1983,

ity in Canada*. 1961 Census Monograph.

New York: Doubleday, 1955.
um Philadelphia." In *The Peoples of*
k Haller. Philadelphia: Temple University,

an Indian Identity: Modern Pan-Indian*
ress, 1971.

Duncan, Otis Dudley, and Stanley Lieberson. "Ethnic Segregation and Assimilation."
American Journal of Sociology 64 (1959): 364-74.

du Preez, Peter. *Social Psychology of Politics*. Oxford: Basil Blackwell, 1980.

Durkheim, Emile. *The Division of Labour in Society*. New York: Free Press, 1955.

Dushkin, L. "Scheduled Caste Politics." In *The Untouchables in Contemporary India*,
edited by J.M. Mahar. Tucson: University of Arizona Press, 1972.

Ebbesen, Ebbe B., Glen L. Kjos, and Vladimer J. Konleni. "Spatial Ecology: Its Effects
on the Choice of Friends and Enemies." *Journal of Experimental Social Psychology* 12
(1976): 505-18.

Edelman, Murray. *The Symbolic Uses of Politics*. Urbana, Ill.: The University of Illinois
Press, 1964.

_____. *Politics as Symbolic Action: Mass Arousal and Quiescence*. New York: Academic
Press, 1971.

Elliot, J.E., ed. *Two Nations, Many Cultures: Ethnic Groups in Canada*. Scarborough:
Prentice-Hall of Canada, Ltd., 1979.

Employment and Immigration Canada. *Background Paper on Future Immigration
Levels*. Ottawa: Minister of Supply and Services Canada, 1984.

_____. *Immigration Statistics, 1983*. Ottawa: Minister of Supply and Services Canada,
1985a.

_____. *Annual Report to Parliament on Future Immigration Levels*. Ottawa: Minister of
Supply and Services Canada, 1985b.

Enloe, Cynthia. "Internal Colonialism, Federalism and Alternative State Development
Strategies." *Publius* (Fall 1977): 145-60.

_____. "The Issue Saliency of the Military-Ethnic Connection." *World Politics* (January
1978): 267-85.

_____. *Ethnic Soldiers: State Security in Divided Societies*. London: Penguin, 1980.

_____. "The Growth of the State and Ethnic Mobilization: The American Experience."
Ethnic and Racial Studies 4 (April 1981): 123-36.

Epp, Frank H. *Mennonites in Canada, 1786-1920*. Toronto: Macmillan of Canada,
1974.

_____. *Mennonites in Canada, 1920-1940*. Toronto: Macmillan of Canada, 1980.

Erbe, Brigitte Mack. "Race and Socioeconomic Segregation." *American Sociological
Review* 40 (1975): 801-12.

Erikson, E. *Childhood and Society*, 2nd ed. New York: Norton, 1963.

_____. *Identity Youth and Crisis*. New York: Norton, 1968.

Etzioni, Amitai. "The Ghetto — A Re-evaluation." *Social Forces* 37 (1959): 255-62.

Fanon, F. *Black Skin, White Masks*. New York: Grove, 1967.

Farley, Renolds. "Residential Segregation in Urbanized Areas of the United States in
1970: An Analysis of Social Class and Racial Differences." *Demography* 14 (1977):
497-518.

Farris, B., and R.A. Brymer. "Differential Socialization of Latin and Anglo-American
Youth; An Exploratory Study of the Self-Concept." In *Mexican Americans in the
United States*, edited by John H. Burma. Cambridge, MA: Schenkman, 1970, pp. 411-
25.

Feagin, J., and D. Eckberg. "Discrimination: Motivation, Action Effects and Context."
Annual Review of Sociology 6 (1980): 1-20.

Filteau, G. *Histoire des Patriotes*, vol. 13. Montreal: 1942, pp. 243-44.

Fischer, Claude S. "Toward a Subcultural Theory of Urbanism." *American Journal of
Sociology* 80 (1975): 1319-41.

_____. *The Urban Experience*. New York: Harcourt, Brace, 1976.

Fisher, Robin. *Contact and Conflict: Indian-European Relations in British Columbia, 1774-1890*. Vancouver: University of British Columbia, 1977.

Fishman, J.A. "An Examination of the Process and Functioning of Social Stereotyping." *Journal of Social Psychology* 43 (1956): 27-64.

Fiske, Adele. "Scheduled Caste Buddist Organizations." In *The Untouchables in Contemporary India*, edited by J.M. Mahar. Tucson: University of Arizona Press, 1972, pp. 113-42.

Fiske, S.T. "Schema-triggered Affect: Application to Social Perception." In *Affect and Cognition: The Seventeenth Annual Carnegie Symposium on Cognition*, edited by M.S. Clark and S.T. Fiske. Hillsdale, N.J.: Lawrence Erlbaum, 1982, pp. 55-78.

Fiske, S.T., and M.A. Pavelchak. "Category-based Versus Piecemeal-based Affective Responses: Developments in Schema-triggered Affect." In *The Handbook of Motivation and Cognition: Foundations of Social Behavior*, edited by R.M. Sorrentino and E.T. Higgins. New York: Guilford Press, 1986, pp. 167-203.

Flint, D. *The Hutterites: A Study in Prejudice*. Toronto: Oxford University Press, 1975.

Fortin, Gérald. "An Analysis of the Ideology of French-Canadian Nationalist Magazines: 1917-1954." Manuscript, Cornell University, 1956.

Fredrickson, George M. *White Supremacy*. Oxford: Oxford University Press, 1981.

Frideres, J.S. *Native People in Canada: Contemporary Conflicts*, 2nd ed. Scarborough: Prentice-Hall Canada, 1983.

Friesen, Richard. "Old Colony Mennonite Settlements in Saskatchewan: A Study in Settlement Change." M.A. thesis, University of Alberta, 1975.

Frisbie, W., and Lisa Neidert. "Inequality and the Relative Size of Minority Populations: A Comparative Analysis." *American Journal of Sociology* 82 (1977): 1007-30.

Galaskiewicz, Joseph. *Exchange Networks and Community Politics*. London: Sage Publications, 1979.

Gans, Herbert. *The Urban Villagers*. New York: Macmillan, 1962.

_____. "Symbolic Ethnicity: The Future of Ethnic Groups and Cultures." *Ethnic and Racial Studies* 2 (1979): 1-20.

Gardner, R.C. "Ethnic Stereotypes: The Traditional Approach, A New Look." *Canadian Psychologist* 14 (1973): 133-48.

Gardner, R.C., and D.M. Taylor. "Ethnic Stereotypes: Their Effects on Person Perception." *Canadian Journal of Psychology* 22 (1968): 267-76.

_____. "Ethnic Stereotypes: Meaningfulness in Ethnic Labels." *Canadian Journal of Behavioural Science* 1 (1969): 182-92.

Gardner, R.C., D.M. Kirby, and J.C. Finley. "Ethnic Stereotypes: The Significance of Consensus." *Canadian Journal of Behavioural Science* 5 (1973): 4-12.

Gardner, R.C., D.M. Taylor, and H.J. Feenstra. "Ethnic Stereotypes: Attitudes or Beliefs?" *Canadian Journal of Psychology* 24 (1970): 321-34.

Gardner, R.C., E.J. Wonnacott, and D.M. Taylor. "Ethnic Stereotypes: A Factor Analytic Investigation." *Canadian Journal of Psychology* 22 (1968): 35-44.

Gardner, R.C., R.N. Lalonde, A.M. Nero, and M.Y. Young. "Ethnic Stereotypes: The Implication of Measurement Strategy." Research Bulletin No. 642, University of Western Ontario.

Geertz, Clifford. "The Integrative Revolution: Primordial Sentiments and Civil Politics in the New States." *Old Societies and New States*, edited by Clifford Geertz. New York: Free Press, 1963, pp. 105-57.

Geographic Board of Canada. *Handbook of the Indians of Canada*. Ottawa: King's Printer, 1913. Reprinted in 1971, Toronto: Coles.

_____. "The Social and Legal Construction of (
sentencing Process." *Social Problems* 22 (197

_____. "Criminal Justice in Rural and Urban (
Bureaucratization of Justice." *Social Forces* 5

_____. "Finding Discrimination: A Question of

Hall, Edward T. *The Hidden Dimension*. Garde

Hamilton, D.L. "A Cognitive-Attributional Ana
Experimental Social Psychology, vol. 12, edit
Press, 1979, pp. 53-84.

_____, ed. *Cognitive Processes in Stereotyping*
Lawrence Erlbaum, 1981.

Hannan, Michael. "The Dynamics of Ethnic Bo
Development of the World System, edited by
University of Chicago Press, 1979, pp. 253-7

Harney, Robert. *Ethnic Forum* (Fall 1982).

Harris, Marvin. *Patterns of Race in the America*

_____. *Cows, Pigs, Wars and Witches*. New Yo

Hawley, Amos. "Dispersion vs. Segregation: A
Papers of the Michigan Academy of Arts and

_____. *Human Ecology*. New York: Ronald Pr

Hawthorn, H.B., ed. *A Survey of the Contempo*
Queen's Printer, 1966, 1967.

Heard, J. Norman. *White Into Red: A Study of*
Captured by Indians. Metuchen, N.J.: Scare

Hearne, Samuel. *Journey from Prince of Wales*
in the Years 1769-1772. London, reprinted i

Hechter, Michael. "Towards a Theory of Ethni
1971): 21-45.

_____. "The Political Economy of Ethnic Chan
(1974): 1151-78.

_____. *Internal Colonialism*. London: Routled

_____. *Internal Colonization: The Celtic Fring*
Berkeley: University of California Press, 197

_____. "Ethnicity and Industrialization: On th
Labour." *Ethnicity* 3 (1976): 214-24.

_____. "Group Formation and the Cultural Di
Sociology 84 (1978): 293-318.

Heinz, Donald. "The Struggle to Define Americ
by Robert C. Liebman and Robert Wuthnow
pp. 133-48.

Henripin, Jacques. *Trends and Factors of Fertil*
Ottawa: Information Canada, 1972.

Herberg, Will. *Protestant — Catholic — Jew*.

Hershberg, Theodore. "Free Blacks in Antebell
Philadelphia, edited by Allen Davis and Mar
1973, pp. 111-33.

Hertzberg, Hazel W. *The Search for an Americ*
Movements. Syracuse: Syracuse University P

Hobsbawm, Eric, and Terence Ranger. *The Invention of Tradition*. Cambridge: Cambridge University Press, 1983.

Hodge, Robert W., Paul M. Siegel, and Peter H. Rossi. "Occupational Prestige in the United States, 1925 to 1963." *American Journal of Sociology* 70, 3 (1964): 286-302.

Hodgkin, Thomas L. *Nationalism in Colonial Africa*. Washington Square, N.Y.: New York University Press, 1956.

Horowitz, Donald. "Ethnic Identity." In *Ethnicity: Theory and Experience*, edited by N. Glazer and D.P. Moynihan. Cambridge: Harvard University Press, 1975, pp. 111-40.

_____. "Cultural Movements and Ethnic Change." *Annals* 433 (September 1977): 6-18.

House of Commons *Debates*. Statement of P.E. Trudeau, October 8, 1971a.

_____. Official Report, vol. 115, no. 187, 3rd Session, 29th Parliament, 1971b.

Hughes, Everett Cherrington. "Dilemmas and Contradictions of Status." *American Journal of Sociology* 50 (1945): 353-9.

_____. *French Canada in Transition*. Chicago: The University of Chicago Press, 1984.

Hughes, Everett Cherrington, and Helen MacGill Hughes. *Where Peoples Meet: Racial and Ethnic Frontiers*. Glencoe, Illinois: The Free Press, 1952.

Hunter, Albert. "The Loss of Community: An Empirical Test Through Replication." *American Sociological Review* 40 (1975): 537-52.

Hurd, W.B. *Ethnic Origin and Nativity of the Canadian People*. 1941 Census Monograph. Ottawa: Queen's Printer, c. 1965.

Hurstfield, Jennifer. "'Internal' Colonialism: White, Black and Chicano." *Ethnic and Racial Studies* 1 (January 1978): 60-79.

International Bill of Human Rights. New York: United Nations, 1978.

Isaacs, Harold R. "Basic Group Identity: The Idols of the Tribe." In *Ethnicity: Theory and Experience*, edited by N. Glazer and D.P. Moynihan. Cambridge: Harvard University Press, 1975a, pp. 29-52.

_____. *Idols of the Tribe: Group Identity and Political Change*. New York: Harper & Row, 1975b.

Isajiw, W.W. "Olga of Wonderland: Ethnicity in Technological Society." *Canadian Ethnic Studies* (1977): 77-85.

_____. "Multiculturalism as Public Philosophy." Unpublished manuscript, 1978.

Isajiw, W.W., and Leo Driedger. "Ethnic Identity: Resource or Drawback for Social Mobility?" Unpublished paper, forthcoming (1987).

Jackson, John. "The Functions of Language in Canada: On the Political Economy of Language." In *The Individual, Language and Society in Canada*, edited by W.H. Coons, Donald M. Taylor, and Marc-Adelard Tremblay. Ottawa: The Canada Council, 1977, pp. 61-76.

Jaenen, Cornelius. *Friend and Foe: Aspects of French-Amerindian Cultural Conflict in the Sixteenth and Seventeenth Centuries*. Toronto: McClelland and Stewart, 1976.

James, Wilmot. "Class Struggle in a Racial Order: South Africa, 1936-1962." Paper presented at the annual meeting of the Midwest Sociological Society, April 7-9, 1982, Des Moines.

_____. "State and Ethnicity in South Africa: From Apartheid to Ethnic Corporation." In *Competitive Ethnic Relations*, edited by S. Olzak and J. Nagel. New York: Academic Press, 1986.

Janowitz, Morris. *The Community Press in an Urban Setting*. New York: Free Press, 1952.

_____. *Social Control of the Welfare State*. New York: Elsevier, 1976.

Jenness, Diamond. *The Indians of Canada*. Ottawa: National Museums of Canada, 1932. Reprinted in 1977, Toronto: University of Toronto.

Jones, E.E., G.C. Wood, and G.A. Quattrone. "Perceived Variability of Personal Characteristics in In-groups and Out-groups: The Role of Knowledge and Evaluation." *Personality and Social Psychology Bulletin* 7 (1981): 523-28.

Kalbach, W.E. *The Impact of Immigration on Canada's Population*. 1961 Census Monograph. Ottawa: Queen's Press, 1970.

_____. "Ethnic Residential Segregation and Its Significance for the Individual in an Urban Setting." Centre for Urban and Community Studies, University of Toronto, Paper No. 4, 1981.

_____. "Growth and Distribution of Canada's Ethnic Populations, 1871-1981." In *Ethnic Canada*, edited by Leo Driedger. Toronto: Copp Clark Pitman, 1987.

_____. *The Effect of Immigration on Population*. Ottawa: Information Canada.

Kalbach, W.E., and W.W. McVey, Jr. "Ethnicity and Race." In *The Demographic Bases of Canadian Society*, 2nd ed. Toronto: McGraw-Hill Ryerson Ltd., 1971, pp. 193-219.

Kalin, R., and R.C. Gardner. "The Cultural Context of Social Psychology." In *A Canadian Social Psychology of Ethnic Relations*, edited by R.C. Gardner and R. Kalin. Toronto: Methuen, 1981, pp. 2-17.

Kallen, E. *Ethnicity and Human Rights in Canada*. Agincourt: Gage Publishers, 1982.

_____. "Ethnicity and Collective Rights in Canada." In *Ethnic Canada*, edited by Leo Driedger. Toronto: Copp Clark Pitman, 1987.

Kane, Paul. *Wanderings of an Artist Among the Indians*. London: Longman, Brown et al., 1859. Reprinted in 1968, Edmonton: Hurtig.

Kantrowitz, Nathan. *Ethnic and Racial Segregation in the New York Metropolis*. New York: Praeger, 1973.

Kapsis, Robert E. "Powerlessness in Racially Changing Neighborhoods." *Urban Affairs Quarterly* 14 (1979): 424-42.

Kardiner, A., and L. Ovesey. *The Mark of Oppression*. New York: Norton, 1951.

Karlins, M., T.L. Coffman, and G. Walters. "On the Fading of Social Stereotypes: Studies in Three Generations of College Students." *Journal of Personality and Social Psychology* 13 (1969): 1-16.

Karning, Albert K. "Black Economic, Political, and Cultural Development: Does City Size Make a Difference." *Social Forces* 57 (1979): 1194-2009.

Kasarda, John. "The Structural Implications of Social System Size." *American Sociological Review* 39 (1974): 19-28.

Kasfir, Nelson. "Explaining Ethnic Political Participation." *World Politics* (March 1979): 365-88.

Katz, D., and K. Braly. "Racial Stereotypes of One Hundred College Students." *Journal of Abnormal and Social Psychology* 28 (1933): 280-90.

_____. "Racial Prejudice and Racial Stereotypes." *Journal of Abnormal and Social Psychology* 30 (1935): 175-93.

Katz, E., and P. Lazarsfeld. *Personal Influence*. New York: Free Press, 1955.

Katzman, Ralph. Brief presented to the Environmental Assessment Panel. In *Public Hearings of the Environmental Assessment Panel on the Proposed Uranium Hexafluoride Refinery at Corman Park, Saskatchewan*, vol. 4. Ottawa: Recorded by International Reporting Inc., 1980, pp. 546-55.

Kearney, R.M. *Communalism and Language in the Politics of Ceylon*. Durham, NC: Duke University Press, 1967.

Kemper, Theodore D. "Why Are the Streets So Dirty? Social Psychological and Stratification Factors in the Decline of Municipal Services." *Social Forces* 58 (1979): 422-42.

Keyfitz, Nathan. "Population Problems." In *French Canadian Society*, vol. 1, edited by M. Rioux and Y. Martin. Toronto: McClelland and Stewart, 1964, p. 227.

Killian, Lewis. "Affirmative Action and Protective Discrimination: A Comparison of the United States and India." Occasional Paper No. 3, Centre for Multicultural Education: University of London, 1981.

Kim, U. "Psychological Acculturation of Korean Immigrants in Toronto: A Study of Modes of Acculturation, Identity, Language and Acculturative Stress." M.A. thesis, Queen's University, 1984.

Kirby, D.M., and R.C. Gardner. "Ethnic Stereotypes: Norms on 208 Words Typically Used in Their Assessment." *Canadian Journal of Psychology* 26 (1972): 140-54.

_____. "Ethnic Stereotypes: Determinants in Children and Their Parents." *Canadian Journal of Psychology* 27 (1973): 127-43.

Knoke, David, and Richard B. Felson. "Ethnic Stratification and Political Cleavage in the United States, 1952-68." *American Journal of Sociology* 80, 3 (1974): 630-42.

Kos-Rabcewicz-Zubkowski, L. *Contribution Made by the Polish Ethnic Group to the Cultural Enrichment of Canada*. Report presented to the Royal Commission on Bilingualism and Biculturalism, 1966.

Kosa, John. "Hungarian Immigrants in North America: Their Residential Mobility and Ecology." *Canadian Journal of Economics and Political Science* 22 (1956): 358-70.

Kralt, J. *Ethnic Origins of Canadians*. Statistics Canada. 1971 Census of Canada Profile Studies, Bulletin 5: 1-9. Ottawa: Information Canada, 1977.

_____. "Ethnic Origin in the Canadian Census 1871-1981." In *Changing Realities: Social Trends Among Ukrainian Canadians*, edited by W.R. Petryshyn. Edmonton: The Canadian Institute of Ukrainian Studies, 1980.

_____. Internal Document, Secretary of State, 1983.

Kroeber, Alfred L. "Native American Population." *American Anthropologist* 6, 1 (1934).

Kuhn, M.H., and T.S. McPartland. "An Empirical Investigation of Self-Attitudes." *American Sociological Review* 19 (1954): 68-76.

Kuhn, T. *The Structure of Scientific Revolutions*. Chicago: University of Chicago Press, 1962.

Kuper, Leo. *An African Bourgeoisie*. New Haven: Yale University Press, 1965.

_____. *Race, Class and Power*. London: Duckworth, 1975.

_____. *Genocide*. New Haven: Yale University Press, 1981.

Kuper, Leo, and M.G. Smith. *Pluralism in Africa*. Berkeley: University of California Press, 1968.

La Gaipa, J.J. "Stereotypes and Perceived Ethnic-Role Specialization." *Journal of Social Psychology* 85 (1971): 285-92.

Lalonde, R.N. "Ethnic Stereotype Processing and Organization as a Function of Group Membership." Ph.D. dissertation, University of Western Ontario, 1985.

Lamarche, L. "Composition d'une liste d'adjectifs ordonnés selon leur degré de polysémie." Paper presented at Canadian Psychological Association meeting, Quebec, 1975.

Lambert, W.E., L. Mermigis, and D.M. Taylor. "Greek Canadian Attitudes Towards Own Group and Other Canadian Ethnic Groups: A Test of the Multicultural Hypothesis." *Canadian Journal of Behavioural Science* 18 (1986): 35-51.

Laumann, Edward O. *Bonds of Pluralism: The Form and Substance of Urban Social Networks*. New York: John Wiley and Sons, 1973.

Laumann, Edward O., and Franz U. Pappi. "New Directions in the Study of Community Elites." *American Sociological Review* 38 (1973): 212-30.

_____. *Networks of Collective Action*. New York: Academic Press, 1976.

Laumann, Edward O., and Peter V. Marsden. "The Analysis of Oppositional Structures in Political Elites: Identifying Collective Actors." *American Sociological Review* 44 (1979): 713-32.

Laumann, Edward O., Lois M. Verbrugge, and Franz U. Pappi. "A Causal Modelling Approach to the Study of a Community Elite's Influence Structure." *American Sociological Review* 39 (1974): 162-74.

Laumann, Edward O., Peter V. Marsden, and Joseph Galaskiewicz. "Community-Elite Influence Structures: Extension of a Network Approach." *American Journal of Sociology* 83 (1977): 594-631.

Lauwagie, B. "Ethnic Boundaries in Modern States." *American Journal of Sociology* 85 (September 1979): 310-37.

_____. "Ethnic Ideology, Boundaries, and Mobilization Among Gypsies in the U.S. and Great Britain." Paper presented at the annual meeting of the Midwest Sociological Society, April 7-9, 1982, Des Moines.

Lay, C.H., and D.N. Jackson. "A Note on the Independence of Stereotypes and Attitude." *Canadian Journal of Behavioural Science* 44 (1972): 146-55.

Lazarsfeld, Paul F., and Robert K. Merton. "Friendship as a Social Process: A Substantive and Methodological Analysis." In *Freedom and Control in Modern Society*, edited by Monroe Berger, Theodore Abel, and Charles Page. New York: D. Van Nostrand, 1954.

Leacock, Eleanor, and Nancy O. Lurie. *North American Indians in Historical Perspective*. New York: Random House, 1971.

Leavy, J. "Working Paper for a Series of Regional Conferences on Minority Rights," for the Canadian Human Rights Foundation, October, 1979.

Lévesque, R. *An Option for Quebec*. Toronto: McClelland and Stewart, 1968.

Levy, J. "In Search of Isolation: The Holdeman Mennonites of Linden, Alberta and Their School." *Canadian Ethnic Studies* 10, 1 (1979): 115-30.

Lewin, K. *Resolving Social Conflicts*. New York: Harper, 1948.

Li, P.S. "Occupational Achievement and Kinship Assistance Among Chinese Immigrants in Chicago." *The Sociological Quarterly* 18 (Autumn 1977): 478-89.

Liddle, R.W. *Ethnicity, Party and National Integration*. New Haven: Yale University Press, 1970.

Lieberson, Stanley. *Ethnic Patterns in American Cities*. New York: Free Press, 1963.

_____. *Language and Ethnic Relations in Canada*. New York: Wiley, 1970.

_____. "Stratification in Ethnic Groups." In *Readings in Race and Ethnic Relations*, edited by A.H. Richmond. London: Pergamon, 1972.

_____. *A Piece of the Pie: Black and White Immigrants since 1880*. Berkeley: University of California Press, 1980.

Lijphart, Arend. *The Politics of Accommodation: Pluralism and Democracy in the Netherlands*. Berkeley: University of California Press, 1968.

_____. "Consociational Democracy." *World Politics* 21 (January 1969): 207-25.

_____. *Democracy in Plural Societies*. New Haven: Yale University Press, 1977.

Linville, P.W. "The Complexity-Extremity Effect and Age-based Stereotyping." *Journal of Personality and Social Psychology* 42 (1982): 193-211.

Linville, P.W., and E.E. Jones. "Polarized Appraisals of Out-group Members." *Journal of Personality and Social Psychology* 38 (1980): 689-703.

Lippmann, W. *Public Opinion.* New York: Harcourt Brace, 1922.

Lipset, S.M. *Political Man: The Social Bases of Politics.* Garden City, NY: Doubleday, 1960.

———. *The First New Nation.* New York: Basic Books, 1963.

Lockwood, D. "Race, Conflict and Plural Society." In *Race and Racialism*, edited by S. Zubaida. London: Tavistock, 1970.

Loken, G. *From Fjord to Frontier: A History of the Norwegians in Canada.* Toronto: McClelland and Stewart, 1980.

Lopreato, Joseph, and Lawrence Hazelrigg. *Class, Conflict and Mobility: Theories and Studies in Class Structure.* San Francisco: Chandler, 1972.

Louvigny de Montigny. *Antoine Gérin-Lajoie.* Toronto: 1849, p. 13.

Lupul, M.R., ed. *A Heritage in Transition: Essays in the History of Ukrainians in Canada.* Toronto: McClelland and Stewart, 1982.

Lyman, Stanford M., and William A. Douglas. "Ethnicity: Strategies of Collective and Individual Impression Management." *Social Research* 40 (1970): 344-65.

Lyons, J. "The (Almost) Quiet Revolution: Doukhobor Schooling in Saskatchewan." *Canadian Ethnic Studies* 8, 1 (1976): 23-37.

Macdonald, R.J. "Hutterite Education in Alberta: A Test Case in Assimilation, 1920-1970." *Canadian Ethnic Studies* 8, 1 (1976): 9-21.

Mackie, M. "Arriving at 'Truth' by Definition: The Case of Stereotype Inaccuracy." *Social Problems* 20 (1973): 431-47.

———. "Ethnic Stereotypes and Prejudice: Alberta Indians, Hutterites and Ukrainians." *Canadian Ethnic Studies* 6 (1974): 234-46.

———. "Stereotypes, Prejudice, and Discrimination." In *Ethnicity and Ethnic Relations in Canada*, 2nd ed., edited by R.M. Bienvenue and S.E. Goldstein. Toronto: Butterworths, 1985, pp. 119-239.

Macmillan, David S. "The 'New Men' in Action: Scottish Mercantile and Shipping Operations in the North American Colonies, 1760-1825." In *Canadian Business History, Selected Studies, 1497-1971*, edited by David S. Macmillan. Toronto: McClelland and Stewart, 1972, pp. 44-103.

———. "The Scot as Businessman." In *The Scottish Tradition in Canada*, edited by W. Stanford Reid. Toronto: McClelland and Stewart, 1976.

Magill, M.L. "William Allan: A Pioneer Business Executive." In *Aspects of Nineteenth Century Ontario*, edited by F.H. Armstrong, H.A. Stevenson, and J.D. Wilson. Toronto: University of Toronto Press, 1974, pp. 101-13.

———. "John Strachan, Schoolmaster, and the Evolution of the Elite in Upper Canada/ Ontario." In *An Imperfect Past: Education and Society in Canadian History*, edited by J. Donald Wilson. Vancouver: 1984, pp. 154-69.

Mann, J. "Group Relations and the Marginal Man." *Human Relations* 11 (1958): 77-92.

———. "Cognitive, Behavioural and Situational Determinants of Ethnic Perception." Ph.D. dissertation, McGill University, 1976.

March, James G., and Johan P. Olsen. *Ambiguity and Choice in Organizations.* Bergen, Norway: Universitetsforlaget, 1976.

Marsden, Peter V., and Edward O. Laumann. "Collective Action in a Community Elite: Exchange, Influence Resources and Issue Resolution." In *Power, Paradigms, and Community Research*, edited by Roland J. Liebert and Allen W. Imershein. London: Sage, 1977, pp. 199-250.

Marston, Wilfred G., and Maxine Baca Zinn. "Impact of Urbanization on Ethnic Subcultures and Assimilation." Unpublished report, 1979.

Marston, Wilfred G., and Thomas L. Van Valey. "The Role of Residential Segregation in the Assimilation Process." *Annals of the American Academy of Political and Social Science* 441 (1979): 13-25.

Massey, Douglas S. "Effects of Socioeconomic Factors on the Residential Segregation of Blacks and Spanish Americans in the U.S. Urbanized Areas." *American Sociological Review* 44 (1979): 1015-22.

_____. "Social Class and Ethnic Segregation: A Reconsideration of Methods and Conclusions." *American Sociological Review* 46 (1981): 641-50.

Matthews, V. *Indians and the Law*. Ottawa: Canadian Corrections Association, 1967.

_____. *Socio-Legal Statistics in Alberta*. Edmonton, Alberta: Human Resources Research Council, 1972.

Mayhew, R.H., R.L. Levinger, J.M. McPherson, and T.F. James. "System Size and Structural Differentiation in Formal Organizations." *American Sociological Review* 37 (1972): 629-33.

Maynard, F.B. *Raisins and Almonds*. Don Mills, Ontario: General Publishing, 1973.

McCarthy, John, and Mayer Zald. "Resource Mobilization and Social Movements: A Partial Theory." *American Journal of Sociology* 82 (1977): 1212-41.

McCauley, C., and C.L. Stitt. "An Individual and Quantitative Measure of Stereotypes." *Journal of Personality and Social Psychology* 36 (1978): 929-40.

McEntire, Davis. *Residence and Race*. Berkeley: University of California, 1960.

McFee, M. "The 150% Man, A Product of Blackfeet Acculturation." *American Anthropologist* 70 (1968): 1096-1103.

McKinnon, J.B., cited in J. Leavy, "Working Paper for a Conference on Minority Rights" held in cooperation with York University (Ontario), October, 1979, pp. 8-11.

McLean, John. *The Indians: Their Manners and Customs*. Toronto: William Briggs,1889. Reprinted in 1970, Toronto: Coles.

_____. *Canadian Savage Folk: The Native Tribes of Canada*. Toronto: William Briggs, 1896. Reprinted in 1971, Toronto: Coles.

McNaught, Kenneth. "The National Outlook of English-speaking Canadians." In *Nationalism in Canada*, edited by Peter Russell. Toronto: McGraw-Hill Ryerson, 1966, pp. 61-71.

Mead, George Herbert. *Mind, Self and Society*. Chicago: University of Chicago Press, 1934.

Mealing, S.R. *The Jesuit Relations and Related Documents*. Toronto: McClelland and Stewart, 1963.

Mede, M.P., cited in J. Leavy, "Working Paper for a Conference on Minority Rights" held in cooperation with York University (Ontario), October, 1979, pp. 3-4.

Meisel, John. "Citizen Demands and Government Response." *Canadian Public Policy* 2 (1976): 564-72.

Merton, R. "Discrimination and the American Creed." In *Discrimination and National Welfare*, edited by R.M. McIver. Port Washington, New York: Kennikat Press, 1949.

Metzger, Paul L. "American Sociology and Black Assimilation: Conflicting Perspectives." *American Journal of Sociology* 76 (1971): 627-47.

Meyer, John W., and James G. Roth. "A Reinterpretation of American Status Policies." *Pacific Sociology Review* 13 (1970): 95-102.

Middlebrook, P.N. *Social Psychology and Modern Life*. New York: Alfred A. Knopf, 1974.

Moodley, Kogila A. "The Predicament of Racial Affirmative Action." *Queen's Quarterly* 91 (1984): 795-806.

Morgan, Lewis H. *Systems of Consanguinity and Affinity of the Human Family.* Cambridge, Mass.: Human Relations Area Files, 1870.

Morris, Ray, and Kenneth A. Price. "The Social Construction of Ethnicity in English Montreal and Toronto." Paper presented at the CSAA meetings in Montreal, 1980.

Multiculturalism and the Government of Canada. Ottawa: Minister of Supply and Services, 1978.

Murdock, George P., and Timothy J. O'Leary. *Ethnographic Bibliography of North America*, vols. 1-5, 4th ed. New Haven: Human Relations Area Files, 1976.

Myers, D.G. *Social Psychology.* New York: McGraw-Hill, 1983.

Myrdal, Gunnar. *An American Dilemma.* New York: Harper, 1944.

Nag, Moni. "The Concept of Tribe in the Contemporary Socio-political Context of India." In *Essays on the Problem of Tribe*, edited by June Helm. Seattle: American Ethnological Society (University of Washington Press), 1968.

Nagel, Joane. "The Ethnic Revolution: The Emergence of Ethnic Nationalism in Modern States." *Sociology and Social Research* 68 (1984): 417-34.

_____. "The Political Construction of Ethnicity." In *Competitive Ethnic Relations*, edited by S. Olzak and J. Nagel. New York: Academic Press, 1986.

Nagel, Joane, and Susan Olzak. "Ethnic Mobilization in New and Old States: An Extension of the Competition Model." *Social Problems* 30 (December 1982): 128-43.

Nagler, Mark. *Perspectives on the North American Indians.* Toronto: McClelland and Stewart, 1963.

Nahirny, V., and J.A. Fishman. "American Immigrant Groups: Ethnic Identification and the Problem of Generations." *Sociological Research* 13 (1965): 311-26.

Nayar, Baldev Raj. *Politics in the Punjab.* New Haven: Yale University Press, 1966.

Nettler, Gwynn. "A Measure of Alienation." *American Sociological Review* 22 (1957): 670-7.

Neuwirth, Gertrud. "A Weberian Outline of a Theory of Community: Its Application to the 'Dark Ghetto'." *British Journal of Sociology* 20 (1967): 148-63.

Newman, Peter C. *The Canadian Establishment.* Toronto: McClelland and Stewart, 1975.

Nielsen, François. "The Flemish Movement in Belgium after World War II." *American Sociological Review* 45 (February 1980): 76-94.

Nolan, Patrick. "Size and Administrative Intensity of Nations." *American Sociological Review* 44 (1979): 110-25.

Nunavut Proposal. *Political Development in Nunavut.* Inuit Tapirisat of Canada: Ottawa, 1979.

Oberg, Kalvero. *The Social Economy of the Tlingit Indians.* Vancouver: J.J. Douglas, 1973.

O'Bryan, K.D., J.G. Reitz, and O.M. Kuplowska. *Non-official Languages: A Study in Canadian Multiculturalism.* Ottawa: Minister Responsible for Multiculturalism, 1976.

Ogbu, John. *Minority Education and Caste.* New York: Academic Press, 1978.

Ogmundson, Rick. "Toward Study of the Endangered Species Known as the Anglophone Canadian." *Canadian Journal of Sociology* 5 (1980): 1-12.

Olzak, Susan. "Ethnic Mobilization in Quebec." *Ethnic and Racial Studies* (July 1982): 253-75.

_____. "Contemporary Ethnic Mobilization." *Annual Review of Sociology* 9 (1983): 355-74.

Ornstein, Michael D. "The Occupational Mobility of Men in Ontario." *Canadian Review of Sociology and Anthropology* 18, 2 (1981): 183-215.

Oswalt, Wendell H. *This Land Was Theirs: A Study of the North American Indian*, 3rd ed. Toronto: John Wiley and Sons, 1978.

Ouellet, F. *Histoire économique et sociale du Québec, 1760-1850*. Paris: Fides, 1966, p. 210.

Owen, Roger C., et al. *The North American Indians: A Sourcebook*. New York: Macmillan, 1967.

Padilla, Felix M. "What is a Latino? Interpretations of an Ethnic Identity in an Urban Context." Paper presented at the annual meeting of the Midwest Sociological Society, April 7-9, 1982, Des Moines.

Palmer, H. "Reluctant Hosts: Anglo-Canadian Views on Multiculturalism in the Twentieth Century." In *Multiculturalism as State Policy*. Report of the Second Canadian Conference on Multiculturalism. Ottawa: Canadian Consultative Council on Multiculturalism, 1976, pp. 81-118.

Panitch, Leo. "The Role and Nature of the Canadian State." In *The Canadian State: Political Economy and Political Power*, edited by Leo Panitch. Toronto: University of Toronto Press, 1977, pp. 3-27.

Park, B., and M. Rothbart. "Perception of Out-group Homogeneity and Levels of Social Categorization: Memory for the Subordinate Attributes on In-group and Out-group Members." *Journal of Personality and Social Psychology* 42 (1982): 1051-68.

Park, Robert E. "The Urban Community as a Spatial Pattern and a Moral Order." In *The Urban Community*, edited by Ernest W. Burgess. Chicago: University of Chicago Press, 1926.

_____. *Race and Culture*. Glencoe, Illinois: Free Press, 1950.

Parkin, Frank. *Marxism and Class Theory: A Bourgeois Critique*. New York: Columbia, 1979.

Patterson, E. Palmer. *The Canadian Indian: A History Since 1500*. Don Mills: Collier-Macmillan, 1972.

Patterson, Nancy-Lou. *Canadian Native Art*. Don Mills: Collier-Macmillan, 1973.

Patterson, Orlando. *Ethnic Chauvinism: The Reactionary Impulse*. New York: Stein and Day, 1977.

Peabody, D. "Trait Inferences: Evaluative and Descriptive Aspects." *Journal of Personality and Social Psychology,* Monograph 7(1967): (4 whole #644).

Peter, Karl. "The Myth of Multiculturalism and Other Political Fables." In *Ethnicity, Power and Politics in Canada*, edited by Jorgen Dahlie and Tissa Fernando. Toronto: Methuen, 1982, pp. 56-67.

Peterson Royce, Anya. *Ethnic Identity*. Bloomington: Indiana University Press, 1982.

Peterson, W., and D. Matza. *Social Controversy*. Bellmont, Calif.: Wadsworth, 1963.

Pineo, Peter C. "Social Mobility in Canada: The Current Picture." *Sociological Focus* 9, 2 (1976): 109-23.

_____. "The Social Standing of Ethnic and Racial Groupings." *Canadian Review of Sociology and Anthropology* 14 (1977): 147-57.

Pineo, Peter C., and John Porter. "Occupational Prestige in Canada." *Canadian Review of Sociology and Anthropology* 4, 1 (1967): 24-40.

_____. "Ethnic Origin and Occupational Attainment." In *Ascription and Achievement: Studies in Mobility and Status Attainment in Canada*, edited by M. Boyd, J. Goyder,

F.E. Jones, P.C. Pineo, and J. Porter. Ottawa: Carleton University Press, 1985.

Plascov, Avi. *The Palestinian Refugees in Jordan, 1948-1957*. London: Frank Cass, 1981.

Ponting, J. Rick, and Robert Gibbons. *Out of Irrelevance*. Toronto: Butterworths, 1980.

Porter, John. *The Vertical Mosaic: An Analysis of Social Class and Power in Canada*. Toronto: University of Toronto Press, 1965.

_____. "Ethnic Pluralism in Canadian Perspective." In *Ethnicity*, edited by Nathan Glazer and Daniel P. Moynihan. Cambridge, Mass.: Harvard University Press, 1975, pp. 267-304.

Power, S. "The Relational Attitudes of Franco-Ontariens in Kingston." B.A. thesis, Queen's University, 1983.

Price, John A. "The Superorganic Fringe: Protoculture, Idioculture, and Material Culture." *Ethos* 1, 2 (1973).

_____. "Sharing: The Integration of Intimate Economies." *Anthropologica* 17, 1 (1975).

_____. *Native Studies: American and Canadian Indians*. Toronto: McGraw-Hill Ryerson, 1978.

_____. *Indians in Canada: Cultural Dynamics*. Scarborough, Ontario: Prentice-Hall, 1979.

Pross, Paul. "Space, Function and Interest: The Problem of Legitimacy in the Canadian State." In *The Administration State in Canada*, edited by O.P. Dwivedi. Toronto: University of Toronto Press, 1982, pp. 107-29.

Public Hearings of the Environmental Assessment Panel on the Proposed Uranium Hexafluoride Refinery at Corman Park, Saskatchewan, vols. 1-22. Ottawa: Recorded by International Reporting Inc., 8-24 January 1980.

Quattrone, G.A. "On the Perception of a Group's Variability." In *The Psychology of Intergroup Relations*, rev. ed., edited by S. Worchel and W.G. Austin. Chicago: Nelson-Hall, 1986.

Quattrone, G.A., and E.E. Jones. "The Perception of Variability Within In-groups and Out-groups: Implications for the Law of Small Numbers." *Journal of Personality and Social Psychology* 38 (1980): 141-52.

Radecki, H. *A Member of a Distinguished Family: The Polish Group in Canada*. Toronto: McClelland and Stewart, 1976.

Rasporich, A.W. *For a Better Life: A History of the Croatians in Canada*. Toronto: McClelland and Stewart, 1982.

Redfield, Robert. *The Little Community*. Chicago: University of Chicago Press, 1955.

Reid, W., ed. *The Scottish Tradition in Canada*. Toronto: McClelland and Stewart, 1976.

Reitz, Jeffrey G. *The Survival of Ethnic Groups*. Toronto: McGraw-Hill Ryerson, 1980.

_____. "Ethnic Group Control of Jobs." Paper presented at the annual meeting of the American Sociological Association, San Francisco, September, 1982.

Rex, John, and Sally Tomlinson. *Colonial Immigrants in a British City*. London: Routledge and Kegan Paul, 1979.

Richmond, Anthony. *Ethnic Residential Segregation in Toronto*. Toronto: Institute of Behavioural Research, York University, 1972.

Richmond, A.H., and W.E. Kalbach. *Factors in the Adjustment of Immigrants and their Descendants*. 1981 Census Analytical Study, Catalogue 99-761E. Ottawa: Minister of Supply and Services Canada, 1980.

Ridge, J.M. "Introduction." In *Mobility in Britain Reconsidered*. Oxford Studies in Social Mobility Working Papers, vol. 2, edited by J.M. Ridge. Oxford: Clarendon Press, 1974, pp. 1-7.

Rioux, Marcel. "The Development of Ideologies in Quebec." In *Communities and Culture in French Canada*, edited by Gerald Gold and Marc-Adelard Tremblay. Toronto: Holt, Rinehart and Winston, 1973.

Roberts, Lance W., and Rodney A. Clifton. "Exploring the Ideology of Canadian Multiculturalism." *Canadian Public Policy*, viii (1982), pp. 88-94.

Rocher, G. "Multiculturalism: The Doubts of a Francophone." *Report of the Second Canadian Conference on Multiculturalism*. Ottawa: Canadian Consultative Council on Multiculturalism, 1977, pp. 47-53.

Roff, Margaret C. *The Politics of Belonging: Political Change in Sabah and Sarawak*. Oxford: Oxford University Press, 1975.

Rogers, Everett M. *A Diffusion of Innovations*. New York: Free Press, 1962.

Roof, W. Clark. "Residential Segregation of Blacks and Racial Inequality in Southern Cities: Toward a Causal Model." *Social Problems* 19 (1972): 393-407.

Rose, A.M. "A Systematic Summary of Symbolic Interaction Theory." In *Human Behavior and Social Processes*, edited by A.M. Rose. Boston: Houghton Mifflin, 1962, pp. 3-19.

Rose, A.M., and C.B. Rose. "Group Identification and the Minority Community." In *Minority Problems*, edited by Rose and Rose. New York: Harper & Row, 1965, pp. 247-52.

Rosenberg, Terry J., and Robert W. Lake. "Toward a Revised Model of Residential Segregation and Succession: Puerto Ricans in New York, 1960-1970." *American Journal of Sociology* 81 (1976): 1142-50.

Rothschild, Joseph. *Ethnopolitics*. New York: Columbia University Press, 1981.

Roy, G. *Ces enfants de ma vie*. Montréal: Stanké, 1977.

Royal Commission on Bilingualism and Biculturalism. *A Preliminary Report*. Ottawa: Queen's Printer, 1965.

_____. *Report: General Introduction*. Ottawa: Queen's Printer, 1967.

_____. Book IV, *The Cultural Contribution of the Other Ethnic Groups*. Ottawa: Queen's Printer, 1969.

Rudolph, Lloyd, and Susanne Rudolph. *The Modernity of Tradition: Political Development In India*. Chicago: University of Chicago Press, 1967.

Sampson, E.E. "Psychology and the American Ideal." *Journal of Personality and Social Psychology* 35 (1977): 767-82.

Sartre, J.P. *Anti-Semite and Jew*. New York: Schocken, 1948.

Schneider, March. *Ethnicity and Politics*. University of North Carolina: Institute for Research in Social Science, 1979.

Schwartz, Walter. *The Tamils of Sri Lanka*. London: Minority Rights Group, 1975.

Seago, D.W. "Before Pearl Harbour and After." *Journal of Psychology* 23 (1947): 55-63.

Service, Elman R. *Primitive Social Organization: An Evolutionary Perspective*, 2nd ed. New York: Random House, 1971.

_____. *Origins of the State and Civilization: The Process of Cultural Evolution*. New York: W.W. Norton, 1975.

Shaffir, W. "The Organization of Secular Education in a Chassidic Jewish Community." *Canadian Ethnic Studies* 8, 1 (1976): 38-51.

Shaw, Marvin E. *Group Dynamics: The Psychology of Small Group Behavior*. New York: McGraw-Hill, 1976.

Silberman, C.E. *Crisis in Black and White*. New York: Random House, 1964.

Simmel, Georg. *The Sociology of Georg Simmel*. Translated and edited by Kurt Wolff. New York: Free Press of Glencoe, 1950.

Simpson, G., and J.M. Yinger. *Racial and Cultural Minorities*. New York: Harper & Row, 1972.

Singer, Lester. "Ethnogenesis and Negro-Americans Today." *Social Research* (Winter 1962): 422-32.

Sinha, A.K.P., and O.P. Upadhyay. "Change and Persistence in the Stereotype of University Students Toward Different Ethnic Groups During a Sino-Indian Border Dispute." *Journal of Social Psychology* 52 (1960): 31-39.

Smiley, Donald. "Reflections on Cultural Nationhood and Political Community in Canada." In *Entering the Eighties: Canada in Crisis*, edited by R. Kenneth Carty and W. Peter Ward. Toronto: Oxford University Press, 1980, pp. 20-43.

Smith, A.D. *Theories of Nationalism*. London: Camelot Press, 1971.

_____. *Nationalism in the Twentieth Century*. Oxford: Martin Robertson, 1979.

Smith, Michael G. *The Plural Society in the British West Indies*. Berkeley: University of California Press, 1965.

Sommerlad, E. "The Importance of Ethnic Identification for Assimilation and Integration: Study of Australian Aborigines' Attitudes." B.A. thesis, University of Sydney, 1968.

Sommerlad, E., and J.W. Berry. "The Role of Ethnic Identification in Distinguishing Between Attitudes Toward Assimilation and Integration." *Human Relations* 23 (1970): 23, 29.

Sowell, T. *Economics and Politics of Race*. New York: William Morrow, 1983, p. 201.

Spindler, G., and L. Spindler. "Identity, Militancy, and Cultural Congruence: The Menominee and Kainai." *The Annals* 436 (March 1978): 73-85.

Srinivas, Mysore N. *Social Change in Modern India*. Berkeley: University of California Press, 1969.

Stanley, Sam, and Robert Thomas. "Current Social and Demographic Trends among North American Indians." *The Annals* 436 (March 1978): 11-120.

Statistics Canada. *1981 Census of Canada*, "Ethnic Origins," Catalogue 92-911. Ottawa: Minister of Supply and Services Canada, 1984.

Steger, Wilbur A. "Economic and Social Costs of Residential Segregation." In *Modernizing Urban Land Policy*, edited by Marion Clawson. Baltimore: Johns Hopkins, 1973, pp. 83-113.

Stein, Janice Gross, and David Dewitt. *The Middle East at the Crossroads: Regional Forces and External Powers*. Oakville: Mosaic Press, 1983.

Steiner, Ivan D. *Group Process and Productivity*. New York: Academic Press, 1972.

_____. "Whatever Happened to the Group in Social Psychology?" *Journal of Experimental Social Psychology* 10 (1974): 94-108.

Steiner, Jurg, and Jeffrey Obler. "Does the Consociational Theory Really Hold for Switzerland?" In *Ethnic Conflict in the Western World*, edited by Milton Esman. Ithaca: Cornell University Press, 1975, pp. 324-42.

Stephan, W.G., and D. Rosenfield. "Racial and Ethnic Stereotypes." In *Contemporary Issues in Stereotyping*, edited by A.G. Miller. New York: Praeger, 1982, pp. 92-136.

Stonequist, E. "The Problem of the Marginal Man." *American Journal of Sociology* 41 (1935): 1-12.

Strauss, Anselm L. *Mirrors and Masks: The Search for Identity*. Glencoe, Ill.: The Free Press, 1959.

Suttles, Gerald. *The Social Order of the Slum*. Chicago: University of Chicago, 1968.

_____. "Anatomy of a Chicago Slum." In *Sociology: Classic and Popular Approaches*, edited by G.T. Marx and N. Goodman. New York: Random House, 1969.

_____. *The Social Construction of Communities*. Chicago: University of Chicago, 1972.

Taeuber, K.E. "Patterns of Negro-White Residential Segregation." *Milbank Memorial Fund Quarterly* 48 (1970): 69-84.

Taeuber, K.E., and A.F. Taeuber. *Negroes in Cities*. New York: Aldine Press, 1965.

Tajfel, H. "Cognitive Aspects of Prejudice." *Journal of Social Issues* 25 (1969): 79-97.

_____. "Experiments in a Vacuum." In *The Context of Social Psychology: A Critical Assessment*, edited by J. Israel and H. Tajfel. London: Academic Press, 1972a, pp. 69-119.

_____. "La Catégorisation sociale." In *Introduction à la psychologie sociale*, edited by S. Moscovici. Paris: Larousse, 1972b, pp. 272-392.

_____. "Social Stereotypes and Social Groups." In *Intergroup Behaviour*, edited by J.C. Turner and H. Giles. Oxford: Basil Blackwell, 1981, pp. 144-67.

Tajfel, H., and J. Turner. "An Integrative Theory of Intergroup Conflict." In *The Social Psychology of Intergroup Relations*, edited by W.G. Austin and S. Worchel. Monterey, CA.: Brooks/Cole, 1979, pp. 33-47.

Taylor, Donald M. "Stereotypes and Intergroup Relations." In *A Canadian Social Psychology of Ethnic Relations*, edited by Robert C. Gardner and Rudolf Kalin. Toronto: Methuen, 1981.

Taylor, D.M., and F.E. Aboud. "Ethnic Stereotypes: Is the Concept Necessary?" *Canadian Psychologist* 14 (1973): 330-38.

Taylor, D.M., and F. Moghaddam. *Theories of Intergroup Relations: International Social Psychological Perspectives*. New York: Praeger, forthcoming.

Taylor, D.M., and L.M. Simard. "Social Interaction in a Bilingual Setting." *Canadian Psychological Review* 16 (1975): 240-54.

_____. "Ethnic Identity and Intergroup Relations." In *Emerging Ethnic Boundaries*, edited by D.J. Lee. Ottawa: University of Ottawa Press, 1979, pp. 155-71.

Taylor, D.M., and R.C. Gardner. "Ethnic Stereotypes: Their Effects on the Perception of Communicators of Varying Credibility." *Canadian Journal of Psychology* 23 (1969): 161-73.

Taylor, D.M., and V. Jaggi. "Ethnocentrism and Causal Attribution in a South Indian Context." *Journal of Cross-Cultural Psychology* 5 (1975): 162-72.

Taylor, Ronald. "Black Ethnicity and the Persistence of Ethnogenesis." *American Journal of Sociology* 84 (1979): 1401-23.

Tedlock, Dennis, and Barbara Tedlock. *Teachings from the American Earth: Indian Religion and Philosophy*. New York: Liveright, 1975.

Tepperman, Lorne. *Social Mobility in Canada*. Toronto: McGraw-Hill Ryerson, 1975.

Terrell, John U., and Donna M. Terrell. *Indian Women of the Western Morning: Their Life in Early America*. Garden City, New York: Anchor, 1976.

Textor, Lucy A. *A Colony of Emigrés in Canada*. Toronto: The University Library, 1905.

Thomas, William I., and Florian Znaniecki. *The Polish Peasant in Europe and America*, vol. 1. New York: Alfred Knopf, 1927.

Thompson, E.T., and E.C. Hughes. *Race: Individual and Collective Behavior*. Glencoe, Illinois: The Free Press, 1958.

Thompson, Fred, and W.I. Stanbury. *The Political Economy of Interest Groups in the Legislative Process in Canada*. Montreal: Institute for Research on Public Policy, Occasional Paper No. 9, 1979.

Tilly, Charles. "Anthropology on the Town." *Habitat* 10 (1967): 20-25.

_____. *From Mobilization to Revolution*. Reading, MA: Addison-Wesley, 1978.

_____. "Community, City, Urbanization." Ann Arbor: Department of Sociology,

University of Michigan, 1979.

Tolbert, C., P.M. Horan, and E.M. Beck. "The Structure of Economic Segregation: A Dual Economy Approach." *American Journal of Sociology* 85 (1980): 1095-1116.

Triandis, H.C., and V. Vassiliou. "Frequency of Contact and Stereotyping." *Journal of Personality and Social Psychology* 7 (1967): 316-28.

_____. *Attitude and Attitude Change.* New York: Wiley, 1971.

Tucker, James, and S. Thomas Friedman. "Population Density and Group Size." *American Journal of Sociology* 77 (1972): 742-49.

Tumin, Melvin. *Caste in a Peasant Society.* Princeton, NJ: Princeton University Press, 1952.

Turner, John C. "Social Comparison and Social Identity: Same Prospects for Intergroup Behaviour." *European Journal of Social Psychology* 5 (1974): 5-34.

Turner, Ralph H. "The Relative Position of Negro Males in the Labor Force of Large American Cities." *American Sociological Review* 16 (1951): 524-29.

_____. "The Self-Conception in Social Interaction." In *The Self in Social Interaction*, edited by Chad Gordon and Kenneth J. Gergen. New York: John Wiley and Sons, 1968, pp. 93-106.

Underhill, Ruth M. *Red Man's Religion: Beliefs and Practices of the Indians North of Mexico.* Chicago: University of Chicago, 1965.

Vallee, Frank G., and Norman Shulman. "The Viability of French Groupings Outside Quebec." In *Regionalism in the Canadian Community, 1867-1967*, edited by Mason Wade. Toronto: University of Toronto Press, 1969, pp. 83-99.

Van den Berghe, Pierre L. *Race and Racism.* New York: Wiley, 1967.

_____. "Ethnic Membership and Culture Change in Quatemala." *Social Forces* 46 (1968): 514-22.

_____. "The Benign Quota: Panacea or Pandora's Box." *The American Sociologist* 6 (Supplementary Issue, 1971): 40-3.

_____. *Human Family Systems: An Evolutionary View.* New York: Elsevier, 1979.

_____. *The Ethnic Phenomenon.* New York: Elsevier, 1981.

Van den Berghe, Pierre L., and George P. Primov. *Inequality in the Peruvian Andes, Class and Ethnicity in Cuzco.* Columbia, MO: University of Missouri Press, 1977.

Vano, Gerard S. *Neo-Feudalism: The Canadian Dilemma.* Toronto: House of Anansi, 1981.

Viatte, Auguste. *Histoire littéraire de l'Amérique française.* Québec: Presses universitaires Laval, 1954.

Vinacke, W.E. "Stereotypes as Social Concepts." *Journal of Social Psychology* 46 (1957): 229-43.

Wade, M. *The French Canadians, 1760-1945*, vol. 1. London: Macmillan, 1967, p. 192.

Wallace, W. Stewart. *The Family Compact.* Toronto: Glasgow, Brook & Company, 1915, pp. 4-5.

Wallerstein, Immanuel. *The Modern World System.* New York: Academic Press, 1976. *The Modern World System II.* New York: Academic Press, 1980.

Warner, W. Lloyd. "Introduction." In *Deep South*, edited by Allison W. Davis, B.B. Gardner, and M.R. Gardner. Chicago: University of Chicago Press, 1941.

_____. *American Life.* Chicago: University of Chicago Press, 1953.

_____. *The Living and the Dead: A Study of the Symbolic Life of America.* New Haven: Yale University Press, 1959.

Weber, Max. *Economy and Society.* New York: Bedminster, 1968 (first published in 1922).

      . "Ethnic Groups." In *Max Weber, Economy and Society*, edited by Guenther Roth and Claus Wittich. Berkeley: University of California Press, 1978.

Wellman, Barry. "The Community Question: The Intimate Ties of East Yorkers." *American Journal of Sociology* 84 (1979): 1201-31.

Wellman, Barry, and Barry Leighton. "Networks, Neighbourhoods, and Communities." *Urban Affairs Quarterly* 14 (1979): 363-90.

Wellman, Barry, Peter Carrington, and Alan Hall. "Networks and Personal Communities." Toronto: Centre for Urban and Community Studies, University of Toronto, 1983.

Werner, W., B. Connors, T. Aoki, and J. Dahlie. *Whose Culture? Whose Heritage?* Vancouver: University of British Columbia, 1977.

Westen, P. "The Empty Idea of Equality." *Harvard Law Review* 95 (1982): 537.

Westhues, Kenneth. "Public vs. Sectarian Legitimation: The Separate Schools of the Catholic Church." *Canadian Review of Sociology and Anthropology* 13 (1976): 137-51.

Why People Say No to a Uranium Refinery at Warman, Saskatchewan. Warman: Warman and District Concerned Citizens Group, 1980.

Wiberg, H. "Self-determination as an International Issue." Paper presented at the 9th General Conference of the International Peace Research Association, Orillia, Ontario (Canada) June 21-26, 1981.

Wickberg, E., ed. *From China to Canada: A History of the Chinese Communities in Canada*. Toronto: McClelland and Stewart, 1982.

Wiebe, R.H. *Peace Shall Destroy Many*. Toronto: McClelland and Stewart, 1962.

Wiley, Norbert F. "The Ethnic Mobility Trap and Stratification Theory." *Social Problems* 15 (1967): 147-59.

Williams, Robin. *The Reduction of Intergroup Tensions: A Survey of Research on Problems of Ethnic, Racial, and Religious Group Relations*. New York: Social Science & Research Council, 1947.

      . *Strangers Next Door*. Englewood Cliffs, N.J.: Prentice-Hall, 1964.

Williams, W. "On Discrimination, Prejudice, Racial Income Differentials and Affirmative Action." In *Discrimination, Affirmative Action and Equal Opportunity*. Vancouver: Fraser Institute, 1982.

Wilson, Bruce G. *The Enterprises of Robert Hamilton*. Ottawa: Carleton University Press, 1983.

Wilson, J. Donald, ed. *An Imperfect Past: Education and Society in Canadian History*. Vancouver: University of British Columbia, 1984.

Wilson, Robert A. "Anomie in the Ghetto: a Study of Neighborhood Type, Race and Anomie." *American Journal of Sociology* 77 (1971): 67-88.

Wilson, William J. *Power, Racism and Privilege*. New York: Macmillan, 1973.

      . *The Declining Significance of Race*. Chicago: University of Chicago Press, 1978.

Winship, Christopher. "A Revaluation of Indexes of Segregation." *Social Forces* 55 (1938): 1058-66.

Wirth, Louis. "Urbanism as a Way of Life." *American Journal of Sociology* 34 (1938): 1-24.

      . *On Cities and Social Life: Selected Papers*, edited by Albert J. Reiss. Chicago: University of Chicago Press, 1964.

Wolfgang, M.E. "The Social Scientist in Court." *Journal of Criminal Law and Criminology* 65 (1974): 239-47.

Yancey, William L., Eugene P. Ericksen, and Richard N. Juliani. "Emergent Ethnicity: A Review and Reformulation." *American Sociological Review* 41 (1976): 391-403.

Yinger, J.M. "Prejudice: Social Discrimination." *International Encyclopedia of the Social Sciences*, edited by D.E. Sills. New York: Macmillan, 1968.

Young, Crawford. *Politics in the Congo*. New Haven: Yale University Press, 1965.

_____. *The Politics of Cultural Pluralism*. Madison, WI: University of Wisconsin Press, 1976.

_____. "Nationalizing the Third-World War State: Categorical Imperative a Mission Impossible?" *Polity* 15 (Winter 1982): 161-81.

_____. "Cultural Pluralism in the Third World." In *Competitive Ethnic Relations*, edited by S. Olzak and J. Nagel. New York: Academic Press, 1986.

Young, M. "Patterns of Psychological Acculturation among Azorean Portuguese-Canadian Families in Kingston." B.A. thesis, Queen's University, 1984.

Contributors

Frederick H. Armstrong, Department of History, University of Western Ontario, London

T.R. Balakrishnan, Department of Sociology, University of Western Ontario, London

Thomas Berger, former Justice and now lawyer, Vancouver

John W. Berry, Department of Psychology, Queen's University, Kingston

Reginald Bibby, Department of Sociology, Lethbridge University, Lethbridge

Raymond Breton, Department of Sociology, University of Toronto, Toronto

Jean Burnet, Department of Sociology, York University, Toronto

A. Gordon Darroch, Department of Sociology, York University, Toronto

Arnold Dashefsky, Department of Sociology, University of Connecticut, Storrs

Leo Driedger, Department of Sociology, University of Manitoba, Winnipeg

John Hagan, Faculty of Law, University of Toronto, Toronto

Warren Kalbach, Department of Sociology, University of Toronto, Toronto

Evelyn Kallen, Department of Anthropology, York University, Toronto

John Kralt, Social Trends Analysis Directorate, Ottawa

Richard N. Lalonde, Department of Psychology, McGill University, Montreal

Wilfred G. Marston, Department of Sociology, University of Michigan, Flint

Kogila A. Moodley, Faculty of Education, University of British Columbia, Vancouver

Joane Nagel, Department of Sociology, University of Kansas, Lawrence

Peter C. Pineo, Department of Sociology, McMaster University, Hamilton

John A. Price, Department of Anthropology, York University, Toronto

Marcel Rioux, Department of Sociology, University of Montreal, Montreal

Donald M. Taylor, Department of Psychology, McGill University, Montreal

Pierre van den Berghe, Department of Sociology, University of Washington, Seattle

Acknowledgments

An honest attempt has been made to secure permission for all material used, and if there are errors or omissions, these are wholly unintentional and the Publisher will be grateful to learn of them.

Max Weber, "Ethnic Groups." Reprinted from *Economy and Society*, vol. 1, edited by Guenther Roth and Claus Wittich (Berkeley: University of California Press, 1978), pp. 385–87 and 393–98. Copyright © 1978 The Regents of the University of California. Used by permission of the University of California Press.

Joane Nagel, "The Ethnic Revolution: The Emergence of Ethnic Nationalism in Modern States," *Sociology and Social Research* 68 (1984): 417–34. Reprinted by permission of the author and journal.

Raymond Breton, "The Production and Allocation of Symbolic Resources: An Analysis of the Linguistic and Ethnocultural Fields in Canada," *Canadian Review of Sociology and Anthropology* 21, 2 (1984): 123–44. Reprinted by permission of the author and journal.

Jean Burnet, "Multiculturalism in Canada." Revised from "Myths and Multiculturalism," *Canadian Journal of Education* 4, 4 (1979): 43–58. Reprinted by permission of the author and journal.

A. Gordon Darroch and Wilfred G. Marston, "Patterns of Urban Ethnicity." Revised from "Patterns of Urban Ethnicity: Toward a Revised Ecological Model," in *Urbanism and Urbanization: Views, Aspects and Dimensions*, edited by Noel Iverson (Leiden, The Netherlands: E.J. Brill, 1984). Reprinted by permission of the authors and publisher.

Arnold Dashefsky, "Theoretical Frameworks in the Study of Ethnic Groups: Toward a Social Psychology of Ethnicity," *Ethnicity* 2 (1975): 10–18. Reprinted by permission of the author and journal. Copyright © 1975 Academic Press, Inc.

John A. Price, "Indian Cultural Diversity," in *Indians of Canada: Cultural Dynamics* (Scarborough, Ontario: Prentice-Hall Canada Inc., 1975). Revised and reprinted by permission of the author and publisher.

Marcel Rioux, "The Development of Ideologies in Quebec," in *Communities and Culture in French Canada*, edited by Gerald Gold and Marc-Adelard Tremblay (Toronto: Holt, Rinehart and Winston, 1973). Reprinted by permission of the author.

Pierre van den Berghe, "Ethnicity and Class: Bases of Sociality." Reprinted by permission of the publisher from "Ethnicity and Class: Bases of Sociality," by Pierre van den Berghe, *The Ethnic Phenomenon*. Copyright 1981 by Elsevier Science Publishing Co., Inc.

Peter C. Pineo, "The Social Standing of Ethnic and Racial Groupings," *Canadian Review of Sociology and Anthropology* 14, 2 (1977): 147–57. Revised and reprinted by permission of the author and journal.

Frederick H. Armstrong, "Ethnicity and the Formation of the Ontario Establishment." Reprinted from "Ethnicity in the Formation of the Family Compact: A Case Study in the Growth of the Canadian Establishment," by Frederick H. Armstrong, *Ethnicity, Power and Politics in Canada*, Jorgen Dahlie and Tissa Fernando, eds. Copyright © 1981 by Methuen Publications, Toronto. Reproduced by permission.

Leo Driedger, "Minority Conflict: Ethnic Networks versus Industrial Power." Reprinted from "Community Conflict: The Eldorado Invasion of Warman," *Canadian Review of Sociology and Anthropology* 23, 2 (1986): 247–69. Reprinted by permission of the author and journal.

John Hagan, "Finding and Defining Discrimination." Revised from "Finding Discrimination: A Question of Meaning," *Ethnicity* 4 (1977): 167–76. Reprinted by permission of the author and journal. Copyright © 1977 Academic Press, Inc.

Donald M. Taylor and Richard N. Lalonde, "Ethnic Stereotypes: A Psychological Analysis." Revised from "Stereotypes and Intergroup Relations," by Donald M. Taylor, *A Canadian Social Psychology of Ethnic Relations*, Robert C. Gardner and Rudolf Kalin, eds. Copyright © 1981 by Methuen Publications, Toronto. Reproduced by permission.

Thomas Berger, "The Banished Japanese Canadians." Revised from *Fragile Freedoms* by Thomas R. Berger © 1981 by Irwin Publishing Inc. Used by permission of the publisher.

Kogila Moodley, "The Predicament of Racial Affirmative Action," *Queen's Quarterly* 91: 795–806. Reprinted by permission of the author and journal.

Index

1 2 3 4 5   132300   91 90 89 88 87